entertaining
for a
veggie planet

250
down-to-earth
recipes

entertaining

for a

veggie
planet

Didi Emmons

Houghton Mifflin Company

Boston • New York • 2003

Visit our Web site: www.houghtonmifflinbooks.com.

Library of Congress Cataloging-in-Publication Data
Emmons, Didi, date.
Entertaining for a veggie planet :
250 down-to-earth recipes / Didi Emmons.
p.   cm.
ISBN 0-618-10451-8
1. Vegetarian cookery. 2. Entertaining.   I. Title.
TX 837.E485 2003 641.5'636 — dc21
2002191287

Design by Melissa Lotfy

Printed in the United States of America

MP 10 9 8 7 6 5 4 3 2 1

To Dad

the consummate entertainer

My dad has mastered the not-so-easy art of entertaining.
He entertains friends and family not only at parties but also
on the tennis court, on the ski slopes, on the phone, in the
kitchen, ad infinitum. He has a one-of-a-kind, well-honed,
homespun sense of humor, the kind that makes you not just
chuckle but laugh deep in your belly. Once you're engaged in
conversation with my dad, you feel as if you're being heard
for real, because he wants to get to know you, no matter
who you are.

acknowledgments

Thanks to

Lori Galvin-Frost, my editor, for dreaming up the idea for this book and for your intelligent comments and edits along the way.

Nancy Kohl, for your perseverance and good humor while editing these recipes over the course of eighteen months and for your mostly unrequited love for my cat, Henry.

Doe Coover, for getting into the nitty-gritty and determining what should stay and what should go. It takes a tough agent to make a decent cookbook.

Roz Cummins, for your swift writing, sensitive edits, and uncanny feel for the spirit of this book.

Rux Martin, for polishing, purging, and pulling it all together with a seasoned and sensitive hand.

My mother, Roz, for your frequent e-mails, your diligent recipe testing, and your relentless promotion of my first book to everyone you meet as I stand by and cringe.

My sister Polly Tilghman, for always being just a phone call away, ready to impart a perspective that would have taken me months to arrive at myself.

My sister Lisa Thoren, for trying to find cilantro at two supermarkets and for your savvy business and art advice.

My cat, Henry, for being at my side. Despite your manipulative, high-pitched cries for food throughout the day and your swatting and hissing to ward off potential friends and suitors, you get cuter and more precious to me every day.

Eden Stone, for your wine acumen and your enlightening wine recommendations.

Cathi DiCocco, Maine's best veggie chef, for inspiring me with your spontaneity, passion, and entrepreneurial spirit.

Paul Hollings, for being my top recipe tester and confidence booster.

Marla Felcher, for your straight-A, Ivy League approach to recipe testing. Even better, you make moves like bringing your large dog onto your lap at the end of dinner seem not only appropriate but progressive.

John Strymish, for being a dear friend who continues to hand-sell my first cookbook, *Vegetarian Planet,* to every customer who walks into your bookstore.

Ann Gallager, for sowing the seeds at Houghton Mifflin back in the late 1990s.

Adam Penn, my partner at Veggie Planet, for working in my stead during all the weeks I was glued to the book and for teaching me your fine and gentle style of management.

Veggie Planet staff Lazaro, Paul, Pat, Alex, Graham, and Jason, for allowing me the time necessary to write this book and for entertaining me whenever I am at V.P.

Jack MacDonald, for swapping journalistic trials and for giving my dad a good run for his title as the consummate entertainer.

Germana Fabbri and Ann O'Brien, for being the cocaptains of my personal and professional cheerleading squad.

Lauren Chandler, for your enthusiasm while typing my recipes and for your steady stream of postcards thereafter.

My downstairs neighbors Scott and Brian, for your "what's mine is yours" attitude. If I could marry two men, it would be you two.

Deirdre Davis, for our passionate, food-based friendship that goes far beyond food.

Max Bazerman, for your ardent support.

Catherine Dickey, for your wisdom in guiding me along the way.

Sam Tan, for being my restaurant informant and for steadfast support.

Jessica Sherman, who, word by word, made this book easy to read and understand.

Jen Goldsmith, who could host a party blindfolded and never miss a beat, for connecting me to many helpful and wonderful people who helped me write this book.

P. J. Burke, for your good attitude and hard work.

Rosalind Reiser, for your swift and sharp editing.

Kelly Horan Jones, for your lively and humorous edits.

Monica Velgos, for your insightful editing.

Tammy Kennedy, for your enthusiastic and thorough recipe tests.

Jean Berg, for being the party girl of Brookline.

Steven Raichlen, for being an enthusiastic and supportive boss in the early nineties.

Becky Sue Epstein, for writing the piece on dessert wines.

Mary Scully, for your supportive and enlightening e-mails and friendship.

Dina Aronson, M.S., R.D., L.D., for generous nutritional advice.

Harvest Cooperative Supermarket, for selling local organic produce without attitude or price hikes.

Rob Beattie, for computer help and friendship.

St. John's Church in Jamaica Plain, for support.

acknowledgments

Operation Frontline (a social service agency), for offering me the opportunity to teach cooking to adults while writing the book.

Pat Montandon, for writing a delightful book on entertaining, *How to Be a Party Girl* (McGraw-Hill, 1968), that is equally poignant and humorous.

Evelyn Kimber, president of the Boston Vegetarian Society, for tirelessly promoting vegetarian eating.

My trusty testers: Kara at Grateful Farm, Jenn Kelley, Jenn McHonagle, Jean McCutcheon, Jane Schulman, Hillary Farber and Joanne, Karen Masterson, Felicity, Dian, Deborah Marlino, Christine Evans, Charles Darwell, Cathy Walthers, Brian Beattie, Bess Hochstein, Cousin Andy, Michael Staub, Adam Penn, Linda Chin, Karen Farrell, Katie, Tiffany, Laura Douglass, Laurie Salzman, Meredith Moore, Julia Grimaldi, the Rad Betties, Lois, Carolyn Heller, Norma, Charlie Bandy, Ron and Judy Blau, and Rosemary Melli.

Deborah Madison, Patti Polisar, Marjorie Williams, and Lisa Tuttle, for giving me insight into their entertainment strategies.

Henry ♥

Contents

Introduction

To have patience with imperfection is almost to guarantee a good time.

—MOLLY O'NEILL

In my experience, the most enjoyable gatherings are simple, unorthodox, and occasionally even botched. One of my favorites was a fiesta-style indoor block party to which I invited the entire neighborhood by tucking flyers into their mail slots. "Come me neighbors and tally me bananas!" I proclaimed to the twenty houses on my street. I cooked enough for sixty and patiently awaited the throngs. An hour after everyone was supposed to be there, only two people had shown up. But the food was spicy, the conversation lively, and by the end of the night, I unexpectedly gained a new best friend. Then there was the time I served *gula malaca,* a Malaysian pudding, for dessert. It came out viscous and gray. As I spooned it into bowls, one of my guests suggested that I rename it bronchitis. Although my ego was bruised for a moment, the jab was too funny not to laugh

at, and the rest of the meal was a smashing success.

There are two essential ingredients for a successful party:

1. **To feed people (yourself included).**
2. **To enjoy people (yourself included).**

Whatever gets you to that place most comfortably is the key. Perhaps it's being superorganized and making a masterpiece dish from Thomas Keller's *The French Laundry Cookbook.* Or maybe it's not planning at all and cooking creatively from your fridge, or serving an entrée you've cooked many times before. Or it could be asking everyone to bring food while you supply the wine, or inviting people over for just ice cream. All parties don't have to be perfectly planned, and they don't have to make sense. The truth is, there are no rules.

Who says that you have to pass hors d'oeuvres, offer alcohol at a cocktail party, or serve a green vegetable at a dinner party? My friend Patti has a strict policy against appetizers. They're too much work, and people fill up on them and have no room for dinner. She'd rather concentrate on making the meal, where everyone is seated around the table and can converse in something other than small talk. Another friend, Jane, has a similar rule regarding the end of the evening: no coffee. She hates leaving the table to rush around and brew a fresh pot, and she wants everyone to linger over wine and enjoy the evening. (One time I saw someone sneak in a thermos of coffee — which just added to the fun.)

All the unspoken "shoulds" of entertaining can ruin a good time. Most of us love good food and look forward to being with others, but the thought of having people over makes us hyperventilate. We have a picture of the perfect party-giver in our heads. She or he has a gorgeous home, serves fab food without getting frazzled, and carries the conversation with razor-sharp wit. This TV image makes us freeze up. But my dining room doubles as my office, my "china" is from a thrift shop, and my significant other is a cat. None of this stops me from having friends over for a good time.

In this book, I want to lower the bar for entertaining and help get people to gather together more often. Sure it's sometimes nice to spend half the day in the kitchen preparing a four-course meal, but a good bowl of soup or a cup of chai and some cookies make most people happy. Why not invite some friends over for creamed spinach over whole wheat toast and watch a favorite film? Or host a dinner party in your driveway, as one of my friends once did when she was faced with the problem of fitting twelve guests into her tiny studio apartment.

introduction

manageable meals for friends

There are few culinary rights and wrongs these days when it comes to planning a dinner. Still, there is some advice worth heeding:

- Strive for balance in flavors, colors, temperatures, and textures.

- Repetition does not appeal to the palate. For example, not every course should be pan-fried, and a pureed soup followed by a pureed sauce in the main course is a no-no. Another common error is using an abundance of cream and cheese throughout the menu. One exception: If you want to celebrate a special ingredient, say garlic or a bumper crop of zucchini, it can be fun to incorporate it into each course.

- Bypass convention if you don't feel up to preparing a "fancy" entrée—serve soup, a substantial salad, and dessert. You can always buy dessert at a nearby bakery or ice cream shop.

- Keep it simple—have one complicated course and keep the rest relatively simple, both for your own sanity and for the well-being of your guests' digestive tracts.

- If you feel uncomfortable about mixing and matching dishes from around the globe, stick to the same country or at least the same continent.

- Finally, on a more practical note, don't choose dishes that all require a lot of last-minute attention. Include some dishes that can be prepared ahead of time so you won't be overwhelmed right before dinner.

Parties should be whatever you want them to be. Casual and spontaneous doesn't mean boring and mediocre. If you're relaxed, your guests will be too. Sometimes I end up inviting four or five extra people a few hours before a dinner party. I don't spend a lot of time planning my menu. Usually I peruse my favorite cookbook of the moment for recipes that grab me. If one dish doesn't fit in seamlessly, I'll throw caution to the wind and make it anyhow. No one will care about the cohesiveness of the menu, and this way I'll have more fun cooking. Chances are the food will taste better too. I find it exciting to mix and match dishes that aren't normally served together when the combination makes sense to me. If you aren't feeling up to making a fancy entrée, just serve soup, salad, and dessert.

This book is meant to inspire. It reflects my passions: Vietnamese, Malaysian, Indian and French cooking, as well as many other cuisines. The menus will satisfy both serious vegetarians and meat-eaters. More and more people are opting to serve vegetarian meals. Vegetarian eating is a way to help the planet, and entertaining helps us make connections and creates a feeling of community.

But the main reason I entertain is even more basic: to make the people I care about happy and to save them the time and trouble of cooking something for themselves.

This is No Big Deal Entertaining. Add a few friends, get ready for the unexpected, and learn that less than perfect is where the fun is.

How to Have Great Food on Hand

When a friend drops by and you'd like to make dinner but you don't know what to have, a well-stocked pantry and freezer and a few good recipes on hand will pay off. The emergency entertaining recipes (see pages 166–167) should give you some good ideas.

Keep in mind that many of the recipes in this book — and of course others — can be approximated with ingredients that aren't perfect substitutes. If you want to make Tofu, Broccoli, and Tomatoes with Curried Peanut Sauce and all you have is frozen tempeh and spinach, you can still make the dish. You'll just have to free-fall and make an educated guess about whether tempeh and spinach should be cooked in the same manner as tofu and broccoli. You will soon become adept at adapting. Combine the ingredients you have on hand with your recipes and see if there's something you can make with a substitution or two. No vegetable stock for a risotto? Use more onions and garlic and

freezer tips

- Double-wrap everything superduper airtight in plastic (buy plastic wrap that is made for the freezer) to prevent freezer burn. Even in its advanced stages, freezer burn won't hurt you, but it does impart a flavor that reminds me of wet feet.

- Delicate herbs such as basil, tarragon, and cilantro do not freeze well in their fresh state. If you have a lot on hand, the best thing to do is process the leaves (and stems in the case of cilantro) in a food processor with a cup or so of oil. Freeze the mixture in a zip bag, and cut off bits with a knife to use in soups, pasta dishes, and the like.

From the Freezer

add a carrot or two. No fresh vegetables, but you have pasta? Mix the pasta with beans or lentils. Whatever you do, don't run out of garlic. There's nothing more depressing than a kitchen lacking this fragrant bulb.

About Freezing

I love my freezer. It's nothing huge — just a conventional compartment on top of my refrigerator, but it holds a wealth of convenient supplies and emergency rations. Stashing some Asian noodles or spring roll wrappers in there saves me a trip to the Asian market when the need arises. If I buy one bunch of rosemary, sage, or thyme, I store what I don't use in the freezer, where it can last for six months. Having frozen vegetables such as spinach, peas, and edamame on hand allows me to make dinner without going to the store — all I have to do is combine them with rice or pasta, garlic, and good olive oil or Asian flavorings. Many of the recipes in this book can be made with frozen vegetables in place of fresh.

Some foods keep in the freezer for six months or more, including nuts, lemongrass, and frozen spinach and peas. Breads and chopped herbs don't keep for long.

Ⓥ indicates that a recipe is vegan.
Vegan foods come entirely from the plant kingdom and contain no products or by-products of animal origin.

chapter 1

Nibbles and Drinks

just a bite?

There are several compelling advantages to having people over for nibbles and drinks versus dinner. It's less expensive. You'll spend less time in the kitchen and more time with your friends. The length of the guest list isn't dictated by how many chairs you own, and you and your guests can move freely from conversation to conversation.

But remember, many people view cocktail parties not just as a time to socialize, but also as an opportunity to get dinner into their stomachs. My parents have operated like this for over forty years. They developed the tactic during their early lean years, when their lively social life was instrumental in defraying their weekly food allowance. I remember my mom uttering the same lines again and again upon returning from yet another cocktail party, "Oh, you should have seen your father! He ate every last shrimp at that party! What are we going to do with him?" In the next breath, she

exonerated herself from dinner duty, "We certainly don't need supper now."

So how many hors d'oeuvres should you plan to serve to the hungry hordes?

For a cocktail party (one that lasts three hours or so), prepare four to six different hors d'oeuvres—at least two of the pass-around kind and two of the help-yourself sort. I figure on two "bites" of each hors d'oeuvre per person at the very least. If the party is from 6:00 to 9:00 p.m., guests will hope to make a dinner of it, so increase the quantity to at least three "bites" of each hors d'oeuvre per person.

When I serve appetizers as a prelude to a dinner party, I don't want my guests to wither from hunger, but I don't want them to fill up frivolously either. I usually offer only one light hors d'oeuvre, such as a basket of crudités with Extra-Smoky Baba Gannouj (page 29), Not-Too-Sweet Caramelized Balsamic Dressing (page 156), or another light dip.

star anise pecans

I like all kinds of crunchy spiced nuts, but these star anise pecans are at the head of the class. This recipe works equally well with walnuts, if you can't spring for the higher-priced pecans.

MAKES 5 CUPS

2/3 cup sugar

2 tablespoons ground star anise (see page 451)

1 tablespoon kosher salt

2 teaspoons cayenne pepper

2 teaspoons ground cinnamon

2 large egg whites

5 cups pecan or walnut halves

1 Preheat the oven to 300 degrees. Line two rimmed baking sheets with parchment paper. In a small bowl, combine the sugar, star anise, salt, cayenne, and cinnamon and mix well.

2 In a medium bowl, whisk the egg whites until bubbly on top, about 30 seconds. Add the spice mixture and mix until blended. Add the nuts, stirring to coat.

3 Divide the nuts between the baking sheets, spreading them in a single layer. Bake for 15 minutes. Reduce the oven temperature to 250 degrees and rotate the baking sheets. Bake for 10 minutes more, or until the nuts are crisp. Slide the parchment paper and nuts onto a cooling rack and let cool before serving.

Note The nuts will keep for at least 1 week in an airtight container at room temperature.

popcorn: the real deal

If you think popcorn is something that is cooked in a bag in the microwave or if you're from the school of Jiffy Pop, you're in for a treat. Real popcorn, the kind popped in a pan with oil, makes for some of the finest noshing on earth. Put out a bowl before dinner (it doesn't fill people up as cheese or dips do), serve it at a cocktail party, or, more traditionally, eat it while you watch a movie.

MAKES 3 QUARTS

- 2 tablespoons canola or olive oil
- ½ cup popcorn kernels
- 3 tablespoons butter, melted (optional)
- ½ teaspoon salt, or more to taste

Heat the oil in a large, heavy-bottomed pan over medium-high heat. When it starts to smoke, add the popcorn kernels. Cover the pan and shake it lightly as the kernels pop. When the popping sound slows markedly, remove the pan from the heat. Transfer the popcorn to a large bowl. Add the butter (if using) and salt and toss to coat (I use my hands). Serve immediately.

Variations

Honey or Maple Popcorn: Add 2 tablespoons honey or maple syrup to the melted butter and boil for 30 seconds. Drizzle the mixture over the popcorn, add the salt, and stir well to coat.

Parmesan Popcorn: After you have tossed the popcorn with the butter and salt, add ½ cup grated Parmesan cheese and freshly ground black pepper to taste, if you like, and stir well to coat.

Fish on Fire

Preheat the oven to 350 degrees. In a large bowl, combine 2 teaspoons or more hot sauce (I like Inner Beauty or Melinda's), 2 tablespoons olive oil, and a pinch of salt. Stir in one 6-ounce bag cheddar-flavored Pepperidge Farm Goldfish and toss to coat. Spread the fish in a single layer on a rimmed baking sheet. Bake for 10 minutes. Serve warm or let cool and store in a zip bag for up to 5 days.

Asian-Style Popcorn: My friend Doe likes to season her popcorn with butter and soy sauce. Mix 1 tablespoon soy sauce with the melted butter. Drizzle the mixture over the popcorn and stir well to coat. You won't need additional salt.

Exotic Popcorn: Tangy ground sumac (found in Middle Eastern markets) and nutty toasted rice powder (found in Asian markets) add exotic notes to popcorn. Add 1 teaspoon of either spice to the melted butter. Drizzle the mixture over the popcorn, add the salt, and stir well to coat.

glamorous pickled vegetables

(V) *Spiked with fresh ginger* and glowing in Technicolor glory, these pickles are absurdly easy to make and mighty tasty. I like to serve them before dinner because you can eat more than a few without filling up. Choose one, two, or three vegetables—I include carrots because they turn a brilliant neon orange. I also like to use green radish, which is found in Asian markets. It looks like a green daikon, although fatter and shorter. Take note that these pickles must be made at least 1 day before they are served.

MAKES 5 CUPS

1½ cups white vinegar

1 cup thinly sliced fresh ginger

½ cup sugar

2 teaspoons kosher salt

8 cups sliced vegetables, such as red or yellow bell peppers, carrots, jicama, daikon, asparagus, pickling cucumbers, kohlrabi, and okra; broccoli and/or cauliflower florets; and halved red radishes

1 In a large, nonreactive saucepan, bring the vinegar, ginger, sugar, and salt to a boil. Remove from the heat and allow the mixture to stand for 15 minutes.

2 Place the vegetables in a large, shallow bowl. Bring the vinegar mixture to a boil again and pour it over the vegetables. Toss the vegetables well and transfer them and the liquid to a container with a tight-fitting lid. Allow the mixture to cool before covering. Refrigerate overnight. Serve the pickled vegetables in a glass bowl or on a tray to show off their beautiful colors.

Note The pickles will keep in the fridge for at least 2 weeks stored in an airtight container, covered with their pickling liquid.

hot spinach-cheese dip

Since it's likely that you already have these ingredients on hand, this dip can be whipped up at the last minute if company shows up unexpectedly. Serve with crackers such as stoned wheat thins or slices of baguette.

MAKES ABOUT 3 CUPS

2 10-ounce boxes frozen, chopped spinach, thawed

1 medium onion, chopped

2 plum tomatoes, chopped

1/4 cup sour cream

1 large garlic clove, minced

8 ounces cream cheese, softened, cut into 8 pieces

1 cup grated Pecorino Romano cheese

1 tablespoon capers, drained

1/2 teaspoon kosher salt

1/2 teaspoon freshly ground black pepper

1 Preheat the oven to 425 degrees (or use the microwave). Place the spinach in a colander set in the sink and press out most of the liquid with a rubber spatula.

2 In a food processor, puree the spinach, onion, tomatoes, sour cream, and garlic. Add the cream cheese, Romano, capers, salt, and pepper and process until smooth.

3 Transfer the dip to a 1 1/2-quart casserole dish. Bake for 20 minutes or microwave on high for 4 to 5 minutes, or until piping hot. Serve.

Note The dip can be prepared through step 2 up to 3 days ahead and stored in an airtight container in the fridge. Transfer to the casserole dish and continue as directed.

nibbles and drinks

crudités as art

Raw vegetables are just raw vegetables, but when you arrange them artfully and pair them with a sauce that rocks, they become crudités. Successful crudités are evidenced by your guests parked by the vegetables, oblivious to the commotion around them, meditatively dipping away.

The Composition

Choose a small variety of vegetables and position them upright in an attractive bowl or basket, *not* a platter. Arrange crudités as you would flowers in a vase—standing up, not lying flat and lifeless. It's better to have a brimming crudité bowl than a sparse one, so err on the smaller side. I prefer wooden salad bowls, funky freeform baskets, handmade ceramic bowls, or anything that is clean and not run-of-the-mill. If you want more height, give your veggies a boost by placing a folded clean dishtowel or two in the basket or bowl before filling it.

The fewer types of vegetables you use, the more attractive the composition will be. Each vegetable need not be a different color. Some of the prettiest arrangements I've seen have been varying shades of green.

Group each vegetable together—the broccoli in one patch, the red pepper in another, the carrots in a third. Think of a crudité basket as the Irish countryside—patches of colors and textures.

The Dip

A common mistake is to choose too large a bowl to hold the dip; a little dip goes a long way. I like to hollow out smallish sturdy vegetables or fruits, such as an acorn squash half, a grapefruit half, or a red bell pepper with its top sliced off. Although I think vegetable vessels are more handsome, sometimes I use a small bowl.

Choosing the Vegetables

Choose only vegetables that are impeccably fresh. There is no place to hide blemished or dried-out vegetables in crudités. If you're looking for something different, shop for your vegetables at an Asian market. They sell basic vegetables like carrots and broccoli as well as more exotic vegetables such as jicama and baby bok choy. Look for flowering chives, which are a decorative addition to your arrangement.

Dip-Worthy Veggies

- **Steamed artichoke leaves** (Steam the artichokes, pull the leaves out, and nestle them in the basket.)
- **Blanched or grilled asparagus**
- **Baby bok choy** (Pull apart like celery; hold the leaf and eat the white part.)
- **Bok choy** (Slice the white part on the bias and keep the green leafy part for garnishing.)
- **Broccoli** (Cut into florets, blanch for just 1 minute, then shock with cold water.)
- **Button mushrooms** (Buy big ones.)
- **Cabbage** (Use only stiff leaves near the core and blanch as for broccoli.)
- **Carrots*** (Wash, peel, then cut thinly on the bias—also good grilled.)
- **Celery*** (Trim and slice into long, thin spears the length of the stalk.)
- **Cherry or pear tomatoes**
- **Cucumbers or pickling cucumbers** (Cut into lengthwise spears, with the skin on.)
- **Daikon radishes*** (Cut into long spears.)
- **Endive leaves*** (Cut 1 inch off the base, then separate the leaves.)
- **Fennel bulb*** (Cut into thin, dippable pieces—also good grilled.)
- **Green beans or pole beans** (Blanch or leave raw.)

(continued)

nibbles and drinks

- **Jicama*** (My favorite dipper! Peel and cut into thin pieces.)
- **Kohlrabi*** (Peel and cut in half, then cut into thin slices.)
- **Bell peppers** (Cut into long, thin or thick slices.)
- **Radicchio** (Cut into 1-inch slices.)
- **Radishes*** (Cut in half or leave whole.)
- **Raw yellow beans** (Trim the tails but leave the tips intact.)
- **Snap peas or snow peas**
- **Zucchini** (Cut into thin, lengthwise spears—also good grilled.)

If preparing these vegetables more than 3 hours ahead, immerse them in cold water, and refrigerate until ready to use.

The Dips

Dress up your crudités with these knock-'em-dead dips:

Not-Too-Sweet Caramelized Balsamic Dressing (page 156)

Gorgonzola Dressing (page 161)

Goat Cheese–Walnut Dressing (page 160)

Saffron Aïoli (page 17)

Alternative Spinach Dip (page 18)

Hip Dip (page 36)

Extra-Smoky Baba Gannouj (page 29)

Green Skordalia (page 20)

Avocado-Tomatillo Guacamole (page 35)

Curried Walnut Dip (page 28)

Goat Cheese and Roasted Garlic Fondue (page 72)

Any one of my peanut sauces (pages 221, 350, and 351)

saffron aïoli

(V) *Aïoli is a garlic mayonnaise* from the South of France. It makes a killer crudité dip. My eggless version made with silken tofu is a bit lighter than the traditional version, and I prefer it this way.

MAKES 1 CUP

2 tablespoons fresh orange juice

Big pinch of saffron threads

2 garlic cloves

½ cup silken tofu

½ cup extra-virgin olive oil

1 tablespoon fresh lemon juice

Kosher salt and freshly ground black pepper to taste

1 In a small saucepan over low heat, combine the orange juice and saffron threads, stirring until the saffron starts to dissolve. Set aside to cool.

2 In a food processor, mince the garlic. Add the tofu and cooled saffron mixture and process well. With the machine running, slowly add the olive oil through the feed tube and process until the mixture thickens and lightens in color. Add the lemon juice and season with salt and pepper.

Note
The aïoli will keep for up to 2 weeks stored in an airtight container in the fridge.

alternative spinach dip

We already have alternative medicine and alternative radio stations, so now I think the world is ready to take on alternative spinach dips. I've seen more than a few traditional spinach dips in my day, most of them dull in flavor and weighed down with gobs of mayonnaise. Here's my alternative—a spinach dip with zest and pep. Serve with crudités and crackers.

MAKES ABOUT 3 CUPS

1 10-ounce box frozen, chopped spinach, thawed, or 10 ounces fresh spinach, finely chopped

1 cup finely chopped red onion

1/2 cup low-fat small-curd cottage cheese

1 large garlic clove, minced

1 1/2 cups cubed firm tofu (about two thirds of a 16-ounce carton)

1/4 cup sour cream

2 tablespoons mayonnaise

2 tablespoons fresh lemon juice (1/2 juicy lemon)

1/2 teaspoon sugar

1/2 teaspoon ground cumin

1 teaspoon kosher salt, plus more if necessary

Freshly ground black pepper to taste

1 tablespoon toasted sesame seeds for garnish (optional; see page 450)

Note

The dip can be prepared 2 days ahead and stored in an airtight container in the fridge.

entertaining for a veggie planet

1 If using frozen spinach, place it in a colander set in the sink and press out most of the liquid with a rubber spatula. In a medium bowl, combine the thawed or fresh spinach, onion, cottage cheese, and garlic and mix well.

2 Wrap the tofu cubes in a clean dishtowel and press firmly with your hands until you feel the towel become damp. Transfer the tofu to a food processor. Add the sour cream, mayonnaise, lemon juice, sugar, cumin, and salt and process until smooth.

3 Fold the tofu mixture into the spinach mixture until well combined. Add the pepper and more salt, if necessary.

4 Serve the dip at room temperature, or cover and refrigerate and serve chilled. Garnish with the sesame seeds, if desired, just before serving.

the pappadam—new chip on the block

Sick of the ever present potato and tortilla chips? Pappadams, the crispy, paper-thin wafers from India, are on the rise. Made from *urad dal* (lentils), their nutty-peppery flavor and crunchy texture (reminiscent of Pringles) make them far more sophisticated than any chip sold in a cardboard tube. They are available at Indian grocery stores and are sometimes labeled "papad." If you want to get fancy, buy prepared chutney to serve with the pappadams. You can crisp them easily ahead of time in the microwave. Place one pappadam on a plate and microwave on high for 50 to 60 seconds. You can heat two or three at the same time; just make sure they don't overlap. They will stay crisp for hours.

green skordalia (potato dip)

Ⓥ *An elderly Greek neighbor* named Ana introduced me to skordalia, a puree of potatoes, olive oil, and garlic. I kept trying to engage her in conversation because I'd heard she was an excellent cook, but she didn't respond to my steady efforts. One day, out of the blue, she waved me into her apartment. There I was, finally sitting in her cozy kitchen, watching her putter around. As I asked her questions, I found out why she'd kept her distance — she could hardly speak English. She fed me an innocent-looking topping on toast that was as white as virgin snow but laced with a lethal dose of garlic. Fortunately, I was able to get her to write down the ingredients of her skordalia. Since then, I've found that I like adding scallions and basil, since they cut the garlic a bit and add good flavor.

MAKES ABOUT 3 CUPS

1⅓ pounds large red or Yukon Gold potatoes, peeled and halved

Kosher salt

½ cup extra-virgin olive oil

3–4 garlic cloves, minced

⅔ cup packed chopped fresh basil or cilantro

½ cup chopped scallions, green parts only

1 tablespoon fresh lemon juice

Freshly ground black pepper to taste

Grilled or toasted bread

Note The dip can be prepared up to 2 days ahead and stored in an airtight container in the fridge.

1 Place the potatoes in a large saucepan and add cold water to cover and salt. Bring to a boil, then reduce the heat and simmer until tender, about 25 minutes. Drain the potatoes and return them to the pan.

2 Add the olive oil and garlic to the hot potatoes and mash with a potato masher until smooth. Add the basil or cilantro, scallions, and lemon juice, and mash until everything is incorporated and smooth. Stir in 1 1/2 teaspoons salt and the pepper.

3 Transfer the skordalia to a serving bowl and serve warm or at room temperature with the grilled or toasted bread.

cleaning up

At the end of the party, some people prefer cleaning up all by themselves after everyone has gone. Others like it when their friends help out. There's no right or wrong way — it's about having a positive attitude. If you're among good friends and you don't feel like doing all the cleanup yourself, ask everyone to pitch in for fifteen or twenty minutes. This can be the best part of the party, since everyone is usually relaxed by then. If the party is formal, this isn't viable, of course. I hate to be stuck with piles of dishes and sticky surfaces once the guests have gone home. But sometimes, if the party was either long or stressful, I like to do the cleanup alone, or with the voices of Lucinda Williams or Emmylou Harris filling the room.

roasted red pepper dip

 Serve this dip with artichoke leaves for an elegant version of "chips and dip." Other appropriate dippers include endive, celery, fennel, blanched asparagus, and bread sticks. This dip can also double as a formidable pasta sauce.

MAKES 1½ CUPS

3 roasted red bell peppers (see page 23)

2 tablespoons capers, drained

½ cup extra-virgin olive oil

2 tablespoons balsamic vinegar

1 teaspoon kosher salt

Freshly ground black pepper to taste

8 large basil leaves torn into small pieces, plus 1 whole basil leaf for garnish

1 In a food processor, coarsely puree the roasted peppers and capers. With the machine running, slowly pour the olive oil through the feed tube, then add the vinegar, salt, and pepper. Transfer to a serving bowl and stir in the torn basil.

2 Cover and refrigerate for at least 2 hours. Remove from the fridge at least 30 minutes before serving to take the chill off. Garnish with a fresh basil leaf and serve.

Note The dip can be made up to 2 days ahead and stored in an airtight container in the fridge.

roasting red peppers is a snap

Roasting red bell peppers at home is easier than you think, and the flavor far surpasses the store-bought version. Roast several peppers at a time because they keep well in the fridge and can be used in so many ways. Use roasted peppers in sandwiches, pasta dishes, pizzas, salads, and salsas, or puree them for sauces.

For gas stoves: Place the whole red bell peppers on a gas burner on low heat. Roast, using tongs to turn the peppers every few minutes, until they're blackened all over but not too charred (you should see a bit of red peering through). Cool the peppers for 10 minutes, then halve them and remove the seeds. Rub the skins off with your fingers until only the red flesh remains. (Do not rinse the peppers with water or they will lose their roasted flavor.)

For electric stoves: Preheat the oven to 450 degrees. Place the whole red bell peppers in an oiled roasting pan and roast for 30 minutes, turning every 10 minutes, until blackened all over but not too charred (you should see a bit of red peering through). Continue with the instructions above.

The roasted peppers will keep for up to 1 month in an airtight container with olive or canola oil to cover.

ruby walnut dip with artichokes

 For an elegant alternative to chips and salsa, try a beautiful bowl of jewel-like dip surrounded by artichoke leaves for scooping. You can also turn this dip into a salad by cutting the beets into larger pieces.

MAKES 3 CUPS

½ cup chopped walnuts

3 artichokes

2 large beets (about 1 pound total), unpeeled

¼ cup finely chopped fresh basil or mint

2 scallions, white and green parts, finely chopped

3 tablespoons extra-virgin olive oil

1 tablespoon fresh lemon juice, or more to taste

Kosher salt and freshly ground black pepper to taste

1 Preheat the oven to 350 degrees. Spread the walnuts in a single layer on a rimmed baking sheet and toast for 5 minutes, or until golden brown.

2 Bring two large pots of water to a boil. Drop the artichokes in one pot and the beets in the other. Lightly boil until both vegetables are tender — when a knife can easily pierce a beet and when a leaf can be easily removed from an artichoke, 30 to 40 minutes.

3 Drain the artichokes in a colander, rinse with cold water, and set aside. Drain the beets, rinse with cold water, and peel off their skins with your hands. Cut the beets into ¼-inch cubes and transfer to a large bowl.

4 Add the toasted walnuts, basil or mint, scallions, olive oil, and lemon juice to the beets, tossing until well mixed. Season with salt and pepper.

Note The dip can be prepared up to 2 days ahead and stored in an airtight container in the fridge. Don't pull the leaves off the artichokes until just before serving, or they will lose their flavor.

making people comfortable

When you're gearing up for company, keep in mind that the most important thing isn't the food. One of my catering clients was an elegant woman named Jean. When I arrived at her house with food in hand, she told me that Yo-Yo Ma would be one of her guests.

"Wow!" I said. "You mean the famous conductor?"

She replied, "Well, he might conduct, but I believe he also plays the cello."

This was a considerate way for her to correct my fumble, sparing me the awkwardness of being corrected directly. I ended up sitting next to Yo-Yo Ma at the dinner table, and he was inspiring as well—generous, modest, and compassionate. He even insisted on clearing the table and wouldn't let me help!

Cover and refrigerate until chilled, then taste for seasoning, adding more salt and pepper if necessary.

5 Meanwhile, pull the leaves off the artichokes (reserve the artichoke hearts and eat them with any leftover beet dip and a drizzle of olive oil and lemon juice). Transfer the dip to a serving bowl and place it in the center of a platter. Arrange the artichoke leaves around the bowl, and serve. Be sure to have a discard bowl for the scraped artichoke leaves.

muhammara (pomegranate-walnut dip)

(V) I only recently discovered muhammara—a crunchy, sour, sweet, and spicy dip—and its ability to drastically improve one's quality of life in minutes. I brought two containers of muhammara and a box of Triscuits to a baseball game at Fenway Park, where I was meeting friends. To my surprise, the muhammara spurred a feeding frenzy. The dip was nearly gone fifteen minutes after I took my seat. Everyone was coming at me with Triscuits as I tried to hold the container steady. While a bit frightened by their zeal, I also felt extremely popular! Even when you don't offer muhammara in a culinary vacuum, amid peanuts, hot dogs, pretzels, and lite beer, it seems to have a magnetic pull. Jars of Turkish red pepper paste can be found in Middle Eastern markets.

MAKES 1½ CUPS

- 1 6-inch pita bread
- 1 cup chopped walnuts
- 2½ tablespoons Turkish seedless red pepper paste or 1–2 teaspoons hot sauce
- 1½ tablespoons pomegranate molasses (see page 449 or markets), or balsamic vinegar
- 1 garlic clove
- ½ teaspoon ground cumin

- ⅔ cup extra-virgin olive oil
- 1 teaspoon kosher salt

Note

The dip can be made up to 2 days ahead and stored in an airtight container in the fridge. Leftovers will keep for 2 weeks. To help preserve it (and to make it more authentic—this version is much less oily than most), I pour ¼ inch of olive oil over it before closing the lid.

1 Preheat the oven to 325 degrees. Carefully separate the pita bread into 2 disks, and place them rough side up on a rimmed baking sheet. Toast for 10 minutes, or until golden. Set the toasted pita bread aside. Spread the walnuts in a single layer on the same baking sheet and toast for 5 minutes, or until golden brown. Transfer the walnuts to a large bowl.

2 In a food processor, pulse 1 of the pita disks until finely chopped but not pasty. Transfer to the bowl with the walnuts. Process the remaining pita, then add the red pepper paste or hot sauce, pomegranate molasses or vinegar, garlic, and cumin to the processor and puree until smooth.

3 With the machine running, slowly add the olive oil through the feed tube and process until well incorporated. Transfer the pita mixture to the bowl with the walnuts and stir in the salt. Serve the muhammara at room temperature.

Walnuts

curried walnut dip

Since the ubiquitous onion soup dip has become dated (along with TV dinners, John Denver, and pet rocks), here's a dip that's ready and willing to take its place. Like the dip from the soup package, it's very fast. Unlike that dip, it's sophisticated and lively in flavor and a lot prettier to look at.

MAKES ABOUT 2 CUPS

½ cup finely chopped walnuts

2 cups sour cream

4 scallions, white and green parts, finely chopped

2 tablespoons finely chopped fresh cilantro or parsley (optional)

1 rounded tablespoon Madras-style curry paste (see page 448)

Kosher salt and freshly ground black pepper to taste

1 Preheat the oven to 350 degrees. Spread the walnuts in a single layer on a rimmed baking sheet and toast for 5 minutes, or until golden brown. Set aside to cool.

2 In a medium bowl, combine the sour cream, scallions, cilantro or parsley (if using), and curry paste and mix well. Stir in the walnuts. Season liberally with salt and pepper and serve.

Note This dip will keep up to a week in an airtight container.

Parsley

extra-smoky baba gannouj

 This is the dip I make most often, and it's what I usually bring to parties. Intense, smoky flavor from cooking the eggplant over a flame for a long time makes this baba gannouj a cut above others. Serve with crackers, Pita Chips (page 43), or crudités.

MAKES ABOUT 3 CUPS

- 1 1-pound eggplant
- 1 medium onion, chopped
- 2–3 garlic cloves
- 3 tablespoons sesame tahini (see page 451)
- 2 tablespoons extra-virgin olive oil
- 2 tablespoons fresh lemon juice (1/2 juicy lemon)
- 1 teaspoon kosher salt
- 1/2 teaspoon freshly ground black pepper

1 Preheat the oven to 400 degrees. Cook the eggplant over a gas burner on low or grill it over a low fire, using tongs to turn the eggplant every few minutes, until it's blackened all over and very soft and limp, 25 to 30 minutes. Err on the side of overcharring the eggplant rather than undercharring it.

2 Place the eggplant in a small baking dish, and bake until soft but not mushy, 15 to 20 minutes.

3 In a food processor, puree the onion and garlic until smooth. When the eggplant is cool enough to handle, remove the skin with your hands. (It's fine if there are little black specks left on the eggplant.) Add the whole skinless eggplant, tahini, olive oil, lemon juice, salt, and pepper and puree until smooth. Transfer the baba gannouj to a serving bowl. Serve at room temperature or cold.

Note
The baba gannouj can be prepared up to 2 days ahead and stored in an airtight container in the fridge.

nibbles and drinks

29

seven-layer mexican bean dip

Here's my take on the layered Mexican dip that people attack like hungry vultures at cocktail parties. It can be made ahead and baked just before serving. If you have fresh corn on hand, you can roast the kernels from two ears along with the zucchini. The guacamole can be made beforehand as well. Serve with sturdy tortilla chips.

SERVES 10 TO 12

3 small zucchini, cut into ⅓-inch cubes

1 tablespoon extra-virgin olive oil

Kosher salt and freshly ground black pepper to taste

salsa

1 pint cherry or grape tomatoes, halved

4 scallions, white and green parts, finely chopped

2 tablespoons coarsely chopped fresh cilantro

1–2 small, skinny chile peppers, finely chopped

2 tablespoons fresh lime juice (1 juicy lime)

Kosher salt to taste

beans

1 garlic clove

2 13-ounce cans black beans or adzuki beans, rinsed and drained

2 tablespoons coarsely chopped fresh cilantro

1 teaspoon ground cumin

Kosher salt to taste

2½ cups grated cheddar or Monterey jack cheese (about 10 ounces)

guacamole

3 ripe Hass avocados

2 tablespoons coarsely chopped fresh cilantro

1 garlic clove, minced

1 tablespoon extra-virgin olive oil

Kosher salt and freshly ground black pepper to taste

garnishes

1 cup sour cream

4 scallions, white and green parts, finely chopped

Hot sauce (optional; I use Melinda's Hot Sauce)

1 Preheat the oven to 400 degrees. In a small roasting pan, toss the zucchini with the oil to coat lightly and season with salt and pepper. Roast until lightly browned, about 10 minutes. Set aside. Reduce the oven temperature to 350 degrees.

2 **Meanwhile, to make the salsa:** In a food processor, pulse the tomatoes, scallions, cilantro, chiles, and lime juice just until the tomatoes are in small pieces (do not overprocess; it should be rugged and chunky). Transfer the salsa to a small bowl and season with salt. Don't bother washing the processor bowl or blade.

3 **To make the beans:** Pulse the garlic once or twice in the food processor to chop it. Add the beans, cilantro, and cumin, and process until fairly smooth. Transfer the bean mixture to a medium bowl and add salt to taste.

4 **To assemble the dip:** Spread the bean mixture evenly over the bottom of a 9-inch square baking pan. Distribute 1¼ cups of the cheese and half of the salsa over the beans, setting aside the remaining salsa. Then add the zucchini and top with the remaining 1¼ cups cheese. Cover the baking pan with foil and bake for 40 minutes, or until piping hot.

5 **Meanwhile, to make the guacamole:** Pit and peel the avocados, then coarsely mash them in a medium bowl with a fork. Add the cilantro, garlic, and olive oil, and continue mashing until well blended. Season liberally with salt and pepper.

6 When the dip is hot, remove the foil and drop spoonfuls of guacamole and sour cream on top, interspersing the two. Garnish with the remaining salsa and the scallions and shake on hot sauce, if desired. Serve hot.

Note

The dip can be assembled up to 1 day before baking, covered with plastic wrap, and stored in the fridge. The guacamole can be made up to 24 hours ahead and stored with a piece of plastic wrap against its surface in the fridge.

nibbles and drinks

zesty, smoky cherry tomato– oregano salsa

Ⓥ *I could have called this* just "Tomato Salsa," but that would have been like calling the Sistine Chapel just a church. I find cherry tomatoes to be much sweeter and more flavorful than just about any tomato. In wintertime, they're the only fresh tomatoes I use. Lime rind adds zest to the salsa, while canned chipotle chiles add smokiness. Serve with U-Do-It Tortilla Chips (page 44) and sour cream. This recipe easily doubles and is great to have on hand.

MAKES 1½ CUPS

- ½ pint cherry tomatoes, halved, or 2 medium tomatoes, cut into wedges
- ¼ red onion, coarsely chopped
- 1–2 chipotle chiles in adobo
- 1 tablespoon chopped fresh oregano, plus 1 sprig of fresh oregano for garnish (optional)
- 1 rounded teaspoon grated lime rind
- 2 tablespoons fresh lime juice (1 juicy lime)
- 2 tablespoons extra-virgin olive oil
- Kosher salt and freshly ground black pepper to taste

1 In a food processor, pulse the tomatoes, onion, chipotles, chopped oregano, lime rind, and lime juice until finely chopped.

2 Transfer the tomato mixture to a serving bowl. Add the olive oil and season with salt and pepper. Serve, garnished with an oregano sprig, if you like.

Note
The salsa can be made up to 2 days in advance and stored in an airtight container in the fridge.

toasted pumpkin seed and red pepper salsa

(V) Here's a chance to enjoy the good flavor of freshly toasted pumpkin seeds. The seeds are chopped in the processor along with all the ingredients and contribute a terrific nuttiness and crunchiness.

Serve with tortilla chips and sour cream, if you like.

MAKES 2 CUPS

1 red bell pepper

1 small onion, quartered

½ cup lightly packed fresh cilantro leaves

½ cup toasted pumpkin seeds (see page 449)

1–2 small, skinny chile peppers

2 tablespoons fresh lime juice (1 juicy lime)

1 tablespoon extra-virgin olive oil

Kosher salt and freshly ground black pepper to taste

In a food processor, pulse all the ingredients until coarsely chopped. Transfer to a serving bowl and serve.

Note The salsa is best served the day it's made.

the importance of lists

Attending to both the organization and timing of my cooking and shopping before my friends arrive does me a lot of good. Over the years, I've learned to be realistic about how many dishes I can take on without feeling rushed. I write a shopping list, then a checklist of the recipes and the order in which I want to conquer them. I figure out how long each dish will take, and I block out some downtime to make phone calls, hug my cat, read a book, bathe, or maybe take a catnap myself. Even still, I sometimes abandon one of the recipes if things are taking longer than expected. I keep my checklist visible at party time so I can make sure I remember to serve everything I've made.

sweet potato–black bean salsa

 This black and orange salsa is great for Halloween parties. Please note that this recipe makes *a lot* of salsa—all the better because in addition to a great party snack with tortillas it also makes a great filling for quesadillas, burritos, or tacos—combined with cheddar cheese, if you like, and served with hot sauce.

MAKES 7 CUPS

1 Place the sweet potatoes in a medium saucepan and add cold water to cover. Bring to a boil, then reduce the heat and simmer until just tender, about 15 to 20 minutes. Drain well and allow to cool.

2 Finely chop the sweet potatoes and put them in a large bowl. Add the remaining ingredients and mix well. Serve.

Note The salsa can be made up to 2 days ahead and stored in an airtight container in the fridge.

- 2 pounds sweet potatoes (2 medium), peeled and quartered
- 2¼ cups finely chopped tomatoes
- 1 13-ounce can black beans, rinsed and drained
- 1 large onion, finely chopped
- 1 green bell pepper, finely chopped
- ½ cup coarsely chopped fresh cilantro leaves and stems
- ½ cup toasted pumpkin seeds (see page 449)
- 1 jalapeño pepper, seeded (if desired) and finely chopped
- 1 garlic clove, minced
- ⅓ cup fresh lime juice (about 6 juicy limes)
- 2 tablespoons extra-virgin olive oil

  Kosher salt and freshly ground black pepper to taste

avocado-tomatillo guacamole

(V) *Tomatillos, tart green fruits* wrapped in papery husks, lend zest and verve to guacamole. I thought I had invented this combination until I picked up a book on Mexican cuisine and found that it had been discovered many years ago. Well, at least I'm in sync with how Mexican cooks think. I like this guacamole with Pita Chips (page 43), but the traditional tortilla chip works just as well.

MAKES 4 CUPS

3 ripe Hass avocados (the dark, bumpy kind), pitted and peeled

½ pound fresh tomatillos, husks removed, finely chopped

1 small red onion, finely chopped, 1 teaspoon reserved for garnish

½ cup chopped fresh cilantro leaves and stems

2 garlic cloves, minced

2 plum tomatoes, diced

Kosher salt and freshly ground black pepper to taste

1 In a wide bowl, combine the avocados, tomatillos, onion, cilantro, and garlic and coarsely mash with a potato masher or fork. Fold in the tomatoes, then season liberally with salt and pepper.

2 Cover the bowl tightly with plastic wrap pressed against the surface of the guacamole. Refrigerate for at least 30 minutes to blend the flavors. Garnish with the reserved onion and serve.

Note The guacamole can be prepared 1 day ahead and stored in the fridge tightly covered with plastic wrap pressed against the surface so air doesn't discolor it.

hip dip

The stylish edamame soybean takes the place of avocado in this new-wave dip. Although it's similar in flavor to traditional guacamole, its more rugged texture makes it winning in its own right. Eat with sturdy tortilla chips or dense whole-grain bread sliced into triangles.

MAKES 3½ CUPS

1 Place the edamame in a colander and rinse them under hot running water until they are mostly thawed, about 30 seconds.

2 In a food processor, coarsely puree the edamame and the remaining ingredients with 2 tablespoons water, leaving some chunks. Adjust the seasonings. Transfer to a serving bowl and, if you like, place lime slices on the sides of the bowl as you would for a margarita. Serve immediately or refrigerate and serve within a few hours.

- **16** ounces frozen, shelled (podless) edamame
- **¾** cup chopped fresh cilantro or flat-leaf parsley
- **1** small red onion, finely chopped
- **2** small, skinny chile peppers, minced
- **2–3** garlic cloves, minced
- **¼** cup extra-virgin olive oil
- **¼** cup fresh lime juice (2 juicy limes)
- **1** tablespoon sugar or honey
- Kosher salt and freshly ground black pepper to taste
- Lime slices for garnish (optional)

edamame—the fashion queen

It seems that edamame, the buttery, sultry soybean from the Far East, migrated to the U.S. via sleek Manhattan bars, where the fashionable set plucked them out of their salted pods while sipping martinis. Edamame, pronounced "eh-da-MA-may," are getting a lot of good press these days, and with good reason. They are picked before they have reached maturity, which makes them more digestible than the harder field soybeans. Edamame are high in protein, containing twice that of lima beans.

Edamame are sold in 1-pound bags in the freezer section of Asian markets, whole food stores, and many supermarkets. They are already blanched, so they only need to be reheated (note: the pod is *not* edible). I always buy podless edamame because they're more convenient for cooking. To enjoy edamame at their simplest, steam them and add a drizzle of good-quality olive oil and a pinch of salt. It's hard to believe frozen food can be so good.

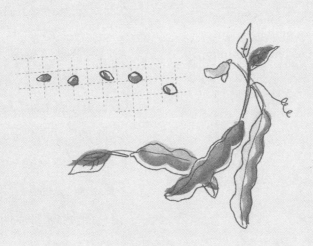

black sesame seed hummus

(V) *Black sesame seeds have the same* nutty flavor as white, but their jet-black color gives a festive visual appeal. Found in Asian markets, they must be toasted to develop their flavor. Toast the whole bag of seeds at once and store what you don't use in the freezer, so you can have them on hand to add drama and flavor to slaws, salads, and stir-fries.

Serve with Pita Chips (page 43), U-Do-It Tortilla Chips (page 44), or plain crackers.

MAKES 1²/₃ CUPS

In a food processor, puree the chickpeas, 3 tablespoons sesame seeds, garlic, tahini, and lemon juice until smooth. With the machine running, add the olive oil through the feed tube, processing until well incorporated. Add the salt and pepper. Transfer to a serving bowl, garnish with the remaining 1 teaspoon sesame seeds, and serve.

- 1 15-ounce can chickpeas, rinsed and drained
- 3 tablespoons toasted black sesame seeds (see page 444), plus 1 teaspoon for garnish
- 2 garlic cloves
- ¹/₃ cup sesame tahini (see page 451)
- ¹/₄ cup fresh lemon juice (1 juicy lemon)
- 2 tablespoons extra-virgin olive oil
- 1 teaspoon kosher salt
- Freshly ground black pepper to taste

Note The hummus can be prepared up to 2 days ahead and stored in an airtight container in the fridge. Let stand at room temperature for 30 minutes before serving.

smoky red lentil spread

(V) *Don't underestimate the diminutive red lentil.* These tiny legumes cook in minutes and are fabulous carriers of flavor. The recipe works equally well with brown or French green lentils, in which case the lentils will need to be boiled for 25 minutes. Serve with crackers or grilled bread.

MAKES 3 CUPS

1½ cups dried red lentils

1 onion, quartered

2 garlic cloves

2 canned chipotle chiles in adobo

¼ cup extra-virgin olive oil

2 tablespoons fresh lemon juice (½ juicy lemon)

1 teaspoon kosher salt

Freshly ground black pepper

1 tablespoon snipped chives or finely chopped scallions, white and green parts, for garnish

1 In a medium saucepan, cook the lentils in at least 2 quarts of boiling water until tender, 5 to 7 minutes. Drain and rinse briefly under cool water. Drain again very well.

2 In a food processor, finely chop the onion and garlic. Add the lentils and chipotles and process until smooth. With the machine running, slowly add the olive oil through the feed tube, processing until well incorporated. Add the lemon juice and salt and pepper. Transfer to a serving bowl, garnish with the chives or scallions, and serve.

Note The spread can be prepared up to 2 days ahead and stored in an airtight container in the fridge. Let stand at room temperature for 30 minutes before serving.

swimming goat cheese

Swimming in a sea of delectable sauces, goat cheese logs are gobbled up by hungry guests. I offer three sauces that the log can swim in: a tomato-oregano salsa, an olive tapenade, and a basil pesto. I like this arrangement because people can decide for themselves the cheese-to-sauce ratio they want.

SERVES 6 TO 8

Spoon about $3/4$ cup of the salsa or tapenade or $1/4$ cup of the pesto into a shallow bowl and place the goat cheese on top. Offer a spoon and knife for serving, with the French bread. Replenish the sauce as necessary.

Zesty, Smoky Cherry Tomato-Oregano Salsa (page 32), Tapenade (page 41), or Pesto (page 42), at room temperature

1 **8-ounce log fresh, mild, creamy goat cheese, at room temperature**

Thinly sliced French bread

indian nachos

A woman I know from India has developed her own radical version of nachos. Here's the skinny:

Preheat the oven to 350 degrees. Cut 4 small flour tortillas into quarters, to make 16 wedges. Place them on a baking sheet and bake until they are crisp and browned. Mash 1 cup chopped and cooked potatoes, 1 cup drained canned chickpeas, a spoonful of butter, a splash of milk, and salt and pepper to taste until smooth. (Both the chips and potatoes can be prepared 1 day ahead and reheated in the microwave.) Top each chip with a spoonful of the hot potato mixture, a small dollop of plain yogurt, and a tiny dab of tamarind pulp (see page 452) or your favorite store-bought chutney. Pass around while still warm.

tapenade

(V) *Okay, I am biased.* This is my favorite of all three swimming sauces. I'm not fond of ordinary tapenades, because they're too pulverized. Here, the components of the sauce—the tomato, basil, and olives—are visible, so it's pretty and texturally interesting. Add some finely chopped red onion, if you like. If the olives are not pitted, see instructions below. Tapenade is also great as a sandwich spread or spooned over a baked potato.

MAKES ABOUT 1¹/₂ CUPS

In a food processor, pulse all the ingredients until finely chopped (do not puree). Serve at room temperature.

Note

> The tapenade is best if eaten within 3 days but will keep for up to 7, stored in an airtight container in the fridge. Let stand at room temperature for 30 minutes before serving.

- 1¹/₂ cups kalamata olives, pitted
- 1 medium ripe tomato
- 10 large fresh basil leaves
- 2 garlic cloves
- ¹/₃ cup extra-virgin olive oil
- 2 tablespoons fresh lemon juice (¹/₂ juicy lemon)
- Freshly ground black pepper to taste

how to pit an olive

Middle Eastern, Italian, Greek, and Armenian markets are excellent places to buy loose olives at a reasonable price. No matter where you buy them, you will probably have to pit them yourself. Here's how:

Place 1 olive on a clean work surface. Put one thumb on top of your other thumb and place the lower thumb on the top of the olive. Putting your weight behind your thumbs, press down on the olive until it cracks and releases its pit. The pit should dislodge itself, but sometimes you must pry it out with your fingers. There will likely be olive meat left on the pit. The only sensible thing to do is to pop the pit into your mouth and enjoy.

nibbles and drinks

pesto

Fresh pesto and goat cheese make a stellar combination. Serve with thinly sliced French bread.

MAKES ABOUT 1½ CUPS

¼ cup pine nuts

2 cups fresh basil leaves

4 garlic cloves

⅓ cup extra-virgin olive oil

¼ cup freshly grated Parmesan cheese

Kosher salt and freshly ground black pepper to taste

1 In a small skillet over medium heat, toast the pine nuts, shaking the skillet often, until they are golden brown in spots, about 3 minutes.

2 In a food processor, coarsely puree the basil, 3 tablespoons of the pine nuts, and the garlic into a rough paste. With the machine running, slowly add the olive oil through the feed tube and process until well incorporated. Add the Parmesan and process until blended. Season liberally with salt and pepper. Serve at room temperature, garnished with the remaining 1 tablespoon pine nuts.

Note The pesto can be made up to 3 days ahead and stored with a thin layer of olive oil on its surface in an airtight container in the fridge. Let stand at room temperature for 30 minutes before serving.

pita chips

(V) *The flavor of fresh pita chips* is so good that they make even store-bought dips and salsas taste great. I especially like them with Extra-Smoky Baba Gannouj (page 29) and Avocado-Tomatillo Guacamole (page 35). Broken into smaller pita "croutons," they also make excellent additions to salads.

MAKES 48 TO 64

12-ounce package 7-inch pita bread

Extra-virgin olive oil

Kosher salt and freshly ground black pepper

1 Preheat the oven to 350 degrees. Carefully separate each pita bread into 2 disks. Cut each disk into 6 or 8 wedges. Place the wedges rough side up on rimmed baking sheets in a single layer, as close together as possible without overlapping. Drizzle olive oil over the wedges, using about 3 tablespoons oil per baking sheet and making sure to get some oil on each wedge. Liberally season the wedges with salt and pepper.

2 Bake the wedges until golden, especially around the edges, about 15 minutes. Serve warm or at room temperature.

Note

The pita chips can be made up to 2 days ahead and stored in an airtight container.

u-do-it tortilla chips

(V) *Why would you bother* making your own tortilla chips? If you try these, you'll find out. Flour tortillas make delicious chips; I don't know why they're not sold commercially. I made these flour tortilla chips when I ran the Delux, a funky bar where bike messengers and artsy types downed pint after pint of Guinness stout and microbrews all night. These trendsetters needed something to counter their liquid diet, and chips and salsa were a common solution. I pan-fried each batch to order, but the same effect can be had by baking the chips.

MAKES 80 CHIPS

10 8-inch flour tortillas

¼ cup canola or extra-virgin olive oil

Kosher salt to taste

1 Preheat the oven to 350 degrees. Stack 5 of the tortillas. Cut the stack in half, then into quarters. Then cut each quarter in half again. You should have 8 triangles per tortilla. Repeat with the remaining 5 tortillas.

2 Pour the oil into a small bowl. With a pastry brush, brush three rimmed baking sheets with some oil (if you have only one or two sheets, just bake the chips in batches). Place the tortilla wedges on the sheets, leaving a little room between them. Drizzle the remaining oil over the wedges (if you're doing this in batches, save some oil for the next batch). Salt the chips generously and evenly.

3 Bake the wedges for 10 minutes, or until the chips are lightly browned. Transfer the chips to a plate or bowl and serve warm.

Note The chips will keep on a baking sheet in a warm (220-degree) oven for up to 2 hours.

parmesan-caraway crackers

You can have homemade crackers lickety-split if you keep the dough in your freezer. It's hard to stop eating them once you start. They are also good with anise seeds (or no seeds at all) in lieu of the caraway.

MAKES 20 CRACKERS

1 cup all-purpose flour

1 tablespoon caraway seeds

4 tablespoons ($\frac{1}{2}$ stick) cold unsalted butter, cut into small pieces

$\frac{2}{3}$ cup freshly grated Parmesan cheese

2 garlic cloves, minced

1 teaspoon kosher salt

Freshly ground black pepper to taste

1 In a food processor, pulse the flour and caraway seeds to blend. Add the butter and pulse until the mixture resembles coarse meal. Add the Parmesan, garlic, salt, and pepper and pulse to incorporate. With the machine running, add $\frac{1}{4}$ cup water through the feed tube and process until the dough comes together.

2 Transfer the dough to a large sheet of plastic wrap and shape it into a 2-inch-diameter log. Wrap the dough tightly in the plastic wrap and freeze for at least 1 hour or refrigerate for at least 24 hours.

3 Preheat the oven to 400 degrees. Unwrap the dough and slice the log crosswise into $\frac{1}{4}$-inch-thick rounds. Arrange the slices 1 inch apart on an ungreased baking sheet.

4 Bake until the crackers are golden brown and firm in the center, about 10 minutes, rotating the pan halfway through for even baking. (Do not allow the crackers to get too dark around the edges.) Use a spatula to transfer the crackers to a cooling rack. Serve at room temperature.

Note
The crackers can be made 1 day ahead and stored in an airtight container. The dough can be frozen for up to 2 months.

new potatoes stuffed with olive salad

V *This recipe wouldn't be out of place* in a glossy, big-name chef's cookbook. However, along with the glitz comes the behind-the-scenes sweat factor—each tiny potato must be hollowed out and stuffed with a lively basil, tomato, and green olive salad. Their elegance and flavor are worth it.

MAKES 12

1 Place the potatoes in a small saucepan and add cold water to cover and salt. Bring to a boil, then reduce the heat and gently simmer just until a paring knife can penetrate a potato with no resistance, 10 to 15 minutes. Do not overcook. Drain the potatoes and rinse quickly under cold water.

2 Meanwhile, chop the olives, slicing the meat off the pits. In a medium bowl, combine the olives, tomatoes, basil, garlic, olive oil, and vinegar. Season liberally with salt and pepper.

3 Cut the potatoes in half. With a small spoon or melon baller, make a well in the cut side of each potato half. If the potato half cannot stand cut side up on its own, slice a small bit off the base to make it stand upright. Fill each well with a generous mound of the olive salad. Serve at room temperature.

6 very small red or white potatoes (about 1 inch in diameter)

Kosher salt

8 Bella di Cerignola olives (or any jumbo green Mediterranean olives; increase to 16 if they aren't jumbo)

4 cherry tomatoes, chopped

6 fresh basil leaves, thinly sliced

1 garlic clove, minced

1 tablespoon extra-virgin olive oil

½ teaspoon balsamic vinegar

Freshly ground black pepper to taste

Note The potatoes can be made up to 1 day ahead and stored in an airtight container in the fridge. Let stand at room temperature for 30 minutes before filling them and serving. The basil-olive mixture can be made up to 2 hours in advance.

calling all women

Stop gabbing on the phone with your girlfriends and invite them over for a girl-talk party! What could be more fun than divulging secrets and desires or commiserating with a group of supportive women you can trust—all while noshing on good food?

What do girls eat when they gab?

Women on the whole enjoy grazing on food rather than consuming it in one fell swoop, so ditch the idea of a sit-down dinner. Instead, serve a selection of tasty foods that can be eaten at will throughout your gabfest. Here are some girl-friendly food ideas. Make two, three, or four of these selections, and adjust the portions to the size of your party.

Crudités with: Extra-Smoky Baba Gannouj (page 29), **Curried Walnut Dip** (page 28), or **Romesco Sauce** (page 345).
U-Do-It Tortilla Chips (page 44) or **Pita Chips** (page 43) with **Avocado-Tomatillo Guacamole** (page 35), **Hip Dip** (page 36), or **Alternative Spinach Dip** (page 18)
Swimming Goat Cheese (page 40)
Pink Eggs (page 52)

Twice-Baked Potatoes (page 197)
Welsh Rabbit (page 69)
Veggie burgers (pages 170–174) with **Lo-Stress Onion Rings** (page 195) or **Steak Fries** (page 196)
Pizza (pages 175–188)

Killer Chocolate Chip Cookies (page 399)
Nutella Fondue (page 424)
Hermit Bars (page 402)
Ice cream with "Seizing" Hot Fudge Sauce (page 422) or **World's Best Peanut Butter Hot Fudge Sauce** (page 421)
Store-bought cookies, such as Oreos or Mrs. Fields Chocolate Chip Cookies

shiitakes stuffed with goat cheese, cranberries, and pecans

These stuffed mushrooms are an elegant but quick nosh, taking no more than 30 minutes to put together. Be sure to choose shiitakes with concave caps so they will hold their stuffing. If it's a festive occasion such as a holiday party, serve on a plate strewn with fresh thyme or sage sprigs and/or fresh cranberries.

If you can't spring for shiitakes, substitute large white mushrooms —not as fancy, but still very tasty.

MAKES 35

35 medium fresh shiitake mushrooms, stems removed

4 tablespoons extra-virgin olive oil

1 medium onion, finely chopped

1 garlic clove, minced

1/4 cup dried, sweetened cranberries

1/4 cup port or dry sherry

1 tablespoon coarsely chopped fresh thyme or sage

4 slices white sandwich bread, stale or toasted

4 ounces soft goat cheese

Kosher salt and freshly ground black pepper to taste

1/3 cup pecans or skinned hazelnuts, untoasted

Note

The mushrooms can be made through step 4 up to 1 day ahead and stored on the baking sheet covered with plastic wrap in the fridge. You can also store the roasted shiitakes and the filling separately in airtight containers in the fridge for up to 3 days. Bake as directed in step 5.

1 Preheat the oven to 400 degrees. Oil a roasting pan large enough to hold the mushrooms in a single layer. In the roasting pan, toss the shiitakes with 1 tablespoon of the olive oil and 2 tablespoons water. Spread the shiitakes stem side down in a single layer and roast until cooked through, about 15 minutes. Set the shiitakes aside to cool. Leave the oven on if you'll be serving the stuffed shiitakes immediately.

2 In a large skillet, heat the remaining 3 tablespoons olive oil over medium heat. Add the onion and sauté until soft, about 5 minutes. Add the garlic and sauté for 1 minute more. Stir in the cranberries and port or sherry. Reduce the heat to low and simmer until the liquid has evaporated and the cranberries have softened, about 5 minutes. Add the thyme or sage and cook for 1 minute more. Remove from the heat.

3 Break the bread slices into a food processor and process them into crumbs. Transfer the crumbs to a large bowl and stir in the onion mixture and goat cheese. Season liberally with salt and pepper.

4 Oil a baking sheet and arrange the shiitakes stem side up on it. Divide the stuffing evenly among the mushrooms, using about 1 teaspoon for each. Use your fingers to press the stuffing into the shiitake caps. Top each with a pecan or hazelnut.

5 Bake the stuffed shiitakes until piping hot, about 10 minutes. Serve immediately.

the devil's eggs

I doubt the devil would ever bother to make anything for a party (he'd buy take-out and say he made it himself), but if he ever did cook anything, these chipotle-spiked stuffed eggs would be right up his alley.

MAKES 16

- 3 tablespoons coarsely chopped pine nuts
- 8 large eggs
- ½ cup mayonnaise
- ½ cup seeded and finely chopped green bell pepper
- ¼ cup finely chopped fresh cilantro leaves and stems
- 6 canned chipotle chiles in adobo
- 1 teaspoon kosher salt

  Freshly ground black pepper to taste

1 In a small skillet over medium heat, toast the pine nuts, shaking the skillet often, until they are golden brown in spots, about 3 minutes. Transfer to a small bowl and set aside.

2 Place the eggs in a medium saucepan and add cold water to cover. Bring to a boil, then immediately reduce the heat to a simmer and set a timer for 12 minutes.

3 Meanwhile, in a small bowl, combine the mayonnaise, bell pepper, cilantro, chipotles, and salt.

4 When the eggs have simmered for exactly 12 minutes, drain them quickly, rattling the eggs around in the pan to crack their shells. Immediately fill the pan with cold water and peel the hot eggs under cold running water.

5 Carefully cut the peeled eggs in half lengthwise and pop out the yolks, reserving the whites. In a medium bowl, mash the yolks with a fork until very smooth (a pastry blender also works well for this), and stir in the mayonnaise mixture. Season with pepper.

campfire confessional
(candles set the scene)

I once went to a birthday party where seven of us (all nearly strangers) sat around the dinner table divulging stories that we might not normally share. One woman had kissed her best friend's boyfriend when they were in college. Another had recently stolen a lipstick from a department store. And a third had skipped a daylong couples therapy session in favor of a late-summer lounge at the beach with her fiancé (she then worried that this meant it would rain on her wedding day, which it did). We went around the table, none of us holding back a word.

The next day I wondered what had caused all this confessing. One factor was that the birthday girl was a very open person. Another factor that contributed was the lighting. The room was dark: there were only two candles on the table, and not another light was on in the house. Is it easier to divulge things when people can barely see you? The campfire atmosphere certainly helped the juicy stories ooze right out.

6 Arrange the egg white halves on a serving platter. Using a small spoon, mound some of the yolk mixture into each egg white cavity. Sprinkle the stuffed eggs with the pine nuts and serve at once.

Note
The stuffed eggs can be made up to 24 hours ahead, without the pine nuts, and stored covered lightly with plastic wrap in the fridge. Let stand at room temperature for 30 minutes, then add the pine nuts and serve.

nibbles and drinks

pink eggs

Adding chopped beets to the yolk mixture means that not only will their pinkness tint the stuffing but the sweet beet flavor will be infused throughout. It's fun to see people's reactions when they're offered a rather shocking-pink egg—they're usually tentative at first and then feel grateful after having tried one.

MAKES 16

2 small beets, unpeeled

8 large eggs

¼ cup mayonnaise

¼ cup finely chopped fresh basil

Kosher salt and freshly ground black pepper to taste

4 finely chopped scallions, green parts only, for garnish

1 Place the beets in a small saucepan and add water to cover. Bring to a boil, then immediately reduce the heat and simmer until the beets are soft when pierced with a paring knife, about 20 minutes. Drain and rinse under cold water, peeling off the skins with your fingers. Cut the beets into ¼-inch cubes.

2 Meanwhile, place the eggs in a medium saucepan and add cold water to cover. Bring to a boil, then immediately reduce the heat to a simmer and set a timer for 12 minutes.

3 When the eggs have simmered for exactly 12 minutes, drain them quickly, rattling the eggs around in the pan to crack their shells. Immediately fill the pan with cold water and peel the hot eggs under cold running water.

4 Carefully cut the peeled eggs in half lengthwise and pop out the yolks, reserving the whites. In a medium bowl, mash the yolks with a fork until very smooth (a pastry blender also works well for this). Stir in the mayonnaise, then fold in the beets and basil and season with salt and pepper.

5 Arrange the egg white halves on a serving platter. Using a small spoon, mound some of the yolk mixture into each egg white cavity. Garnish the stuffed eggs with the chopped scallions and serve at once.

Note The stuffed eggs are best eaten the same day they're made. However, they can be made up to 1 day ahead, without the scallions, and stored covered lightly with plastic wrap in the fridge. Let stand at room temperature for 30 minutes before serving. Add the scallions just before serving.

snack shopping at an asian market

Asian markets can provide entertaining snacks to keep on hand for yourself and your friends. Like American junk food, most of it will last for centuries in your pantry:

Hot green peas: Addictive, crunchy, fried wasabi-coated peas. Check the ingredient label if you're allergic to MSG.

Rice crackers: Japanese crackers, usually shiny, that come in all sorts of shapes and flavors. Some are wrapped in nori seaweed or are flavored with wasabi or curry powder.

Gummy candies: Individually packaged candies similar to gummy bears but made from real fruit juice (such as kiwi, grape, peach, and melon).

Pocky: Skinny bread sticks coated with chocolate or various other flavors.

Jelly shots: Similar to Jell-O but served in small plastic thimbles that you squeeze into your mouth. My favorite flavor? Litchi.

Jackfruit chips: Crunchy, deep-fried chips made from jackfruit, which tastes like a cross between mango and pineapple. Sold in small foil bags.

Sizzling rice crusts or cakes: Dried cakes of glutinous rice that must be deep-fried in hot oil until they puff up. Sold in plastic bags.

mashed potato spring rolls
with peanut sauce

Mashed potatoes and peanut sauce? Bear with me—I won't steer you wrong! The potatoes are mashed with lots of fresh ginger and some cream cheese and then rolled in the spring roll with some watercress. The mashed potatoes are a treat all by themselves, so make extra if you're hungry.

MAKES 20

1 pound red potatoes

Kosher salt

4 ounces cream cheese, at room temperature

2 tablespoons peeled and minced fresh ginger

Freshly ground black pepper to taste

20 8-inch rice-paper wrappers

Small handful of pickled sliced ginger (see page 449)

1 bunch fresh mint, stems removed

1 bunch watercress, larger stems removed

1 cup All-Purpose Peanut Sauce (page 350)

1 Place the potatoes in a large saucepan and add water to cover and salt. Bring to a boil, then reduce the heat and simmer until tender, 25 to 30 minutes. Drain well and return the potatoes to the pan. Add the cream cheese and ginger and season liberally with salt and pepper. Mash the mixture with a potato masher until well blended and smooth.

2 Bring a large pot of water to a boil. Once it boils, reduce the heat to low and cover the pot.

3 Transfer the pot of boiling water to a trivet on a clean work surface. Quickly dip 1 rice-paper wrapper into the hot water. Rotate the wrapper in the water to fully wet it. Lay the wrapper on your work surface. Do a few more (however many will fit on your work surface). Let the wrappers stand for 1 minute to become tacky.

4 Spread about 2 tablespoons of the potato mixture on the bottom third of each wrapper. Top the potatoes with 2 pickled ginger slices. Place a few mint leaves and a watercress sprig on the wrapper above the potatoes. Starting with the end closest to you, roll the wrapper tightly around the stuffing. When it's rolled halfway up, fold the sides of the wrapper toward the center and continue rolling to the end of the wrapper. You should be able to see the herbs through the wrapper. Continue in the same fashion for the other rolls. Cut the spring rolls in half diagonally and serve on a platter with a bowl of All-Purpose Peanut Sauce for dipping.

expanding your spring roll horizons

Cold rice-paper spring rolls make an elegant appetizer. Sometimes I fill them with an already dressed salad or slaw—a good way to finish off a left-over salad in the fridge. The dressing acts as a built-in dipping sauce. Just cut each roll in half on the bias, arrange on an attractive plate, and serve.

How to make rice-paper spring rolls:

1   Purchase round rice-paper wrappers. I usually buy the medium (8-inch) width.

2   Bring a large pot of water to a boil. Once it boils, reduce the heat to low and cover the pot.

3   Transfer the pot of boiling water to a trivet on a clean work surface. Quickly dip 1 rice-paper wrapper into the hot water. Rotate the wrapper in the water to fully wet it. Lay the wrapper on your work surface. Do a few more (however many will fit on your work surface). Let the wrappers stand for 1 minute to become tacky.

4   Spread about 2 tablespoons of the salad of your choice on the bottom third of each wrapper. Starting with the end closest to you, roll the wrapper tightly around the salad. When it's rolled halfway up, fold the sides of the wrapper toward the center and continue rolling to the end of the wrapper. Continue in the same fashion for the other rolls.

NOTE: The spring rolls can be made 3 hours ahead and stored covered in plastic wrap in the fridge (in addition, they can be left at room temperature for up to 1 hour before serving). Do not refrigerate for more than 3 hours, since they will harden and lose their delicate nature. Wrap any unsoftened rice paper wrappers well in plastic wrap and store at room temperature.

Salads for Spring Roll Fillings

Forkless Artichoke Salad (page 128)

Chard and Eggplant Salad with Miso-Sesame Vinaigrette (page 134)

Crispy, Spicy Tofu and Peanut Slaw (page 136)

Green Bean–Sweet Potato Salad with Peanut Dressing (page 142)

Sweet Heat Cucumber Salad (page 122)

Watercress, Cabbage, and Tomato Slaw with Ginger Dressing (page 124)

Malaysian Fruit and Vegetable Salad (page 140)

popiah (malaysian spring rolls)

(V) Traditionally, <u>popiah</u> are soft, fresh spring rolls filled with sautéed jicama, shrimp, peanuts, fried garlic, and a dozen other goodies. The best version I ever tasted was a vegetarian one from a street cart in Malaysia. The vendor had a friendly face, marked by an unlikely catlike whisker looming straight out of a clean-shaven chin. He tried to sell me his spring rolls, but I resisted. I told him I was too full to eat and I just wanted to watch him work. He kept at me, saying that they would stay fresh for 6 hours. So I caved in just to make him happy. Hours later on the bus to Singapore, I remembered my stash. They were off-the-chart delicious.

These spring rolls take about an hour to prepare, with the one consolation that there is no dipping sauce to make because they contain their own within the filling. Have lots of friends over, double this recipe, and have everybody roll them up with you.

If you can't find jicama, substitute turnips.

MAKES 18

1 16-ounce carton firm tofu

3 tablespoons canola oil

Kosher salt

4 large shallots, minced

1 jicama (1–1¼ pounds), peeled and grated

3 garlic cloves, minced

2 tablespoons dark miso (see page 448)

2 tablespoons sugar

18 popiah skins (see page 449) or mu-shu pancakes (see page 448)

18 Boston or red leaf lettuce leaves

⅓ cup unsalted roasted peanuts, chopped

2 cups bean sprouts

Hoisin sauce (I prefer Lee Kum Kee brand)

Asian chili sauce (see page 443)

1 Wrap the block of tofu in a clean dishtowel and press it firmly with your hands until you feel the towel become damp. Unwrap the tofu and cut it into 1/4-inch cubes. In a large, well-seasoned skillet, heat 2 tablespoons of the canola oil over medium-high heat. Add the tofu and salt it liberally. Fry the tofu undisturbed until it forms a dark golden crust on the bottom, then use a spatula to turn it and brown it well on at least one more side. Drain well on paper towels.

2 In the same skillet, heat the remaining 1 tablespoon canola oil over medium heat. Add the shallots and stir-fry for 3 minutes. Add the jicama and stir-fry until it starts to become translucent, about 5 minutes. Add the garlic and cook for 1 minute more. Stir in the miso and sugar, cook for 1 minute, then season with salt and remove from the heat. Transfer the jicama mixture to a bowl.

3 Place 1 popiah skin or mu-shu pancake on a clean work surface. Pile a bit of each ingredient across the center, leaving a 1-inch border on both sides, in the following order: the jicama mixture, tofu, lettuce, peanuts, and bean sprouts. Dot generously with hoisin and chili sauce. Roll up the popiah skin or mu-shu pancake, folding the sides in as you roll. Taste your first spring roll to decide if you are using the right amount of hoisin and chili sauce. If desired, decorate the spring rolls with dots or squiggles of Asian chili sauce. Serve.

Note

Popiah can be made up to 6 hours ahead and stored in an airtight container in the fridge. If you do make them ahead, omit the bean sprouts and lettuce from the filling to keep them from getting soggy.

crispy sweet potato–tempeh spring rolls with all-purpose peanut sauce

(V) *Spiked with ginger, scallions, and chili paste,* these crunchy spring rolls are tasty little nuggets. You can find lumpia spring roll wrappers in the frozen section of larger Asian markets. Buy a few packages to stock your freezer. Once pan-fried, they make flaky and tender wrappings for all the goodies inside.

MAKES 20

3 tablespoons canola oil

8 ounces tempeh (see page 452), cut into 1/4-inch cubes

1 bunch scallions, white and green parts, finely chopped

2 rounded tablespoons peeled and minced fresh ginger

3 garlic cloves, minced

1 large sweet potato, peeled and cut into 1/4-inch cubes

3 cups mung bean sprouts

1/2 cup chopped canned water chestnuts

2 teaspoons chili paste, or more to taste

1 teaspoon kosher salt

20 8-inch square lumpia spring roll wrappers (see page 451)

All-Purpose Peanut Sauce (page 350)

1 In a large, well-seasoned skillet (preferably not nonstick), heat 2 tablespoons of the canola oil over medium heat. Add the tempeh and fry until golden brown on the bottom, then shake the skillet to turn the cubes and brown another side. Add the scallions, ginger, and garlic and sauté for 1 minute. Stir in the sweet potato and 1/2 cup water and reduce the heat to low. Simmer until the sweet potato is just tender, 5 to 10 minutes. Transfer the tempeh mixture to a large bowl and add the bean sprouts, water chestnuts, chili paste, and salt. Taste to correct the seasonings.

2 Lay one of the spring roll wrappers on a work surface with one of the corners pointing toward you (like a diamond, not a square). Arrange 2 rounded tablespoons of filling across the center (too much filling will cause the wrappers to tear). Fold the left and right points inward over the filling, then roll the skin up from the bottom to enclose the filling tightly. Repeat with the remaining wrappers and filling, keeping the wrappers covered with a damp cloth so they don't dry out.

3 In a large, heavy skillet, heat the remaining 1 tablespoon canola oil over medium heat. Working in batches if necessary to avoid crowding the skillet, pan-fry the spring rolls, turning once, until golden brown. Drain on paper towels. Leave the spring rolls whole so they retain the heat or cut them in half on the bias. Serve with All-Purpose Peanut Sauce for dipping.

Note

The spring rolls can be kept warm on a baking sheet in a warm (220-degree) oven for up to 30 minutes before serving. If you are frying the spring rolls right before serving, let them cool for a few minutes before setting them out, since they can scorch the tongue. (I count myself as one of the walking wounded.)

sesame-scallion pancakes

(V) *These scallion pancakes stand out* from the others mainly because they contain baking powder, which makes them lighter and a bit less chewy. Try engaging children in the rolling process, since it's easy and gives them a sense of "can do." These can be pan-fried an hour before a party and kept warm in the oven. The recipe can be easily doubled or tripled.

MAKES EIGHT 4-INCH PANCAKES

1 cup all-purpose flour, plus more
   if needed

1 teaspoon baking powder

1/2 teaspoon kosher salt

3 tablespoons canola oil, plus more
   as needed

3 scallions, white and green parts,
   chopped

3 tablespoons toasted black or white
   sesame seeds (see pages 444
   and 450)

dipping sauce

3 small, skinny chile peppers, minced

1 teaspoon sugar

1/4 cup soy sauce

2 tablespoons black vinegar (see
   page 445) or balsamic vinegar

1 In a medium bowl, combine the flour, baking powder, salt, and 1 tablespoon of the oil. With a wooden spoon, stir in 1/2 cup boiling water to form a soft dough. (Add additional flour or boiling water if necessary.) Turn the dough out onto a lightly floured surface and knead until smooth, about 3 minutes. Cover the dough with its bowl and let stand for 30 minutes.

2 Dust the dough with a bit of flour and roll it into an 8-x-16-inch rectangle. Brush 1 tablespoon of the oil over the surface of the dough and sprinkle it with the scallions and sesame seeds. Starting on one long side, roll up the dough like a jelly roll. Cut the roll into 8 even slices. One at a time, lay a slice of dough on the work surface. Flatten it with a floured hand, then roll it into a 4-inch disk.

3 **To make the dipping sauce:** In a small bowl, combine all the ingredients and stir until the sugar dissolves. Set aside.

4 In a large, nonstick skillet, heat the remaining 1 tablespoon canola oil over medium-high heat. Working in batches if necessary to avoid crowding the skillet and adding oil as necessary, pan-fry the pancakes until crispy and brown, turning once, about 1 minute per side. As the pancakes are done, transfer them to a baking sheet and keep them warm in a 250-degree oven while you fry the rest. Serve the pancakes warm with the dipping sauce.

Note

The pancakes can be rolled out and stacked, separated by small pieces of plastic wrap, and well wrapped in plastic wrap. At this point they can be stored for up to 3 days in the fridge or up to 2 months in the freezer. The sauce can be made up to 24 hours ahead and stored in an airtight container in the fridge. My friend Bess reheats leftovers in foil in a toaster oven the next day.

Scallions

asian eggplant pakoras with scallion raita

These spiced pakoras have such a lovely flavor that it's worth the fuss and calories of deep-frying. It's best to make them when your guests are present. Assign yourself the job of dipping the eggplant in the batter and have a friend do the frying. That way you'll have the messy, thankless job and your friend will have the important, rewarding, and slightly thrilling job.

Buy a good-quality, whole-milk, organic yogurt for the raita, because the flavor will be better. Wash these down with good beer.

SERVES 6 TO 8

scallion raita

- 2 cups plain yogurt
- 1 tablespoon Asian chili sauce, or to taste (see page 443)
- 6 scallions, white and green parts, finely chopped
- 2 teaspoons sugar
- ½ teaspoon kosher salt

pakora batter

- 2⅔ cups chickpea flour (see page 445)
- 2 tablespoons finely chopped shallots
- 2 tablespoons chopped fresh cilantro leaves and stems
- 2 teaspoons ground coriander
- 1 teaspoon garam masala (see page 447) or ground cumin
- 1 teaspoon kosher salt
- ½ teaspoon baking soda
- ¼ cup plain yogurt

  About 1 cup canola oil
- 3 Asian eggplants (about 1½ pounds total; see page 443), halved lengthwise and cut into ⅓-inch-thick half-moons

1 **To make the raita:** In a medium bowl, combine the yogurt, chili sauce, scallions, sugar, and salt. Transfer to a serving bowl just large enough to hold it, cover it, and refrigerate until serving time.

2 **To make the pakora batter:** In a large bowl, combine the chickpea flour, shallots, cilantro, coriander, garam masala or cumin, salt, and baking soda. Add the yogurt and $1^2/3$ cups water, stirring to form a smooth batter that has the consistency of yogurt. If it seems too thick, stir in more water.

3 In a large skillet, heat at least $1/2$ inch canola oil over medium-high heat until a drop of batter sizzles immediately on contact. Dip 1 slice of eggplant into the batter to coat it evenly, letting the excess drip back into the bowl, and place it carefully into the skillet. Continue with the remaining eggplant, working in batches to avoid crowding the pan. After the eggplant has cooked for about 1 minute and the bottoms are golden brown, turn the slices and brown the other sides, about 1 minute more. Drain on paper towels. Serve the pakoras immediately with the Scallion Raita.

Note Both the raita and the pakora batter can be made up to 1 day ahead, although it is important to leave the baking soda out of the pakora batter until right before frying. Store the raita and batter separately in airtight containers in the fridge. Bring the pakora batter to room temperature before using. The eggplant can be sliced up to 1 day ahead and stored in an airtight container in the fridge.

nibbles and drinks

black bean–corn cakes

(V) *These casual hors d'oeuvres* resemble simple breakfast pancakes, but once you bite into them, a panoply of rich flavors emerges. The cakes must be fried just before serving. Find a willing friend to flip the cakes so you can take care of your other hosting duties. This recipe comes from my friend Cathi DiCocco of Bethel, Maine.

MAKES ABOUT THIRTY 2-INCH CAKES

2/3 cup stone-ground cornmeal, preferably organic

3/4 cup whole wheat flour

1/4 cup all-purpose flour

2 teaspoons baking powder

1/2 teaspoon baking soda

1 teaspoon ground cumin

1 1/2 teaspoons kosher salt

1 10-ounce box frozen corn kernels, thawed and drained well

1 cup cooked, rinsed, and drained black beans (canned are fine)

2 tablespoons chopped fresh cilantro leaves and stems

2 tablespoons thinly sliced scallions, green parts only

1 3/4 cups soy milk mixed with 2 teaspoons cider vinegar

5 tablespoons canola oil

Your favorite salsa (I recommend Frontera's Tangy Two-Chile Salsa) or Asian chili sauce (see page 443)

Sour cream (optional)

Note The batter can be made up to 1 day ahead and stored in an airtight container in the fridge.

1 In a dry cast-iron skillet, toast the cornmeal over low heat until fragrant. Transfer to a large bowl and add the whole wheat and all-purpose flours, baking powder, baking soda, cumin, and salt and mix well. Add the corn, beans, cilantro, and scallions and toss to coat with the flour mixture. Gradually stir in the soy milk and 3 tablespoons of the canola oil to make a thick batter. Do not overstir.

2 In a large skillet, heat the remaining 2 tablespoons oil over medium heat. Drop a spoonful of batter into the pan to form a 2-inch cake and repeat to fit as many cakes in the skillet as possible without crowding. Fry until bubbles form on the surface of the cakes and the edges begin to brown, about 2 minutes. Turn and brown the other sides. When the cakes are done, transfer them to a serving platter. If you want to cook more before passing them around, transfer the finished cakes to a baking sheet and keep them warm in a 250-degree oven while you fry the rest. Serve hot or warm with a spoonful of salsa or Asian chili sauce and sour cream, if you like.

crispy quesadilla triangles

Crunchy on the outside and gooey on the inside, a well-made quesadilla is comfort food at its finest. For crispy quesadillas, use a full tablespoon of oil when pan-frying each one. Each quesadilla makes 4 cocktail-size wedges, and they are best pan-fried just before serving.

MAKES 16

2 plum tomatoes, finely chopped

1½ cups grated Monterey jack cheese or sharp cheddar cheese (about 6 ounces)

½ medium red onion, finely chopped

½ teaspoon ground cumin, or more to taste

2 tablespoons canola oil

4 8-inch flour tortillas

2 tablespoons chipotle chile sauce or your favorite hot sauce

1 Preheat the oven to 350 degrees. Lightly oil a rimmed baking sheet. Spread the chopped tomatoes in a single layer on the baking sheet. Bake the tomatoes for 10 minutes, then reduce the oven temperature to 250 degrees and leave the tomatoes in the oven (they will help the cheese melt).

2 In a medium bowl, combine the cheese, onion, and cumin and mix well.

3 In a medium skillet, heat 1 tablespoon of the canola oil over medium heat. Place 1 tortilla in the skillet and sprinkle half the cheese mixture evenly over it. When the tortilla is crisp and golden on the bottom and the cheese is starting to melt, 2 to 3 minutes, spread half of the tomatoes over the cheese. Place another tortilla on top and lightly press to seal. Flip the quesadilla with a spatula and cook until the bottom side has browned, 2 to 3 minutes. Transfer the finished quesadilla to a clean baking sheet in the oven. Repeat with the remaining ingredients to make a second quesadilla. To serve, cut each quesadilla into 8 wedges and top each wedge with 2 or 3 drops of chile or hot sauce. Serve the quesadillas on cocktail napkins.

welsh rabbit

Welsh Rabbit is a great party dish since it can be made ahead. Unlike most fondues, it reheats like a gem. Make sure you use a high-quality sharp cheddar. And though the curry paste is optional, I urge you to try it—it's what really makes this version special.

SERVES 4 TO 6

½ cup light-colored ale or beer

2 teaspoons Worcestershire sauce

1½ teaspoons dry mustard

1 teaspoon Madras-style curry paste (optional; see page 448)

2⅓ cups packed grated extra-sharp cheddar cheese (about 12 ounces)

1½ teaspoons all-purpose flour

Kosher salt and freshly ground black pepper to taste

Toast points, cubes of French bread, and/or green apple slices

1 In a medium saucepan, combine the ale or beer, Worcestershire sauce, mustard, and curry paste, if using, over medium heat. Cook, stirring, until the mixture is heated through and well blended.

2 Reduce the heat to low and add the cheese in 3 batches, whisking vigorously until each is melted before adding the next. Add the flour and whisk until the mixture is smooth, hot, and bubbling. Season with salt and pepper. Serve the Welsh Rabbit in a crock, surrounded by toast points, bread cubes, and/or green apple slices.

Note
The Welsh Rabbit can be made 2 days ahead and stored in an airtight container in the fridge. Reheat it in the microwave for 2 to 3 minutes, or until hot. Pour the Welsh Rabbit into a crock and serve. The toast points should be prepared within 1 hour of serving.

hot tortilla and cheese spirals

Three cheeses are rolled into a flour tortilla and baked until they have melted and the tortilla is crispy. Dotted with your favorite hot sauce, it's easy to eat more than just a few. But more than two or three will ruin guests' appetites if dinner is to follow—so don't serve too many.

MAKES 42 TO 48

1 15-ounce can black beans, rinsed and drained

1½ cups grated extra-sharp cheddar cheese (about 6 ounces)

6 ounces cream cheese, at room temperature

4 ounces blue cheese, crumbled

1 cup chopped scallions, white and green parts (about 1 bunch)

1 small onion, finely chopped

½ red bell pepper, finely chopped

2 tablespoons chopped pickled jalapeños or 1–2 minced small, skinny chile peppers

Kosher salt and freshly ground black pepper to taste

6 8-inch flour tortillas, preferably tomato- or spinach-flavored

Hot sauce (optional; I recommend Mo Hotta Mo Betta's Chipotle Adobo Hot Sauce or Frontera's Chipotle Hot Sauce)

1 Preheat the oven to 350 degrees.

2 In a large bowl, combine the beans, cheddar, cream cheese, blue cheese, scallions, onion, bell pepper, and pickled jalapeños or chiles and mix well. Season liberally with salt and pep-

Note The uncut rolls can be prepared up to 2 days ahead through step 2 and stored covered with plastic wrap in the fridge.

per. Spread an even, thin layer on one side of each tortilla and roll them up tightly like jelly rolls.

cooking under the influence

Lisa says no way:

"When throwing a dinner party, I hold off on drinking alcohol for the first hour or so. It takes only one glass of wine for me to lose track of what needs to be done. It used to be that as soon as my party started, I would be engaged in one animated conversation after another, laughing and drinking and carrying on. An hour would whiz by, and then I'd find a guest scavenging for crumbs in the kitchen, looking weak from hunger. I'd think, 'Yikes, I completely forgot about getting dinner on the table!' So now my rule is no wine for Lisa until dinner is served."

But Kelly says yes:

"Usually I host a dinner party as motivation to clean my house, and that means that before I get to the cooking I'm already in a bad mood from all the last-minute scrubbing and dusting and hiding piles of dirty clothes. Because I fear I may injure my guests when they arrive, I pour myself a glass of red wine and sip it as I cook. This restores my good humor, inclines me toward creativity, and relaxes me to the point of sanity again. Of course, if my in-laws are the guests, I break out the whiskey."

3 Lightly oil a baking sheet. Using your sharpest knife, slice the tortilla rolls crosswise into 7 or 8 pieces each, discarding the ends. Arrange the slices on the baking sheet. Bake until lightly browned, about 10 minutes.

4 Transfer the spirals to a serving plate with a small bowl of hot sauce for dipping, if you like (if the hot sauce is thick, I just spoon a little dollop on top of each spiral). Serve immediately.

goat cheese and roasted garlic fondue

You don't need a fondue pot to make this savory fondue. (But if you want one, spend a Saturday afternoon cruising local thrift shops — I bet you'll find a few specimens in eye-catching flame-orange enamel and even a copper one now and again.) You can use a small, heavy casserole dish or cast-iron skillet, and the fondue will stay warm for 30 minutes or so even without being set over a flame. If it's within easy reach of your guests, it will get scarfed down in less time than that, and it tastes just as good cool. Unlike many fondues, this one can be made the day before and reheated. If you like, you can add chopped canned green chiles. Use fondue forks or ordinary forks for dipping.

SERVES 6 TO 10

1 Preheat the oven to 375 degrees. Peel just the outer skin from the upper half of the garlic heads. Arrange the heads root end down in a baking dish just large enough to hold them in a single layer. Add water to reach about 1/4 inch up the sides of the garlic heads and drizzle them with the olive oil. Sprinkle with salt, cover tightly with foil, and roast until the garlic is soft, 35 to 40 minutes. Remove the foil. If all the water has evaporated, add 1 to 2 table-

2 large heads of garlic, plus 1 garlic clove, minced

1 tablespoon extra-virgin olive oil

Kosher salt to taste

1 cup heavy cream

11 ounces fresh creamy goat cheese

1 rounded teaspoon minced fresh herbs, such as rosemary, sage, or thyme

Freshly ground black pepper to taste

1 French baguette, cut into cubes

spoons more and continue to roast, uncovered, for 5 to 10 minutes. Let stand until cool enough to handle.

2 In a medium saucepan, heat the cream and minced raw garlic over medium heat. Bring to a boil, then reduce the heat to low. Squeeze the roasted garlic cloves out of their skins and into the cream mixture. It will be somewhat lumpy. Whisk in the goat cheese a little at a time, stirring with a fork until smooth. Add the herbs and season with salt and pepper. Serve with the cubed baguette. Use a trivet to protect the table from the fondue pot.

Note

The fondue can be made up to 3 days ahead and stored in an airtight container in the fridge. Reheat it in a small flameproof casserole dish, a cast-iron skillet, or a small, heavy saucepan, stirring frequently.

nibbles and drinks

ten sound pieces of advice on buying wine

God gave me the ability to keenly remember my food experiences, but short-changed me in the wine department. But I *do* have my favorites—namely, Pinot Noir, Fumé Blanc, Sancerre, Riesling, and Côtes du Rhône. When I buy wine, I rely on store employees who seem knowledgeable to lead me to the better vineyards and years. To keep track of the wines you enjoy, keep a piece of paper tacked to the fridge and jot down the necessary info on it so you'll have a handy record.

1. If you care about wine, go to a wine store that cares about wine.

2. Don't be embarrassed about asking for a $10 (or less expensive) bottle of wine.

3. Steer clear of Merlot and California wines in general, since they are usually overpriced relative to their quality. Six areas that produce wines that are a good bang for the buck are Portugal, southern France, New Zealand, South Africa, Chile, and Argentina.

4. If the food is heavy, you want a heavy wine. Use the inherent quality of the food as well as the style of preparation to determine if it is heavy— if it's deep-fried, it's heavy; if it's steamed, it's light. Sweet wines are heavier than dry.

5. Likewise, match the flavor of the food to the wine—if the dish is sweet, acidic, bland, bold, herbal, spicy, or fruity, pair it with a wine that has a similar flavor. For instance, if you're serving a salad, choose a wine with a crisp, acidic quality, such as Pinot Grigio. Departing briefly from this rule, it's helpful to know that sweet wines such as Riesling and Vouvray go well with spicy foods.

6. With that said, don't worry about perfect matching—just about any food tastes better with almost any wine. It's hard to make an egregious mistake.

7. Light and versatile Pinot Noir pairs nicely with vegetarian food (Cabernet Sauvignon, on the other hand, is best reserved for bloody steaks and the like).

8. Heavily oaked New World Chardonnays may taste good to the untrained palate, but they pair well with a very narrow range of food. If you like Chardonnay, try branching out to something similar but more food-friendly—say, Pinot Blanc, Viognier, or Sémillon.

9. Plan on one half to three quarters of a bottle per person. It's better to buy too much than too little. Also, drink from big wineglasses so you can swirl and smell and hopefully not spill.

10. Drink two kinds of wines if the dinner is on the fancy side—one with the first course and the other with the main course. It's generally best to move from a lighter wine to a heavier one.

beer, bathtubs, and vegetarian food

Want to offer a good brew but don't have a clue? Two types of beer, pilsner and India Pale Ale (IPA), work especially well with flavorful vegetarian food. IPA, which is the more full-bodied of the two, has a hoppy, assertive flavor that can stand up to spicy, robust food. Some good choices are Hop Devil, Wild Goose, and Pike. Pilsner is a bit lighter in color and body than IPA, but is still quite hoppy, meaning, for lack of a better word, zippy. Czechvar and Pilsner Urquell are good.

If your party is large and you have no place to put your beer (and your white wine, for that matter), buy a dozen bags of ice and fill your bathtub with them. Or use your recycling bin, in which case you'll need only eight bags or so. Sticking the beer in either keeps everyone out of the kitchen and out of your hair.

bloody marys

 Asian chili sauce makes a bloody mary that is very aromatic and intense. About twelve years ago, when I was a bit of a hellion, I carried a jar of Asian chili sauce in my purse. One night when I was drinking with friends at a bar, I added some of the chili sauce to my bloody mary, and I couldn't believe the stellar results. I was so pleased that I started dropping spoonfuls of it into everyone else's bloody mary. My friends tried to stop me, but I told them resolutely that I was making the world a better place. They agreed once they tasted it.

SERVES 4 OR 5

In a tall pitcher, combine all the ingredients (except for the celery or asparagus). Stir well and taste for seasoning, adding more of any of the ingredients, if desired. Refrigerate for 1 hour, if possible. Serve in tall glasses over ice, inserting a celery stalk or an asparagus spear into each glass.

1 28-ounce can tomato puree, preferably organic

1 cup vodka

⅓ cup fresh lime juice (about 3 juicy limes)

1 tablespoon Asian chili sauce (see page 443)

2 teaspoons Worcestershire sauce

1 tablespoon prepared horseradish

Kosher salt and freshly ground black pepper

Celery stalks or raw asparagus spears for stirring

southeast asian white wine sangria

(V) *Wine aficionado Walter Clay* created this concoction when we opened Pho République, a French-Vietnamese bistro in Cambridge, Massachusetts. It's much lighter than traditional red wine sangria, making it a perfect warm-weather refreshment. Using Melon Ice Cubes (page 85) instead of conventional ones makes it even more fun.

SERVES 8

1 750-ml bottle Chardonnay

⅓ cup sugar

2 cups chilled sparkling water

2 tablespoons fresh lime juice (1 juicy lime)

½ lime, cut into thin slices

1 kiwi, peeled and sliced

1 cup small honeydew melon cubes (or any other fruit, such as oranges, kumquats, litchis, star fruit, lemons, or mangoes)

Ice cubes

In a large, chilled pitcher, combine the wine and sugar and stir until the sugar dissolves. Refrigerate for 30 minutes. Add the sparkling water, lime juice, and fruit and stir well. Serve in large wineglasses with lots of ice. (If using Melon Ice Cubes, serve with spoons or at least have them on hand so your guests can eat the melon.)

punch!

Punch is a funny word. All I can think is that a bunch of guys got tipsy on some spiked juice and then one of them got feisty and started swinging punches at the others.

Growing up, punch meant one thing: our Christmas Eve punch, consisting of 2 cans of Hawaiian Punch mixed with a bottle of ginger ale. But now that I'm a chic urban foodie, I have learned that punch can be an exciting and sophisticated beverage that adds fun and sparkle to the evening. Here are a few punch combinations I like, some of which are inspired by the wonderful cookbook *Lord Krishna's Cuisine: The Art of Indian Vegetarian Cooking* by Yamuna Devi. Serve these punches with ice—but don't put the ice in with the punch. Keep the ice separate to keep the punch from getting watered down. For extra fun, buy some star fruit, slice it into thin stars and drop them into the punch. Or go even more exotic by cutting lemongrass stalks in half lengthwise and using them as stirrers. And, of course, vodka or rum can be added to any of these punches.

Mint Syrup

In a large saucepan, combine 1 bunch mint, 1 quart water, and 2 cups sugar. Bring to a boil then remove from the heat and let stand for 30 minutes. Strain the syrup and store in an airtight container in the fridge. Keeps for weeks, maybe months. (Other uses include smoothies, lassis, lemonade, and hot tea.)

Each punch below makes about 3 quarts.

Mango-Mint De-Lite

2 quarts mango or pear juice, 1 quart sparkling water, ½ cup mint syrup, and lemon slices

Lime-Ginger Crush

2 quarts apple juice, 1 quart pineapple juice, the juice of 5 limes, and 4 inches fresh ginger, grated and squeezed to extract the juice (pulp discarded)

Maple Tonic

3 quarts sparkling water, 1 cup maple syrup, and lemon slices

Tropical-Trees Punch

2½ quarts pineapple juice, 2 cups unsweetened coconut milk, a few pinches of ground cardamom, and lime slices

Passion Punch

1 quart passion fruit nectar, 1 quart pineapple or orange juice, 1 quart sparkling water, and orange slices

lemonade by the pitcher

(V) *The problem with making lemonade* is that unless you make a sugar syrup, vigorous stirring is necessary to dissolve the sugar. In my version, warm water makes dissolving the sugar a bit easier. Whether I'm making a pitcher or just one glass, I always cut some of the already squeezed lemons into slices to add to the prepared lemonade. The peel adds another dimension of flavor.

For an exotic twist, add a few drops of rose water (see page 450) or orange flower water (see page 449) to the lemonade.

MAKES 1½ QUARTS, SERVES 6

³/₄ cup sugar

3 juicy lemons, squeezed, and rind of 1 squeezed lemon cut into thin slices

Ice cubes

In a large pitcher, combine 6 cups very warm tap water and the sugar and stir until the sugar dissolves, about 1 minute. Add the lemon juice, sliced rind, and ice cubes to fill the pitcher and stir again. Wait 1 minute for it to chill, then serve.

Variations

Citron Pressé (or Lemonade by the Glass)
Follow the method above, using these quantities: 2 tablespoons sugar, 8 ounces water, ¹/₂ juicy lemon, and 4 or 5 ice cubes.

For fizzy lemonade, substitute plain seltzer water for the tap water.

homemade ginger ale

(V) *You can't begin to compare* the flavor of homemade ginger ale to store-bought. Real ginger ale actually tastes like ginger and has much more of a bite than any commercial variety. The syrup can also be combined with boiling water to make hot ginger tea.

MAKES 1 QUART SYRUP, SERVES ABOUT 16

ginger syrup

3 **cups coarsely chopped fresh ginger (scrubbed well but not peeled)**

2 **cups sugar**

Sparkling water or seltzer

Lemon wedges for garnish

1 **To make the ginger syrup:** In a food processor, finely chop the ginger pieces. Transfer the ginger to a medium saucepan. Stir in the sugar and 2 quarts cold water. Bring to a boil, then reduce the heat to low and simmer for 1 hour. Cool the syrup so you don't burn yourself, then strain it through a fine sieve.

2 **To serve by the glass:** Briskly stir 1/4 cup ginger syrup into an 8-ounce glass of sparkling water or seltzer. Garnish with a lemon wedge and serve.

To serve by the pitcher: Use 1 cup ginger syrup for each quart of sparkling water or seltzer. Stir together in a pitcher, float a few lemon wedges in it, and serve.

Note The ginger syrup can be stored in an airtight container in the fridge for up to 2 months.

Variation **Hot Ginger Tea:** Briskly stir 3 to 4 tablespoons ginger syrup in an 8-ounce mug of boiling water and serve.

peach-rose cooler

(V) *A simple summer cooler.*

SERVES 4

2 bags peach-flavored herbal tea
(I like Celestial Seasonings)

2 tablespoons sugar

A few splashes of rose water
(see page 450)

½ ripe but firm peach, pitted and
sliced (optional)

In a medium saucepan, bring 4 cups water to a boil. Remove from the heat, add the tea bags and sugar, and stir until the sugar dissolves. Steep the tea for 30 minutes. Remove the tea bags and discard. Add the rose water to taste and the peach slices, if using. Transfer the tea to a pitcher and refrigerate for at least 2 hours. Pour into four ice-filled glasses and serve immediately.

not the same old water

If you're looking for something a little more exciting than ice water to drink during a meal, try lemon water: combine a pitcher of water with half a lemon's worth of lemon slices an hour or so before people arrive, so the lemon has time to flavor the water (I usually squeeze the other lemon half into the water for extra zip). Pour the water into glasses filled with ice and drop in a lemon slice. The puckery quality of the lemon cuts the richness of the meal.

cinnamon iced tea

 Cinnamon is a spice with timeless appeal. This tea is sassy and quenching.

SERVES 4

2 bags apple-cinnamon-flavored herbal tea (I like Celestial Seasonings)

2 tablespoons sugar

Orange slices from 1/2 orange

In a medium saucepan, bring 4 cups water to a boil. Remove from the heat, add the tea bags and sugar, and stir until the sugar dissolves. Steep the tea for 30 minutes. Remove the tea bags and discard. Transfer the tea to a pitcher, add the orange slices, and refrigerate for at least 2 hours. Pour into four ice-filled glasses and serve immediately.

express yourself through cubism

Flavored ice cubes: they're fun, unusual, and tasty, giving you good mileage for your effort. They add panache to seltzer water, iced tea, lemonade, and store-bought sodas, not to mention mixed drinks. These cubes will keep for up to 3 months in your freezer. Just choose your cube and go!

Lemon Ice Cubes

1 juicy lemon

Using the fine holes of a box grater, grate the lemon rind into a large bowl. Juice the lemon, and strain the juice into the bowl of rind. Stir in 3 cups cold water, then ladle the lemon water into ice-cube trays. Freeze until firm, about 3 hours.

Orange–Mint Ice Cubes

To me, these orange-mint ice cubes are the pinnacle of extravagance, yet they cost almost nothing to make. If you dare, add a drop of green food coloring and the cubes will become emerald, making a beautiful contrast to lemonade. This recipe was created by Danny Wisel.

1 pound freshly cut mint (preferably orange or lemon mint
   if you can find it)
   orange slices from $1/2$ orange
2–3 drops green food coloring (optional)

1 In a large saucepan, combine the cut mint, orange slices, and $1\frac{1}{2}$ quarts cold water. Bring slowly to a simmer, then remove from the heat. Let the mint mixture steep for 1 to 2 hours.

2 Strain the mint mixture, add the green food coloring, if using, and let cool. Ladle into ice-cube trays. Freeze until firm, at least 4 hours.

Melon Ice Cubes

These are the easiest of the three cubes to make. All you need is a ripe melon. The best way to tell when a melon is ripe is to press against the stem area. If it's somewhat soft, it's ripe. Also smell the stem area, which should smell like melon.

1 ripe cantaloupe or honeydew melon

1 With a large knife, cut the ends off the melon and stand it on one end. Cut the skin away in slabs. When all the skin is removed, cut the melon in half and spoon out the seeds.

2 Cut the melon into 1-inch cubes. Place the cubes on a baking pan or sheet that fits in the freezer. Freeze the cubes until frozen through, about 3 hours.

lime aid

I have a friend from Mexico who believes that limes are a tonic for the body. She calls it citro-therapy. She says that the average person should start therapy by drinking the straight juice of 2 limes on an empty stomach before bed every night. Over the course of a few months, one works one's way to 50 limes per night. I, too, think that limes have a curative value, but my therapeutic drink is less rigorous. Here it is.

Limeade

2 tablespoons sugar
Juice of 3 limes
1 glass of ice

Stir the sugar into 1 cup hot water and let stand for 1 minute. Pour the lime juice over the ice. Stir the water and sugar one last time, then pour it over the ice as well. Stir well and drink up!

watermelon lassi

Lassis are thirst-quenching drinks from India. I came up with this indulgent and nontraditional lassi (note the ice cream) for an article on watermelons in a magazine. The recipe can be easily doubled.

In a blender, mix the water-melon, yogurt, sugar, cardamom, and salt on high speed until smooth. Pour into an ice-filled glass. Rub a lime wedge around the rim of each glass and squeeze its juice into the lassi. Add the ice cream, if desired, and serve imme-diately.

SERVES 2

4 cups seeded watermelon chunks

1 cup plain yogurt

4–6 tablespoons sugar

    Large pinch of ground cardamom

    Large pinch of salt

    Ice cubes

2 lime wedges

2 scoops vanilla ice cream (optional)

Variation

Thick Watermelon Lassi "Shake": Add the ice cream to the blender with the other ingredients and blend until smooth.

pineapple lassi

Here's a more traditional lassi than the watermelon recipe. Pineapple juice works wonders with yogurt, and the ginger adds a refreshing zing. The recipe can be easily doubled.

SERVES 2

In a blender, mix pineapple juice, yogurt, ginger, cardamom (if using), salt, sugar, and ice cubes on high speed until smooth. Serve immediately, garnished with the pineapple slices, if desired.

2 cups pineapple juice

1 cup plain yogurt

2 tablespoons peeled and chopped fresh ginger

Pinch of ground cardamom (optional)

Pinch of salt

2 tablespoons sugar

Ice cubes

Pineapple slices for garnish (optional)

Pineapple

christmas eve at the emmonses'

For nearly forty years, my parents have hosted a wonderful party on Christmas Eve. The same people have been coming since the sixties, and it's gained a bit of notoriety among the neighbors (it was even in *Connecticut Magazine* one year).

First we sing carols up and down our candlelit street, then Santa comes and hands out gifts, and we all make our way back to the house, where the fireplaces are roaring and the tree is always fat and glowing in the corner of the den, stuffed to the gills with old dolls and popcorn strings. Little kids are speeding through the halls at dangerous rates, and old friends are reconnecting over wine and nibbles.

What everyone seems to love about the party is the very thing that drives me crazy: the food is *exactly* the same every year. Considering that my mom is a wonderful cook, one would think the food would be tops. But she hasn't changed the menu since 1959, since everyone expects their favorites to be there.

The worst thing is the feature attraction: Austrian fondue. Guests hover over the fondue, adults and kids alike, and eat until they are nearly drunk. I sip my drink on the sidelines, conducting my usual silent boycott. I have no problem with melted cheese or white wine, but I don't know what compelled someone to use a cheese with as little personality as Emmenthaler.

One day I'm going to replace the Emmenthaler with a more exciting cheese, such as raclette. This small change would make the difference between ho-hum and thrilling. The children might be a little put off by the personality of the cheese, so I'll dress up as Santa's helper and thank them for leaving more fondue for me, as they know I'll have a rough night of hard work ahead of me and my belly must be full.

chapter 2

Sociable Soups

Eat Soup!

Black Beans

CHIPOTLE
ADOBO SAUCE

Pick flowers

soup sense

In my book (no pun intended), soup is usually not a first course but the main event. It's the perfect food for a casual lunch or dinner with friends while watching the Grammys or after taking a walk in the woods.

Keep in mind a few things when deciding how to serve soup or whether to serve soup at all. If the meal will be served buffet style, it's unwise for guests to carry their bowls hither and yon and then perch uncomfortably on the edge of a futon while trying not to spill any on the slipcover or themselves. Even the most delicious soup can't be enjoyed under these conditions. If the soup you have in mind is one that doesn't have a lot of "stuff" in it (i.e., noodles, vegetables), you could serve it in mugs. But if you have any doubts about your guests' hand-eye coordination or if toddlers or pets will be roaming around, stick to dishes with less "spillability."

It's preferable to serve soup to guests seated at a table. You can either fill the bowls in the kitchen and then carry them to the table (slightly tricky—watch out for doorsill and throw rugs), or you can bring a tureen to the table and ladle the soup into the bowls right there. If you don't have a suitable tureen, poke around for one in secondhand stores, and see if you can find a nice ladle and some real soupspoons while you're at it. True soupspoons have a nice round "bowl" shape instead of the oblong shape of a regular spoon, and it's much easier to sip soup from them. If you can't find your dream tureen, remember to tell people that you'd like one whenever anyone asks you what you want from Santa, for your birthday, or as a wedding gift. Just smile sweetly and say "a soup tureen." If none of these methods produces a tureen, just bring the pot to the table.

Here are a few soup and bread and/or salad combinations to spur you on to feature soups in your menus. For desserts, make one yourself or just buy one.

Top-Dog Gazpacho (page 94)
Potato Salad Niçoise (page 144)
French bread

Carrot, Rosemary, and Ginger Minestrone (page 98)
Simple Cauliflower Salad with Creamy Cilantro Dressing (page 138)
Whole Wheat Communion Bread with butter (page 384)

Baked Onion Cheese Soup (page 106)
Crispy Chickpea Salad with Roasted Eggplant and Feta (page 148)
Crusty Italian or French bread with olive oil or butter

Butternut and Ginger Soup (page 110)
Watercress, Cabbage, and Tomato Slaw with Ginger Dressing (page 124)
Roti Jala (Malaysian Crepes) (page 358)

Acorn Squash, Spinach, and Roasted Garlic Soup (page 111)
Big Couscous and Clementine Salad (page 139)
French bread

chilled celery soup

This soup is smooth, refreshing, and understated.
When celery is cooked, its flavor becomes sweeter and more intense.
Pureeing the soup and passing it through a sieve is a vestige of the
classic French cooking that Julia Child popularized in the sixties.
Serve with Ruby Walnut Dip with Artichokes (a beet-walnut salad;
page 24), made without the artichokes, and crusty bread.

SERVES 6 TO 8

3 tablespoons extra-virgin olive oil

1 leek, white and light green part only,
   halved lengthwise, washed well,
   and thinly sliced

2 large bunches celery, trimmed and
   chopped into 1/2-inch pieces
   (about 9 cups)

2 garlic cloves

4 cups plain yogurt

   Kosher salt and freshly ground
      black pepper to taste

   Sour cream for garnish

1/4 cup chopped shallot or red onion
   for garnish

1 In a large pot, heat the olive oil
over medium heat. Add the leek and
sauté, stirring occasionally, until soft,
about 5 minutes. Add the celery, garlic
cloves, and 8 cups water. Bring to a boil,
then reduce the heat and simmer for
20 minutes, or until the celery is very
tender.

2 In a blender, puree the soup
until very smooth. Or use an immersion
blender to puree the soup in the pot.
Strain through a sieve set over a large
bowl, then whisk in the yogurt. Let cool
to room temperature. Cover tightly with
plastic wrap and refrigerate for at least 3
hours, or until chilled. To serve, season
the soup liberally with salt and pepper.
Transfer to serving bowls and garnish
each with a spoonful of sour cream and
a sprinkle of shallot or onion.

Note The soup can be made up to 2 days
ahead and stored in an airtight container in the fridge. Add the garnish
just before serving.

chilled curried pea soup

You're likely to have most or all of the ingredients for this spunky soup on hand. If you have edamame (see page 446) in your freezer, you can use them in place of the peas. A glass of Lemonade (page 80) or Cinnamon Iced Tea (page 83) would complement this soup perfectly.

SERVES 4

1 In a large saucepan, heat the canola oil over medium heat. Add the onion and sauté, stirring occasionally, until transparent, 7 to 9 minutes. Add the garlic, ginger, and curry powder and cook, stirring, for 1 minute more.

2 In a blender, puree the onion mixture, peas, sour cream or yogurt, and 1½ cups water until smooth but slightly coarse. Transfer to a large bowl, cover tightly with plastic wrap, and re-frigerate until chilled, about 2 hours. Garnish each bowl with a small spoon-ful of sour cream or yogurt and crushed peanuts, if desired.

1 tablespoon canola oil

1 large onion, chopped

4 garlic cloves, minced

1 tablespoon peeled and minced fresh ginger

2 teaspoons curry powder

2 cups thawed frozen peas

¼ cup sour cream or plain yogurt, plus more for garnish

2 tablespoons crushed peanuts for garnish (optional)

Note The soup can be made up to 3 days ahead and stored in the fridge. Add the garnishes just before serving.

top-dog gazpacho

Ⓥ *This combination was loosely inspired by* ajo blanco, the Spanish grape-and-almond gazpacho. I veered off the track by using tomatoes instead of grapes, and the result was so good that I've given it the name Top Dog. To do this gazpacho justice, use only local ripe tomatoes and serve the soup in chilled bowls.

SERVES 4

1/3 cup almonds, skin on

2 ears corn, shucked

4 ripe tomatoes, chopped

1 orange, red, or yellow bell pepper, seeded and coarsely chopped

2–3 tablespoons chopped fresh cilantro

1 garlic clove, chopped

2 1/2 tablespoons red wine vinegar

2 tablespoons extra-virgin olive oil

Kosher salt and freshly ground black pepper to taste

Hot sauce to taste

4 fresh cilantro sprigs for garnish

1 Preheat the oven to 350 degrees. Spread the almonds in a single layer on a rimmed baking sheet and toast for 10 minutes, stirring occasionally, until golden brown. Set aside to cool.

2 Bring a medium saucepan of water to a boil. Cut the corn kernels off the cobs. You should have about 1 1/3 cups. Blanch the kernels in the boiling water for 1 minute, then drain.

3 In a food processor, process the almonds until finely chopped. Add the tomatoes, bell pepper, chopped cilantro, garlic, vinegar, and olive oil and pulse until chunky. Transfer to a large bowl and stir in the corn. Add up to 1 cup cold water if the soup is too thick for your liking. Season the gazpacho with salt, pepper, and hot sauce. Cover tightly with plastic wrap and refrigerate until chilled, at least 1 hour. Garnish with the cilantro sprigs and serve.

Note The gazpacho can be made up to 2 days ahead and stored in an airtight container in the fridge. Add the garnish just before serving.

ana's yellow tomato gazpacho

(V) *Yellow tomatoes taste sweeter* than red ones because they are less acidic. This gazpacho is adapted from a recipe by Ana Sortun, the chef/owner of Oleana, who is renowned for her ambitious Eastern Mediterranean cuisine and commitment to working with local farms. I like to follow this soup with Chard and Eggplant Salad with Miso-Sesame Vinaigrette (page 134) and crusty bread.

SERVES 4

1 Break the bread slices into a food processor and process them into crumbs. Add the tomatoes, olive oil, vinegar, and 1 teaspoon salt and process until smooth.

2 Strain the tomato mixture through a sieve into a large bowl. Gradually add the sparkling water and stir until the mixture reaches soup consistency. Stir in the cilantro or basil, if using, and season with salt and pepper. Cover tightly with plastic wrap and refrigerate until chilled, at least 1 hour. Ladle the gazpacho into bowls, garnish with cilantro or basil, if desired, and serve.

4 slices white sandwich bread, stale or toasted

2 pounds ripe yellow tomatoes (about 6 medium), quartered

3 tablespoons extra-virgin olive oil

2 tablespoons good-quality Champagne vinegar or white wine vinegar (Chardonnay vinegar if you can find it)

1 teaspoon kosher salt, plus more to taste

½ cup sparkling water

2 tablespoons chopped fresh cilantro or basil, plus more for garnish (optional)

Freshly ground black pepper to taste

Note The gazpacho can be made up to 1 day ahead and stored in an airtight container in the fridge. Add the garnish, if using, just before serving.

rachel and felicity's minestrone

(V) *My friend Felicity* has been a professional cook for years, and she makes a formidable minestrone. I asked for the recipe, but she said I had to watch it being made. When I showed up months later, Felicity's childhood friend Rachel was there. Years earlier, she had fallen in love with a young Italian in Manhattan, who took her to Siena, where she became the chef at his parents' restaurant. They taught her how to make this soup, and she in turn taught it to Felicity. Rachel eventually broke it off with her Italian lover, but this recipe is still with her.

For a fancy meal, serve the minestrone with French bread as a first course before Goat Cheese Flan with Arugula Salad (page 296).

Although I took an oath to preserve the recipe just as Felicity had taught it to me, I confess that I like fresh rosemary in the minestrone. About a teaspoon of finely chopped rosemary will do, added at the same time as the parsley.

SERVES 6 TO 8

2/3 cup extra-virgin olive oil

1/2 pound carrots, peeled and cut into 1/3-inch-thick slices (fat carrots should be halved lengthwise as well; about 1 2/3 cups)

1 head of garlic, cloves separated and peeled

1 small onion, chopped

3 28-ounce cans whole peeled tomatoes (Felicity prefers organic ones)

1/2 cup finely chopped fresh flat-leaf parsley

4 cups vegetable broth or water

1 15-ounce can cannellini or navy beans, drained and rinsed

Kosher salt and freshly ground black pepper

1 In a large, heavy pot, heat the olive oil over medium-low heat. Add the carrots and garlic, and sauté, stirring occasionally, until they soften, about 10 minutes. Add the onion and sauté, stirring until the onion begins to turn golden, about 10 minutes more. Be careful not to burn the carrot mixture; you're aiming for a slow caramelization. Using a fork, mash the garlic cloves coarsely in the pot. They don't need to be totally mashed because they'll break down further as the soup continues to cook.

2 Meanwhile, strain the tomatoes over a large bowl; reserve the juice. Into a separate large bowl, squeeze the tomatoes through your fingers to break them apart. Add one third of the tomatoes to the carrot mixture and cook, stirring occasionally, until most of the liquid evaporates, about 10 minutes more.

3 Add the parsley and the remaining tomatoes to the pot, and cook, stirring often, for 10 minutes more, or until quite thick. Stir in the vegetable broth or water, reserved tomato juice, and beans and bring to a simmer. Season with salt and pepper, ladle into bowls, and serve.

Note

The soup can be made up to 3 days ahead and stored in an airtight container in the fridge.

soup base spawns new dishes

The base of Rachel and Felicity's Minestrone (before the liquid and beans are added) can be the mother of an array of fine meals.

For starters, it can make a lip-smackin' bolognese-style pasta sauce. To mimic the ground beef, you can crumble a package of tempeh, sauté it in olive oil for a few minutes, then add it to the soup base. Then boil your spaghetti and drain it, top with the soup base, and grate some Parmesan on top.

For an afternoon snack, Rachel likes to mash some white beans and garlic into the soup base and eat it with crusty bread. The base is also great as a pizza topping. If these suggestions appeal to you, make a double batch of the soup base and freeze half, then continue with the soup recipe as written.

carrot, rosemary, and ginger minestrone

Ⓥ *Ginger and rosemary are both* strong flavors, yet they are harmonious side by side. Carrots, macaroni, and red bell pepper give the minestrone sweet substance. Feel free to add other vegetables, such as chopped green beans, edamame, corn, fennel, or potatoes, although I'd limit the total number of vegetables to five. Serve with warm focaccia or sourdough bread. This recipe comes from Jason Fishman, a creative dynamo in the kitchen.

SERVES 6

1 In a large pot, heat the canola oil over medium heat. Add the carrots, onions, ginger, and garlic and sauté for 8 to 10 minutes, or until the onions are translucent. Add the bell pepper and sauté until slightly softened, about 5 more minutes.

2 Add 12 cups water and the rosemary and bring to a boil. Reduce the heat and simmer until the carrots are tender, about 10 minutes. Stir in the miso mixture, macaroni, scallions, salt, and pepper. Serve immediately.

2 tablespoons canola oil

1 pound carrots, peeled and cut into ¼-inch pieces

3 medium onions, chopped

½ cup peeled and coarsely chopped fresh ginger

4 garlic cloves, minced

1 red bell pepper, cut into ¼-inch pieces

2 tablespoons minced fresh rosemary

¼ cup red miso (see page 448) dissolved in ½ cup warm water

4 cups cooked elbow macaroni

6 scallions, white and green parts, minced

2 teaspoons kosher salt

Freshly ground black pepper to taste

cambodian tomato soup

(V) *A friend who thought she disdained* all tomato soups found this one revelatory. It's my not-all-that-authentic version of a tomato-shrimp soup I had ten years ago at Elephant Walk, a Cambodian restaurant in Boston. I like to serve this soup in pretty Asian bowls that I bought at an Asian market.

SERVES 8

1 In a large pot, heat the canola oil over medium heat. Add almost all the leek (reserve a handful for the garnish) or all the onion, the chiles, garlic, and ginger and sauté until the leek or onion is translucent, 7 to 9 minutes. Add the tomatoes, their liquid, zucchini or summer squash, lime leaves or lime rind, and 4 cups water and bring to a boil. Reduce the heat to medium and simmer for 15 minutes.

2 Add the coconut milk and salt and cook, stirring, until heated through. Ladle the soup into soup bowls and garnish each serving with some of the reserved leek, if using.

- 1 tablespoon canola oil
- 1 large leek, chopped and washed well, or 1 large onion, chopped
- 1–3 small, skinny chile peppers, minced
- 1 tablespoon minced garlic
- 1 tablespoon peeled and minced fresh ginger
- 1 28-ounce can diced tomatoes
- 1 zucchini or summer squash, halved lengthwise and cut into thin half-moons
- 6 fresh or dry kaffir lime leaves (see page 447) or the grated rind of 1 lime
- 1 13.5-ounce can unsweetened coconut milk (see page 446)
- 1–2 teaspoons kosher salt

Note
The soup can be made up to 3 days ahead and stored in an airtight container in the fridge. Add the garnish just before serving.

sociable soups

eight menus in tribute to mother nature

Only that day dawns to which we are awake.
—Henry David Thoreau

Sometimes I get so bogged down with the details of my life that I don't even notice the changes that are happening outside. I often feel as if I've missed the boat, or to be more accurate, the trees. Inviting friends over allows me to celebrate the current or upcoming season before it speeds past.

How does one celebrate a season at a dinner party? Mainly by using seasonal food. Don't feel hemmed in by these suggestions. You may want to opt for cheese and crackers instead of preparing an hors d'oeuvre. Or perhaps you'd rather not bother with the first course. If you want, buy something at a local bakery or ice cream store for dessert. I've heard that Julia Child has been known to serve Häagen-Dazs ice cream bars at her dinner parties. I opt for Ben & Jerry's Peace Pops.

Make your table come to life, as this will help enliven conversation. If you have time, bring the outdoors to your table with pretty leaves, flowers, chestnuts, shells from the beach, or even twigs.

Buy local. Using produce that is grown locally (always ask your grocer if it's not labeled as such) means your food will be fresher and tastier. Buying locally is also good for the planet because it reduces the use of nonrenewable resources for transportation, it reduces air pollution, and it supports growers who care about and preserve the land.

Fall

Menu I

Extra-Smoky Baba Gannouj (page 29) with crudités and/or **Pita Chips** (page 43)
Butternut and Ginger Soup (page 110)
Root Stew with Millet Cakes (page 308)
Hazelnut-Pear Torte (page 440)

Menu II

Shiitakes Stuffed with Goat Cheese, Cranberries, and Pecans (page 48)
Acorn Squash, Spinach, and Roasted Garlic Soup (page 111)
Spaghetti Squash Wedges with Roasted Vegetable–Feta Stuffing (page 330)
Lemon Square Cake (page 432) with whipped cream

Winter

Menu I

Hip Dip (page 36) with crudités or **Goat Cheese and Roasted Garlic
Fondue** (page 72) with bread
Rachel and Felicity's Minestrone (page 96)
Butternut Risotto Cakes with Portobellos and Stilton Butter (page 312)
Mexican Flan (page 406)

Menu II

Muhammara (page 26) with crackers
Carrot, Rosemary, and Ginger Minestrone (page 98)
Roti Jala (page 358) with **Saag Paneer** (page 226) or **Curried Cauliflower
with Tomatoes and Tofu** (page 224)
Crunchy Almond Rice Pudding (page 408), **Hilde's Berry Pudding**
(page 409) or **Bionic Chocolate Pudding** (page 404)

Spring

Menu I

Sesame–Scallion Pancakes (page 62)—use local leeks or spring onions
instead of scallions
Mashed Potato Spring Rolls with Peanut Sauce (page 54) with a side of
Mango Slaw (page 120)
Five-Spice Seitan and Asparagus (page 228) over rice or couscous—
add 1 cup fresh peas in addition to the asparagus in celebration of
spring.
Blueberry-Peach Cranachan (page 403) or **Macadamia–Tropical Fruit Salad
with Ice Cream** (page 412)

(continued)

Menu II

Curried Walnut Dip (page 28) with artichoke leaves for dipping (see **Ruby Walnut Dip with Artichokes,** page 24)

The Prettiest Little Salad Around (page 125)—use blanched fresh peas instead of the fried Japanese peas

Portobello–Goat Cheese Lasagna with Flashy Green Sauce (page 292) —add ½ pound blanched asparagus, cut into 1-inch pieces, when assembling the lasagna

Melon Sago (page 410), strawberries with **One-Bite-Won't-Suffice Lemon Ice** (page 418) or **Pavlova** (page 416)

Summer

Menu I

Swimming Goat Cheese (page 40) with **Zesty, Smoky Cherry Tomato–Oregano Salsa** (page 32)—make the salsa without the chipotles to allow the flavor of the tomatoes to come through; you can substitute chopped jalapeños if you like.

Ana's Yellow Tomato Gazpacho (page 95)

Spaghetti with Green Olive Pesto (page 288)

Melon Sago (page 410) or **Peach Upside-Down Cake** (page 434)

Menu II

Crudités with Avocado-Tomatillo Guacamole (page 35) or **Saffron Aïoli** (page 17)

Heirloom tomatoes and arugula with Goat Cheese–Walnut Dressing (page 160) or **Top-Dog Gazpacho** (page 94)

Smoky Corn Risotto (page 322) or **Bumper Crop Risotto with Herb Butter** (page 324)

Blueberry-Peach Cranachan (page 403) or **Michel Richard's Fruit "Salad" with Melted Ice Cream** (page 414)—use local fruits in season

black bean soup in a hurry

Ⓥ *Although I'm generally not a fan* of canned beans or of being in a hurry, this soup comes in handy. It's something you can make even if your fridge is empty. Serve it as a light dinner, perhaps with a salad and bread.

SERVES 4

3 tablespoons extra-virgin olive oil

2 medium onions, chopped

3 garlic cloves, minced

2 teaspoons ground cumin

2 13-ounce cans black beans, undrained

Fresh lemon juice or red wine vinegar to taste

Kosher salt and freshly ground black pepper

Diced tomato and chopped scallions and/or optional sour cream for garnish

1 In a large saucepan, heat the olive oil over medium heat. Add the onions and sauté, stirring occasionally, until softened, about 7 minutes. Add the garlic and cumin and sauté for 3 minutes more. Stir in the black beans with their liquid and 2 canfuls of water. Bring to a simmer and cook for 10 minutes to blend the flavors. Remove from the heat.

2 In a blender, coarsely puree the soup in batches. Or use an immersion blender to coarsely puree the soup in the pot. Return the soup to the pot, if necessary, and heat through. Season with the lemon juice or vinegar and salt and pepper. Ladle the soup into bowls and serve, with tomato and scallions, if desired.

Note The soup can be made up to 3 days ahead and stored in an airtight container in the fridge. Add the garnish just before serving.

mulligatawny soup

(V) To me, mulligatawny, which means "pepper water," sounds more like the name of a river in the Deep South than a spiced soup from southern India. Mulligatawny usually contains beef stock. This version, however, relies on vegetables and freshly ground aromatic spices for flavor. It's the perfect starter to a meal full of bright Asian flavors, such as Cashew Korma (page 206) or Tempeh Rendang (page 232).

SERVES 4

1 In a large spice mill or using a mortar and pestle, grind the coriander seeds, cumin seeds, and peppercorns. In a large saucepan, heat the canola oil over medium heat. Add the onion and sauté until soft, about 7 minutes. Add the ground spices, ginger, and garlic and cook, stirring, for 2 minutes more.

2 In a small bowl, whisk the flour and 1 cup cold water until well blended. Stir the flour mixture into the onion mixture. Add the carrots, potatoes, and 3 cups water and bring to a boil. Reduce the heat to a simmer and cook for 30 minutes, or until the vegetables have softened. Remove from the heat.

1 tablespoon coriander seeds

1 teaspoon cumin seeds

1 teaspoon black peppercorns

1 tablespoon canola oil

1 large onion, chopped

1 rounded tablespoon peeled and minced fresh ginger

2 garlic cloves, minced

1 tablespoon all-purpose flour

3 carrots, peeled and diced

2 small new potatoes, peeled

Sherry vinegar or apple cider vinegar to taste

Kosher salt to taste, at least 1 rounded teaspoon

2 tablespoons chopped fresh cilantro leaves for garnish (optional)

3 In a blender, coarsely puree the soup in batches. Or use an immersion blender to coarsely puree the soup in the pan. Return the soup to the pan, if necessary, and heat through. Season with vinegar and salt. Serve the soup in mugs or small bowls, garnished with the cilantro, if desired.

Note

The soup can be made up to 3 days ahead and stored in an airtight container in the fridge. Add the garnish, if using, just before serving.

Ginger

baked onion cheese soup

This recipe is adapted from one in the Time-Life The Good Cook series. It was compiled by the legendary Richard Olney, an American food writer who lived in France for most of his life. This soup combines caramelized onions, garlic, and hearty bread with cheddar or Gruyère cheese. When baked, it becomes thick, rich, and delicious. You can add a pinch of saffron threads to the broth, if you like. Serve with watercress and sliced apple salad tossed with a good olive oil and a touch of balsamic vinegar.

SERVES 6

3 tablespoons butter

6 medium onions, thinly sliced

1 large head of garlic, separated into cloves, peeled, and sliced

2/3 cup white wine

Kosher salt and freshly ground pepper to taste

12 slices sturdy peasant bread

2 cups grated sharp cheddar (I like Grafton Vermont sharp cheddar or Canadian cheddar) or grated Gruyère cheese (about 8 ounces)

1 In a large, heavy pot, melt the butter over medium heat. Add the onions and sauté, stirring occasionally, until they begin to brown, about 25 minutes. Add the garlic and cook, stirring occasionally, for 5 minutes more.

2 Preheat the oven to 375 degrees. Increase the heat under the pot to medium-high, add the wine, and boil for 1 minute. Stir in 5 cups water. Bring to a boil, then reduce the heat to a simmer and cook for 10 minutes. Season with salt and pepper. Remove from the heat.

Note If you want some time between preparation and serving, the soup can be prepared, layered into the tureen, and baked in a 275-degree oven for at least 1 hour and up to 1 1/2 hours. It can also stand for 1 hour before baking. Or, if you prefer, make the soup through step 2 and store in an airtight container in the fridge for up to 3 days.

3 In an ovenproof soup tureen or 2-quart casserole, place 6 slices of the bread and sprinkle them with 1 cup of the cheese. Carefully ladle half the soup over the bread. Repeat with the remaining 6 slices of bread and 1 cup cheese. Carefully ladle the remaining soup over the bread. (Use a large spoon to immerse the bread, if necessary.) Cover the tureen or casserole and bake until piping hot, about 25 minutes. Ladle the soup into bowls at the table and serve.

focaccia meets edward scissorhands

Try cutting focaccia with kitchen scissors instead of a knife. You can cut the focaccia into fun shapes before adding it to the breadbasket or plates.

creamy parsnip soup
with horseradish

(V) *Parsnips impart a nutty yet sweet* flavor and possess a rich texture that makes this soup especially creamy. Don't buy extra-large parsnips, since they tend to be woody in the center. This is a filling soup, so serve it in small bowls if a main course will follow.

SERVES 6 TO 8

1 In a large pot, heat the olive oil over medium heat. Add the onion and sauté, stirring occasionally, until translucent, 8 to 10 minutes. Add the garlic and cook for 2 minutes more. Add the potatoes, parsnips, sage, thyme, or rosemary, and 7 cups water. Bring to a boil, then reduce the heat to a simmer and cook until the potatoes and parsnips are tender, about 25 minutes. Remove from the heat.

2 In a blender, puree the soup in batches. Or use an immersion blender to puree it in the pot. Return the soup to the pot, if necessary, and heat through. If the soup is too thick, add $1/2$ to 1 cup water. Stir in the vinegar and the horseradish to taste, then season liberally with salt and pepper. Whisk in the sour cream, if desired. Don't let the soup boil or the sour cream will curdle. Ladle into bowls and serve.

- 2 tablespoons extra-virgin olive oil
- 1 large yellow onion, chopped
- 8 garlic cloves, minced
- $1^{1}/_{2}$ pounds russet potatoes, peeled and cut into 1-inch cubes
- $1^{1}/_{2}$ pounds parsnips, peeled or scrubbed and cut into 1-inch pieces
- 1 tablespoon minced fresh sage, thyme, or rosemary
- 1 teaspoon sherry vinegar or red wine vinegar

  About 2 tablespoons prepared or freshly grated horseradish

  Kosher salt and freshly ground white or black pepper to taste
- $1/4$ cup sour cream (optional)

Note The soup may be made up to 2 days in advance. Reheat it slowly if using the sour cream; do not boil.

sweet potato soup with chipotle and sage

(V) *The pinelike flavor of sage* stands up beautifully to the smoky heat of the chipotle, and the sweet potatoes allow the sage and chipotle to come through without losing their own buttery, honeyed personality. It's a quick and easy soup to make if you have only a little time before your guests arrive.

SERVES 4

1 tablespoon canola oil

2 onions, chopped

3 large garlic cloves, minced

2 sweet potatoes (about 1½ pounds total), peeled and cut into 1-inch cubes

1 tart apple, such as Granny Smith, peeled, cored, and chopped

1 tablespoon chopped fresh sage, or more if needed

1 canned chipotle chile in adobo, or more if needed

Kosher salt to taste

1 In a large saucepan, heat the canola oil over medium heat. Add the onions and sauté, stirring occasionally, until soft, about 7 minutes. Add the garlic and sauté for 2 minutes more.

2 Add the remaining ingredients and 6 cups water and simmer for 30 minutes, or until the sweet potatoes are very tender. Remove from the heat.

3 In a blender, puree the soup in batches. Or use an immersion blender to puree the soup in the pot. Return the soup to the pan, if necessary, and heat through. Adjust the seasonings, adding more sage, chipotle, or salt, if desired. Ladle into bowls and serve.

Note The soup can be made up to 3 days ahead and stored in an airtight container in the fridge.

butternut and ginger soup

 This soup is so fast and easy that you'll feel guilty accepting the compliments. You can substitute sweet potatoes for the squash. Serve it with a salad of mixed greens tossed with Goat Cheese–Walnut Dressing (page 160) and hearty whole wheat bread.

SERVES 4

1 In a large saucepan, heat the oil over medium heat. Add the onions and sauté, stirring occasionally, until soft, about 7 minutes. Add the ginger and garlic and sauté for 1 minute more.

2 Add the squash, coconut milk, and 5 cups water. Bring to a boil, then reduce the heat and simmer, stirring occasionally, until the squash is cooked through, about 20 minutes. Remove from the heat.

3 In a blender, puree the soup in batches. Or use an immersion blender to puree the soup in the pan. Return the soup to the pan, if necessary, and heat through. Add the chili sauce, chopped cilantro, and salt and pepper. Ladle into four bowls, garnish each with chopped peanuts and a cilantro sprig, and serve.

1 tablespoon canola oil

2 onions, chopped

¼ cup peeled and minced fresh ginger

3 garlic cloves, minced

1 2-pound butternut squash, peeled, seeded, and cut into 1-inch cubes

1 13.5-ounce can unsweetened coconut milk (see page 446)

1 teaspoon Asian chili sauce (see page 443), or more to taste

3 tablespoons chopped fresh cilantro, plus 4 sprigs for garnish

Kosher salt and freshly ground black pepper to taste

3 tablespoons chopped roasted peanuts for garnish

Note The soup can be made up to 2 days ahead and stored in an airtight container in the fridge. Add the garnish just before serving.

acorn squash, spinach, and roasted garlic soup

I served this soup as part of a four-course dinner at an extravaganza five years ago, and people still tell me how much they loved it. Use heavy cream if everyone can swing with the fat.

MAKES 6 SMALL BOWLS

2 acorn squash

Extra-virgin olive oil

4 heads of garlic, 3 left whole, 1 separated into cloves and peeled

2 tablespoons butter

2 onions, chopped

4 cups vegetable stock

$^2/_3$ cup dry sherry

1 bunch spinach (about $^2/_3$ pound), stemmed

$^2/_3$ cup light or heavy cream

1 teaspoon kosher salt

Pinch of freshly ground nutmeg

Freshly ground black pepper to taste

1 Preheat the oven to 375 degrees. Cut the acorn squash in half with a large, sharp chef's knife. Remove and discard the seeds and strings. Brush the cut sides with olive oil. Arrange the squash cut side down on a rimmed baking sheet. Cut off the top thirds of the 3 whole heads of garlic and brush the cut sides with olive oil. Place on the baking sheet with the squash. Roast until the squash and garlic are very tender, about 45 minutes. Let stand until cool enough to handle.

2 Meanwhile, in a large, heavy pot, melt the butter over medium heat. Add the onions and sauté, stirring occasionally, until lightly browned, about 15 minutes. Add the unroasted garlic cloves and sauté for 3 minutes more. Stir in the vegetable stock, sherry, and spinach. Bring to a boil and boil for 5 minutes. Remove from the heat.

3 Scoop the squash flesh into a food processor. Squeeze the roasted garlic cloves out of their skins and add to the food processor. Puree the squash and garlic, adding a bit of the liquid from the soup, if necessary. Transfer to a clean, large saucepan.

4 In the food processor, puree the spinach mixture in batches, adding each batch to the squash mixture. Or use an immersion blender to puree the spinach mixture in the pot, then add it to the squash mixture. Add the cream, salt, and nutmeg and mix well. Heat through and season with pepper. Ladle into bowls and serve.

Note
The soup can be made up to 2 days ahead and stored in an airtight container in the fridge.

chapter 3

Side Salads and Stand-Alone Salads

Endive

Mint

salad buffets:
the ultimate crowd-pleasers

When I'm having a large group over for a meal, a buffet is the only way to go. And I always try to serve a variety of salads.

Here's why. First, they're usually visually striking. In salads, the beauty of the vegetables isn't hidden by a layer of sauce; everything glistens. The salad that gets the most oohs and aahs at my house is Mango Slaw, with vibrant orange mango, red pepper, and red cabbage doing the fandango in the serving bowl. Second, salads can be prepared beforehand and don't need any last-minute attention except for tossing.

For salads it's important to adapt the recipes according to which vegetables are freshest at the market. If the beets or the green beans look best, incorporate some into one of the salads or use them as replacements for other vegetables that have similar qualities.

For serving utensils, tongs are best, since people are usually holding their plates in one hand and serving themselves with the other. Here are a few salad combos that have met with great success:

A salad of watercress, Bibb lettuce, and cucumbers (alfalfa sprouts optional) with Classic Lemon Dressing (page 154)
French Lentil Salad with Dried Currants and Walnuts (page 150)

Simple Cauliflower Salad with Creamy Cilantro Dressing (page 138)
Mango Slaw (page 120)

New Millennium Waldorf Salad (page 130)
Big Couscous and Clementine Salad (page 139)

Green Bean–Sweet Potato Salad with Peanut Dressing (page 142)
Sweet Heat Cucumber Salad (page 122)

side salads and stand-alone salads

asparagus slaw

(V) *Here's a slaw with class.* Halved spears of asparagus tossed with slivers of red bell pepper, black olives, and mint make an elegant first course for a spring dinner. If you find superthin asparagus, you won't need to cut the spears in half. If you want to get really fancy, you can garnish the slaw with crumbled goat cheese.

SERVES 6

1½ pounds asparagus

¼ cup fresh lemon juice (1 juicy lemon)

¼ cup extra-virgin olive oil

20 kalamata olives, pitted and coarsely chopped

⅓ cup chopped packed fresh mint leaves

1 red bell pepper, very thinly sliced

1 small red onion, thinly sliced

Kosher salt and freshly ground black pepper to taste

1 Bring a large pot of salted water to a boil. Meanwhile, break off and discard the tough bottom quarter of each asparagus spear. Blanch the asparagus in the boiling water for 3 minutes. Drain and immediately rinse under cold running water until cool; drain again. Cut the spears in half lengthwise.

2 In a large bowl, whisk together the lemon juice, olive oil, olives, and mint. Add the asparagus, bell pepper, and onion and toss well to coat. Season with salt and pepper. Serve at room temperature, or refrigerate for up to 6 hours and serve cold, tossing again just before serving.

Mint

fennel slaw

(V) *In this refreshing slaw,* anise seeds accentuate the flavor of the fennel. If you don't have a plastic vegetable slicer (see page 119) or a fine slicing disk for your food processor, use a very sharp chef's knife.

SERVES 4 TO 6

⅓ cup white vinegar

1 tablespoon extra-virgin olive oil

1 tablespoon sugar

2 teaspoons anise seeds

3 cups finely shredded green cabbage (about ⅓ head)

2 cups finely shredded fresh fennel bulb (about 1 medium bulb)

1 large carrot, peeled and grated

½ red onion, thinly sliced

Kosher salt and freshly ground black pepper

In a large bowl, whisk together the vinegar, olive oil, sugar, and anise seeds. Add the cabbage, fennel, carrot, and onion and toss well to coat. Season with salt and pepper. Serve at room temperature or refrigerate for up to 24 hours and serve cold, tossing again just before serving.

side salads and stand-alone salads

summer slaw with poppy-mustard dressing

(V) In slaws, I prefer summer squash to zucchini because of its soft, silky texture. Zucchini can be almost as delicate and tender, though, as long as you choose small ones. The simple dressing will perform well on many other raw vegetables. For added flavor, substitute extra-virgin olive oil for the canola oil. If you have fresh mint on hand, add a few handfuls of leaves to the salad just before serving.

SERVES 6 TO 8

dressing

- 2½ tablespoons red wine vinegar
- 1 tablespoon honey or 1 tablespoon sugar
- 1 tablespoon Dijon mustard
- 1 garlic clove
- ⅓ cup canola oil
- ½ teaspoon kosher salt
- 2 tablespoons poppy seeds

slaw

- 2 medium summer squash or 2 small zucchini
- 1 large carrot, peeled and grated
- 1 small red bell pepper, cut into matchsticks
- 1 small red onion, thinly sliced
- 1 jalapeño pepper, seeded and thinly sliced (optional)

Kosher salt and freshly ground black pepper to taste

1 **To make the dressing:** In a food processor, combine the vinegar, sugar or honey, mustard, and garlic and process until smooth. With the machine running, slowly add the canola oil through the feed tube, processing until incorporated. Add the salt and the poppy seeds.

plastic vegetable slicers

Can't cut cabbage as razor-thin as the kind you get in restaurants? The plastic slicers sold in Asian markets will cut your cabbage, onions, daikon, carrots, apples, celery, and dozens of other foods thinner and faster than an Iron Chef ever could. The slicers are about 12 inches long and 4 inches wide and are sold in slim rectangular boxes. I like the "New Benriner" slicer with the photo of a smiling Japanese woman on the box. Besides slaws, I also use it to slice vegetables for spring roll fillings, stir-fries, and roasted vegetables (Jerusalem artichokes are great thinly sliced and roasted with olive oil and garlic). Plastic slicers are a fraction of the price of the bulkier stainless-steel mandolines used in French kitchens, and their blades seem to stay sharper longer. But beware, these slicers can slice through anything, including your fingers! Use the guard religiously—I nearly lost the upper part of my pinky one afternoon while I was slicing carrots without the guard. Four stitches later, I now use the guard.

2 **To make the slaw:** Cut off about one third of each squash or zucchini in a single, lengthwise strip, as close to the seed core as possible without touching it. You should be able to see the seeds. Holding the cut side up, make another lengthwise cut in the same manner. Do this two more times, so you end up with 4 long strips of squash or zucchini and 1 long core of seeds. Discard the core of seeds. Julienne the squash or zucchini flesh.

3 In a large bowl, toss together the squash or zucchini, carrot, bell pepper, onion, and jalapeño, if using, and mix well. Gradually add just enough dressing to ensure the slaw is well coated but not soupy. Season with salt and pepper. Serve at room temperature or chill the slaw, but serve within 6 hours so the squash doesn't exude too much water into the dressing.

mango slaw

 This slaw is full of healthy veggies pulled together by mango and mint. If you can't find jicama, 6 thinly sliced celery stalks will do just fine. This slaw is great served on a buffet table, next to a veggie burger, on top of a pile of brown rice, or as a sort of "relish" alongside an Indian curry.

SERVES 8

slaw

- 6 cups thinly sliced savoy or napa cabbage (about 1/2 head)
- 1 cup thinly shredded red cabbage (optional)
- 1 small jicama, peeled and cut into matchsticks or half-moons
- 1 red bell pepper, diced
- 6 scallions, white and green parts, chopped
- 1/2 cup thin strips fresh mint leaves
- 1 ripe but firm mango, cut into thin strips (see note); pit reserved

dressing

- 1 cup chopped fresh cilantro leaves and stems
- 1 3-inch piece fresh ginger, peeled and minced
- 1/4 cup lime juice (2 juicy limes)
- 1 tablespoon white vinegar
- 1 tablespoon sugar
- 1 teaspoon kosher salt
- 1/2 teaspoon freshly ground black pepper
- 1/4 teaspoon hot sauce
- 1 teaspoon Dijon mustard
- 1/4 cup canola oil

Note
To cut the mango, first peel it with a sharp veggie peeler. Then make 2 straight cuts down the length of the fruit, on opposite sides of the pit. Holding the pit, cut away any flesh you can.

entertaining for a veggie planet

120

1 **To make the slaw:** In a large bowl, combine the savoy or napa cabbage, red cabbage (if using), jicama, bell pepper, scallions, and mint and toss until well mixed. Fold in the mango.

2 **To make the dressing:** Chop the mango trimmings from the reserved pit. In a medium bowl, combine the mango trimmings, cilantro, ginger, lime juice, vinegar, sugar, salt, pepper, and hot sauce and whisk until the sugar dissolves. Whisk in the mustard. When it is incorporated, gradually add the canola oil, whisking until well blended. Pour the dressing over the slaw, tossing until well coated. Serve immediately. The salad and dressing can be refrigerated in separate containers up to 24 hours ahead and combined just before serving.

RED Cabbage

beauty tip

Thinly sliced red cabbage adds beautiful color to plain green salads. Use a plastic vegetable slicer or a Y-shaped vegetable peeler to get the cabbage slices paper-thin. Whole cabbages will keep for more than 1 week in the fridge.

sweet heat cucumber salad

 This sweet, spicy cucumber salad draws on three popular Thai ingredients — lime juice, peanuts, and chiles. Pickling cucumbers don't need to be peeled and have a crisper texture than conventional ones. This salad loses its pep after 24 hours, so leftovers must be attended to swiftly.

SERVES 4 TO 6

dressing

- 1–3 small, skinny chile peppers, minced
- 2 tablespoons sugar
- 1 garlic clove, minced
- ¼ cup fresh lime juice (2 juicy limes)
- 2 tablespoons Asian fish sauce (see page 444) or 1 teaspoon kosher salt

salad

- 2 cups cherry tomatoes, halved
- 4 pickling cucumbers, very thinly sliced
- 1 cup sugar snap peas
- 4 scallions, white and green parts, thinly sliced
- ¼ cup chopped unsalted roasted peanuts
- ⅓ cup chopped fresh cilantro leaves and stems for garnish

1 **To make the dressing:** In a small bowl, whisk together the chiles, sugar, garlic, lime juice, and fish sauce or salt until the sugar dissolves.

2 **To make the salad:** In a large bowl, combine the tomatoes, cucumbers, sugar snap peas, scallions and peanuts. Add the dressing and toss well to coat. Chill before serving and garnish with the cilantro.

Variation Instead of using cucumbers, try thinly sliced jicama or zucchini or diced raw green beans.

jicama-grape salad

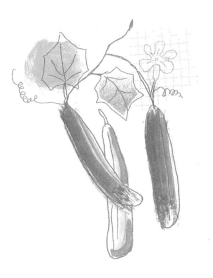

(V) *This salad contains so much flavor* and texture that it doesn't need even a drop of oil. The soft, tart grapes, crunchy jicama, roasted peanuts, mint and chiles form a perfectly orchestrated marching band in your mouth.

SERVES 4

In a large bowl, whisk together the vinegar, sugar, and chiles until the sugar dissolves. Add the jicama, grapes, cucumber, peanuts or cashews, scallions, and mint and toss to coat well. Season with salt and pepper. Serve at room temperature or refrigerate and serve cold.

Note
The salad can be prepared up to 1 day ahead and stored in an airtight container in the fridge.

2 tablespoons rice vinegar

1 teaspoon sugar

2 small, skinny chile peppers (seeded, if you like), minced

1 pound jicama, peeled and cut into matchsticks

2 cups coarsely chopped seedless green grapes

1 pickling cucumber, peeled, seeded, and chopped

½ cup chopped roasted peanuts or cashews (see page 449)

⅓ cup finely chopped scallions, white and green parts

⅓ cup chopped fresh mint leaves

Kosher salt and freshly ground black pepper to taste

watercress, cabbage, and tomato slaw with ginger dressing

Something supernatural happens when you combine these ingredients. The dried coconut adds crunch, and even coconutphobes love this salad. I like to add a teaspoon of toasted rice powder to this dish (available at Asian markets) or a handful of mint leaves.

SERVES 4

1 Cut off and discard the bottom $1/2$ inch of the watercress stems. Chop the entire bunch, including the remaining stems, into 1-inch pieces. In a medium bowl, combine the watercress, cabbage, tomato, peanuts, and coconut.

2 To make the dressing: In a small bowl, combine the lime juice, salt or fish sauce, ginger, and sugar, stirring until the sugar dissolves.

3 Pour the dressing over the salad and toss well to coat. Sprinkle the salad with the sesame seeds and serve at room temperature, or refrigerate for up to 2 hours and serve cold.

1 small bunch watercress

2 cups green cabbage, sliced as thinly as possible

1 large tomato or 2 plum tomatoes, cut into $1/2$-inch cubes

$1/4$ cup chopped unsalted roasted peanuts (see page 449)

2 tablespoons dried, unsweetened coconut

dressing

$1/4$ cup fresh lime juice (2 juicy limes)

2 teaspoons kosher salt or Asian fish sauce to taste

$3^1/2$ tablespoons peeled and minced fresh ginger

1 tablespoon sugar

2 tablespoons toasted sesame seeds (see page 450) for garnish

the prettiest little salad around

(V) *If I cared about appearances*, I'd want to be seen with this glamorous medley of pastel fruits and vegetables. A strawberry papaya's flavor is sweeter than a conventional papaya's. The exterior should be more yellow than green, and if it has no blemishes, it's probably not quite ripe—it should be soft like a ripe peach. Well-stocked supermarkets often carry strawberry papayas. I have found extremely large ones in Asian markets, in which case I use only half a papaya for this recipe.

SERVES 6

1 Cut off the bulbous bottom third of each lemongrass stalk. (Save the rest of the stalks for stocks, soups, stews, or even tea.) Remove and discard the tough outer leaves. With a large, sharp chef's knife or a plastic vegetable slicer, cut the lemongrass bottoms into thin rounds.

2 In a large bowl, combine the lemongrass, papaya or cantaloupe, bok choy, bell pepper, onion, mint, lemon juice, olive oil, and salt and toss well to coat. Serve on large plates lined with the reserved bok choy leaves, garnished with the fried Japanese peas.

4 fat lemongrass stalks

1 strawberry papaya or ½ very ripe cantaloupe, seeded, peeled, and cut into small cubes

1 small head bok choy, stems cut into half-moons and leaves reserved

1 yellow bell pepper, seeded and thinly sliced

½ small onion, very thinly sliced and separated into rings

½ cup fresh mint leaves

¼ cup fresh lemon juice (1 juicy lemon)

2 tablespoons extra-virgin olive oil

Kosher salt to taste

Handful of crunchy fried Japanese "peas," either wasabi (hot) or plain

Note The salad can be made up to 8 hours ahead and stored in an airtight container in the fridge. Add the garnish before serving.

side salads and stand-alone salads

roasted pear, blue cheese, and bibb salad with cranberry vinaigrette

When I taught a vegetarian food and wine-tasting class with my wine buddy Eden, we practically knocked all the students' socks off with this salad. Fresh cranberries are generally in season from September through November. If you can't find Maytag blue cheese, a blue that's made in Wisconsin, you can use French Roquefort. Because the cranberry dressing is so pretty, drizzle it over the salad rather than tossing it in.

SERVES 4

vinaigrette

- 1½ cups fresh cranberries
- ½ cup extra-virgin olive oil
- 2 tablespoons balsamic vinegar
- 1 tablespoon honey
- Squeeze of fresh lemon juice
- 1 teaspoon Dijon mustard
- Kosher salt and freshly ground black pepper to taste

salad

- 2 Bosc pears (if they're still firm, that's fine)
- 1 small head Bibb lettuce
- 4 ounces Maytag blue or Roquefort cheese
- ¼ cup toasted chopped pecans (see page 283)

1 **To make the vinaigrette:** Preheat the oven to 350 degrees. Oil a rimmed baking sheet. Place the cranberries on the baking sheet and roast until they begin to soften and wilt, about 15 minutes. Set aside to cool. Increase the oven temperature to 375 degrees.

> I have one friend who entertains nicely, but rather minimally. He doesn't offer a lot of courses, and he doesn't serve a lot of food, but he always has excellent wines. There are times when it's been a bit close to the bone — once we actually went home hungry — but at one dinner his style suddenly made sense: it was so simple, and he and his wife were so relaxed even though they are very busy people. As a result, I started paring back my menus, and I found that it has made for very relaxed entertaining all the way around.
>
> **—Cookbook author Deborah Madison**

2 Meanwhile, in a medium bowl, combine the olive oil, vinegar, honey, lemon juice, and mustard. Stir in the roasted cranberries and season with salt and pepper. Set aside.

3 **To make the salad:** Halve the pears (leave the skins on) and spoon out the seeds. Oil a small baking pan and place the pears in it cut side down. Bake the pears until tender, about 30 minutes, or until a knife pierces the pears easily. Let cool.

4 Arrange the Bibb lettuce leaves on four salad plates. Cut the pear halves lengthwise into thin slices, keeping them in their pear shape. Pick up the slices with a chef's knife or spatula and place each half on a salad plate. Crumble the blue cheese evenly over the salads.

5 Spoon at least 2 tablespoons of the vinaigrette over each salad (you'll have some left over). Top with the pecans and serve.

side salads and stand-alone salads

forkless artichoke salad

The idea for this salad grew out of practicality. I had piles of leftover artichoke leaves just aching to be eaten after I'd put the artichoke hearts into a salad. The artichoke leaves form a dramatic wreath around this excellent salad of artichoke hearts, oranges, walnuts, goat cheese, and black olives. The leaves act as "forks" to bring the salad to your mouth. What could be better than bucking the tradition of silverware? Just remember to scrape the meat from the leaf as you eat the salad it carries. Serve with crusty bread. For dessert, make a double batch of Michel Richard's Fruit "Salad" with Melted Ice Cream (page 414).

SERVES 8

7 large artichokes, bottom ½ inch of stems trimmed

1 cup finely chopped fresh fennel bulb (about ½ medium bulb)

1 medium red onion, chopped

⅔ cup pitted, chopped kalamata olives

3 tablespoons finely chopped fresh mint or basil, plus 8 sprigs for garnish

¼ cup fresh lemon juice (about 1 large lemon)

3 tablespoons extra-virgin olive oil

6 ounces soft goat cheese

2 navel oranges, peeled, membranes removed, and separated into segments

¼ cup toasted chopped walnuts (see page 283)

Kosher salt and freshly ground black pepper

1 **Cook the artichokes:** Place the artichokes stem side up in a saucepan wide enough to hold all of them side by side. Fill the pan with about 2 inches of water. Bring to a boil over high heat. Cover the pan (use a large dinner plate if your pan doesn't have a cover) and steam the artichokes until the tip of a sharp knife can slide easily into the base of each one, about 45 minutes. Remove from the heat and let cool in the pan.

2 Meanwhile, in a large bowl, combine the fennel, onion, olives, and mint or basil and mix well. Drizzle with the lemon juice and olive oil and toss well to coat.

3 When the artichokes are cool enough to handle, pull off the leaves and set aside. Discard the tiny yellow leaves toward the middle of the choke. With a spoon, remove the hairy choke from the hearts. Trim around each stem with a paring knife. Cut the hearts and stems into $1/2$-inch pieces.

4 At serving time, crumble the goat cheese over the salad. Add the artichoke hearts and stems, orange segments, and walnuts. Season with salt and pepper and toss gently just to incorporate. Arrange the artichoke leaves in a circular pattern on eight salad plates, leaving room for the salad in the center of each plate. Spoon on the salad and serve. Offer an empty bowl for discarded artichoke leaves.

artichokes—the difficult vegetable

Artichokes are notoriously difficult to match with wines. James Beard once said, "There is a great feeling among serious wine drinkers that artichokes spoil the flavor of fine wines and therefore should be forbidden at great dinners." After some research, scientists found a unique acid in artichokes called cynarin, which alters the flavor of foods that follow in its path. When artichokes are mixed with other foods, however, the effects are much less noticeable. There are, in fact, a few wines that can retain their flavors when consumed with artichokes: a rich Sancerre, a white Burgundy, and Tavel (a French rosé).

new millennium waldorf salad

I love the apples, walnuts, and celery in Waldorf salad, but who needs the mayonnaise-laden dressing? This is my mayo-free, twenty-first-century version. It's a perfect salad for fall, when the apples are local, crisp, and tart. For a vegan version, substitute Pan-Fried Tofu (page 217) for the blue cheese and use sugar instead of honey. If you want to prepare the dish ahead, hold off on cutting up the apples until you're ready to serve.

SERVES 8

1 cup coarsely chopped walnuts

3 tablespoons extra-virgin olive oil

2 tablespoons fresh lemon juice (1/2 juicy lemon)

1 tablespoon honey

2 cups thinly sliced celery

1 large Fuji or Gala apple, unpeeled, cut into 1/4-inch cubes

1/3 cup golden raisins soaked in hot water for 10 minutes and drained

3 ounces good-quality crumbly blue cheese, such as Great Hill Blue or Maytag

1 small red onion, chopped

Kosher salt and freshly ground black pepper to taste

1 Preheat the oven to 350 degrees. Spread the walnuts in a single layer on a rimmed baking sheet and toast for 5 minutes, or until golden brown. Let cool.

2 In a small bowl, combine the olive oil, lemon juice, and honey and mix well.

3 In a large bowl, combine the celery, apple, walnuts, and raisins. Pour the dressing over the salad, add the blue cheese, onion, and salt and pepper and toss until well combined. Serve at room temperature right away or combine everything except the apple and refrigerate for up to 24 hours. Cut and add the apple bits just before serving.

grilling without animals

If you prefer to hear the birds sing in the trees rather than singe on the grill, try these vegetarian alternatives for your summer barbecue.

Grilled Vegetable Salad with Tarragon-Sherry Vinaigrette (page 132).

Grilled Vegetables with Romesco Sauce (page 345)—for directions on grilling vegetables, see Grilled Vegetable Salad with Tarragon-Sherry Vinaigrette (page 132).

Portobello "Burgers" with Chipotle Ketchup (page 174).

Amy's Burgers—found in the freezer section of supermarkets. I also like Trader Joe's burgers. Serve with Zesty, Smoky Cherry Tomato–Oregano Salsa (page 32); substitute mangoes for the cherry tomatoes.

Grilled pizza—roll out a piece of pizza dough, rub both sides with a spoonful of olive oil. Throw it on a hot grill for a few seconds then turn it with tongs. It should have black grill marks on it. Cook the other side, then top with grilled veggies and a sauce (or cheese) of your liking such as Saffron Aïoli (page 17).

Grilled slices of hearty bread brushed with olive oil (before grilling)—wonderful with Romesco Sauce (page 345) or with Zesty, Smoky Cherry Tomato–Oregano Salsa (page 32), with a few more tablespoons of extra-virgin olive oil added for good measure.

Extra-Smoky Baba Gannouj (page 29)—follow the directions for cooking the eggplant, but cook it on the grill. Once it's made, grill some pita bread and serve with the baba gannouj.

Peach Chutney (page 343)—wonderful with any burger.

Fresh Cilantro Chutney (page 344)—great with grilled veggies.

Caramelized Garlic Sambal (page 348)—serve with a veggie burger or grilled veggies (especially corn that has been grilled unhusked) and jasmine rice.

Raisin Ketchup (page 342)—a good burger dress-up.

Chipotle Ketchup (page 341)—ditto.

grilled vegetable salad with tarragon-sherry vinaigrette

V *Grilled vegetables, like many foods,* taste best when served at room temperature, and that's what I recommend here. When grilling vegetables, my friend Tony, an avid griller, advises, "Do not grill them uncovered, or there will be a lot of char. If you cover them, they will melt in your mouth." Tony uses Nature's Own Chunk Charwood for charcoal because it imparts a lovely smoky flavor. Serve the salad with any cooked grain or crusty bread.

SERVES 4

vinaigrette

- ½ cup extra-virgin olive oil
- 3 tablespoons sherry vinegar
- 1 tablespoon fresh lime juice (½ juicy lime)
- 1 tablespoon Dijon mustard
- 1 tablespoon packed fresh tarragon leaves
- Kosher salt and freshly ground black pepper to taste

grilled vegetables

- 4 pounds mixed vegetables, such as fennel, red onion, eggplant, boiled red potatoes, red bell peppers, leeks, cherry tomatoes, and asparagus
- Extra-virgin olive oil or canola oil
- Kosher salt and freshly ground black pepper to taste

Note The salad is best served immediately. The dressing can be made up to 24 hours ahead and stored in an airtight container in the fridge.

1 **To make the vinaigrette:** In a food processor, combine the olive oil, vinegar, lime juice, mustard, and tarragon and process until smooth. Season with salt and pepper. Set aside.

2 **To make the grilled vegetables:** Prepare a medium-hot fire in a grill. Meanwhile, cut the vegetables into small pieces for grilling. Cut the fennel in half from top to bottom, then cut it into quarters or eighths, making sure that a piece of the core remains on all the wedges so they will hold together; cut the onion in a similar fashion. Cut the eggplant into $1/2$-inch-thick disks. Halve the new potatoes. Halve and seed the bell peppers and cut each half into 3 fat strips. Cut the leeks in half lengthwise and wash them well. Cherry tomatoes can be left whole. The asparagus spears need only be trimmed at the ends. In a large bowl, combine the vegetables. Add enough olive or canola oil to lightly coat the vegetables. Season liberally with salt and pepper.

3 Grill the vegetables with the cover closed. When grill marks form on the bottoms, turn and grill, covered, until tender. Transfer the vegetables to a serving platter and drizzle with as much of the vinaigrette as you like. (You'll have more than enough dressing, so refrigerate what you don't use.) Allow the vegetables to cool to room temperature before serving.

chard and eggplant salad with miso-sesame vinaigrette

(V) *This tasty salad is a permutation* of the irresistible cold sesame spinach offered in Japanese restaurants. You can eat it as a light lunch or dinner on a bed of watercress or over hot jasmine rice and/or Pan-Fried Tofu (page 217).

SERVES 2

1 Preheat the oven to 350 degrees. In a large bowl, toss the eggplant and canola oil and season with salt and pepper. Spread in a single layer on a rimmed baking sheet and roast until tender but not mushy, 15 to 20 minutes.

2 In the same bowl used for the eggplant, whisk together the black or balsamic vinegar, sesame oil, rice vinegar, sugar, miso, and garlic.

3 In a large saucepan, bring 2 inches of water to a simmer over medium-high heat. Add the Swiss chard, cover, and cook just until the chard wilts, 4 to 5 minutes. Drain and rinse under cold running water. Squeeze out as much liquid as possible. Add the chard to the vinaigrette, stirring to separate the leaves.

3 Asian eggplants or 1 medium Italian eggplant, cut into $1/2$-inch cubes (about 6 cups)

3 tablespoons canola oil

Kosher salt and freshly ground black pepper to taste

3 tablespoons Chinese black vinegar (see page 445) or balsamic vinegar

2 tablespoons toasted sesame oil

1 tablespoon rice vinegar

$1^1/2$ tablespoons sugar

1 tablespoon red or barley miso (see page 448)

2 garlic cloves, minced

1 large bunch Swiss chard (preferably red or ruby), leaves cut into $1/2$-inch-long shreds, stems cut into $1/4$-inch pieces

2 tablespoons toasted sesame seeds (see page 450)

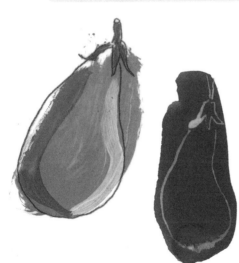

4 Add the eggplant to the chard mixture. Cover with plastic wrap, refrigerate for a few hours and serve cold. Sprinkle with the sesame seeds just before serving.

crispy, spicy tofu and peanut slaw

Ⓥ *This slaw is a perfect example* of how chiles can transform something as mundane as cabbage into a truly special dish. The texture of the slaw is best when the cabbage is sliced paper-thin. To get the thinnest possible shreds, use a Y-shaped vegetable peeler or a plastic vegetable slicer (see page 119). If you don't have either, a very sharp knife will do the trick.

SERVES 4 TO 6

1 In a large colander, combine the cabbage and 1 teaspoon salt and toss to coat. Let stand for 30 minutes in the sink to leach out excess water. Rinse well with cold running water and drain.

2 Wrap the block of tofu well with a clean dishtowel and press firmly with your hands until you feel the towel become damp. Unwrap the tofu and cut it into ½-inch cubes. In a large, well-seasoned skillet, heat the canola oil over medium-high heat. Add the tofu and salt it liberally. Fry the tofu undisturbed until it forms a dark golden crust on the bottom, then use a spatula to turn it and brown it well on at least one more side. Drain well on paper

- 3 cups very thinly sliced green cabbage (see above)
- 1 teaspoon kosher salt, plus more to taste
- 1 16-ounce carton firm or extra-firm tofu
- 2 tablespoons canola oil
- 1 cup bean sprouts
- 3 scallions, white and green parts, coarsely chopped (optional)
- 1 tablespoon minced small, skinny chile peppers, or more to taste
- 1 tablespoon peeled and minced fresh ginger
- 2 garlic cloves, minced
- 2 tablespoons sugar
- 3 tablespoons white vinegar
- 1 cup chopped unsalted roasted peanuts (see page 449) for garnish

Note

The slaw is best served the same day it's made, but the slaw and dressing can be prepared up to 1 day ahead and stored in separate airtight containers in the fridge. Toss together and add the garnish just before serving.

towels. Transfer the tofu to a large bowl and add the cabbage, bean sprouts, and scallions.

3 In a small bowl, whisk together the chiles, ginger, garlic, sugar, and vinegar. Pour the dressing over the tofu mixture and toss to coat well. Just before serving, season the slaw with salt and garnish it with the peanuts.

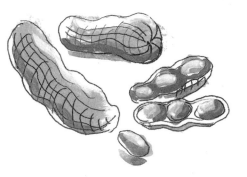

simple cauliflower salad with creamy cilantro dressing

Some people don't like cauliflower. However, many of these people only *think* they don't like cauliflower. Serving this salad to your guests will give potential cauliflower lovers a chance to discover the taste and texture of cauliflower at its best. If you want leftovers, you might have to make a second batch and stash it away before your guests arrive.

SERVES 6

1 Bring a large pot of salted water to a boil. Add the cauliflower and boil for 7 minutes, or until the florets are fairly tender. (Bite into a piece to check; it should be translucent, not white, inside.) Drain and rinse the cauliflower under cold running water. Drain well, then transfer to a large bowl. Add the bell pepper and onion.

2 In a small bowl, whisk together the lemon juice, olive oil, sour cream, cilantro and garlic. Let it sit for 5 minutes for the flavors to blend. Pour the dressing over the vegetables and toss well to coat. Season with salt and pepper. Serve at room temperature or refrigerate for a few hours and serve cold.

1 head cauliflower, separated into small florets

1 red bell pepper, cut into 1/2-inch pieces

1 red onion, finely chopped

3 tablespoons fresh lemon juice (about 1 juicy lemon)

2 tablespoons extra-virgin olive oil

2 tablespoons sour cream

1/2 cup chopped fresh cilantro leaves and stems

1 garlic clove, minced

Kosher salt and freshly ground black pepper to taste

big couscous and clementine salad

(V) *This is a light summer salad*, but it is filling enough to be a meal. Israeli couscous—the couscous with larger grains—can be found in Eastern Mediterranean markets and well-stocked supermarkets. Substitute regular (instant) couscous if you can't find the Israeli type. Additions to this salad are welcome. You could add artichoke hearts, tomatoes, or black olives, or use basil, mint, or dill instead of parsley.

SERVES 6 TO 8

1¼ cups uncooked Israeli couscous (see page 447)

¼ cup fresh lemon juice (1 juicy lemon)

2 tablespoons extra-virgin olive oil

4 clementines or 2 oranges, peeled and divided into segments

1 small red onion, finely chopped

½ cup chopped fresh flat-leaf parsley

½ cup toasted sliced almonds or pecans (see page 283)

Kosher salt and freshly ground black pepper to taste

1 Bring a large pot of salted water to a boil. Add the couscous and boil until tender, about 12 minutes. (Or cook regular couscous according to the package directions.) Drain the couscous and rinse it with cold running water. Drain well.

2 Meanwhile, in a large bowl, combine the lemon juice and olive oil. Add the clementine or orange segments, onion, parsley, and almonds or pecans and mix well. Stir in the couscous. Season liberally with salt and pepper. Serve at room temperature or refrigerate and serve cold within a few hours.

side salads and stand-alone salads

malaysian fruit and vegetable salad

 Even children love this salad. Tamarind can be found in Asian markets and *some* large supermarkets. Serve this salad as part of a buffet or as a light meal with miso soup or spring rolls.

SERVES 6 TO 8

dressing

- 1 2-inch square piece of tamarind (see page 452)
- ¼ cup unsweetened coconut milk (see page 446)
- 1 tablespoon fresh lime juice (½ juicy lime)
- ½ cup finely chopped toasted almonds (see page 283)
- 2–4 small, skinny chile peppers, minced
- 1 garlic clove, minced
- 1 teaspoon sugar
- 1 teaspoon kosher salt

salad

- 1 16-ounce carton extra-firm tofu
- 2 tablespoons canola oil

  Kosher salt to taste
- 1 Asian pear or Bosc pear, peeled, cored, and cut into ½-inch pieces
- 2 Fuji or Gala apples, peeled, cored, and cut into ½-inch pieces
- ½ red onion, finely chopped
- 3 stalks bok choy, cut into ½-inch pieces
- 3 tablespoons toasted sesame seeds for garnish (see page 450)

Note
The tofu can be fried up to 5 hours ahead and left at room temperature. The rest of the salad and the dressing can be made up to 1 day ahead and stored in separate airtight containers in the fridge. Toss and add the sesame seeds just before serving.

1 **To make the dressing:** In a small bowl, cover the tamarind with ³⁄₄ cup boiling water. Let stand for 15 minutes, then use your fingers to loosen the tamarind pulp from the seeds. Strain through a sieve, discarding the seeds and fibrous pulp. The remaining tamarind pulp should be the consistency of thick gravy. You should have about ²⁄₃ cup.

2 In a medium bowl, combine the tamarind pulp, coconut milk, lime juice, almonds, chiles, garlic, sugar, and salt and mix well. Set aside.

3 **To make the salad:** Wrap the block of tofu well with a clean dishtowel and press firmly with your hands until you feel the towel become damp. Unwrap the tofu and cut it into ¹⁄₂-inch cubes.

In a large, well-seasoned skillet, heat the canola oil over medium-high heat. Add the tofu and salt it liberally. Fry the tofu undisturbed until it forms a dark golden crust on the bottom, then use a spatula to turn it and brown it well on at least one more side. Drain well on paper towels. Transfer the tofu to a large bowl.

4 Add the pear, apples, onion, and bok choy to the tofu and toss to combine. Pour the dressing over the salad and toss to coat well. Sprinkle with the sesame seeds and serve immediately.

green bean–sweet potato salad with peanut dressing

(V) *This salad travels especially well,* whether it's for a picnic or to take to a party. After tasting this dish, a friend made an odd but accurate comment: "It's fruity and complex, like a fine wine." Speaking of which, don't serve wine with this salad, because the green beans and raw cabbage make it difficult to find a good match. Better to have beer or lemonade.

SERVES 6

1 large sweet potato, peeled and cut into 1/2-inch cubes

1 pound green beans, stem ends trimmed

3 cups thinly sliced green cabbage (about 1/4 head)

1/2 red onion, diced

1 lemongrass stalk

1 tablespoon ground coriander

1 garlic clove, minced

1 teaspoon peeled and minced fresh ginger

1/2 cup unsweetened coconut milk (see page 446)

1/2 cup unsalted roasted peanuts (see page 449)

2 teaspoons sugar or honey

2 tablespoons fresh lime juice (1 juicy lime)

1 teaspoon kosher salt or fish sauce to taste

1 Bring a pot of salted water to a boil. Add the sweet potato and boil until tender but still slightly firm, about 12 minutes. Use a slotted spoon to transfer the sweet potato to a colander (leave the water in the pot). Rinse with cold running water and drain well. Transfer the sweet potato to a large bowl.

2 Add the green beans to the same cooking water and boil for 4 minutes, or

peanut sauce diaries

I develop intense, high-school-girl-like crushes on peanut sauces. I'm often inspired by a sauce I taste in a restaurant or a recipe I see in a new cookbook, and before you know it, I'm puttering around in my kitchen, concocting yet another peanut sauce. This isn't a bad thing, though, since my friends are always happy to try yet another version.

As you'll see, not all peanut sauces are alike. Each of the recipes in this book has its special place and use. Let your senses (and, if necessary, my recommendations) guide you. Check out the other equally splendid peanut sauces featured in the recipes Tofu, Broccoli, and Tomatoes with Curried Peanut Sauce (page 220), All-Purpose Peanut Sauce (page 350), and Peanut Dressing (page 351).

until tender. Drain and rinse with cold running water. Drain well. Add to the sweet potato, along with the cabbage and onion.

3 Cut off the bulbous bottom third of the lemongrass stalk. Remove and discard the tough outer leaves. With a large, sharp chef's knife, cut the lemongrass bottom crosswise into thin rounds.

4 In a blender or food processor, puree the lemongrass, coriander, garlic, ginger, and coconut milk for 30 seconds, or until fairly smooth. Add the

peanuts, sugar or honey, lime juice, and salt or fish sauce and process for a few more seconds until slightly chunky. Add to the salad and toss to coat well. Serve at room temperature or refrigerate and serve cold.

Note

The salad can be made up to 1 day ahead and stored in an airtight container in the fridge.

potato salad niçoise

This beautiful salad of contrasting colors and shapes is well suited for a warm-weather buffet or lunch. Feel free to add other blanched vegetables, such as asparagus, carrots, beets, or fennel. If the tomatoes at the store don't look good, buy cherry tomatoes and halve them.

SERVES 6 TO 8

vinaigrette

- ½ cup extra-virgin olive oil
- ¼ cup fresh lemon juice (1 juicy lemon)
- 2 tablespoons capers, drained
- 1 garlic clove, minced
- 1 teaspoon Dijon mustard
- 1 teaspoon kosher salt
- Freshly ground black pepper to taste

salad

- 2 pounds red or Yellow Finn potatoes (the smaller the better)
- ⅓ pound green beans, stem ends trimmed
- 3 tomatoes, cut into wedges
- 1 cup thinly sliced fresh basil leaves
- ½ red onion, thinly sliced
- ½ cup pitted niçoise or kalamata olives
- Kosher salt and freshly ground black pepper to taste
- 6 hard-boiled eggs (see page 145; optional), peeled and quartered

Note

The vinaigrette and the salad components can be made up to 2 days ahead and stored separately in airtight containers in the fridge. Tossing together the ingredients is best done just before serving, or the salad will lose its vibrancy.

1 **To make the vinaigrette:** In a small bowl, whisk together all the ingredients and set aside.

2 **To make the salad:** In a large pot, put the potatoes and enough cold water to cover. Bring to a boil, then reduce the heat to a simmer and cook until just tender, 12 to 15 minutes. Add the green beans and cook for 30 seconds more. Drain and rinse with cold running water until cool. Drain well. Cut the cooled potatoes into 1-inch cubes.

3 In a large bowl, combine the potatoes, green beans, tomatoes, basil, onion, and olives. Add the vinaigrette and toss gently to combine. Season with salt and pepper. Arrange the wedges of hard-boiled eggs decoratively on top. Serve at room temperature.

it's not hard to hard-boil eggs

In a saucepan, cover the eggs with cold water. Bring just to a boil, reduce the heat, and simmer for exactly 12 minutes. Drain them quickly, rattling the eggs around in the pan to crack their shells. Immediately fill the pan with cold water, and peel the hot eggs under cold running water.

pantry tabbouleh

(V) *Since I love to overpopulate my tabbouleh* with mint and parsley, I never thought I'd like it without them. One day, however, I really craved tabbouleh but didn't have the herbs on hand. I improvised by using raisins and capers in their place, and it turned out to be much better than I had expected. Tabbouleh is best right after it's made, while it's still warm. (This is partly because the flavor of citrus alters when chilled.) I prefer the fine bulgur available at whole food stores and Mediterranean markets (medium-grind bulgur will do, but it will need a longer softening period).

SERVES 6

1¼ cups fine bulgur (the finer the better)

Kosher salt to taste

¼ cup fresh lemon juice (1 juicy lemon)

3 tablespoons extra-virgin olive oil

2 plum tomatoes, coarsely chopped (optional)

1 small onion, finely chopped

¼ cup raisins or dried currants

2 tablespoons capers, drained

Freshly ground black pepper to taste

1 In a large bowl, pour 1⅔ cups boiling water over the bulgur. Add 1 teaspoon salt and stir well. (Coarse bulgur may need to be cooked or microwaved for 1 to 2 minutes with the water to soften it before it stands.) Let the bulgur stand until the water is absorbed, about 10 minutes. Fluff the bulgur with a fork.

2 Add the lemon juice, olive oil, tomatoes (if using), onion, raisins or currants, and capers and mix well. Season with salt and pepper. Serve at room temperature or refrigerate and serve cold.

Note The salad can be made up to 1 day ahead and stored in an airtight container in the fridge.

barley salad with dill and lemon

(V) *Turn this salad into a meal* by adding blanched asparagus, diced roasted sweet potatoes, or pan-fried tofu. My friend Tami makes it with quinoa instead of barley. Since quinoa expands more, start with only 1¼ cups of raw quinoa and cook it according to the directions on page 201.

SERVES 6

1²/₃ cups dried pearl barley

1 bunch scallions, white and green parts, chopped

1 large Granny Smith, Fuji, or Gala apple, unpeeled, cored and cut into small dice

1 cup chopped fresh dill

½ cup dried currants or raisins

1 teaspoon ground coriander

¼ cup fresh lemon juice (1 juicy lemon) plus 1 teaspoon grated fresh lemon rind

3 tablespoons extra-virgin olive oil

Kosher salt and freshly ground black pepper to taste

1 In a medium saucepan, combine the barley and 6 cups water. Bring to a boil. Reduce the heat to a simmer, cover, and cook until tender, 35 to 40 minutes. Drain and rinse the barley under tepid water. Drain well; the barley should still be warm.

2 In a large bowl, combine the scallions, apple, dill, currants or raisins, coriander, lemon juice and rind, and olive oil. Add the warm barley and mix well. Let stand for 20 minutes to give the barley a chance to absorb the seasonings. Season with salt and pepper. Serve at room temperature or refrigerate for a few hours and serve cold.

side salads and stand-alone salads

crispy chickpea salad with roasted eggplant and feta

The element of surprise is an important part of this salad. Your friends have probably had chickpeas before, but I bet few have encountered the crispy chickpea. The chickpeas' crunchy texture contrasts nicely with that of the silky eggplant.

SERVES 3 OR 4

½ large Italian eggplant or 1 Asian eggplant, unpeeled, cut into ½-inch cubes

1 cup cherry tomatoes, halved

1 tablespoon extra-virgin olive oil

Kosher salt and freshly ground black pepper to taste

½ cup canned chickpeas, rinsed and drained

1 large bunch arugula

½ red onion, thinly sliced

½ cup coarsely chopped fresh basil or mint leaves

¼ cup crumbled feta cheese (I like a soft French goat's milk feta)

¼ cup Classic Lemon Dressing (page 154)

1 Preheat the oven to 350 degrees. Spread the eggplant and tomatoes in a single layer in a baking dish just large enough to hold them. Drizzle with the olive oil and season with salt and pepper. Roast until the eggplant is very soft, 15 to 20 minutes. Set aside to cool to room temperature.

2 Increase the oven temperature to 400 degrees. Spread the chickpeas in a single layer on a rimmed baking sheet and roast until crunchy, about 30 minutes. Alternatively, you can microwave them: spread the chickpeas on a double thickness of paper towels and sprinkle with salt. Microwave on medium until they are firm and crunchy, 16 to 20 minutes, stirring and checking them every 5 minutes. Set aside to cool to room temperature.

coping with intellectual overload

One night I attended a friend's dinner party where two Harvard University professors were debating the efficacy of domestic politics in the eighteenth century. I developed a slight throb on one side of my head because I couldn't even understand the words they were using, let alone the points they were making. I had a pen and a piece of paper in my pocket, so I began to jot down the words I didn't know: lachrymose, ululate, hegemony, undulation. Someone asked me what I was doing, and the conversation became hushed. I meekly read my collection of words, and everyone began shouting differing definitions. This little list spawned a much more interesting debate than the politics! When I said my goodbyes, I left the paper there, asking the host to jot down any additional words that I might have missed and e-mail them to me. The next day I received an e-mail that included the words shoals, quorum, draconian, onomatopoeia, fricative, and "filthy-broke."

Lesson: admitting one's shortcomings is almost always entertaining.

3 In a large bowl, toss the roasted vegetables, chickpeas, arugula, onion, basil or mint, and feta until well combined. Drizzle with the dressing, toss again, and season with salt and pepper. Serve immediately or refrigerate for a few hours and serve cold.

Eggplant

french lentil salad with dried currants and walnuts

(V) *French green lentils are a marvel* in their raw state. They're mottled green, like pebbles on a beach. Pass up the mint and feta for this salad if it means a special trip to the market; the salad tastes just fine without them. For an even faster version, replace the French green lentils with red lentils, which require only 5 minutes of cooking.

SERVES 4

1 cup French green lentils or brown lentils

¼ cup dried currants

¼ cup fresh lemon juice (1 juicy lemon)

2 tablespoons extra-virgin olive oil

1 small onion, finely chopped

¼ cup toasted chopped walnuts (see page 283)

Kosher salt and freshly ground black pepper to taste

½ cup crumbled feta cheese (optional)

¼ cup chopped fresh mint (optional)

1 In a small saucepan, combine the lentils and 2 cups water. Bring to a boil, then reduce the heat and simmer until the lentils are tender but still slightly chewy, 20 to 25 minutes. (Add more water if necessary to prevent scorching.) Add the currants and simmer for 2 minutes more. Drain well.

2 In a medium bowl, combine the lentil mixture, lemon juice, olive oil, onion, and walnuts and mix well. Season liberally with salt and pepper. Stir in the feta and mint, if using, just before serving. This salad tastes great warm, at room temperature, or cold.

entertaining for a veggie planet

150

peanut udon salad

(V) *One day I finally bought* the fattest fresh noodles the Asian market had to offer. They were as thick as pencils, and when boiled, they plumped up even more. I pulled one out of the colander and just kept pulling and pulling and pulling. I could have jumped rope with what I pulled out. You can substitute the thinner fresh Chinese noodles found at the supermarket.

SERVES 8

1 Bring a large pot of water to a boil. Cook the noodles until soft but slightly al dente. Drain and rinse with cold running water until cool, then drain well. Transfer the noodles to a large bowl.

2 Add the peanuts, cilantro stems, and Peanut Dressing to the noodles and mix well. Add the bean sprouts and season liberally with salt. Serve at room temperature or refrigerate and serve cold. Garnish with the cilantro leaves and lime wedges just before serving.

2 **pounds fresh udon noodles**

1½ **cups unsalted roasted peanuts (see page 449)**

½ **cup chopped cilantro stems, plus** ½ **cup cilantro leaves for garnish**

Peanut Dressing (page 351)

3 **cups bean sprouts**

Kosher salt to taste

1 **lime, cut into 8 wedges for garnish**

Note This salad is best if eaten within 24 hours.

side salads and stand-alone salads

rice noodle salad with grapefruit, watercress, and peanuts

(V) Here's a cool and refreshing salad for a balmy summer day. Feel free to change the fruit according to your whim; instead of grapefruit, try thinly sliced pineapple, orange sections, or sliced mango. The essentials in this dish are the herbs, dressing, and peanuts.

SERVES 6

1 large grapefruit, peeled, separated into segments, seeded, and chopped

1 bunch watercress, leaves left whole, stems finely chopped

4 scallions, white and green parts, finely chopped

1/2 cup coarsely chopped fresh mint leaves

1/2 cup coarsely chopped fresh cilantro leaves

1/2 cup unsalted roasted peanuts, coarsely chopped (see page 153)

1–4 small, skinny chile peppers, seeded and minced

2 teaspoons sugar

1/4 cup fresh lime juice (2 juicy limes)

2 tablespoons canola oil

8 ounces rice vermicelli, soaked in hot water for 10 minutes and drained well

Kosher salt to taste

1 Bring a large pot of water to a boil. Meanwhile, in a large bowl, combine all the ingredients except for the vermicelli and salt and toss until well combined.

Note The salad can be made up to 1 day ahead and stored in an airtight container in the fridge.

peanuts in the raw

No peanut can rival the flavor of those that have been recently roasted. I've learned to buy my peanuts raw and roast them. Their flavor is richer and deeper than factory-roasted peanuts. You can buy raw peanuts in Asian markets in 1-pound bags. Store them in the freezer raw, and roast the quantity you need (or you can roast the whole bag; they will be fine in a zip bag in the freezer for up to 5 months).

Preheat the oven to 350 degrees. Spread the peanuts in a single layer on a rimmed baking sheet and roast for 12 to 15 minutes, stirring occasionally, or until golden brown. Don't be afraid to roast them darker than you see them in the supermarket. Underroasting the peanuts is a common but unfortunate mistake.

2 When the water boils, add the vermicelli to the pot and return to a boil. Quickly drain the vermicelli and rinse with cold running water, stirring with your fingers until the vermicelli is thoroughly chilled, about 2 minutes. Drain very well (or the salad will be watery).

3 Add the vermicelli to the grapefruit mixture. Toss until well combined. Season with salt. Serve at room temperature or refrigerate and serve cold.

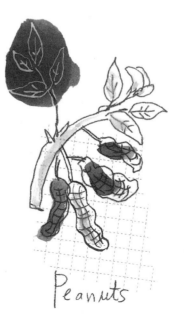

Peanuts

side salads and stand-alone salads

classic lemon dressing

(V) *This versatile dressing enlivens* cold pasta, couscous, bulgur, barley, rice, beans, lentils, and yes, even lettuce. Drizzle it on soft lettuces or over a grilled vegetable salad. Or toss some with room-temperature pan-fried tofu, tomatoes, onions, and peanuts and put it in a wrap or pita sandwich. You can use olive oil instead of canola oil, if you like.

MAKES ²/₃ CUP

In a food processor, combine the lemon rind and juice, mustard, sugar or honey, and garlic and process until smooth. With the machine running, slowly add the canola oil through the feed tube. Season with salt and pepper. Serve.

Finely grated rind and juice of 1 lemon

1 teaspoon Dijon mustard

1 teaspoon sugar or honey

1 garlic clove

½ cup canola oil

Kosher salt and freshly ground black pepper to taste

Note The dressing can be made up to 1 week ahead and stored in an airtight container in the fridge.

mint vinaigrette

 I toss this refreshing and elegant vinaigrette with a mélange of vegetables, such as sliced tomatoes, julienned summer squash or zucchini, blanched corn kernels, and chopped onion. It's also terrific tossed with torn pita bread, tomatoes, red onion, and feta cheese.

MAKES 1½ CUPS

- **2 cups fresh mint leaves**
- **6 tablespoons fresh lemon juice (1½ juicy lemons)**
- **1 cup extra-virgin olive oil**
- **Kosher salt and freshly ground black pepper to taste**

In a food processor, pulse the mint until finely chopped. With the machine running, slowly add the lemon juice and then the olive oil through the feed tube and process until incorporated. Season with salt and pepper. Serve.

Note
The vinaigrette can be made up to 1 week ahead and stored in an airtight container in the fridge, but it's best if you serve it within 1 day.

not-too-sweet caramelized balsamic dressing

(V) *This dressing is delicious* with greens, roasted vegetables, and grain salads, drizzled on pizza or goat cheese, or served as a sleek dip for crudités. The possibilities abound. Thanks to Matthew Campbell, who created the original dressing.

MAKES 1¼ CUPS

½ cup sugar

6 tablespoons balsamic vinegar

1 tablespoon Dijon mustard

2 garlic cloves, minced

⅔ cup extra-virgin olive oil

Kosher salt and freshly ground black pepper to taste

1 In a small saucepan, combine the sugar and 3 tablespoons water. Bring to a boil and boil until it turns a light golden color. Immediately remove from the heat and add the vinegar (but stand back; it might spit at you if you're too close!). Whisk well and add the mustard and garlic.

2 Add the olive oil to the vinegar mixture in a thin stream, whisking constantly. The mixture should stay nearly homogeneous (if not, add the oil more gradually). Add 1 tablespoon water, season with salt and pepper, and whisk again. Serve at room temperature if you want to use it as a salad dressing. But sometimes it's nice chilled and thick for drizzling (on a goat cheese log, for instance).

Note

The dressing will last for several months stored in an airtight container in the fridge. Let it come to room temperature or warm slightly in the microwave before serving.

tahini lemon dressing

This worthy recipe is from my friend Angelo, who lives in the deep woods of Maine. To me Angelo embodies the message you see as you enter the state on the highway: "Maine: The way life should be." At seventy-two, he lives without a telephone or electricity in a home he built himself. He runs on positive energy and hosts family and friends for weeks at a time, lovingly preparing vegetarian meals for them from his large, well-tended garden. If everyone could live this kind of life, we'd be less stressed and so would our planet.

He uses this dressing as a dipping sauce for artichokes and in a salad of artichoke hearts, pine nuts, and tomatoes. I use it to dress a romaine lettuce salad. You and I can make this dressing in a food processor. Angelo does it by hand, of course.

MAKES 2/3 CUP

2	**garlic cloves**
1/4	**cup fresh lemon juice (1 juicy lemon)**
1/4	**cup sesame tahini (see page 451)**
1/4	**cup plain yogurt**
1/3	**cup extra-virgin olive oil**
	Kosher salt and freshly ground black pepper to taste

In a food processor or blender, puree the garlic. Add the lemon juice, tahini, and yogurt. With the machine running, slowly add the olive oil and 1 teaspoon water. Season with salt and pepper. Serve.

Note

The dressing can be made up to 5 days ahead and stored in an airtight container in the fridge, but it's best within 2 days.

thai coconut-lime dressing

 Coconut milk makes a sumptuous salad dressing. Toss this Southeast Asian dressing with a combination of any of the following: finely shredded green or napa cabbage, grated carrots, crushed peanuts, thinly sliced green apple, tomatoes, julienned endive, shaved red onion, and/or baby spinach. For paper-thin slicing, see page 119.

MAKES 2 CUPS

In a food processor, puree the cilantro, ginger, and garlic. Add the coconut milk, lime juice, and sugar. With the machine running, slowly add the canola oil through the feed tube. Season with chili sauce and salt.

- 1 cup coarsely chopped fresh cilantro
- 2 tablespoons peeled and coarsely chopped fresh ginger
- 2 garlic cloves
- 2/3 cup unsweetened coconut milk (see page 446)
- 1/4 cup fresh lime juice (2 juicy limes)
- 2 teaspoons sugar
- 1 cup canola oil
- Asian chili sauce (see page 443) to taste
- Kosher salt to taste

Note
The dressing can be made up to 1 week ahead and stored in an airtight container in the fridge.

creamy tofu-lime dressing

 This winning recipe comes from Chris Huang, a talented cook and artist who has worked with me in Boston. It's creamy and limy, and you would never guess that tofu plays a part. It's great with hearty salads and slaws.

In a food processor, pulse the cilantro, ginger, and garlic until smooth. With the machine running, add the tofu through the feed tube, then the lime juice, the oil in a thin stream, the Asian chili sauce, sugar or honey, and salt. Serve.

Note

The dressing can be made up to 1 week ahead and stored in an airtight container in the fridge.

MAKES 2 CUPS

- ½ cup coarsely chopped fresh cilantro
- 2 rounded tablespoons peeled and coarsely chopped fresh ginger
- 3 garlic cloves
- 1 cup firm tofu, broken into small pieces (about ½ an 8-ounce carton)
- ⅓ cup fresh lime juice (3 juicy limes)
- ¾ cup canola oil
- 1 teaspoon Asian chili sauce (see page 443)
- 1 teaspoon sugar or honey
- 2 teaspoons kosher salt

goat cheese–walnut dressing

If I had to commit to one dressing for the rest of my life, this would be it. The goat cheese provides almost enough acidity to balance the olive oil, so only a small amount of lemon juice is needed. I love it drizzled over cold or warm steamed green beans or asparagus. It's also tasty on any lettuce. Be sure to eat it with plenty of bread for sopping up runaway dressing. This dressing doubles as a compelling dip when served with crudités and Pita Chips (page 43).

MAKES ABOUT 1 CUP

½ cup walnuts

1 large garlic clove

4 ounces fresh, creamy goat cheese

1 lemon wedge

½ cup extra-virgin olive oil

Kosher salt and freshly ground black pepper to taste

1 Preheat the oven to 350 degrees. Spread the walnuts in a single layer on a rimmed baking sheet and toast for 5 minutes, or until golden brown. Let cool.

2 In a food processor, finely chop half of the walnuts and all of the garlic. Add the goat cheese and the juice of the lemon wedge and process until smooth. With the machine running, slowly add the olive oil through the feed tube. Add the remaining walnuts and pulse until the nuts are coarsely chopped. Season with salt and pepper. Serve.

Note The dressing can be made up to 1 week ahead and stored in an airtight container in the fridge.

gorgonzola dressing

When restaurants offer Gorgonzola in a dish, it's usually low-quality, often domestic, sometimes Italian. The flavor of these Gorgonzolas pales in comparison to those from smaller, artisanal Italian producers. It's best to buy this cheese (and all cheeses) from a cheesemonger, who will cut it from a wheel. Avoid presliced and prewrapped cheese. For this dressing, be sure to buy Gorgonzola dolce with a foil wrapping, a cream-colored hue, and scant blue veins. Drizzle this dressing on boiled or roasted beets, potatoes, leeks, green beans, or practically any vegetable—or even hot pasta or grilled bread. It's good over endive or watercress, although it will need to be thinned slightly with light cream for these delicate greens.

MAKES ABOUT 1 CUP

4 ounces Gorgonzola dolce

1 garlic clove

1 tablespoon sherry vinegar or Champagne vinegar

⅓ cup extra-virgin olive oil

Kosher salt and freshly ground black pepper to taste

In a food processor, puree the Gorgonzola, garlic, and vinegar until very smooth. With the machine running, slowly add the olive oil through the feed tube and process until incorporated. Season with salt and pepper. Serve.

Note

The dressing can be made up to 4 days ahead and stored in an airtight container in the fridge.

picnics—eat with nature at your feet

A picnic can be a most pleasant alternative to having a friend over. For one, it gets you outside, and Lord knows we all spend too much time indoors. And the outdoors does something to the food—somehow, no matter how simple the food may be, it tastes much better when eaten outside. Furthermore, my friends are always intrigued when I invite them on a picnic, and it inevitably ends up being a memorable and bonding experience. On a picnic, there's plenty of time to talk and few distractions—just the wisp of the passing breeze and some good food.

The three factors that determine a restaurant's success apply to picnics as well: that is, location, location, and location. Choosing a spot can be half the fun. Select a place where no one would ever expect to find you or one that gives you a sense of pleasure or adventure.

Potential Picnic Spots

- On a baseball field (not during a game)
- On a large rock or ledge above the highway
- On a friend's roof (or your own)
- On the commercial shipping docks in a city
- In a graveyard
- In a canoe, rowboat, or sailboat
- At some random spot at the end of a bus or subway line
- On a beach in the off-season
- On the lawn of a well-groomed church
- On a playground
- On a park bench in a neighboring town

The Food

When you're eating in the middle of nature, vegetarian food seems only fitting. Sandwiches or wraps are a fine idea. Quiche is also a good choice, since it's delicious cold. I have a soft place in my heart for cold gourmet pizza—nothing wrong with it, especially if it's homemade. I don't recommend green salads, since they wilt in no time. I favor grain salads (such as tabbouleh or wild rice salad) or sturdy vegetable salads (such as potato salad or tomato and fresh mozzarella salad). Homemade cookies and brownies and fresh whole fruit are always a fitting finale. If you want to picnic and you have no time to prepare food, stop at a gourmet store and pick up calzones, sandwiches, cookies, and so on. When it comes to beverages, drink what you like. I prefer wine unless it's early in the day.

Don't forget linen or paper napkins, silverware (if necessary), and your less valuable plates or sturdy paper plates. Bring an old blanket, quilt, or sheet to sit on, if you like. If you're drinking wine, real wineglasses are a necessity. If you don't have a picnic basket, use a sturdy paper or plastic shopping bag. One step up from this is a cooler with ice blocks. The premium solution is to buy a real picnic basket. I've also seen knapsacks outfitted with plates, glasses, and utensils in kitchen stores.

Here are some dishes that work well for picnics:

Snacks
(to be eaten with crackers—any bland cracker will do)

Extra-Smoky Baba Gannouj (page 29)
Muhammara (page 26)
Hip Dip (page 36)
Smoky Red Lentil Spread (page 39)

Other Snacks

Popiah (without the bean sprouts) (page 58)
Mashed Potato Spring Rolls with Peanut Sauce (page 54)

Main Meal

Sandwich filled with Escalivada (page 346)
Tea Sandwiches (lots of 'em!) (see page 191)
Luscious Seitan Sandwich (page 189)
Tomato-Tarragon Quiche (page 388)
Hazelnut-Mushroom Burgers in a bun (already fried and at room temperature; page 170)

(continued)

side salads and stand-alone salads

Main Dish Salads
(serve with bread)

Barley Salad with Dill and Lemon (page 147)
French Lentil Salad with Dried Currants and Walnuts (page 150)
Pantry Tabbouleh (page 146)
New Millennium Waldorf Salad (page 130)
Potato Salad Niçoise (page 144)
Big Couscous and Clementine Salad (page 139)
Crispy Chickpea Salad with Roasted Eggplant and Feta (page 148)

Lighter Salads

Asparagus Slaw (page 116)
Fennel Slaw (page 117)
Jicama-Grape Salad (page 123)

Desserts

Hermit Bars (page 402)
Killer Chocolate Chip Cookies (page 399)
Cardamom Pound Cake (page 438)
Stowe Brownies (page 400)
Figgy Walnut Bread (page 382)
Almond Butter Cake (page 430)
Vegan Chocolate Cake (page 429)

Don't Forget

Insect repellent
Bottle opener (for wine)
Knife
Garbage bag
Napkins
Bottle of water
Cloth to sit on

chapter 4

Rent-a-Video Burgers, Pizzas, Sandwiches, and Snacks

emergency cooking for last-minute get-togethers

It's Friday night, and it's been a long week. Your brain is fried, but your stomach is starving. You can't fathom cooking up a big meal, much less shopping for food, but you'd love to invite a friend over to watch a movie and eat something good. Here are some painless but delectable meals you can make with a near-empty fridge.

All these meals serve 2.

Spaghetti with Olive Oil and Garlic

Boil 8 ounces of spaghetti. Meanwhile, in a medium skillet over medium heat, sauté 6 minced garlic cloves in 4 tablespoons extra-virgin olive oil. Stir for 1 minute, then remove from the heat. Drain the spaghetti and toss it with the garlic-oil mixture. Add 1 teaspoon kosher salt and freshly ground black pepper to taste (add crushed red pepper flakes as well, if desired) and transfer to a plate. Drizzle with 4 more tablespoons extra-virgin olive oil and serve immediately.

Spaghetti with Olive Oil, Portobellos, and Parmesan

Boil 8 ounces of spaghetti. Meanwhile, in a medium skillet over medium-high heat, sear 2 thinly sliced portobello mushroom caps in 4 tablespoons extra-virgin olive oil. Do not stir. Sear the portobellos for at least 2 minutes, then turn and sear the other sides. Add 6 minced garlic cloves and stir for 1 minute. Drain the spaghetti and toss it with the portobello mixture. Add 2 more tablespoons extra-virgin olive oil, 6 tablespoons freshly grated Parmesan cheese, and plenty of kosher salt and freshly ground black pepper to taste, and toss again. Transfer to a plate and serve immediately.

Mashed Sweet Potatoes with Chipotle

In a large saucepan of water, boil 2 to 3 peeled and cubed sweet potatoes for about 10 minutes, or until a fork can pierce the cubes. Drain and return to the pot. Mash with a fork or potato masher, adding a few tablespoons of butter or olive oil and about $2/3$ of a minced canned chipotle chile in adobo. Add kosher salt and freshly ground black pepper to taste. Transfer to a bowl and serve immediately.

Eggs and Cheddar on Browned Onions

In a medium skillet, sauté 1 large thinly sliced yellow onion in 2 tablespoons extra-virgin olive oil over medium heat for 7 minutes, or until it begins to brown. Crack 4 eggs over the onions, add kosher salt and freshly ground black pepper to taste, then lay some sliced cheddar cheese over the eggs. Cover the skillet and cook for 3 minutes, or until the eggs are set. Divide the eggs and onions evenly between two plates and serve immediately with toast and your favorite hot sauce, if desired.

Other Good Couch Potato Food

Curried Walnut Dip (page 28)

Black Bean Soup in a Hurry (page 103)

Chilled Curried Pea Soup (page 93)

Smoky Lentil Chili (page 272)

Tempeh and Spinach in Peanut Sauce (page 229)

Chinese Noodles in Chile Oil (page 244)

Pantry Tabbouleh (page 146)

Shiitake Risotto with Edamame (page 320)

veggie sloppy joes

(V) *This recipe gives you the opportunity* to clean out your vegetable bin. That doesn't mean it's fine to use shriveled carrots or sprouting potatoes, but you can use practically any combination of vegetables in place of or in addition to the bell peppers. If you leave the cilantro out, fine. If you want to add more ketchup, go right ahead. The only things I wouldn't play around with are the tempeh and the canned tomatoes. One bit of advice: Sloppy joes are sloppy, so eat these with people you know well.

SERVES 6

1 tablespoon canola oil

1 large onion, chopped

1 green bell pepper, chopped

1 red bell pepper, chopped

3 garlic cloves, minced

2 tablespoons chili powder

2 8-ounce packages tempeh

1 28-ounce can diced tomatoes, with their juice

¼ cup ketchup

1 teaspoon vegetarian Worcestershire sauce or Worcestershire sauce

¼ cup chopped fresh cilantro leaves and stems

Hot sauce to taste

Kosher salt and freshly ground black pepper to taste

6 toasted bulky rolls

1 In a large skillet, heat the canola oil over medium heat. Add the onion and sauté, stirring occasionally, until soft, about 7 minutes. Add the bell peppers, garlic, and chili powder, and cook for 2 minutes more.

2 Crumble the tempeh into the pan (it will crumble more as it cooks, with the help of a wooden spoon). Add the tomatoes, ketchup, Worcestershire sauce, and 1 cup water and mix well. Simmer, stirring occasionally, until

Two friends of mine, Bess and Kipp, found themselves ignoring their lovely dining room and eating dinner on their living room rug, where they could be near the fireplace and their cat and dog. They thought about buying a café table and placing it near the fire so they could eat in a more civilized fashion. Then Kipp saw an inexpensive Japanese-style dinner table at a local furniture store. Bess bought lots of colorful antique pillows to sit on. Now they have two rooms in which to dine, and their friends and pets love it.

heated through and the flavors are well blended, about 10 minutes. Remove from the heat.

3 Stir in the cilantro and hot sauce. Season with salt and pepper. Serve over toasted bulky rolls.

Note

The sloppy joe mixture can be made up to 3 days ahead and stored in an airtight container in the fridge. Reheat in the microwave or on the stove.

hazelnut-mushroom burgers

(V) *Don't flip by this burger—make it!* The flavor and crunch of roasted hazelnuts mixed with earthy mushrooms turn out a burger tasty enough to serve to your most sophisticated guests. I think it's best eaten solo (no bun) with a bit of hot sauce and a delicate salad. If you do invite your most sophisticated friends over, serve a full-bodied Italian red such as Montepulciano d'Abruzzo. It's similar to Chianti but has more pep.

MAKES FOUR 5-INCH PATTIES

- 1 cup hazelnuts
- 2 tablespoons extra-virgin olive oil
- 1 medium onion, chopped
- 12 ounces fresh mushrooms, coarsely chopped
- 3 garlic cloves, minced
- 4 ounces tempeh, crumbled
- 3 slices whole wheat or white bread
- 1/2 teaspoon kosher salt
- Hot sauce to taste

1 Preheat the oven to 350 degrees. Spread the hazelnuts in a single layer on a rimmed baking sheet and toast for 10 to 15 minutes, or until golden in the center (you'll need to cut into one to see). While the nuts are still hot, pour them onto a clean dishtowel, form a sack, then rub the nuts in the towel to remove the skins. Don't worry about removing every last bit of skin. Open the towel and transfer the hazelnuts to a small bowl with your hands, leaving the paperlike skins behind.

2 In a large skillet, heat 1 tablespoon of the olive oil over medium heat. Add the onion and sauté, stirring occasionally, until softened, about 7 minutes. Add the mushrooms and garlic and sauté, stirring frequently, until the mushrooms soften and begin to brown, about 5 minutes more. Add the tempeh, cook for 1 minute, then remove from the heat.

3 In a food processor, pulse the bread into coarse crumbs. Add the hazelnuts and pulse until they are chopped. Add the mushroom mixture and salt and pulse again until the mixture just comes together. Gently form into four 5-inch patties.

4 In a large skillet, heat the remaining 1 tablespoon olive oil over medium heat. Add the patties and cook until they form a golden brown crust on the undersides, 4 to 5 minutes. Turn and brown the other sides. Serve the burgers hot, passing the hot sauce at the table.

Note
The patties can be formed up to 2 days ahead and stored in an airtight container in the fridge, or frozen for up to 2 months (if you stack the patties, layer them with plastic wrap). Thaw overnight in the fridge or for at least a few hours at room temperature before frying.

Mushrooms

kasha-crunch burgers

(V) *I find most commercial veggie burgers* wanting, especially with their dull, pasty texture. Well, this burger with a crunch that rivals KFC has it all over them. Beware of nonstick pans, which don't have the capacity to form a thick crust. Any heavy-bottomed, well-seasoned skillet (especially cast-iron) will work.

Try this burger bunless with a dash of hot sauce or in a pita with lettuce and tomato. You can also make meatball-size burgers to serve on top of spaghetti with tomato sauce. For a satisfying brunch dish, make a rather large and flat burger for each person and sit a poached egg or two atop it.

SERVES 8

2 tablespoons olive oil, plus more for pan-frying

1 small onion, coarsely chopped

1 carrot, peeled and coarsely chopped

2 garlic cloves, minced

2 cups raw short- or long-grain brown rice

1½ cups coarsely chopped white mushrooms

2 teaspoons kosher salt

1 cup raw kasha (whole buckwheat groats)

1 cup chopped cashews, toasted if you like (see page 283)

3–4 tablespoons chopped fresh tarragon

All-purpose flour for dredging

Hot sauce or ketchup

1 In a medium saucepan, heat 2 tablespoons of the olive oil over medium heat. Add the onion and carrot and sauté, stirring occasionally, until the onion is soft, about 7 minutes. Add the garlic and cook for 2 minutes more.

2 Add the rice, mushrooms, salt, and 5 cups water, and bring to a boil. Reduce the heat to a simmer, cover, and simmer for 25 minutes. Stir in the kasha, cover, and cook until the rice and kasha are tender and the liquid has been absorbed, about 20 minutes more. Remove from the heat and stir in the cashews and tarragon.

3 In a food processor, coarsely puree the rice mixture in three batches. Transfer the rice mixture to a bowl, and cover and refrigerate it if you aren't forming the burgers right away.

> I see entertaining as an extension of my life, not an interruption.
> —**Roz Cummins**

4 Dust your hands with flour and form the rice mixture firmly into 8 patties, each about 1 inch thick and 4 inches in diameter. Lightly coat the patties with flour.

5 In a large, heavy skillet, heat $1/8$ to $1/4$ inch olive oil over medium heat. Pan-fry the burgers until the undersides are dark golden brown, about 5 minutes, checking frequently to prevent burning. Flip the burgers and brown the other sides, about 5 minutes more. Serve with hot sauce or ketchup.

Note
The patties can be formed up to 2 days ahead and stored in an airtight container in the fridge, or frozen for up to 2 months (if you stack the patties, layer them with plastic wrap). Thaw overnight in the fridge or for at least a few hours at room temperature before frying.

portobello "burgers" with chipotle ketchup

The portobello mushroom itself is the "burger," which makes things simple. Serve on bulky rolls and melt cheddar on the burgers if you desire.

SERVES 4

1 Prepare a hot fire in a grill. Meanwhile, in a small bowl, combine the olive oil and garlic and season liberally with salt and pepper. Brush the top of the portobello caps with the garlic mixture.

2 Grill the portobellos for about 5 minutes per side, or until cooked through. If using the cheese, add a slice to each mushroom after it has been flipped. Transfer the portobellos to a plate and keep warm.

3 Grill the bulky rolls. Spoon the Chipotle Ketchup onto the rolls, and add the lettuce and onion. Place a portobello on top of each one, cover with the top of the roll, and serve.

2 tablespoons extra-virgin olive oil

2 garlic cloves

Kosher salt and freshly ground black pepper to taste

4 large portobello mushrooms, stems removed

4 thin slices cheddar cheese (about 3 ounces; optional)

4 bulky rolls

Chipotle Ketchup (page 341)

4 lettuce leaves

Thinly sliced onion

creative pizza

The difference between a cheese pizza from the local pizzeria and one you can make at home is a mile wide. We all know what pizza-shop pizza is usually like: cheesy, salty, greasy, and cheap. But if you buy pizza dough (or make it) and prepare your own toppings, pizza can be altogether a different experience.

The best part is that pizza-making is straightforward and suited for groups of people, with endless room for creative participation. You don't need to make the dough yourself unless you enjoy the process. Just about every supermarket carries pizza dough, either frozen or fresh. Once the dough is home (and thawed), just roll it out with a sprinkling of flour and transfer it to a cornmeal-dusted baking sheet. I like to roll the dough before the guests arrive (I keep the rounds of dough in the fridge, separated with parchment paper).

All the guests need to do is top their pizzas. I usually offer four or five roasted vegetables, Caramelized Onions (page 354), Roasted Garlic (page 353), Roasted Tomato Sauce (page 179), grated sharp cheddar and creamy goat cheese, olives, pine nuts or cashews, and fresh herbs such as thyme, oregano, and basil. For other ideas for pizza toppings, see page 187.

As for tomato sauce, our country is stuck in a terrible rut! There are two different and better alternatives to the ubiquitous prepared tomato sauces. Both are easier and tastier. The first sauce is barely a sauce at all, just raw tomatoes in a marinade, but oh, is it good. See pages 178 and 179.

pizza

haley house pizza dough

(V) *This elite pizza dough* comes from D. A. Ekstrom, who runs the Haley House, a nonprofit bakery training program in the South End of Boston. What's wonderful is that the *poolish* (the French name for a Polish starter) and a long fermentation give the dough a complexity that everyday pizza dough lacks. You need to start the dough at least 1 full day before you intend to serve the pizza. Organic white flour with the germ intact can be found at whole food stores.

MAKES ENOUGH FOR SIX 8-INCH PIZZAS

poolish (starter)

- 1 pinch of active dry yeast
- 1½ cups white flour (organic if possible, with the germ intact)

dough

- 3¼ cups white flour (organic if possible, with the germ intact), plus more for rolling
- ½ cup whole wheat flour
- ¼ cup semolina, plus more for stacking
- 1 tablespoon salt
- ¼ teaspoon active dry yeast
- 1 tablespoon extra-virgin olive oil

1 **To make the poolish:** In a large bowl, sprinkle the yeast over ³/4 cup warm water. Add the flour and mix with a spoon until fully combined. Cover with a damp dishtowel or plastic wrap and let stand in a mildly warm place for 5 to 6 hours, or until tripled in size and bubbly.

2 **To make the dough:** In a medium bowl, combine the white flour, whole wheat flour, semolina, and salt and mix well. In a large bowl, sprinkle the yeast over 1 cup warm water. Stir to dissolve. Add the *poolish* and the olive oil, stirring with a spoon until the *poolish* is broken up. Add the flour mixture and stir with a sturdy spatula or plastic dough scraper, "cutting" into the mixture until the dough comes together. Cover with a damp dishtowel or plastic wrap and let rise in a warm place for 30 to 45 minutes, or until it doubles in size.

3 On a lightly floured surface, knead the dough for 5 to 8 minutes, or until the dough bounces back easily. The dough will be a bit moist, so flour your hands and the surface minimally but as needed. Return the dough to the bowl, and cover with the dishtowel or plastic wrap as before. Let rise until doubled in size, 3 to 5 hours, or let rise for just 1 hour and refrigerate overnight.

4 Divide the dough into 6 pieces and form each piece into a ball. On a lightly floured surface, roll out one ball of dough into a round about 8 inches in diameter. Sprinkle on more flour if it sticks. Roll out the remaining balls of dough in the same fashion. Stack the rounds, sprinkling them with semolina to prevent them from sticking. Use right away or let rise again for 30 minutes before topping and baking. If you want to freeze some or all of the dough, do so at this point.

5 Bake the pizza dough following the instructions for each topping.

Note

The dough freezes well, and you can easily double this recipe so that you can freeze some. I like to roll the dough into individual rounds and stack them with parchment paper. Double-wrap the whole lot in plastic wrap. The dough keeps for up to 2 months.

fresh tomatoes for pizza

This sauce is in tribute to the colorful Caruso's Pizza in Melrose, Massachusetts. I finally discovered Don Caruso's secret to his outstanding pizza. He doesn't precook his tomatoes! They develop their own sauce when they bake on the dough. After about fifty pizzas and three years, I had to ask him point-blank, and he showed me (with reluctance and slight irritation) a bowl of freshly sliced, vine-ripened tomatoes seasoned with the ingredients below. Don't prepare this mixture more than 30 minutes before you plan to use it, as it does not keep well.

MAKES ENOUGH FOR SIX 8-INCH PIZZAS

In a medium bowl, combine all of the ingredients. Let stand for at least 10 minutes. Place the tomatoes directly on the pizza dough. (There will be "juice" left in the bottom of the tomato bowl. You can either consume it—it's delightful—or spoon it over the baked pizza.)

3 large or 6 small ripe tomatoes, cut into thin wedges

⅓ cup extra-virgin olive oil

8 garlic cloves, minced

3 tablespoons chopped fresh basil

Kosher salt and freshly ground black pepper to taste

tomatoes—seize the day

Don't dilly-dally when late-summer tomatoes arrive. Buy them feverishly, like a stockbroker with insider knowledge. Uncooked ripe tomatoes have a sweet, delicate taste, and they can make a remarkable difference. (Canned tomatoes have been cooked, which alters their flavor.)

Tomatoes that are picked green and ripened off the vine can't compare to the locally grown, just-picked kind. One exception is cherry tomatoes, which I sometimes buy in the winter. They travel well and remain sweet.

roasted tomato sauce

 This sauce more closely resembles your standard tomato sauce. It's perfect for pizzas where you want a thin layer of sauce, not the chunky tomatoes of the raw tomato "sauce."

**MAKES 2½ CUPS,
ENOUGH FOR SIX 8-INCH PIZZAS**

Preheat the oven to 350 degrees. In a small baking pan, combine the tomatoes, garlic, olive oil, and salt and pepper. Bake for 30 minutes, or until the tomatoes have softened and broken down.

10 plum tomatoes, cut into ¼-inch-thick slices, or 2 pints cherry tomatoes, halved

6 garlic cloves, minced

2 tablespoons extra-virgin olive oil

Kosher salt and freshly ground black pepper to taste

Note

This sauce will keep in an airtight container in the fridge for up to 4 days.

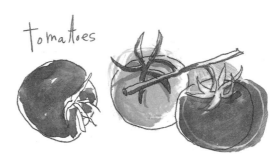

tomatoes

portobello redhead pizza

This pizza makes use of the divine Romesco Sauce. Yes, the sauce contains bread crumbs, and it's served on bread. You'll see why when you taste it. Garlicky portobellos and caramelized onions are nestled under the sauce and, if you desire, feta is sprinkled on top.

MAKES SIX 8-INCH PIZZAS

- **6 large portobello mushrooms**
- **⅓ cup extra-virgin olive oil**
- **6 garlic cloves, minced**

  Kosher salt and freshly ground black pepper to taste
- **4 medium onions, thinly sliced**

  Cornmeal for sprinkling
- **6 rounds of Haley House Pizza Dough (page 176)**
- **6 tablespoons crumbled sheep or goat feta cheese (optional)**
- **2 cups Romesco Sauce (page 345), at room temperature**

1 Remove the portobello stems. Cut the dirt from the stems, then cut the stems lengthwise into ⅓-inch-thick slices. Cut the caps into ⅓-inch-thick slices.

2 In a large skillet, heat 4 tablespoons of the oil over medium heat. Add the portobellos and sauté, stirring frequently, until darkened, about 5 minutes. The mushrooms will soak up all the oil quickly, but don't worry. Add the garlic and cook for 1 minute more, stirring constantly. Season with salt and pepper. Transfer the mushroom mixture to a plate.

3 Rinse out the skillet and heat the remaining oil over medium heat. Add the onions and sauté, stirring occasionally, for 15 to 20 minutes, or until browned and caramelized. Season with salt and pepper. Transfer to the plate with the mushrooms.

4 Preheat the oven to 500 degrees. If you don't have a pizza stone, sprinkle some cornmeal on a baking sheet and place the dough rounds on it side by side. If you have a pizza stone, place the dough rounds (perhaps one at a time) on a pizza peel. Distribute the portobellos and onions over the dough. Top with the feta, if using. Bake the pizzas until the crust is browned in spots, about 10 minutes. Spoon the Romesco Sauce on top of the pizzas, cut into slices, and serve immediately.

dinner for henry (butternut squash–goat cheese pizza)

This pizza is named for my stunningly handsome cat, Henry. Although the bulk of his diet is cat food (top of the line, of course), he's an avid gourmet. He enjoys many unusual foods, such as beet salad, Israeli couscous salad, and fried rice. This pizza, topped with roasted butternut squash, goat cheese, sage, and caramelized onions, is his favorite meal of all time—and all my other friends' favorite pizza too.

MAKES SIX 8-INCH PIZZAS

2 large butternut squash, peeled and cut into ¼-inch-thick slices

6 garlic cloves, minced

6 tablespoons extra-virgin olive oil

Kosher salt and freshly ground black pepper to taste

5 medium onions, thinly sliced

Cornmeal for sprinkling

6 rounds of Haley House Pizza Dough (page 176)

18 fresh sage leaves, chopped

12 ounces creamy goat cheese

6 tablespoons freshly grated Asiago or Parmesan cheese

1 Preheat the oven to 400 degrees. In a large bowl, combine the squash, garlic, and 3 tablespoons of the olive oil and toss well. Season with salt and pepper and toss to coat. Spread the squash in a single layer on a rimmed baking sheet and roast for 25 minutes, or until tender and slightly browned at the edges. Remove from the oven and set aside. Increase the oven temperature to 500 degrees.

2 In a large skillet, heat the remaining 3 tablespoons olive oil over medium heat. Add the onions and sauté, stirring occasionally, for 15 to 20 minutes, or until browned and caramelized.

OH Henry!

Note

The squash and onions can be cooked up to 2 days ahead and stored in airtight containers in the fridge.

3 If you don't have a pizza stone, sprinkle some cornmeal on a baking sheet and place the dough rounds on it side by side. If you have a pizza stone, place the dough rounds (perhaps one at a time) on a pizza peel. Distribute the squash over the dough. Don't overload it; one layer is plenty (you may not need all the squash). Add the onions and sage, then spoon the goat cheese on top. Sprinkle on the Asiago or Parmesan. Bake the pizzas until the crust is browned in spots, about 10 minutes. Cut the pizzas into slices and serve immediately.

butternut squash and tom cruise

Butternut squash is the Tom Cruise of winter squashes—easily recognizable and universally popular. But unlike Tom Cruise, butternut squash can be enjoyed in the privacy of your home—in the flesh.

This is how I usually prepare butternut: Halve the squash, scoop out the seeds, then peel with a good vegetable peeler. I use an inexpensive, plastic, Y-shaped peeler. It makes peeling squash as easy as peeling carrots. My favorite brand is Kuhn Rikon from Switzerland. Thinly slice (about 1/8 inch) the squash with a sharp knife. Toss it with rosemary, garlic, olive oil, and salt and pepper, and spread in a single layer on a rimmed baking sheet. Bake the squash in a preheated 400-degree oven for about 30 minutes, flipping the pieces so that they're browned on all sides—this is crucial. Roasted butternut squash can be eaten as is or used in burritos, tacos, salads, pasta dishes, or pizza toppings.

In addition to roasting butternut squash, try grating it raw and using it in place of carrots and sweet potatoes in cakes, breads, and muffins.

tofu pesto and roasted tomato sauce pizza

(V) *Don't turn up your nose* at tofu pesto until you try it! Tofu lightens pesto's richness, which can be overwhelming. It works better than ricotta in pesto, because it allows the olive oil and basil flavors to come through cleanly (you'll also be getting more protein and less fat, but that wasn't my motive). If you want to get fancy, you can top the pizza with Caramelized Onions (page 354) and pine nuts.

MAKES SIX 8-INCH PIZZAS

tofu pesto

- 3 cups coarsely chopped fresh basil leaves
- 3/4 cup pine nuts or coarsely chopped walnuts
- 9 garlic cloves
- 12 ounces soft or firm tofu (not silken)
- 1/3 cup extra-virgin olive oil
- 1 1/2 teaspoons kosher salt

  Cornmeal for sprinkling
- 6 rounds of Haley House Pizza Dough (page 176)
- 3 tablespoons extra-virgin olive oil
- 1 cup Roasted Tomato Sauce (page 179)
- 3/4 cup pitted kalamata olives (optional), chopped

1 **To make the tofu pesto:** In a food processor, pulse the basil, nuts, and garlic until finely chopped. Transfer to a bowl, add the tofu, 1/3 cup olive oil, and salt, and mix well.

2 Preheat the oven to 500 degrees. If you don't have a pizza stone, sprinkle some cornmeal on a baking sheet and place the dough rounds on it side by side. If you have a pizza stone, place the dough rounds (perhaps one at a time) on a pizza peel. Drizzle the 3 tablespoons olive oil over the dough rounds, spreading it with the back of a spoon. Bake for 5 minutes.

the advantages to a small party

I enjoy socializing most with a small group—two or three people. More things get revealed and shared, especially if the guests know one another well. Cooking for fewer people is less hectic, too, which helps me relax and enjoy the conversation.

3 Remove the crusts from the oven and evenly spread the Roasted Tomato Sauce then the Tofu Pesto over them, leaving a $^1/_2$-inch border around the edges. Bake the pizzas until the crust is browned in spots, about 4 to 5 minutes. Sprinkle with the olives, if you like. Cut the pizzas into slices and serve immediately.

Note The pesto can be made up to 2 days ahead and stored in an airtight container in the fridge, with a piece of plastic wrap placed right against the surface of the pesto.

curried sweet potato and cheddar pizza with pickled red onions

This pizza satisfies many urges —curry, sweet, sour, crunchy, rich, and cheesy. You can use curry powder instead of the spices, and it will still make a fine pizza. I've also added seared spinach, with excellent results.

MAKES SIX 8-INCH PIZZAS

1 Preheat the oven to 400 degrees. In a large bowl, combine the sweet potatoes, garlic, and canola oil and toss well. Add the spices and salt and toss to coat the cubes. Spread the cubes in a single layer on a rimmed baking sheet and bake for 15 to 20 minutes, or until tender. Increase the oven temperature to 500 degrees.

2 If you don't have a pizza stone, sprinkle some cornmeal on a baking sheet and place the dough rounds on it side by side. If you have a stone, place the dough rounds (perhaps one at a time) on a pizza peel. Distribute the sweet potato over the dough. Distribute the cheddar among the pizzas. Bake the pizzas until the crust is browned in spots, about 10 minutes. Top with the Pretty Pickled Red Onions, cut into slices, and serve immediately.

2 very large sweet potatoes, peeled and cut into $1/2$-inch cubes

6 garlic cloves, minced

4 tablespoons canola oil

2 teaspoons ground star anise or garam masala (optional)

2 teaspoons ground coriander

1 teaspoon ground cinnamon

1 teaspoon kosher salt or more to taste

Cornmeal for sprinkling

6 rounds of Haley House Pizza Dough (page 176)

3 cups grated sharp white cheddar cheese

$3/4$ cup Pretty Pickled Red Onions (page 352)

freewheeling pizza combos

Make these pizzas according to the directions on page 180.

Indian Mash Make the mashed potato–ginger mixture from Mashed Potato Spring Rolls with Peanut Sauce (page 54), spread it over an uncooked dough round, and bake. Spoon Fresh Cilantro Chutney (344) over the baked pizza.

Bumper Crop Place a thin layer of Fresh Tomatoes for Pizza (page 178), pan-fried zucchini, blanched corn kernels, and bits of creamy goat cheese and pitted black olives, if you like, on the uncooked dough round, and bake.

Garlicky Shiitakes Sauté sliced fresh shiitake mushroom caps and minced garlic in extra-virgin olive oil. Dot the uncooked dough round with Roasted Tomato Sauce (page 179) and fresh mozzarella and bake. Top the baked pizza with the hot shiitakes.

Seared Spinach and Goat Cheese Pan-fry spinach with extra-virgin olive oil and lots of garlic. Place the spinach on the uncooked dough round. Add a bit of Roasted Tomato Sauce (page 179) or Caramelized Onions (page 354) and dollops of creamy goat cheese, and bake.

Fennel Blues Slice the fennel, then roast it like the butternut squash on page 182, until the fennel begins to color. Place the fennel on the uncooked dough round. Add some crumbled creamy Gorgonzola and grated Parmesan and bake. Top with toasted walnuts. (Try this with leeks in place of the fennel.)

White Pizza Mix fresh ricotta with minced garlic. Place the ricotta on the uncooked dough round. Add grated Parmesan, fresh mozzarella, and freshly ground black (or white) pepper, and bake.

(continued)

rent-a-video burgers, pizzas, sandwiches, and snacks

Trees on Cheese Place blanched broccoli on an uncooked white pizza (see previous page), then bake.

Saag Paneer Place Saag Paneer (page 226) on the uncooked dough round. Add Caramelized Onions (page 354), then bake.

Mexican Pizza Top the uncooked dough round with refried beans and grated Monterey jack cheese and bake. Dot the baked pizza with Zesty, Smoky Cherry Tomato–Oregano Salsa (page 32) and Hip Dip (page 36).

Puttanesca Spoon Roasted Tomato Sauce (page 179) spiked with extra garlic, olives, capers, crumbled tempeh, and chiles onto an uncooked dough round. Top with fresh mozzarella, then bake.

Smoky Eggplant Spoon Roasted Tomato Sauce (page 179) onto the uncooked dough rouond and bake. Top with Extra-Smoky Baba Gannouj (page 29) and toasted pine nuts.

Provençal Place Fresh Tomatoes for Pizza (page 178) and fresh mozzarella on the uncooked dough round and bake. Top with Tapenade (page 141).

Margherita Place fresh mozzarella, Fresh Tomatoes for Pizza (page 178), minced garlic, fresh basil, and extra-virgin olive oil on an uncooked dough round, then bake.

luscious seitan sandwich

(V) *It was a long time before* I got the nerve to try seitan. But one day my friend Kat was eating a sandwich of it, layered with sprouts and a creamy dressing, and I found myself aching for a taste. She handed it over, and I took an enormous bite. Now I get cravings for it.

MAKES 2

1 In a small saucepan, combine the seitan, barbecue sauce, and 3 tablespoons water over medium heat. Reduce the heat to low and simmer for 10 minutes, adding a little water if the liquid completely evaporates. Remove from the heat and set aside.

2 In a small bowl, combine the mayonnaise and sprouts. Spread over one slice of the bread. Top with the hot seitan, then the second slice of bread, and serve.

6–8 ounces seitan (see page 450), thinly sliced

4 tablespoons smoky barbecue sauce (mesquite-flavored is best)

2 tablespoons vegan mayonnaise or ordinary mayonnaise or more to taste

4 tablespoons bean or alfalfa sprouts

4 slices whole-grain bread, as fresh as possible

seitan: the great impersonator

Seitan is a concentrated source of protein made by cooking the gluten extracted from wheat flour. Many people think its texture is similar to that of bread, but the flavor is richer and it's much juicier. Seitan comes already marinated in soy sauce and kombu (a sea vegetable) and therefore does not need to be further salted.

Seitan can usually be found next to the refrigerated tofu at well-stocked supermarkets and whole food stores. My favorite brand is Upcountry. Seitan can be pan-fried, deep-fried, braised, or ground and added to sauces, chilies, sandwiches, or stuffings. It works especially well as a meat or chicken substitute with Asian noodles. It doesn't need to be cooked, although it's awfully good served hot.

rent-a-video burgers, pizzas, sandwiches, and snacks

emmons egg salad sandwich

Whenever I was sick and home from school when I was growing up, I made a warm egg salad sandwich on toast for lunch. In case you don't know, *warm* egg salad has more flavor, more soul and much more clout in my book than chilled egg salad. There are many optional ingredients here, but all you need for the real deal is eggs, mayonnaise, salt and pepper, and bread.

Choosing your bread is a highly personal matter — I like a Pepperidge Farm white, toasted. Sometimes, I like an untoasted whole wheat (try the Whole Wheat Communion Bread, page 384). It's also nice in pita bread or on a toasted sesame-seed bagel.

MAKES 2

2 large eggs

3 tablespoons mayonnaise

Kosher salt and freshly ground black pepper to taste

optional ingredients

1 inner celery stalk with leaves, finely chopped

2 tablespoons chopped onion or shallot

A few dashes of hot sauce

2 tablespoons chopped fresh basil, cilantro, or tarragon

A dab of mustard

4 slices of your favorite bread (I prefer Pepperidge Farm white)

1 Place the eggs in a small saucepan and add cold water to cover. Bring to a boil, then immediately reduce the heat to a simmer and set a timer for 12 minutes.

2 Meanwhile, in a small bowl, combine the mayonnaise and any optional ingredients of your choice.

3 When the eggs have simmered for exactly 12 minutes, drain them quickly, rattling the eggs around in the pan to crack their shells. Immediately fill the pan with cold water and peel the hot eggs under cold running water.

> I love egg salad. To jazz it up, I put the egg salad on a piece of lightly toasted bread, cover it with a slice of Swiss cheese, broil it, then cut it into four squares. —**Suzie Mclean**

4 In a medium bowl, mash the eggs with a fork (don't be fastidious—chunks are good), and stir in the mayonnaise mixture. Season with salt and pepper.

5 Toast the bread slices and divide the warm egg salad between two of them. Top with the remaining toast, cut the sandwiches in half, and serve immediately.

peanut butter and jelly sandwich

On one of many visits to my vegetarian chef friend Cathi DiCocco at her restaurant Café DiCocoa, in Bethel, Maine, I noticed that a peanut butter and jelly pu-pu platter was on the brunch menu. She had listed a choice of nut butters—hazelnut, cashew, almond or soy—and jellies ranging from orange-lime marmalade to rhubarb jam and Maine blueberry jam. There were add-in options as well, such as chopped nuts, banana, and mango. People loved it not only because of the nostalgia factor but because of the far-from-boring flavor combinations.

So this got me to thinking—why not use extra-thin bread and serve PB&J tea sandwiches at parties? If you go the peanut butter route, be sure to use the crunchy style; it adds essential crunch. Here are some great combinations:

- Peanut butter/mango slices/roasted peanuts
- Hazelnut butter/apricot jam
- Cashew butter/peach jam/cashews
- Almond butter/strawberry jam
- Soy butter/chopped Medjool dates/banana slices
- Your favorite nut butter/orange marmalade/chocolate chips
- Cashew butter/ginger marmalade/ripe pear slices

tempeh fajitas with pretty pickled red onions

(V) If you order a fajita in Mexico, you'll get skirt steak stuffed in a flour tortilla—never mind fajitas with shrimp or chicken, which to Mexicans aren't fajitas at all. So, I'm sure the idea of tempeh fajitas would have them in a moral uproar. No matter—you can make these tasty fajitas in the safety of your own home.

SERVES 2

1 In a medium skillet, heat the olive oil over medium heat. Add the garlic and cumin and sauté for 1 minute. Crumble in the tempeh bit by bit. Add the salt and cook until the tempeh becomes brown and crunchy, about 15 minutes. Add the chipotle and lime juice and mix well.

2 In a large, dry skillet, heat the tortillas one at a time until soft and warm. Divide the tempeh mixture, Pretty Pickled Red Onions or salsa, and avocado slices between the tortillas. Fold one side in as for an egg roll, and roll the tortillas up tightly. Serve with the sour cream (if using), lime wedges, and hot sauce.

1 tablespoon extra-virgin olive oil

2 garlic cloves, minced

1 teaspoon ground cumin

8 ounces tempeh

Generous pinch of kosher salt

1 canned chipotle chile in adobo, chopped

1 tablespoon fresh lime juice (1/2 juicy lime)

2 8-inch flour tortillas

Pretty Pickled Red Onions (page 352) or store-bought salsa

1 ripe avocado, peeled and sliced

2 tablespoons sour cream (optional)

2 lime wedges

Hot sauce to taste

leftovers? wrap them!

A wrap can transform leftovers into a new meal. Flatbreads can envelop a rather wet mixture of food, which would ooze out the sides of a conventional sandwich. Many of my dips, dressings, and salads make excellent fillings for wraps. Some of my favorites are Saag Paneer (page 226), Chard and Eggplant Salad with Miso-Sesame Vinaigrette (page 134), Forkless Artichoke Salad (page 128), and Green Skordalia (page 20) with ripe tomatoes.

You can find flatbread (also called lavash, roll-ups, or mountain bread) in well-stocked supermarkets, whole food stores, or Middle Eastern markets. The bread is usually rectangular, about 10 inches by 12 inches, and about $1/8$ inch thick. If you can't find this kind of bread, use large pita breads, separating them like an English muffin and using each half as a wrap. Or you can always use a large flour tortilla.

Keep a pack of flatbread in your freezer so you can make spur-of-the-moment wrap sandwiches. If you're taking a wrap sandwich to go, wrap it well in foil and bring along a napkin or two.

emergency quesadillas

Quesadillas are quick and easy, and if you have tortillas or lavash in the freezer, all you need is some cheese. Here is what you'll need to have quesadilla capability in your home. Also, you'll want to read the directions for Crispy Quesadilla Triangles (page 68) for cooking quesadillas.

Whatever cheese you've got: Even cream cheese will work—grated or thinly sliced.

Tortillas: My favorite option here is to substitute lavash for tortillas. They're made from the same ingredients but are more convenient to freeze since they aren't stuck together like tortillas. If you prefer tortillas, freeze them as follows: when you first buy them, separate all the tortillas from each other. Put them back into their bag, seal, and freeze. They sometimes need to be thawed slightly to separate.

Salsa or hot sauce: I like ones that contain chipotle chiles.

Add-ins: Canned black beans, drained and rinsed, sliced scallions, black olives, diced tomatoes, canned green chiles, frozen spinach, thawed, and any stray vegetables, blanched.

creamed spinach and shiitakes on toast

This dish is similar to the creamed spinach we grew up with, but updated—and more delicious—due to the shiitakes and a cream sauce that's easier and lighter than the traditional one. This is for one of those nights when you want to have a close friend over for an above-average film, which you watch on the couch with an old quilt over your legs.

SERVES 2

2 tablespoons canola oil

1 medium onion, chopped

3 garlic cloves, minced

2 tablespoons pine nuts (optional)

2 cups sliced shiitake mushroom caps (about 4 ounces)

¼ teaspoon freshly grated nutmeg

1 bunch spinach (about ⅔ pound), stemmed

¼ cup sour cream

Kosher salt and freshly ground black pepper to taste

4 slices whole-grain bread

Hot sauce (optional)

1 In a large skillet, heat the canola oil over medium heat. Add the onion and sauté, stirring occasionally, until soft, about 7 minutes. Add the garlic and pine nuts, if using, and cook until fragrant, about 1 minute more. Reduce the heat to medium. Add the mushrooms and sauté for 5 minutes more, stirring frequently, adding the nutmeg during the last minute.

2 Increase the heat to high and add the spinach all at once, stirring constantly until wilted. Remove from the heat and stir in the sour cream. Season with salt and pepper. Cover loosely to keep warm.

3 Toast the bread slices and cut them into diagonal halves. Divide the toast between the two plates, and spoon the spinach mixture over the toast. Serve, passing hot sauce on the side, if you like.

lo-stress onion rings

These rings are as crispy and taste as sinful as the fried version, but without the last-minute hassle of batter-dipping and deep-frying. Serve with veggie burgers, quesadillas, or grilled sandwiches. Ketchup is optional.

SERVES 6

1 Preheat the oven to 400 degrees. In a large bowl, combine the flour, baking powder, chili powder, and salt and mix well.

2 Toss the onions with the flour mixture, then remove them, knocking any excess flour back into the bowl, and place them in a large clean bowl. Pour the eggs over the onion rings, tossing with your hands until the onions are well coated. Lift out the onions, letting the excess egg drip back into the bowl. Transfer the onions to the flour mixture and wipe your hands with a dishtowel.

3 With clean, dry hands, toss the onions with the flour mixture until most of it adheres to the onions. Divide the onions between 2 rimmed baking sheets, drizzle them with the canola oil, and toss to coat. Arrange the onion rings in an even layer.

- 1 cup all-purpose flour
- 2 teaspoons baking powder
- 1 tablespoon chili powder
- 2 rounded teaspoons kosher salt, plus more if needed
- 3 large onions, sliced into thin rounds
- 2 large eggs, beaten
- ½ cup canola oil

4 Bake the onion rings until they are crisp and brown, 30 to 40 minutes. Salt again if necessary (it usually is) and serve.

Note The onion rings can be made up to 4 hours ahead. Transfer the baked onion rings to a clean rimmed baking sheet lined with a brown paper bag and set aside. Re-crisp them in a 300-degree oven for 15 to 20 minutes before serving.

steak fries

(V) *I learned how to make these* toothsome fries at Hamersley's Bistro in Boston. These hefty fries, with a crisp outer skin, ache to be dipped. I like dipping them into tomato ketchup or Chipotle Ketchup (page 341).

SERVES 4

4 large russet or Yukon Gold potatoes

3 tablespoons canola oil

Kosher salt and freshly ground black pepper to taste

1 Preheat the oven to 400 degrees. Scrub the potatoes well. Halve them lengthwise, then cut in half again lengthwise to form spears.

2 In a large skillet, heat the canola oil over medium-high heat. When the oil is just starting to smoke, add the potato spears, flesh side down. You should be able to fit in all of the potatoes, but if you can't, don't worry.

3 Pan-fry the potatoes on one side until they are golden brown, about 5 minutes. Using tongs, turn the spears over, flesh side down. Pan-fry until that side is also golden brown. When both sides have browned, transfer the spear to a rimmed baking sheet. At this point,

if you have more spears to pan-fry, add them as the first batch leaves the pan. Continue with the browning process until all the spears are done and are on the baking sheet.

4 Salt the spears very liberally and season with pepper. Bake for 15 minutes, or until the insides are very tender and the outsides are crisp. Let cool for at least 5 minutes before serving.

Variation If you're feeling decadent, make cheese fries. During the last minute of baking, toss a few handfuls of grated cheddar cheese over the fries. Continue baking for about 1 minute, or until melted.

twice-baked potatoes

There's nothing more soothing to me than curling up with friends to enjoy a good film and eat a twice-baked potato. Many thanks to *Cooks Illustrated* magazine, which published an article on twice-baked potatoes that helped me devise this recipe. For a real treat, try one of the variations on page 198.

SERVES 2

1 Preheat the oven to 400 degrees. Scrub the potatoes well and prick them with a sharp knife or fork. Bake them until they can be pierced easily with a knife, about 1 hour. Leave the oven on. Let the potatoes cool for 10 minutes; if they are still too hot to handle, use a dishtowel to hold them. Cut a thin, lengthwise slice from one side of each potato. Use a small spoon to scoop the flesh into a medium bowl, leaving a thin layer of potato in the shell.

2 Return the shells to the oven for 10 minutes to crisp. Meanwhile, mash the potato flesh with a fork until smooth.

3 Stir in the remaining ingredients, and pile the filling back into the crisped shell. Turn the oven to broil. Broil the potatoes 4 to 5 inches from the broiler until they are spotty brown and crisp on top, 5 to 10 minutes. Serve.

2 large baking potatoes, such as russet or Yukon Gold

¼ cup chopped scallions, white and green parts

4 tablespoons sour cream

4 tablespoons buttermilk or plain yogurt

2 tablespoons butter

¼ cup grated cheddar or Monterey jack cheese

2 tablespoons freshly grated Parmesan cheese

Kosher salt and freshly ground black pepper to taste

Potatoes

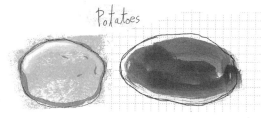

Combine any of the following with the ingredients on the previous page.

Fried Caper Garnish: Rinse 1 tablespoon capers and pat dry inside a folded paper towel. Fry in olive oil until the capers "bloom," then sprinkle them on top of the stuffed potatoes after broiling.

Horseradish: Add 2 tablespoons prepared horseradish and 1 tablespoon Worcestershire sauce or vegetarian Worcestershire sauce to the filling mixture.

Garlicky Mushrooms: Sauté sliced shiitake mushroom caps and minced garlic in butter or olive oil until tender. Pile the mushrooms on top of the potato after boiling.

Garlicky Broccoli: Sauté chopped, blanched broccoli or broccoli rabe with minced garlic in olive oil. Season with kosher salt and crushed red pepper flakes. Add to the filling.

Caramelized Onion: Sauté 1 small sliced onion in olive oil with a pinch of sugar until soft and golden brown. Fold into filling.

Florentine: Sauté chopped spinach (I use frozen for convenience) with minced garlic in olive oil; add to the filling along with $1/4$ cup ricotta cheese.

Purely Vegan: Mash the potato with 6 ounces firm tofu, 2 minced garlic cloves, 3 tablespoons each sliced scallion, white and green parts, and chopped fresh basil, and 4 tablespoons extra-virgin olive oil.

Blue Cheese: Omit the buttermilk and add 3 ounces crumbled or mashed good-quality blue cheese, such as Gorgonzola dolce or Bleu d'Auvergne to the filling mixture, along with 4 tablespoons cottage cheese.

Goat Cheese: Substitute goat cheese for the cheddar in the filling. This is particularly good with the broccoli or caramelized onion options above.

chapter 5

Nice over Rice

happy landings

Whenever I cook rice in my house, I make twice as much as needed. The leftover rice acts as a fine landing pad for curries, kormas, ragouts, stir-fries—and many other satisfying mélanges. It reheats like a gem in the microwave. That way, I'm halfway done preparing the meal when friends drop in.

Long-Grain White Rice

In a medium saucepan, bring 4 cups water and a scant 1 teaspoon kosher salt to a boil. Add 2 cups raw white long-grain rice, cover, reduce the heat to a simmer, and cook for 15 minutes. Remove from the heat and let stand, covered, for 10 to 15 minutes. Makes 6 to 7 cups cooked rice.

White Basmati Rice

In a sieve or colander, rinse 2 cups raw white basmati rice with cold running water for 1 to 2 minutes to keep it from becoming sticky. Let drain for a few minutes. In a medium saucepan, bring 2⅔ cups water and a scant 1 teaspoon kosher salt to a boil. Add the rice, cover, reduce the heat to a simmer, and cook for 15 minutes. Remove from the heat, and let stand, covered, for 10 minutes. Makes 6 cups cooked rice.

Long-Grain Brown Rice or Brown Basmati Rice

In a colander or sieve, rinse 2 cups raw rice with cold running water for 1 to 2 minutes to keep it from becoming sticky. Let drain for a few minutes. In a medium saucepan, bring 4 cups water and a scant 1 teaspoon kosher salt to a boil. Add the rice, cover, reduce the heat to a simmer, and cook the rice for 20 minutes. Remove from the heat and let stand, covered, for 15 minutes. Makes 6 cups cooked rice.

Short-Grain Brown Rice

In a medium saucepan, bring 4 cups water and a scant 1 teaspoon kosher salt to a boil. Add 2 cups raw short-grain brown rice, cover, reduce the heat to simmer, and cook for 45 minutes. Makes 6 to 7 cups cooked rice.

Jasmine Rice

In a medium saucepan, bring 3 cups water and a scant 1 teaspoon kosher salt to a boil. Add 2 cups raw white jasmine rice, cover, reduce the heat to a simmer, and cook for 15 minutes. Remove from the heat and let stand, covered, for 10 minutes. Makes 6 cups cooked rice.

Speedy Couscous

In a medium saucepan, bring 2^1/2 cups water to a boil. Add 2 cups instant or quick-cooking couscous and 1^1/2 teaspoons kosher salt, stir once or twice, cover, and remove from the heat. Let stand for at least 5 minutes. Fluff thoroughly with a fork and serve. Makes 6 cups cooked couscous.

Quinoa

In a medium saucepan, bring 2 cups water, 1 cup quinoa, and ^{1}/2 teaspoon salt to a boil. Cover, reduce the heat to low, and simmer for 15 minutes. Remove the pan from the heat and let it sit for 5 minutes, until all the liquid is absorbed. Makes 3 cups.

coconut rice

This coconut rice gets its rich flavor from dried, unsweetened coconut. It's much lighter than rice cooked in coconut milk. Serve with curries.

SERVES 4

Scant 1 teaspoon kosher salt

2 cups jasmine rice

½ cup dried, unsweetened coconut

10 cardamom pods

In a medium saucepan, bring 3½ cups water and the salt to a boil over medium-high heat. Add the rice, coconut, and cardamom pods and return to a boil, stirring occasionally. Reduce the heat to a simmer, cover, and simmer gently for 15 minutes. Remove from the heat and let stand, covered, for 5 minutes. Stir well and remove the cardamom pods before serving.

Coconut

Variations

For a moister, richer version, use 2 cups unsweetened coconut milk (see page 446) and 2 cups water instead of 3½ cups water in the basic recipe. This is still lighter than many Indian recipes for coconut rice.

Stir 2 teaspoons red curry paste into the boiling water. When the rice is done, stir in a few tablespoons chopped fresh cilantro stems. Serve with roasted vegetables and tofu.

cauliflower, cashew, and cardamom pilaf

Infused with cardamom, ginger, and cumin, this fragrant pilaf is best with the irresistible, crepelike Roti Jala (page 358). It's a casual meal that's perfect for cool weather.

SERVES 4

12 cardamom pods

1½ tablespoons butter

½ cup raw unsalted cashews

1 small onion, chopped

1 cup basmati or jasmine rice

1 tablespoon peeled and minced fresh ginger

1 teaspoon whole cumin seeds

3 cups small cauliflower florets

1 teaspoon kosher salt, plus more to taste

1 cup frozen peas, thawed

Freshly ground black pepper to taste

3 scallions, white and green parts, thinly sliced

1 Place the cardamom pods on a cutting board and whack them with a heavy pan to crush them lightly. Separate the seeds, discarding the pods.

2 In a large skillet, melt the butter over medium heat. Add the cashews and sauté until golden but not browned, about 2 minutes. With a slotted spoon, transfer the cashews to a plate and set aside.

3 Add the onion to the skillet and sauté for 2 minutes. Add the rice, ginger, cumin, and cardamom seeds and sauté, stirring constantly, for 1 minute. Add the cauliflower, salt, and 2 cups water and bring to a boil. Reduce the heat to a simmer, cover, and cook for 15 minutes. Remove from the heat and let stand, covered, for 10 minutes. Fold in the peas and cashews and season with salt and pepper. Transfer to a serving dish, garnish with the scallions, and serve.

Note The pilaf can be made up to 2 days ahead and stored in an airtight container in the fridge. Reheat in a covered casserole dish in a 350-degree oven for about 25 minutes, or in the microwave.

nice over rice

pilafs—thinking out of the box

Even though I know better, I'm apt to think of pilaf as those overpriced boxes half filled with rice and a flavor packet. Pilafs can be so much more, and they're a delightful way to expand one's vegetarian repertoire. Technically, a pilaf is any rice or bulgur dish that begins by sautéing the grain in butter or oil.

Basic method for making a pilaf: In a large saucepan, melt 1 to 2 tablespoons butter (vegans can use canola oil) over medium heat. Add the onion, garlic, and spices and sauté, stirring occasionally, until the onion is soft, about 7 minutes. Add the rice, cook, stirring, for 1 minute. Add the water and salt and bring to a boil. Reduce the heat to a simmer, cover, and simmer gently for at least 20 minutes (brown rice will take 35 to 40 minutes).

If you're using nuts in the pilaf, brown them in the butter, then transfer them to a small bowl and set aside. Add the nuts to the cooked pilaf before serving. Traditionally, fresh chiles are added to pilafs, so feel free to do so.

Great combinations: I've called for white basmati rice, but you can use jasmine or brown rice. For jasmine rice, use 2 cups rice and 3 cups water. For brown rice (either basmati or long-grain), use 2 cups rice and 4 cups water. If you want to add brown or French green lentils to any of these pilafs, add ½ cup raw lentils along with the rice and 1 cup extra water. Add at least ½ teaspoon salt along with the water and season to taste at the end.

Other Fun Add-Ins

- Raisins or dried currants, cashews, pistachios, or sliced or slivered almonds: add these at the start with the butter, then remove them and stir in before serving.

- Curry powder, minced fresh lemongrass stalk, minced chiles, tamarind, star anise pods, or fennel seeds: add these with the butter.

- Chopped fresh cilantro, 1 teaspoon garam masala, thawed frozen peas, or toasted dried, unsweetened coconut: add these at the end.

Potato-Lentil Pilaf

Sauté 2 teaspoons ground coriander, 1 teaspoon whole cumin seeds, and 1 cup chopped red onion in the butter. When the onion is soft, add 2 cups basmati rice, $1/2$ cup raw brown lentils, 1 cubed waxy potato, and 4 cups water.

Saffron Pilaf

Sauté 2 tablespoons pine nuts in the butter until golden brown. Transfer them to a small bowl and set aside. Add 1 tablespoon peeled and minced fresh ginger, 1 teaspoon brown or black mustard seeds, and a few cardamom pods and sauté until fragrant. Add a pinch of saffron threads, 1 chopped tomato, 2 cups basmati rice, and $2^2/3$ cups water. Stir in the pine nuts before serving.

Spiced Green Bean Pilaf

Sauté 1 cup chopped onion, $1/2$ teaspoon whole cumin seeds, and a pinch of ground cinnamon in the butter. When the onion is soft, add 2 cups chopped green beans, 2 cups basmati rice, and $2^2/3$ cups water.

Spinach Pilaf

Sauté $1^1/2$ cups ($1/2$-inch cubes) firm tofu in the butter until golden brown. Add 3 minced garlic cloves, 1 teaspoon ground coriander, and a pinch of freshly ground nutmeg and sauté until fragrant. Add 1 chopped tomato, 2 cups basmati rice, and $2^2/3$ cups water. Stir in a small bunch of spinach leaves after 15 minutes of cooking. Add a squeeze of fresh lemon juice before serving.

cashew korma

Asian eggplant, tomatoes, kohlrabi, and lots of cashews make an unusual and healthy korma, an Indian stew that uses nuts as a thickener and flavoring. It takes only 25 minutes to pull together.

Kohlrabi looks like a pale green baseball with stems sprouting from the top and sides. It's in the Asian-broccoli family and can be eaten raw or cooked. Look for it at Asian markets. You can use peeled and sliced broccoli stems instead. Garnish with a sprinkle of poppy seeds, if you have some on hand.

SERVES 4

3/4 cup cashew halves

3 tablespoons canola oil

1 small onion, chopped

1 teaspoon ground cardamom

1 Asian eggplant, cut into half-moons

1/2 kohlrabi, cut into 1/2-inch cubes

2 plum tomatoes, cut into 1/2-inch cubes

1 garlic clove, minced

2 teaspoons garam masala (see page 447)

1 teaspoon red wine vinegar or cider vinegar

1 1/2 cups plain yogurt

Kosher salt to taste

Basmati Rice (page 200) or Jasmine Rice (page 201)

1 Preheat the oven to 350 degrees. Spread the cashews in a single layer on a rimmed baking sheet, and toast for 5 minutes, or until golden brown. Cool slightly, then grind 1/2 cup of the cashews in a food processor. Set aside the ground cashews and cashew halves separately.

2 In a large skillet, heat the canola oil over medium heat. Add the onion and sauté, stirring occasionally, until soft, about 7 minutes. Add the cardamom and stir until the onion is coated and the mixture is fragrant, 1 to 2 minutes more.

3 Stir in the ground cashews, eggplant, kohlrabi, tomatoes, and garlic, and cook for 4 minutes, stirring occasionally. Add $^1/_2$ cup water, cover, reduce the heat to a simmer, and cook until the vegetables are tender, 10 to 15 minutes. Reduce the heat to its lowest setting and stir in the garam masala and then the vinegar and yogurt, stirring until heated through. Do not let the mixture boil, or the yogurt will curdle. Season well with salt. Serve the korma over hot rice, garnished with the halved cashews.

garam masala–gilded vegetables

Ⓥ *I am very fond of this simple dish* that showcases garam masala, a delicious blend of Indian spices (see page 447). I've used some of my favorite vegetables here, but feel free to choose your own. Chopped green beans, parboiled cubed potatoes, diced fennel bulb, or diced jicama would all work well. But keep the cherry tomatoes, because they help form the sauce.

SERVES 4

1 In a large skillet, heat the canola oil over medium heat. Add the mushrooms, garlic, and ginger and sauté for 2 minutes. Add the sweet potato or carrots, edamame, scallions, and ¼ cup water, cover, and cook until the vegetables are soft, about 6 minutes.

2 Stir in the cherry tomatoes, garam masala, and brown sugar and cook for 1 minute more. Season with salt and pepper. Serve hot over rice or couscous.

Note

This dish can be prepared up to 1 day ahead and stored in an airtight container in the fridge. Reheat only until it's hot, to prevent the vegetables from overcooking.

2 tablespoons canola oil

2 cups thinly sliced shiitake mushroom caps (about 4 ounces)

3 garlic cloves, minced

1 tablespoon peeled and minced fresh ginger

1 sweet potato or 2 large carrots, peeled and cut into ¼-inch cubes

1 cup frozen shelled (podless) edamame (see page 446)

8 scallions, white and green parts, cut into 1-inch lengths

2 cups halved cherry tomatoes

1 tablespoon Garam Masala (page 209)

2 teaspoons brown sugar

Kosher salt and freshly ground black pepper to taste

Basmati Rice (page 200) or Speedy Couscous (page 201)

garam masala

(V) *Think of garam masala as* a cross between apple-pie spice and curry powder. Consisting mainly of ground coriander, cumin, and cinnamon, it originated in the colder areas of India, where it is believed to generate internal body heat. It is most often added to vegetable dishes near the end of the cooking to boost the aroma and flavor. Garam masala can be substituted for curry powder, if you like, since it works fine in the beginning phase of cooking as well.

I often add 6 to 8 star anise pods or 1 tablespoon fennel seeds to this mix. If you find breaking open the cardamom pods cumbersome, just add 1 teaspoon ground cardamom along with the nutmeg.

MAKES ¾ CUP

- 1 tablespoon whole cloves
- 1 3-inch-long cinnamon stick
- 1 tablespoon cardamom pods
- 2 tablespoons cumin seeds
- ⅓ cup coriander seeds
- 2 tablespoons black peppercorns
- 2 teaspoons ground nutmeg

1 In a small, dry skillet, toast the spices (except for the nutmeg) over low heat, stirring frequently, until fragrant and slightly browned, 8 to 10 minutes. Transfer to a plate and let cool slightly.

2 On a cutting board, pound the cinnamon stick with a hammer or the bottom of a heavy pan to crush it. Lightly crush the cardamom pods to release the black seeds inside; discard the pods.

3 In a spice grinder or with a mortar and pestle, grind the toasted spices in small batches until they are powdered. Stir in the nutmeg.

Note
The garam masala can be stored in a tightly sealed jar for up to 5 months in a cool, dark place.

sweet potato badi

A badi is an Indian lentil dish in which the lentils (*dal*) have been fried in oil or butter until crunchy before liquid is added and the remaining ingredients cooked to completion. Don't buy the sticky, sweetened shredded coconut that you find in the baking section of supermarkets. You want dried, unsweetened coconut sold in Asian markets and whole food stores. Its nutty taste adds a dazzling dimension.

SERVES 4

$\frac{1}{2}$ cup dried, unsweetened coconut (see page 446)

$\frac{1}{4}$ cup canola oil

$\frac{1}{2}$ cup raw red lentils

8 curry leaves (see page 446) or 1 teaspoon ground cumin

1 medium yellow, white, or new potato, peeled and cut into $\frac{1}{2}$-inch cubes

1 large sweet potato, peeled and cut into $\frac{3}{4}$-inch cubes

2 small zucchini, cut into $\frac{1}{4}$-inch-thick rounds

2 plum tomatoes, cut into $\frac{1}{2}$-inch cubes

$\frac{1}{2}$ cup frozen baby peas

$\frac{1}{2}$ cup plain yogurt

1–2 small, skinny chile peppers, minced

1 teaspoon kosher salt

4 pita breads, split, toasted, and buttered, Basmati Rice (page 200) or Jasmine Rice (page 201)

1 In a small, dry skillet, toast the coconut over medium heat, shaking the skillet often, until the coconut is uniformly light brown, about 5 minutes. Transfer the coconut to a small bowl and set aside.

2 In the same skillet, heat the canola oil over medium heat. Add the lentils and sauté for 5 to 10 minutes, stirring, until they begin to brown. Stir in the curry leaves or cumin. Add the potato, sweet potato, and $1\frac{1}{2}$ cups water and bring to a boil. Reduce the heat to a simmer, cover, and simmer, stirring occasionally, for 15 minutes. Add the zucchini, tomatoes, and peas, and cook until the vegetables are fork-tender and the liquid is almost gone, about 10 minutes more. If the liquid evaporates too quickly, add a little more water. Remove from the heat.

Lentils

3 Measure out 2 tablespoons of the toasted coconut and set aside. In a large bowl, combine the remaining coconut, yogurt, chiles, and salt, and whisk until smooth. Fold the yogurt mixture gently into the vegetables. Cover the skillet and let stand for a few minutes until warmed through. Transfer the *badi* to a serving bowl and sprinkle the remaining 2 tablespoons coconut on top. Serve immediately with the pita bread or rice.

Note

This dish can be prepared ahead through step 2 up to 2 days ahead and stored in an airtight container in the fridge. To serve, reheat the mixture in a large skillet and remove from the heat before starting step 3.

curried jack-o'-lantern

(V) *When Halloween is over,* eat your jack-o'-lantern! The flesh of a cutting pumpkin is semisweet and juicy, similar to summer squash. It tastes best roasted. I've used Indian spices here, but it's equally good roasted with sage, rosemary, or thyme. If you want to cook your Halloween jack-o'-lantern, the pumpkin must be freshly cut (within the last 24 hours). Alternatively, after 24 hours cut the jack-o'-lantern into pieces, wrap them in plastic, and refrigerate for up to 1 week.

SERVES 4

1 jack-o'-lantern or cutting pumpkin

¼ cup canola oil

1 medium onion, chopped

1 green bell pepper, chopped

1 tablespoon curry powder

2 tomatoes, chopped

2 garlic cloves, minced

Kosher salt and freshly ground black pepper to taste

Jasmine Rice (page 201) or Basmati Rice (page 200)

1 Preheat the oven to 375 degrees. If the base of the pumpkin has melted wax on it, cut it out and discard it. Cut a few large slabs from the uncarved sides of the pumpkin. Peel the slabs with a sharp knife and cut the flesh into 1-inch cubes. You will need 8 cups. In a colander, rinse the cubes well under cold running water. Set aside.

2 In a large skillet, heat the canola oil over medium heat. Add the onion and bell pepper and sauté, stirring occasionally, until the onion begins to brown, 9 to 11 minutes. Add the curry powder and sauté for 1 minute more.

Note This dish can be prepared up to 2 days ahead, but refrain from roasting the pumpkin. Instead, store the pumpkin mixture in an airtight container in the fridge and roast it just before serving.

3 Transfer the onion mixture to a roasting pan or large casserole dish, add the pumpkin, tomatoes, and garlic, and toss with your hands until the pumpkin is coated with the onion mixture. Season liberally with salt and pepper. Roast until the pumpkin is tender, 50 to 60 minutes. Serve hot with the rice.

spinach, crunchy chickpea, and hazelnut ragout

Ⓥ *This ragout was inspired by* a traditional Spanish dish of spinach with raisins and pine nuts. I built this into a meal by adding crisp baked chickpeas, which add a "meaty" crunch (they taste like fried chicken to me!). Add a few chopped tomatoes in step 3 if you desire, or use Swiss chard or kale instead of the spinach.

SERVES 2 OR 3

1 15-ounce can chickpeas, rinsed
   and drained

¼ cup whole hazelnuts

2 tablespoons raisins

1 tablespoon extra-virgin olive oil

2 garlic cloves, minced

1 bunch spinach, stemmed

3 plum tomatoes, cut into ½-inch
   cubes

2 tablespoons capers or caperberries,
   with a bit of the brine

A squeeze or two of fresh lemon juice

Kosher salt and freshly ground
   black pepper to taste

Speedy Couscous (page 201) or
   Jasmine Rice (page 201)

1 Preheat the oven to 350 degrees. Spread the chickpeas in a single layer on a rimmed baking sheet and roast until crunchy, about 30 minutes. Transfer to a plate and set aside. Meanwhile, spread the hazelnuts on a second rimmed baking sheet and roast for 10 to 15 minutes, or until golden in the center (you'll need to cut into one to see). While the nuts are still hot, pour them onto a clean dishtowel, form a sack, then rub the nuts in the towel to remove the skins. Don't worry about removing every last bit of skin. Open the towel and transfer the nuts to a cutting board with your hands, leaving the paperlike skins behind. Coarsely chop the nuts and set aside.

2 In a small bowl, pour $^{1}/_{2}$ cup boiling water over the raisins. Let stand for at least 10 minutes, or until plump. Set aside.

3 In a large skillet, heat the olive oil over medium-low heat. Add the garlic and cook for 1 minute; do not let it brown. Increase the heat to medium-high and stir in the spinach, tomatoes, capers or caperberries with their brine, and raisins with about 1 tablespoon of the soaking liquid. Cook, stirring frequently, until the spinach is completely wilted, about 3 minutes. Stir in the roasted chickpeas and hazelnuts and heat through. Season to taste with lemon juice, salt, and pepper. Serve immediately over the couscous or rice.

Hazelnuts

sesame-crunch tofu

(V) *This tofu is crunch-a-licious.* It's marinated in ginger and soy sauce, coated with sesame seeds and flour for maximum crunch power, then pan-fried. Serve it over rice with chili sauce on the side, or with a lightly dressed watercress salad or steamed Swiss chard.

SERVES 2 OR 3

1 16-ounce carton firm tofu

2 tablespoons soy sauce

1 tablespoon toasted sesame oil

1 tablespoon peeled and minced fresh ginger

1 tablespoon minced garlic

½ cup all-purpose flour

2 tablespoons toasted sesame seeds (see page 450)

3 tablespoons canola oil

Jasmine Rice (page 201)

1 Wrap the block of tofu well in a clean dishtowel and press it firmly with your hands until you feel the towel become damp. Unwrap the tofu and cut it into ½-inch cubes.

2 In a bowl large enough to accommodate the tofu, combine the soy sauce, sesame oil, ginger, and garlic and mix well. Add the tofu, turning gently to coat. Cover with plastic wrap and marinate in the refrigerator for at least 1 hour or up to 24 hours.

3 In a pie pan or wide bowl, combine the flour and sesame seeds and mix well. Drain the tofu pieces in a colander set over a bowl, saving the marinade. In a large well-seasoned skillet, heat the canola oil over medium-high heat. Dredge the tofu cubes in the flour mixture, knocking any excess flour back into the bowl. Use a slotted spoon to transfer the tofu to the skillet. Pan-fry the tofu until it is golden brown on one side, working in batches if necessary to avoid crowding the skillet. Use a spatula to carefully turn the cubes and fry on at least one more side, 4 to 5 minutes per side. Drain well on paper towels. Serve the tofu over the rice, drizzled with the reserved marinade.

tofu: the other white meat

People are finally realizing that tofu is good for their health as well as the environment. Soy has anticarcinogens that protect us from cancer, and it can lower our cholesterol levels, protect us from osteoporosis, and alleviate symptoms of menopause and diabetes. It's especially good for the environment—you can get twenty times the usable protein from an acre of soybeans that you can from cattle grazing on the same land.

But as popular as tofu has become, I don't hear people professing their love for this virtuous white "meat." That is, until they try it *my* way. Everyone wants to learn my method once they taste it. I salt the tofu and pan-fry it until it develops a golden crust. Toss the tofu pieces into salads (I call them tofu croutons). They're also good in stir-fries and curries, since their neutral interior takes well to flavorful sauces. Try the tofu pieces in Viet Rice in a Rush with Tofu (page 218) and Sweet Potato Badi (page 210). The tofu pieces will stay crispy for a few hours on a baking sheet in a 250-degree oven. If you're going to use them as croutons, they'll keep at room temperature for up to 4 hours.

Pan-Fried Tofu or Tofu Croutons

Wrap a 16-ounce block firm or extra-firm tofu in a clean dishtowel and press it firmly with your hands until you feel the towel become damp. Unwrap the tofu and cut it into $1/2$-inch cubes. In a large, well-seasoned skillet, heat 2 tablespoons canola oil over medium-high heat. Add the tofu and salt it liberally. Fry the tofu undisturbed until it forms a dark golden crust on the bottom, then use a spatula to turn it and brown it well on at least one more side, 4 to 5 minutes per side. Drain well on paper towels.

In general, it's not worth marinating tofu, and freezing it makes it dry and spongy.

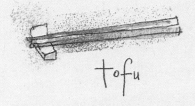

tofu

viet rice in a rush with tofu

 One night when I was hurrying to feed a friend before an early movie, I scrambled together some leftover rice, cooked potatoes, tomato, and tofu with Vietnamese seasonings. From these serendipitous ingredients, I hit upon something worth passing on. Feel free to leave out the potato if you don't have a cooked one handy.

SERVES 2

3 tablespoons canola oil

1 tablespoon peeled and minced fresh ginger

3 garlic cloves, minced

1 16-ounce carton firm tofu

Kosher salt to taste

2 cups cooked white or brown long-grain rice (page 200), at room temperature or cold

1 cup cooked, cubed new potatoes

2 plum tomatoes, diced

3 tablespoons coarsely chopped fresh cilantro

1–2 teaspoons Asian chili sauce (see page 443)

Kosher salt or Asian fish sauce (see page 444) to taste

1 In a large skillet, heat 1 tablespoon of the canola oil over medium heat. Add the ginger and garlic and sauté, stirring constantly, until light brown. Immediately remove the ginger and garlic with a slotted spoon to a plate lined with a paper towel and set aside.

2 Wrap the block of tofu in a clean dishtowel and press it firmly with your hands until you feel the towel become damp. Unwrap the tofu and cut it into 1/2-inch cubes. In a large, well-seasoned skillet, heat the remaining 2 tablespoons oil over medium-high heat. Add the tofu and salt it liberally. Fry the tofu undisturbed until a dark golden crust forms on the bottom, then use a spatula to turn it and brown it well on at least one more side, 4 to 5 minutes per side.

fish sauce—the things we do for love (of food)

I consider myself a "95% vegetarian." The 5% accounts for the fact that I *will* eat seafood once in a while. I don't cook it anymore, but I'll order it when I'm at a nice restaurant, in part because so many chefs have no interesting or viable vegetarian options.

However, fish sauce is something I use every now and again at home because I love Southeast Asian cooking. Fish sauce is a salty liquid produced from the brine of small, salted, fermented fish such as anchovies. Its shelf life is indefinite. It has a sharp pungency that works especially well with chiles, lime juice, garlic, and other common Southeast Asian flavors; without it, the food loses its character. It's economical and practical. It's easier to substitute vegetables or soy products for fish than to find a substitute for fish sauce. Soy sauce is not a good replacement, since it shifts the entire flavor of the dish. Salt, perhaps fish sauce's best substitute, can't offer the depth of flavor of the real thing.

A vegetarian sauce by Lee Kum Kee called Vegetarian Stir-Fry Sauce is based on dried mushrooms. It's quite different from fish sauce (it's thick and sweet), but it can throw an equally powerful punch into sauces. The result is different but usually good.

3 Add the rice, potatoes, and tomatoes to the skillet and increase the heat to high. Cook, stirring constantly, for 4 minutes, or until heated through. Remove from the heat and add the cilantro, chili sauce, and salt or fish sauce. Divide between two bowls and sprinkle each serving with the ginger-garlic mixture.

tofu, broccoli, and tomatoes with curried peanut sauce

(V) *Here's a healthy meal* with lots of good flavor. Instead of the broccoli, you can use chopped bok choy, kale, spinach, or green beans. Also, this dish is equally good with tempeh in place of the tofu.

SERVES 4

1   16-ounce carton firm tofu

2   tablespoons canola oil

    Kosher salt to taste

1   bunch broccoli, cut into florets with 3-inch stems

2   cups whole cherry tomatoes or 4 plum tomatoes, quartered

    Jasmine Rice (page 201) or long-grain brown rice (page 200)

    Curried Peanut Sauce (page 221), warm or at room temperature

1 Wrap the block of tofu in a clean dishtowel and press it firmly with your hands until you feel the towel become damp. Unwrap the tofu and cut it into $1/2$-inch cubes. In a large, well-seasoned skillet, heat the canola oil over medium-high heat. Add the tofu and salt it liberally. Fry the tofu undisturbed until a dark golden crust forms on the bottom, then use a spatula to turn it and brown it well on at least one more side, 4 to 5 minutes per side. Transfer to a plate lined with paper towels.

2 Add the broccoli, tomatoes, and $1/2$ cup water to the skillet and cook, stirring occasionally, until the vegetables are cooked through and the water has nearly evaporated, about 5 minutes. Return the tofu to the skillet and heat through. Serve the tofu mixture over the rice, with the Curried Peanut Sauce spooned over the top.

Note The Curried Peanut Sauce can be prepared up to 5 days ahead and stored in an airtight container in the fridge. Bring the sauce to room temperature before serving.

curried peanut sauce

(V) *This goes well with steamed vegetables.*

MAKES 1⅓ CUPS

In a medium saucepan, heat 1 tablespoon of the oil over medium-low heat. Add the shallots, garlic, and ginger and sauté for 2 minutes. Add the curry powder, and cook for 1 minute more. Remove from the heat and whisk in the peanut butter, gradually adding ¾ cup warm water to smooth the sauce as you go. Stir in the cilantro and lime juice. Season with the salt or fish sauce.

- 1 tablespoon canola oil
- 2 shallots, finely chopped
- 2 garlic cloves, minced
- 2 teaspoons peeled and minced fresh ginger
- 1 tablespoon curry powder
- ⅓ cup crunchy peanut butter
- 2 tablespoons coarsely chopped fresh cilantro
- 2 tablespoons fresh lime juice (1 juicy lime)
- 2 teaspoons Kosher salt or Asian fish sauce (see page 444) to taste

Note The sauce can be made up to 5 days ahead and stored in an airtight container in the fridge. Let it come to room temperature before serving, or warm it slightly in the microwave if it is too thick.

thai red curry with tofu, mango, and sugar snap peas

 This dish is simple and elegant. I feel a bit guilty resorting to prepared curry paste, but the resulting sauce is very good. Be sure to use mangoes that are still on the firm side, or they'll turn to mush in the skillet.

SERVES 4

1½ 16-ounce cartons firm tofu

2 tablespoons canola oil

Kosher salt to taste

1 large red onion, thinly sliced

2 cups sugar snap peas, stem ends removed

2 garlic cloves, minced

½ cup unsweetened coconut milk (see page 446)

2 teaspoons Thai red curry paste, or more to taste

1 mango, peeled and cut into ½-inch cubes (see note)

1 tablespoon fresh lime juice (½ juicy lime)

⅓ cup coarsely chopped unsalted toasted cashews (page 283) for garnish

¼ cup fresh cilantro leaves for garnish (optional)

Basmati Rice (page 200) or Jasmine Rice (page 201)

1 One at a time, wrap the blocks of tofu in a clean dishtowel and press it firmly with your hands until you feel the towel become damp. Unwrap the tofu and cut it into ½-inch cubes. In a large, well-seasoned skillet, heat the canola oil over medium-high heat. Add the tofu and salt it liberally. Fry the tofu undisturbed until a dark golden crust forms on the bottom, then use a spatula to turn it and brown it well on at least one more side, 4 to 5 minutes per side.

veggie cuisine hits small connecticut town

My sister Lisa lives in our Connecticut hometown with her husband and three children. It's a beautiful place, with manicured lawns and picturesque views of the ocean. But it's a town where many of the residents resist the idea of a vegetarian dinner, let alone a vegetarian diet. Nonetheless my sister invited me down from Boston to test recipes on her guests at her annual paddle tennis party. Just before the meatless meal, she offered a blessing. We held hands tightly and lowered our heads as Lisa began her prayer: "Please, Lord, help us eat this food . . ."

2 Add the onion, sugar snap peas, and garlic to the skillet, and cook for 1 minute. Stir in the coconut milk and curry paste, and bring to a simmer. Cook, stirring occasionally, until the peas lose their raw texture, about 2 minutes.

3 Stir in the mango and heat through. Remove from the heat, stir in the lime juice, and season with salt. Transfer to a serving dish and garnish with the cashews and cilantro, if using, just before serving with the rice.

Note

The mango can be cut up to 1 day ahead and stored in an airtight container in the fridge. To dice the flesh of a mango, make 2 straight cuts down the length of the fruit on opposite sides of the pit. Holding one half of the mango cut side up on the work surface, make crosshatch cuts into the flesh about 1 inch apart, down to but not through the skin. Push the skin side of the mango inward, as if you were turning the mango inside out, and cut along the skin to release the cubes of flesh. Repeat with the second half of the mango.

curried cauliflower with tomatoes and tofu

Cauliflower has a lot to offer if we just learn how to tap into its talents. In this dish, tomatoes and yogurt blend with ginger, cilantro, and spices to create a sauce for the cauliflower and pan-fried tofu. This dish is fast and healthy and makes a meal. Feel free to use Garam Masala (page 209) instead of the cumin.

SERVES 4

1 Wrap the block of tofu in a clean dishtowel and press it firmly with your hands until you feel the towel become damp. Unwrap the tofu and cut it into $1/2$-inch cubes. In a large, well-seasoned skillet, heat 1 tablespoon of the canola oil over medium-high heat. Add the tofu and salt it liberally. Fry the tofu undisturbed until a dark golden crust forms on the bottom, then use a spatula to turn it and brown it well on at least one more side, 4 to 5 minutes per side. Transfer to a plate lined with paper towels.

2 Add the remaining 2 tablespoons canola oil to the skillet. Add the chiles, ginger, cumin, and coriander and cook for 2 minutes, stirring constantly. Add the cauliflower and $1/2$ teaspoon kosher

- 1 16-ounce carton firm tofu
- 3 tablespoons canola oil
  Kosher salt
- 1–2 small, skinny chile peppers, minced
- 2 tablespoons peeled and minced fresh ginger
- 2 teaspoons ground cumin
- 1 tablespoon ground coriander
- 1 medium head cauliflower, cut into florets
- 7 plum tomatoes (about 1 pound), cut into $1/2$-inch cubes
- $1/2$ cup plain yogurt
- 3 tablespoons chopped fresh cilantro
- 1 tablespoon butter (optional)

  Basmati Rice (page 200)

My sister, who is a busy woman, drove to two stores to get all the ingredients for one of my simplest recipes. There was no cilantro at the first store.

My mother is another family member who never departs from a recipe, although she's an excellent veteran cook. She and my sister seem to forget that most recipes were created from whims (hopefully tested whims), not scientific formulas.

If you leave out one or two ingredients or make substitutions, chances are the recipe will still work and taste good. (Pastries, cookies, and cakes *don't* follow this logic.) If there's one way I could make a difference in this world, it would be to teach people not to take recipes too seriously.

salt and stir-fry until the florets are slightly browned, 3 to 4 minutes. Add the tomatoes and $1/2$ cup water, cover, and reduce the heat to low. Simmer until the cauliflower stems are just tender, shaking the pan occasionally to keep the vegetables from sticking, about 10 minutes.

3 Just before serving, stir in the tofu and heat through. Add the yogurt, cilantro, and butter, if using. Stir until heated through and season with salt, but do not boil or the yogurt will curdle. Serve with the rice.

saag paneer

Saag is a Hindi word that refers to green leafy vegetables, and paneer is the yogurt-based cheese that is a traditional component of this dish. Using tofu instead of paneer spares you the time it takes to make the yogurt cheese—tofu, after all, is a fresh cheese made from soy milk. For a real treat, serve this dish with Roti Jala (page 358), a quick flatbread.

SERVES 4

1 16-ounce carton firm tofu

2 tablespoons butter

2 tablespoons canola oil

Kosher salt to taste

1 large onion, finely chopped

1½ tablespoons peeled and minced fresh ginger

4 garlic cloves, minced

1 teaspoon ground coriander

1 teaspoon Garam Masala (page 209)

2 pounds fresh spinach, stemmed

4 plum tomatoes, cut into ½-inch cubes

1 teaspoon asafetida powder (see page 443; optional)

2 teaspoons Asian chili sauce (see page 443)

½ cup sour cream

Squeeze of fresh lemon juice

Basmati Rice (page 200)

1 Wrap the block of tofu in a clean dishtowel and press it firmly with your hands until you feel the towel become damp. Unwrap the tofu and cut it into ½-inch cubes. In a large, well-seasoned skillet, heat 1 tablespoon of the butter and 1 tablespoon of the canola oil over medium-high heat. Add the tofu and salt it liberally. Fry the tofu undisturbed until a light golden crust forms on the bottom, then use a spatula to turn it and brown it well on at least one more side. Transfer to a plate lined with paper towels.

2 Reduce the heat to medium and add the remaining 1 tablespoon butter and 1 tablespoon oil to the skillet. Add the onion and sauté until it starts to brown, 9 to 11 minutes. Add the ginger, garlic, coriander, and garam masala and sauté for 2 minutes more. Stir in the spinach by the handful, adding more once the previous batch wilts. Stir in the tomatoes, asafetida, if using, and chili sauce and cook for 5 minutes more. Add the tofu and sour cream. Season liberally with salt and add a squeeze of lemon juice. Stir until heated through, but do not boil or the sour cream will curdle. Serve hot over the basmati rice.

Note The spiced spinach can be prepared up to 1 day ahead, but refrain from preparing the tofu. You can add tofu, as well as the sour cream and lemon juice, within an hour of serving.

five-spice seitan and asparagus

(V) *This Chinese five-spice sauce* is absolutely stellar, so even if you don't love seitan, try the same recipe with tofu or tempeh (using water instead of the seitan juices). You can also substitute broccoli for the asparagus. This is a fast meal to serve to a friend, perhaps after work.

SERVES 2

1 In a medium bowl, combine the ginger, garlic, sesame oil, soy sauce, sugar or honey, and five-spice powder. Add the seitan and reserved liquid and toss to coat. Cover the bowl with plastic wrap and marinate for at least 2 hours and up to 3 days in the fridge.

2 Heat a large skillet over medium-high heat. Add the seitan along with the marinade, the asparagus, and the bell pepper. Stir-fry until the asparagus is bright green and tender but still crunchy, 5 to 7 minutes. Serve over bowls of jasmine rice, garnished with the scallions and a squeeze of lime.

2 rounded tablespoons peeled and minced fresh ginger

3 garlic cloves, minced

2 tablespoons toasted sesame oil

2 tablespoons soy sauce

1 tablespoon sugar or honey

1 teaspoon five-spice powder (see page 446)

8 ounces seitan, cut into bite-size pieces, 2 tablespoons liquid reserved

½ pound asparagus, cut crosswise into ½-inch pieces

1 small red bell pepper, cut into ½-inch pieces

Jasmine Rice (page 201)

6 scallions, white and green parts, chopped, for garnish

2 lime wedges

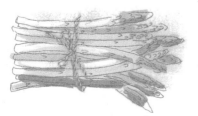

tempeh and spinach in peanut sauce

(V) *If you have friends coming over* and a well-stocked freezer, you can whip up this dish without making a trip to the store. Tempeh is a dream to freeze: it's already wrapped, and it only needs to be left at room temperature for an hour or microwaved to thaw.

SERVES 3

1 Place the spinach in a colander set in the sink and press out most of the liquid with a rubber spatula.

2 In a large, well-seasoned skillet, heat the canola oil over medium heat. Add the tempeh and fry until golden brown on the bottom. Salt the tempeh liberally. Shake the skillet vigorously and brown another side of the tempeh. Stir in the spinach and water chestnuts and heat through. Serve over rice or noodles and spoon the peanut sauce on top. Sprinkle with the scallions or cilantro, if desired.

1 10-ounce package frozen chopped spinach, thawed

2 teaspoons canola oil

8 ounces tempeh, cut into ½-inch cubes

   Kosher salt to taste

½ cup coarsely chopped water chestnuts

   Jasmine Rice (page 201), Coconut Rice (page 202), or cooked Asian noodles

   All-Purpose Peanut Sauce (page 350), at room temperature

   Chopped scallions, white and green parts, or fresh cilantro for garnish (optional)

tempeh and bok choy in black bean sauce

 There aren't many ways to convert the tempeh-phobic, but here's one of them. You can find Chinese fermented black beans at Asian markets.

SERVES 4

1 tablespoon Chinese fermented black beans (see page 445)

3 garlic cloves, minced

1 tablespoon peeled and minced fresh ginger

1 teaspoon sugar

3 tablespoons sherry

1 tablespoon soy sauce, plus more if needed

2 tablespoons canola oil

8 ounces tempeh, cut into ½-inch cubes

Kosher salt to taste

4 cups thinly sliced bok choy or Chinese mustard greens

12 fresh shiitake mushrooms, stems discarded and caps halved

1 teaspoon Asian chili sauce (see page 443)

Jasmine Rice (page 201), Coconut Rice (page 202), or cooked Asian noodles

1 tablespoon toasted sesame seeds (see page 450) for garnish

1 In a small sieve, rinse the beans under cold running water and drain well. Chop them coarsely. In a small bowl, combine the beans, garlic, ginger, sugar, sherry, and soy sauce and mix well. Set aside.

2 In a large, well-seasoned skillet, heat 1 tablespoon of the canola oil over medium heat. Add the tempeh and fry until golden brown on the bottom. Salt it liberally. Shake the skillet vigorously and brown another side of the tempeh. Transfer to a plate.

3 Add the remaining 1 tablespoon canola oil to the skillet. Add the bok choy or mustard greens and the shiitakes and sauté, stirring occasionally, until the shiitakes are soft, about 4 minutes. Return the tempeh to the skillet, add the bean mixture, and stir to coat. Cook for 2 minutes more, or until heated through.

4 Remove from the heat and add the chili sauce. Stir well, and taste for seasoning, adding more soy sauce if necessary. Spoon over bowls of rice or noodles, sprinkle with the sesame seeds, and serve.

Note

The sauce (through step 1) can be prepared and the vegetables chopped up to 1 day ahead. Store in separate airtight containers in the fridge.

tempeh: the next great frontier

Like tofu, tempeh can replace poultry and other meat in many recipes. Unlike tofu, tempeh has real flavor. Tempeh is made with a starter, similar to the process involved in making blue cheese. Cooked soybeans are tossed with a culture (usually derived from mushrooms) and a powdered grain, such as rice or millet, for added flavor. This mixture is left at room temperature for a day or so to ferment and form a cake held together by mycelium, a cottonlike substance that forms from the fermentation. Tempeh's flavor is slightly reminiscent of that of a nutty cheese, and its texture is similar to that of brown rice bread.

But you must try it for yourself. Here's how: Slice an onion and sauté it over medium heat in a bit of oil until it starts to brown, about 10 minutes. Transfer to a plate. Cube 4 ounces of tempeh, salt it, and sauté in a bit more oil until it is brown on one side. Flip with a spatula and brown another side. Eat the tempeh with the onions and your favorite hot sauce (Inner Beauty is great for this) or peanut sauce (pages 221, 350, and 351).

tempeh rendang

(V) *The heady scents of lemongrass,* star anise, cardamom, cinnamon, and cloves act as an inexpensive form of aromatherapy as you prepare this dish. Rendang is a traditional Malaysian recipe for beef (originally for old, overworked buffalo). The Malaysians would cook the buffalo for hours, until the tired meat turned tender. Fortunately, tempeh is naturally tender. I scrub my sweet potatoes clean but leave the skin on for eating.

SERVES 4

lemongrass paste

- 1 lemongrass stalk
- 3 shallots, quartered
- 3 garlic cloves
- 2 small, skinny chile peppers, sliced

tempeh

- 1/4 cup dried, unsweetened coconut
- 2 tablespoons canola oil
- 8 ounces tempeh, cut into 1/2-inch cubes

  Kosher salt to taste

- 1 teaspoon ground star anise, or 1 teaspoon fennel seeds, ground in a spice mill
- 1/2 teaspoon ground cardamom
- 1/2 teaspoon ground cinnamon

- 1/4 teaspoon ground cloves
- 1 sweet potato, cut into 1/2-inch cubes
- 3/4 cup unsweetened coconut milk (see page 446)

  Freshly ground black pepper to taste

- 2 scallions, white and green parts, thinly sliced on the bias, for garnish

  Jasmine Rice (page 201) or Roti Jala (page 358)

Note

The rendang can be made up to 2 days ahead and stored in an airtight container in the fridge. Reheat on the stove, stirring constantly, or in the microwave. Add the scallions just before serving.

1 **To make the lemongrass paste:** Cut off the bulbous bottom third of the lemongrass stalk. (Save the rest of the stalk for another use.) Remove and discard the tough outer leaves. With a large, sharp chef's knife, cut the lemongrass bottom into thin rounds. Transfer to a blender and finely chop. You should have about 3 tablespoons. Add the shallots, garlic, and chiles and puree to form a thick paste, adding 2 to 3 tablespoons water if necessary.

2 **To make the tempeh:** In a large, dry skillet, toast the coconut over medium heat, shaking the pan and stirring constantly until it becomes a uniform dark golden brown (don't let it get too dark), 5 to 7 minutes. Transfer to a plate.

3 In the same skillet, heat the canola oil over medium-high heat. Add the tempeh and fry until golden brown on the bottom. Salt the tempeh liberally. Shake the skillet vigorously and brown another side of the tempeh, 3 to 5 minutes per side. Add the lemongrass paste, ground star anise or ground fennel, cardamom, cinnamon, and cloves and cook for 2 minutes more.

4 Add the sweet potato, coconut milk, and 1 cup water, cover, and boil for 5 minutes. Uncover and boil for 2 minutes more, stirring frequently, until the sweet potato is tender. Remove from the heat and add the coconut. Season with salt and pepper. Garnish with scallions just before serving with the rice or Roti Jala.

it's filo, not fido!

I've noticed that a lot of my friends are naming their pets after foods these days. I only hope the animals outlive the food fad for which they were named.

Okra (dog)
Miso (dog)
Juniper (cat)
Popcorn (poodle)
Tofu (dog)
Chai (dog)
Quinoa (dog)
Nestlé (dog)
Coffee (chocolate lab)
Nori (actually a teenager, but close enough)
Beaujolais (dog)
Saffron (cat)

long-life tempeh stir-fry

(V) *This stir-fry provides* a large range of nutrients in one meal. Broccoli and cabbage are cruciferous vegetables, which help to ward off cancer. Sweet potatoes are high in vitamins A and C, and tempeh is a good source of protein and vitamin A. Peanuts have phosphorus, folic acid, magnesium, and calcium.

SERVES 4

1 In a small bowl, combine the soy sauce, brown sugar, and cornstarch. Set aside.

2 In a large, well-seasoned skillet, heat the canola oil over medium heat. Add the tempeh and fry until golden brown on the bottom. Shake the skillet vigorously and brown another side of the tempeh, 3 to 5 minutes per side. Add the broccoli, cabbage, sweet potato, ginger, and garlic, and cook, stirring, for 1 minute more.

3 Add the soy mixture and ¹⁄₃ cup water and bring to a boil, stirring often. Reduce the heat, cover, and simmer just until the sauce is thickened and the vegetables are cooked through, 4 to 5 minutes. Serve hot over bowls of rice, garnished with the scallions and peanuts.

¹⁄₄ cup soy sauce

1 tablespoon light or dark brown sugar

1 teaspoon cornstarch

2 tablespoons canola oil

8 ounces tempeh, cut into ¹⁄₂-inch cubes

3 cups broccoli florets and sliced stems

3 cups thinly sliced green cabbage

1 sweet potato, peeled and grated

2 tablespoons peeled and minced fresh ginger

1 tablespoon minced garlic

Basmati Rice (page 200) or Jasmine Rice (page 201)

1 bunch scallions, white and green parts, thinly sliced, for garnish

¹⁄₂ cup coarsely chopped unsalted roasted peanuts (see page 449) for garnish

chapter 6

Noodles Unite

Lemongrass

Soy Sauce

Hot!

Soy Sauce

Lime

Mung Bean Sprouts

廣東鷄蛋麵
CHINESE NOODLES

pasta without pressure

Noodles are comfort food that can be easily elevated to party food. It's nice to keep a little collection of your favorite types of noodles on hand so that you'll always be prepared if people come over. Simple meals that can be made in a few minutes are just as delicious as more complex ones.

Many of the Asian noodle dishes in this chapter can be prepared earlier in the day, so you don't have to worry about keeping tabs on the noodles as they boil, having them stick together, getting everyone to the table in split-second timing, or doling out the unruly strands before they cool.

Mediterranean pasta must be cooked just before serving, so things will be infinitely easier if you save it for small groups. Here are a few tips:

- Bring a large pot of water to a boil, then reduce the heat to a low simmer up to 2 hours before cooking the pasta. That way you won't have to wait for the water to boil at the last minute.

- Warm the serving plates in a 200-degree oven.

- Put a tablespoon of olive oil in the pot as the pasta is boiling. To prevent sticking when it's time to drain the pasta, don't rinse it, but add a bit more olive oil right in the colander.

- Serve the pasta from the pot, keeping the pot on a low burner so it stays piping hot once the other ingredients are mixed in. Using tongs makes it easier to serve.

angel hair with peas, walnuts, and mint

The flavors of mint, olive oil, walnuts, garlic, and feta are sublime with angel hair pasta. Serve a salad that is fully prepared in advance, such as Asparagus Slaw (page 116), as a first course, since the pasta will demand your attention at the last minute.

SERVES 4

½ cup walnut pieces

1 cup frozen peas, thawed

½ cup lightly packed coarsely chopped fresh mint leaves

1–2 garlic cloves

7 tablespoons extra-virgin olive oil

Kosher salt to taste

12 ounces dried angel hair

1 cup crumbled feta cheese (creamy French goat's milk feta works well)

Freshly ground black pepper to taste

1 Preheat the oven to 350 degrees. Spread the walnuts in a single layer on a rimmed baking sheet and toast for 5 minutes, or until golden brown. Let cool.

2 In a food processor, puree the walnuts, ½ cup of the peas, the mint, garlic, and 4 tablespoons of the olive oil until smooth.

3 Meanwhile, bring a large pot of salted water to a boil. Add the angel hair and return to a boil, stirring to separate the noodles. Boil for 3 to 5 minutes, or until al dente. Drain, reserving 3 tablespoons of the pasta water. Return the pasta to the pot. Add the walnut mixture, feta, remaining ½ cup peas, remaining 3 tablespoons olive oil, and reserved pasta water and toss until well mixed. Season with salt and pepper. Serve immediately.

Note The walnut mixture can be made up to 1 day ahead and stored in an airtight container in the fridge.

linguine with broccoli rabe, pecans, and feta

This recipe is a pleasure to make because it's simple, yet it nets you a meal worthy of a fine restaurant. The sauce can be prepared ahead of time, so all you'll have to do is cook the pasta just before serving.

SERVES 6

1 **Bring a large saucepan of water** to a boil. Blanch the broccoli rabe just until it turns bright green, about 2 minutes. Drain immediately, and rinse under cold running water, and drain well. Set aside.

2 **Bring a large pot of salted water** to a boil. Add the linguine and return to a boil, stirring to separate the noodles. Boil for 8 to 10 minutes, or until al dente. Drain, reserving ¼ cup of the cooking water, then return the pasta and the reserved cooking water to the pot.

3 **Meanwhile, in a large skillet,** heat the olive oil over medium heat. Add the leek and sauté until translucent, 7 to 9 minutes. Add the garlic and sauté for 1 minute. Add the broccoli

1 bunch broccoli rabe, trimmed and cut crosswise into 1-inch pieces

Kosher salt to taste

1 pound dried linguine

⅓ cup extra-virgin olive oil

1 leek, white and light green parts only, thinly sliced crosswise and washed well

4 garlic cloves, minced

½ teaspoon crushed red pepper flakes

2 teaspoons grated fresh lemon rind

3 tablespoons fresh lemon juice (about 1 juicy lemon)

1 cup chopped toasted pecans (see page 283)

Freshly ground black pepper to taste

1 cup crumbled feta cheese (I prefer French goat's milk feta)

rabe and red pepper flakes and heat through. Remove from the heat and stir in the lemon rind and juice and almost all of the pecans, reserving 2 tablespoons for the garnish. Season liberally with salt and pepper. Add the sauce and the feta to the hot pasta and toss to coat well. Taste for seasoning, adding more salt or pepper if necessary. Serve immediately, garnished with the remaining 2 tablespoons pecans.

Note

The sauce can be made up to 24 hours ahead and stored in an airtight container in the fridge.

Broccoli

how to clean up your home in 30 minutes!*

Friends are coming in two hours. You've finished cooking, and the kitchen is pretty clean. Now all you have to do is tidy up the rest of the place. These seven easy steps will keep you from veering off your path to a clean dwelling.

Step One (30 seconds): Who can clean in silence? Find a CD with a fast tempo and crank it up.

Step Two (5 minutes): Grab a heavy-duty garbage bag. Pick up misplaced belongings: baseball hats, CDs, toys, newspapers, knitting projects, and junk mail and toss it all in the bag (no pets, please). Stash the bag behind your bed or in a vacant closet and deal with it the next day.

Step Three (6 minutes): Attack the bathroom. Take a sponge with spray cleaner and wipe down the floor, sink, and toilet. The bathtub can be avoided if you have a shower curtain. Check to see if your towels are clean, and make sure there's plenty of toilet paper on the roll.

Step Four (3 minutes): Rehydration/pep rally: Pat yourself on the back and treat yourself to a cold drink.

Step Five (8 minutes): Okay, stop lollygagging. Sweep the kitchen and vacuum the rugs and floors, if necessary.

Step Six (3 minutes): Give your home a final glance. Remember, people like a place that looks lived in.

Step Seven (3 minutes): If there are certain parts of your home that are shabby or unkempt, turn off the lights and use candles. No one will be able to determine if the area is condemned or cozy if it's dimly lit. Now calm your pet, whose nerves have been rattled by the vacuum and your frenzied state.

Congratulations! Your house is now clean to the unsuspecting eye—and you still have 2½ minutes to lie down and relax!

*NOTE: This seven-step program of superficial housecleaning has been designed for modest homes and apartments. Homes where one gets easily lost or homes that have been sorely neglected for months are in a different league. Look in the Yellow Pages under housecleaning.

thai rice noodles with cilantro-ginger sauce

(V) *Like pad thai,* this rice noodle dish is in a sauce that contains lime juice and a bit of sugar, but it also includes a hefty amount of ginger and caramelized onions and, unlike pad thai, not even a molecule of garlic. Use a well-seasoned pan, such as a cast-iron skillet.

SERVES 4

- 12 ounces fettuccine-width dried rice noodles
- 3 tablespoons canola oil
- 2 medium onions, thinly sliced
- 2 plum tomatoes, halved lengthwise, then cut crosswise into half-moons
- 1–2 jalapeño peppers, seeded and minced
- 2 tablespoons peeled and minced fresh ginger
- 1 teaspoon ground cumin

- 1 tablespoon sugar
- 3 tablespoons fresh lime juice (1½ juicy limes)
- ½ cup coarsely chopped fresh cilantro leaves and stems
- 1 teaspoon kosher salt or 1 tablespoon Asian fish sauce (see page 444), or more to taste
- ¼ cup crushed peanuts for garnish (optional)

1 In a large bowl of hot water, soak the rice noodles for 20 minutes. Drain well. Set aside.

2 In a large, well-seasoned skillet, heat the canola oil over medium heat. Add the onions and sauté, stirring occasionally, until golden brown, 9 to 11 minutes. Add the tomatoes, jalapeños, ginger, and cumin and sauté for 2 minutes more.

3 Add the noodles, sugar, and ½ cup water and cook, stirring often, until the noodles soften, about 3 minutes. Remove from the heat and add the lime juice, cilantro, and plenty of salt or fish sauce to taste. Divide among four plates, garnish with the crushed peanuts, if using, and serve immediately.

fresh rice noodles with tofu and turnip in malaysian black pepper sauce

In this dish, fresh tofu really makes a difference—its flavor is milder and its texture is softer. You can buy fresh tofu in Asian markets (often packed in plastic tubs, not vacuum-packed) or at whole food stores (in loose blocks stored in a large tub of water). If you're at an Asian market, serve with fresh rice noodles (see page 450), since they are so yummy. Just pan-fry them in a touch of sesame oil right before serving. The dish also works with Jasmine Rice (page 201).

SERVES 4

- 1 16-ounce carton firm tofu (preferably fresh, see above)
- 1 large turnip or small rutabaga (about 1 pound), peeled and cut into 1/2-inch cubes
- 2 shallots or 1 small onion, thinly sliced
- 2–3 small, skinny chile peppers, minced
- 8 curry leaves (see page 446; optional)
- 2 tablespoons vegetarian oyster sauce (see page 453)
- 2 teaspoons miso (see page 448)
- 1 teaspoon freshly ground Sichuan peppercorns (see page 451)

- 1 teaspoon freshly ground black pepper (use a little less for timid tongues)
- 1 teaspoon kosher salt
- 3 tablespoons butter
- 4 garlic cloves, minced
- 3 scallions, white and green parts, cut into 3-inch lengths
- 16 ounces fresh rice noodles, pan-fried

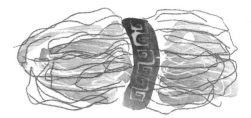

1 Wrap the block of tofu in a clean dishtowel and press it firmly with your hands until you feel the towel become damp. Unwrap the tofu and cut it into $1/2$-inch cubes. In a large bowl, combine the tofu, turnip or rutabaga, shallots or onion, chiles, curry leaves (if using), oyster sauce, miso, Sichuan pepper, black pepper, and salt and mix well.

2 In a large skillet, melt the butter over medium heat. Add the garlic and sauté for 2 minutes; do not let the garlic brown. Stir in the tofu mixture and $1^1/4$ cups water and simmer until the turnip or rutabaga is tender. Add a bit more water if the mixture becomes dry; there should be enough sauce to generously coat the mixture. Stir in the scallions. Serve immediately over the rice noodles, instructing your guests to remove the curry leaves as they eat.

fresh rice noodles

There's no question that these silky, luxurious fresh noodles are one of the treasures of Asian markets. Packaged in plastic bags, the noodles are actually one large, supple sheet, folded over many times. It's easy to improvise with them. I usually cut the noodle into large pieces and fry them in a bit of oil with garlic and a leafy vegetable such as Chinese mustard greens. When the noodles become crisp, I add some soy sauce, a little toasted sesame oil, a chopped chile, and a squeeze of lime.

Fresh rice noodles have no substitute. In a pinch, dried rice noodles are acceptable, but you lose a lot of the velvety texture of the real thing.

chinese noodles in chile oil

(V) *This dish takes barely any effort at all*, yet it's one of my favorites. This is its genesis: about ten years ago, I ordered pasta with chile oil at Biba, a swank restaurant in Boston. Each piece of spaghetti was rolled by hand, and each strand was lumpy and uneven, as if the pasta maker had a bad case of the shakes when rolling it. But the uneven texture (or the uneven personality of the pasta maker) helped me drag the spicy oil right into my mouth. I couldn't get this dish out of my mind.

Unless you want to hand-roll your own pasta, use fresh Chinese wheat noodles (see page 445). They aren't the same, but they hold on to the oil and taste great. If you like, you can add any blanched vegetable to this dish. I like to serve it plain followed by a salad.

SERVES 3 OR 4

5 tablespoons extra-virgin olive oil

1 small onion, chopped

4–6 dried 2-3-inch-long New Mexican chiles, ground with a spice mill or a mortar and pestle

2 garlic cloves, minced

Kosher salt to taste

1 1-pound package fresh Chinese wheat or rice noodles (see page 245) or 8 ounces dried spaghetti

3 tablespoons toasted black or white sesame seeds (see page 450)

1 In a small skillet, heat the olive oil over medium heat. Add the onion and sauté, stirring frequently, until golden brown, 9 to 11 minutes. Stir in the ground chiles and garlic and sauté for 1 minute more; do not brown the garlic. Remove from the heat and season liberally with salt (I recommend at least ¹/₂ teaspoon).

chinese noodles—the affordable fresh pasta

Fresh Chinese wheat noodles, available in most supermarkets, are soft and chewy. They're a treat *and* a deal, often costing half the price of fresh Italian pasta. These versatile noodles, often labeled *mein* or *lo mein,* are sold in 1-pound bags in most supermarkets near the produce. Before using, they must be boiled until tender, about 4 minutes, then drained and rinsed well under cold running water.

In the following recipes, fully cooked Chinese noodles can be tossed with the vegetables and sauce (omit the rice). The noodles are greedy, so you'll have to work to distribute the sauce evenly. They're also bland, so be sure to season liberally with salt and pepper before serving. These recipes require a 1-pound bag of noodles unless otherwise noted.

- **Five-Spice Seitan and Asparagus** (page 228; use ½ pound noodles)
- **Tempeh and Bok Choy in Black Bean Sauce** (page 230)—increase the canola oil to 3 tablespoons and serve this *over* the hot noodles. Boil them just before serving and do not rinse them.
- **Tofu, Broccoli, and Tomatoes with Curried Peanut Sauce** (page 220)
- **Thai Red Curry with Tofu, Mango, and Sugar Snap Peas** (page 222)

2 Meanwhile, bring a large pot of salted water to a boil. Add the noodles or spaghetti and return to a boil, stirring to separate the strands. Boil until tender, 4 to 5 minutes for Chinese noodles or 8 to 10 minutes for spaghetti. Drain and immediately return the noodles to the warm pot.

3 Add the chile oil to the noodles and toss to coat. Taste and add more salt, if desired. Divide between three or four plates, sprinkle with sesame seeds, and serve immediately.

chinese noodles in spicy lemongrass sauce with peanuts

Ⓥ *If you have a green vegetable* in your fridge, this Vietnamese-inspired dish will gladly accommodate it. Just chop it and add it along with the edamame. For a more authentic flavor, add a teaspoon of Asian fish sauce instead of the salt if you aren't a strict vegetarian. Please note that you must freeze the ginger for at least 1 hour before preparing this dish, which will enable you to squeeze out the juice.

SERVES 4

1 5-inch piece fresh ginger, frozen
   Kosher salt

16 ounces thin, fresh Chinese wheat noodles (see page 445) or 8 ounces dried spaghetti

2 lemongrass stalks

1 16-ounce carton firm tofu, cut into 1/2-inch cubes

4 garlic cloves, minced

1 bunch scallions, white and green parts, thinly sliced on the diagonal

1 cup frozen shelled (podless) edamame (see page 446)

1 cup drained sliced water chestnuts

1/2 lime, cut into 2 large wedges

1 cup bean sprouts (optional)

3/4 cup coarsely chopped fresh cilantro or basil leaves

1/2 cup finely chopped unsalted roasted peanuts (see page 449)

2–4 small, skinny chile peppers, minced

Soy sauce and toasted sesame oil

> *Many gatherings have to do with energy. If the people are right and click, it happens. A welcoming atmosphere has a lot to do with it. Good food and drink, whether simple or elegant, make an event work, and a relaxed, open, and genuinely giving host makes everyone feel welcome and comfortable.*
>
> — **Jesse Cool**, author of *Your Organic Kitchen*

1 Thaw the ginger either at room temperature or in the microwave and cut it in two. Over a small bowl, squeeze the pieces of ginger as much as you can, so that the juice runs into the bowl. You should have about ¹/₃ cup.

2 Bring a large pot of salted water to a boil. Add the noodles or spaghetti and return to a boil, stirring to separate the strands. Boil until tender, 4 to 5 minutes for fresh Chinese noodles or 8 to 10 minutes for spaghetti. Drain, rinse quickly under cold running water, and drain again. Set aside.

3 Cut off the bulbous bottom third of the lemongrass stalks (reserve the rest of the stalks for another use). Remove and discard the tough outer leaves. With a large, sharp chef's knife, cut the lemongrass bottom into very thin rounds.

4 In a large saucepan, bring 6 cups water to a boil over medium-high heat. Add the ginger juice, tofu, lemongrass, garlic, and 1 teaspoon salt. Reduce the heat to a simmer, cover, and cook for 8 minutes. Add the scallions, edamame, water chestnuts, and noodles and heat through.

5 Distribute the noodles or spaghetti, vegetables, and broth among four bowls. Squeeze the lime wedges judiciously over each serving. Top each serving with some of the bean sprouts (if using), cilantro or basil, peanuts, and chiles. Serve immediately. Pass the soy sauce and sesame oil at the table for diners to drizzle slowly over the noodles or spaghetti.

crispy bun (noodle) tofu

(V) *As chef at Pho République,* a French-Vietnamese bistro in Cambridge, Massachusetts, I enjoyed taking liberties with traditional Vietnamese dishes. In this dish, I not only replaced the original beef with tofu but used wheat noodles instead of rice noodles and served it hot instead of cold. The sauce, made from fresh mint, lime juice, chili sauce, and garlic, is exceptional. Chinese egg noodles are available at Asian markets. Feel free to substitute your own favorite vegetables, such as zucchini, scallions, jicama, or cucumber.

SERVES 4

Kosher salt

8 ounces very thin fresh Chinese egg noodles or fresh Chinese wheat noodles (see page 445)

1½ teaspoons plus 2 tablespoons canola oil

1 cup packed fresh mint leaves

1½ tablespoons sugar

2 garlic cloves

¼ cup fresh lime juice (2 juicy limes)

1 teaspoon kosher salt or 2 tablespoons Asian fish sauce (see page 444)

Asian chili sauce (see page 443) to taste (I use 2 teaspoons)

1 carrot, peeled and grated or cut into matchsticks

1 cup thinly sliced red cabbage

1 cup bean sprouts

½ small red onion, thinly sliced

2 tablespoons chopped fresh cilantro (optional)

⅓ cup chopped unsalted roasted peanuts (see page 449)

Pan-Fried Tofu (see page 217; optional)

Cilantro sprigs for garnish (optional)

1 Bring a large pot of salted water to a boil. Add the noodles and return to a boil, stirring to separate the noodles. Boil until tender, 2 to 3 minutes for egg noodles or about 4 minutes for wheat noodles. Drain, rinse quickly under cold running water and drain again. Set aside.

2 In a food processor, combine 1½ teaspoons of the canola oil with the mint, sugar, garlic, lime juice, salt or fish sauce, and chili sauce and puree until the mint and garlic are finely chopped. In a large bowl, combine the carrot, cabbage, bean sprouts, onion, and cilantro, if using, pour the sauce over them, and toss to combine. Set aside.

3 About 15 minutes before serving, in a large, well-seasoned skillet (preferably not nonstick), heat 1 tablespoon of the canola oil over medium-high heat. Add half of the cold noodles, patting them into a large pancake with a metal spatula or large spoon. Reduce the heat to medium and fry until lightly browned on the bottom, 8 to 10 minutes. Shake the skillet to loosen any stuck noodles and place a large platter or lid over the skillet. Flip the noodle cake out onto the platter or lid, then

slide it back into the skillet, crispy side up. When the second side has browned, 8 to 10 minutes, slide the noodle cake onto a platter and cover it loosely with a dishtowel to keep warm. Repeat with the remaining noodles and the remaining 1 tablespoon canola oil to make a second noodle cake.

4 Add the peanuts to the carrot mixture and mix lightly. Cut the noodle cakes into wedges, arrange on four plates, and top with the carrot mixture. If using the Pan-Fried Tofu, arrange it around the noodle cakes. When you have finished dividing the carrot mixture, drizzle any remaining sauce in the bottom of the bowl over each plate. Serve immediately, garnished with the cilantro sprigs, if desired.

Note

The carrot mixture must be made on the same day it's served. The noodles can be boiled up to 3 days ahead and fried up to 4 hours ahead (keep the noodle cakes at room temperature and reheat on a baking sheet in a 350-degree oven).

mee goreng (pan-fried noodles)

 Finally, you can burn something and feel good about it. This traditional Malaysian dish calls for slightly burning the noodles, which gives them a wonderful smoky flavor. It's great for entertaining, because the flavor improves with reheating. If you can't find Asian mustard greens, kale or collard greens will do.

SERVES 4

2 cups dried shiitake mushrooms (see page 451)

Kosher salt to taste

16 ounces thick fresh Chinese egg noodles or dried spaghetti

½ 16-ounce carton firm tofu

3 tablespoons canola oil

⅓ pound Asian mustard greens, thinly sliced

3–4 garlic cloves, thinly sliced

1–3 teaspoons Asian chili sauce (see page 443)

5 tablespoons ketchup

3 tablespoons vegetarian oyster sauce (see page 453)

2 tablespoons soy sauce

2 tablespoons sugar

2 cups bean sprouts

¼ cup ground peanuts (optional)

2 scallions, white and green parts, finely chopped, for garnish

2 tablespoons chopped fresh cilantro for garnish (optional)

1 lime, quartered, for garnish

1 In a medium bowl, soak the shiitakes in boiling water for 20 minutes. Drain the shiitakes, squeezing them gently to remove excess liquid. Cut off and discard the stems. Thinly slice the caps. Set aside.

2 Bring a large pot of salted water to a boil. Add the noodles or spaghetti and return to a boil, stirring to separate the strands. Boil until al dente, 2 to 3 minutes for egg noodles or 8 to 9 minutes for spaghetti. Drain, rinse quickly under cold running water, and drain again. Set aside.

3 Wrap the block of tofu in a clean dishtowel and press it firmly with your hands until you feel the towel become damp. Unwrap the tofu and cut it into $1/2$-inch cubes. In a large, well-seasoned skillet or wok, heat 2 tablespoons of the canola oil over medium-high heat. Add the tofu and salt it liberally. Fry the tofu undisturbed until a dark golden crust forms on the bottom, then use a spatula to turn it and brown it well on at least one more side, 4 to 5 minutes per side. Transfer the tofu to a bowl and set aside.

4 Add the remaining 1 tablespoon canola oil to the skillet or wok. Add the mustard greens and garlic and cook, stirring constantly, for 30 seconds. Add the chili sauce and cook until fragrant, about 30 more seconds. Stir in the mushrooms, ketchup, oyster sauce, and soy sauce, then add the noodles or spaghetti and toss to combine with the seasonings. Sprinkle on the sugar and 1 teaspoon salt and cook for 2 minutes more, stirring frequently.

5 Increase the heat to high and add the tofu, bean sprouts, and peanuts, if using. Cook for 10 minutes, stirring the noodles or spaghetti very little so it chars a bit. Use tongs to divide the noodles or spaghetti among four bowls. Top with the scallions, cilantro (if using), and lime wedges, and serve immediately.

wasabi soba noodles

V *These noodles are dressed* in sushi attire: wasabi powder, ginger, rice vinegar, and soy sauce. Add other veggies, such as blanched broccoli or cut asparagus, if you'd like.

SERVES 3 OR 4

1 Bring a large pot of water to a boil. Add the noodles and return to a boil, stirring to separate the noodles. Boil for 5 minutes, or until just barely tender; if you overcook them, they'll get mushy and ruin the salad. Drain, rinse under cold running water until they are cold, and drain well. Transfer to a large bowl and add the bean sprouts, tomatoes, scallions, carrot, and sesame seeds.

2 Meanwhile, in a food processor, puree the ginger and wasabi. With the machine running, add the vinegar, the soy sauce, and the oil in a thin stream, and then the sugar or honey.

3 Pour the dressing over the noodle mixture and toss until all the ingredients are incorporated and well coated. Serve cold or at room temperature.

- 8 ounces dried soba noodles (see page 451)
- 2 cups bean sprouts
- 1 cup halved cherry tomatoes
- 6 scallions, white and green parts, cut into 1/2-inch lengths on the diagonal
- 1 small carrot, peeled and grated
- 3 tablespoons toasted black sesame seeds (see page 444)
- 2 tablespoons peeled and minced fresh ginger
- 5 teaspoons wasabi powder
- 1/4 cup rice vinegar
- 3 tablespoons soy sauce
- 3 tablespoons canola oil
- 2 teaspoons sugar or honey

Note

The noodles can be made up to 2 days ahead and stored in an airtight container in the fridge.

chapter 7

Communal Casseroles, Lasagnas, Chilies, Stews, and Savory Pies

Savory Pie

Mac 'n' Cheese

Lasagna

Chili

Stew

can i bring anything?
yes, please!

There are no rights and wrongs here, but some people like to take care of everything when they throw a party. They want their guests to be guests, and they want to pamper them thoroughly. These people will decline if you ask, "Is there anything I can bring?" More power to them, because there are also people like me, who don't exactly have bragging rights when it comes to their bank accounts. And honestly I appreciate not only the money I save when a guest brings, say, a bottle of wine but the time it's saved me as well. In turn, I always offer to bring something when I am a guest myself. When I'm enjoying a party that a friend has worked hard to make happen, I feel good to know that I've contributed more than just my presence.

If you're organizing a massive potluck, keep a list of who's coming and what they're bringing next to the phone. If three people are already bringing peanut noodles, you can ask the person who's calling to bring a dessert or salad instead.

Ask your guests to bring serving utensils for their dishes, but it's a good idea to have some extras on hand. A restaurant supply store is an excellent place to buy cheap but sturdy ladles and large slotted spoons. Make sure that you have plenty of plates in case guests want to have a clean plate for different courses. If you're using plastic cups and paper plates, strategically place a garbage can in an obvious spot so that people don't end up leaving used cups and plates on the serving table. If you want to recycle plastic glasses or utensils, create a "drop-off" spot that your guests can find easily. Some hosts—especially at large events—ask guests to bring an ingredient list for each dish so people with food allergies don't have to guess about that mysterious but tempting casserole.

Supply your guests with plenty of plastic bags and foil for taking home their leftovers. People sometimes want to take home others' leftovers too, and paper plates are good for that purpose. You can make a "flying saucer" container that would be the envy of any fast-food joint by placing the leftovers on one plate, inverting a second plate over it, and then wrapping the whole deal in foil.

Invariably someone will leave a fork or a plate (or a spouse) behind, so be prepared to make phone calls the next day. Plus that will give you the chance to dish about the party and ask what happened when so-and-so went home with you-know-who. Talk about pot-luck!

mac'n'cheese (with four spins)

There I was, a woman with a mission: to save all the poor souls who purchase macaroni and cheese in a box, bringing them to cheesier and better pastures. I searched high and low for ideas.

A light bulb went on over my head when I was reading a cheese fondue recipe. The Swiss sprinkle flour on the grated cheese to thicken and stabilize the fondue. Why couldn't I do the same for macaroni and cheese? I add cubed sweet potato to provide a bit of relief from the pasta and cheese. Also, be sure to use a good, sharp cheddar. I like those from Vermont and Canada. Pair mac'n'cheese with a simple green salad and serve sorbet or one of my ices (pages 418–420) for dessert. For the deluxe version, make a crumb topping.

SERVES 4 TO 6

2 medium sweet potatoes

Kosher salt to taste

16 ounces (3²⁄₃ cups) grated sharp cheddar cheese

²⁄₃ cup freshly grated Parmesan cheese

2 tablespoons all-purpose flour

8 ounces cream cheese

2 cups milk

1 garlic clove, minced

16 ounces elbow macaroni or similar-size pasta

Freshly ground black pepper to taste

Crumb Topping (page 257; optional)

Note

This dish can be prepared up to 2 days ahead and stored in an airtight container. It can be reheated in a microwave or in a skillet over low heat, stirring frequently.

1 Scrub the sweet potatoes, and pierce them with a knife so they don't burst. Cook them in the microwave until tender, about 7 minutes on high. Cut them into bite-size pieces. I like keeping the skin on. Set aside.

2 Preheat the oven to 350 degrees. Butter a large casserole dish or a 13-x-9-inch baking dish. Bring a large pot of salted water to a boil.

3 In a large bowl, combine the cheddar, Parmesan, and flour and toss until well combined. Set aside.

4 In a small, heavy saucepan, melt the cream cheese over low heat, stirring with a whisk. Slowly whisk in the milk and garlic until smooth. Remove from the heat and set aside.

5 Add the macaroni to the boiling water and return to a boil, stirring to separate the pieces. Boil for 5 minutes, or until just al dente. Drain the macaroni and immediately return it to the pot. Add the cheddar mixture to the macaroni and stir well. Add the cream cheese mixture and sweet potatoes. Season with salt and pepper. Mix well.

6 Transfer the macaroni mixture to the prepared dish. Sprinkle with the crumb topping, if using. Cover the dish tightly with foil and bake for 30 minutes, or until piping hot. To brown the crumb topping, remove the foil during the last 10 minutes of baking. Serve hot.

crumb topping

5–6 slices white or whole wheat sandwich bread
   1 garlic clove
   1 teaspoon dried rosemary or thyme, or 1 sprig fresh, minced
   2 tablespoons extra-virgin olive oil
      Kosher salt and freshly ground black pepper to taste

Tear the bread into smaller pieces. In a food processor, grind the bread into coarse crumbs. Add the garlic and rosemary or thyme and process until finely chopped. Add the olive oil and season liberally with salt and pepper and process for a few seconds until mixed.

Superfast Mac'n'Cheese

• • serves 4

$1/3$ cup milk or light cream

3 tablespoons butter, cut into 6 pieces

3 cups grated sharp cheddar cheese

1 cup freshly grated Asiago or Parmesan cheese

1 tablespoon all-purpose flour

1 garlic clove, minced

    Kosher salt and freshly ground black pepper to taste

1 pound macaroni or similar-size pasta

1 In a medium bowl, combine the milk or cream, butter, cheddar, Asiago or Parmesan, flour, garlic, and salt and pepper and toss well.

2 After boiling the macaroni in salted water, draining it, and returning it to the pot, add the cheese mixture. Stir for a couple of minutes over low heat until the cheeses are melted and the mixture is heated through. Taste for seasoning, adding more salt and pepper, if necessary, and serve hot.

Shiitake Mac'n'Cheese

3 tablespoons butter

$1/2$ pound fresh shiitake mushrooms, stems removed, caps sliced

2 garlic cloves, minced

    Kosher salt and freshly ground black pepper to taste

In a small skillet, melt the butter over medium heat. Add the mushrooms and garlic and sauté until the mushrooms are cooked through, 3 to 4 minutes. Season with salt and pepper and add to the Mac'n'Cheese in step 5.

Gorgonzola Mac'n'Cheese

1 In the basic Mac'n'Cheese, reduce the cheddar to 10 ounces.

2 Cut 6 ounces Gorgonzola dolce (or any other good blue cheese, such as Bleu d'Auvergne) into small pieces. You can remove the rind, if you like, but it's edible and I like it.

3 Add the Gorgonzola or other blue cheese to the Mac'n'Cheese in step 5.

Cowboy Mac'n'Cheese

    1 cup fresh or frozen corn kernels
    2 cups chopped scallions, white and green parts
    1 green bell pepper, finely chopped
  1/4 cup chopped fresh cilantro
    2 canned chipotle chiles in adobo, or canned green chiles, finely chopped

1 If using frozen corn, place it in a colander and run it under warm water to thaw it.

2 Add all of the ingredients to the Mac'n'Cheese in step 5.

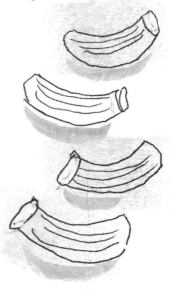

versatile noodle casserole

This casserole is enriched with silken tofu instead of the more predictable heavy cream. It's a better choice because it moistens the casserole without weighing it down. If you like sun-dried tomatoes, soften some in hot water, then chop and add them. If you like green beans, chop a handful and blanch them instead of the broccoli. Almost any vegetable would work in this dish.

SERVES 6

6 tablespoons extra-virgin olive oil

2 large onions, thinly sliced

   Kosher salt and freshly ground black pepper to taste

2 large portobello mushrooms, caps and top half of stems cut into ½-inch cubes

6 garlic cloves, minced

1 16-ounce carton silken tofu

1 cup fresh basil leaves, thinly sliced

12 ounces medium-width egg noodles

3 cups bite-size broccoli pieces, blanched

2 plum tomatoes, seeded and diced

½ cup pitted Mediterranean green olives

1 Preheat the oven to 350 degrees. Lightly oil a 13-x-9-inch baking dish.

2 In a large skillet, heat 1 tablespoon of the olive oil over medium-low heat. Add the onions and sauté, stirring occasionally, until brown and caramelized, about 20 minutes. Season with salt and pepper. Transfer to a plate and set aside.

3 In the same skillet, heat the remaining 5 tablespoons oil over medium-high heat. Add the portobellos and cook, stirring frequently, for 3 to 5 minutes, or until they become wilted. (They will also appear to be starving for oil, but don't add any more.) Add half the garlic and cook, stirring frequently, for 2 minutes or until it cooks through.

Season the portobellos with salt. Remove from the heat and set aside.

4 In a medium bowl, combine the tofu, basil, and remaining garlic. Season liberally with salt and pepper. Use a clean hand to mix the ingredients, squeezing the tofu through your fingers until it resembles scrambled eggs. Set aside.

5 Bring a large pot of salted water to a boil. Add the noodles and return to a boil, stirring to separate the strands. Boil for 6 to 8 minutes, or until al dente. Drain, reserving $1/2$ cup of the cooking liquid. Return the noodles and the reserved cooking liquid to the pot. Add the tofu mixture, broccoli, tomatoes, and olives and mix well. Season with salt and pepper. Gently fold in the mushrooms; don't overstir, or they'll discolor the casserole. Transfer to the prepared baking dish and spread the caramelized onions on top.

6 Bake the casserole until hot and bubbly, about 30 minutes. Let stand for 5 minutes before serving.

Note The casserole can be assembled up to 1 day before baking. Cover with plastic wrap and refrigerate. The chilled casserole will need at least 35 minutes in the oven to become piping hot.

spaghetti casserole

This casserole was one of our family's favorite ways to refuel at the end of a long day of skiing. My mom made it with a pound of sour cream, a pound of ground meat, and half a pound each of cheddar cheese and cream cheese! These days, I prefer a lighter version.

SERVES 6

1 Preheat the oven to 350 degrees. Oil a 13-x-9-inch baking dish. Bring a large pot of salted water to a boil.

2 In a medium saucepan, heat the olive oil over medium heat. Add the onions and fennel seeds and sauté until the onions have softened, about 7 minutes. Add the garlic and sauté for 1 minute. Add the tomatoes and 1/2 cup water, reduce the heat to medium-low, and simmer for 15 to 20 minutes, or until it has thickened slightly. Remove from the heat and stir in the balsamic vinegar. Set aside.

3 In a colander, press out most of the liquid from the spinach with a rubber spatula. Set aside.

Kosher salt to taste

3 tablespoons extra-virgin olive oil

2 onions, chopped

1 teaspoon fennel seeds

5–6 garlic cloves, minced

1 28-ounce can diced tomatoes, with their juice

1 teaspoon balsamic vinegar

1 box frozen, chopped spinach, thawed

6 ounces cream cheese or creamy goat cheese

1/2 cup sour cream

2 cups cottage cheese

1 1/2 cups freshly grated Parmesan

Freshly ground black pepper to taste

12 ounces spaghetti or capellini

Note The casserole can be made but not baked up to 2 days ahead. Cover with plastic wrap and store in the fridge or freeze for up to 1 month.

4 In a large saucepan slowly melt the cream cheese or goat cheese with the sour cream over low heat, stirring frequently with a wooden spoon; do not boil. Stir in the spinach, cottage cheese, 3/4 cup of the Parmesan, and 1/4 cup water. Season well with salt and pepper. Remove from the heat.

5 Meanwhile, in the pot of boiling water, boil the pasta for 1 minute less than as directed on the package; it should be very al dente. Drain, rinse with warm running water, and drain well. Add the pasta to the cottage cheese mixture and toss well.

6 Line the bottom of the prepared dish with the pasta mixture and ladle the tomato sauce evenly over it. Cover with foil and bake until piping hot, about 40 minutes. Sprinkle with the remaining 3/4 cup Parmesan and serve.

swiss chard–eggplant lasagna

Eggplant roasted over a flame imparts smokiness to this satisfying lasagna. If you don't have a gas stove, you can cook the eggplant on a grill. If you like, add chopped kalamata olives to the cooked tomato mixture. For a vegan version, use Tofu Pesto (page 184) in place of the ricotta and the egg-roll wrappers instead of the lasagna noodles.

SERVES 8

1 Preheat the oven to 375 degrees. Lightly oil a 13-x-9-inch baking pan.

2 Cook the eggplant over a gas burner on low, using tongs to turn the eggplant every few minutes until it's blackened all over and very soft and limp, 25 to 30 minutes. Let cool for 15 minutes.

3 Meanwhile, in a large skillet, heat 2 tablespoons of the olive oil over medium heat. Add the onion and sauté, stirring occasionally, until browned and caramelized, 15 to 20 minutes. Add the tomatoes, about three quarters of the garlic, and 1/4 cup water and cook for 5 minutes, or until the tomatoes collapse. If the tomatoes are not collapsing, crush them with a potato masher or pierce them with a fork. Remove from the heat and stir in the balsamic vinegar. Season with salt and pepper. Set aside.

1 large eggplant (about 2 pounds)

5 tablespoons extra-virgin olive oil

1 large onion, chopped

2 pints cherry tomatoes

6 garlic cloves, minced

1 tablespoon balsamic vinegar

Kosher salt and freshly ground black pepper to taste

2 cups ricotta cheese

1/2 cup coarsely chopped fresh cilantro and/or basil

1 large bunch Swiss chard, stems cut into 1/2-inch-thick pieces, leaves left whole

1 pound 8-inch-square fresh egg-roll wrappers or 1 pound lasagna noodles, cooked

4 Peel the eggplant and cut it crosswise into $\frac{1}{2}$-inch-thick slices (if it's too soft to slice neatly, just chop it). In a medium bowl, combine the eggplant, the remaining 3 tablespoons olive oil, and half of the remaining garlic. Add 1 teaspoon salt and season with pepper to taste. Mix well and set aside.

5 In a second medium bowl, combine the ricotta, cilantro and/or basil, and the remaining garlic. Season liberally with salt and pepper. Set aside.

6 Bring a large pot of salted water to a boil. Add the chard stems and boil for 3 minutes. Add the chard leaves and boil until the stems are tender, about 3 minutes more. Drain and rinse quickly under cold running water. Let the chard drain in the colander for 10 minutes, then squeeze it with your hands to remove as much water as possible. Chop the leaves and stems.

7 Spread 1 cup of the tomato mixture on the bottom of the prepared pan. Add a single layer of egg-roll wrappers or noodles, cutting some with scissors if necessary to make a uniform layer. Scatter half of the ricotta mixture on top, then half of the tomatoes (reserving the remaining tomatoes). Layer on half of the eggplant and half of the Swiss chard. Add another layer of egg-roll wrappers or noodles, then the remaining ricotta mixture and Swiss chard. Top with a third layer of egg-roll wrappers or noodles and the remaining eggplant.

8 Cover the pan with foil and bake until heated through, 30 to 40 minutes. Serve hot, topping each serving with some of the reheated reserved tomatoes.

communal casseroles, lasagnas, chilies, stews, and savory pies

broccoli rabe lasagna

I created this lasagna for my friend Steve, who loves broccoli rabe. Most people who clamor for this vegetable avoid blanching it so that it retains some bitterness. But if you want to cut the bitter flavor, blanch it for 1 minute before proceeding with the recipe. If you like, add white beans to the lasagna.

SERVES 8

1 Preheat the oven to 375 degrees. Lightly oil a 13-x-9-inch baking pan.

2 In a large skillet, heat 2 tablespoons of the olive oil over medium heat. Add the onion and sauté, stirring occasionally, until translucent, 7 to 9 minutes. Add the tomatoes and garlic and cook until the tomatoes soften, about 3 minutes more. Stir in the broccoli rabe, sherry, and 1/2 cup water. Season liberally with salt and pepper. Cover partially and simmer for 5 minutes, or until the rabe is tender. Remove from the heat and set aside.

3 Wrap the block of tofu in a clean dishtowel and press it firmly with your hands until you feel the towel become damp. Unwrap the tofu and crumble it into a large bowl. Add the remaining 1 tablespoon olive oil, ricotta, and goat

3 tablespoons extra-virgin olive oil

1 large onion, chopped

8 plum tomatoes, chopped

6 garlic cloves, minced

2 bunches broccoli rabe, 1/2 inch trimmed off the ends, thick stems halved lengthwise

1/3 cup dry sherry

Kosher salt and freshly ground black pepper to taste

1 16-ounce carton firm tofu

2 cups ricotta cheese

3 ounces creamy fresh goat cheese

1 pound 8-inch-square fresh egg-roll wrappers or 1 pound lasagna noodles, cooked

1/2 cup freshly grated Parmesan cheese

freezing lasagna and other foods

Practically every lasagna, chili, or casserole freezes well. But unless you have a spe-cial stand-alone freezer (one that registers below 0 degrees), these foods, like most others, begin to lose their flavors after a couple of months. How much chutzpah they lose depends on how cold your freezer is, how often you open it, and how well you wrap the food. Turn your freezer to its coldest setting to extend the life of your frozen food. Double-wrap the food with plastic wrap that is meant for freezer use (some plas-tic wrap is permeable). You can freeze chilies and soups in airtight plastic containers, which make for easy stacking. Don't use foil, which invites freezer burn because air can easily enter. Thaw in the fridge overnight.

cheese, and mix well. Season liberally with salt and pepper. The mixture should resemble scrambled eggs.

4 Spread half of the tomato mix-ture (leaving behind the broccoli rabe for the next layer) on the bottom of the prepared pan. Add a single layer of egg-roll wrappers or noodles, cutting some with scissors if necessary to make a uni-form layer. Distribute half of the cheese mixture and then half of the broccoli rabe on top. Add another layer of egg-roll wrappers or noodles, then the re-maining broccoli rabe and the remain-ing tomato mixture. Add a third layer of egg-roll wrappers or noodles and top with the remaining cheese mixture and the Parmesan.

Note
The lasagna can be assembled, cov-ered with foil, and refrigerated up to 1 day before baking. The chilled lasagna will need at least 40 minutes in the oven to become piping hot.

5 Cover the pan with foil and bake until heated through, 35 to 40 minutes. Serve hot.

butternut squash–lentil chili

(V) *When I'm pressed for time,* I use fast-cooking lentils rather than long-cooking beans in my chilies. My friend and recipe tester Marla likes to use canned adzuki beans and Fakin' Bacon (smoky tempeh by Lightlife) in lieu of the lentils, regular tempeh, and chipotles in this chili. Although I don't usually like canned beans, Marla's version is excellent.

SERVES 4 OR 5

2¼ cups red lentils (see page 450) or brown lentils

3½ cups peeled butternut squash, cut into 1-inch cubes

4 garlic cloves, minced

Kosher salt to taste

2 tablespoons extra-virgin olive oil

2 teaspoons ground cumin

1 teaspoon ground coriander

8 ounces tempeh

1 cup raw bulgur

2–3 canned chipotle chiles in adobo

1 12-ounce bottle pale ale or beer

3 tablespoons chopped fresh cilantro leaves and stems, plus a few leaves for garnish

Freshly ground black pepper to taste

2 tablespoons grated unsweetened chocolate

1 lime, cut into wedges

1 Preheat the oven to 400 degrees. Bring a large saucepan of water to a boil. Add the lentils and boil until they are just tender, about 5 minutes for red lentils and about 25 minutes for brown lentils. Drain, rinse with cold running water, and drain well. Set aside.

2 In a large baking pan, combine the squash, half of the garlic, a pinch of salt, and 1 tablespoon of the olive oil and toss well. Bake the squash until tender, about 25 minutes. Let cool.

getting heard

It can be an uphill climb to make yourself heard at your own dinner table if you need to stop multiple conversations and address everyone. No one hears your announcement because everyone is talking right over you.

Regardless of who's drowning you out, however, there's a way to cut through the chatter. I created this tactic and believe it's foolproof, although it takes some nerve. Full throttle, sing what you need to say—for instance, "Just thought you should know, I'm getting married." If you concentrate and continue to sing, people will quickly close their mouths and turn their attention to you in bewilderment. If you have a good voice, they may clap at the end (but they didn't when I sang).

In the unlikely case that this doesn't work, plant a new fly swatter within easy reach of your chair. When your voice fails you, take the fly swatter and swat the talking guests either directly on their heads or on their shoulders (all bald men should be whacked on the head; the impressive sound it makes is attention-grabbing and ego-boosting for the host). Once you have successfully slapped your guests, you pretty much have the floor. Your guests will secretly admire you for your sassy and dramatic behavior.

3 Meanwhile, in a large, heavy saucepan, heat the remaining 1 tablespoon olive oil over medium heat. Stir in the remaining garlic, the cumin, and coriander. Crumble the tempeh into the pan and sauté for 1 minute. Add the bulgur, chipotles, ale or beer, and $3^{1}/_{2}$ cups water and bring to a simmer. Add the lentils, squash, and cilantro. Season with salt and pepper. Simmer for about 4 minutes, or until very hot. Stir in the chocolate until melted. Taste for seasoning, adding more salt and pepper if necessary. Serve the chili in bowls and garnish each with the cilantro leaves and a fresh lime wedge.

Note The chili can be made up to 2 days ahead and stored in an airtight container in the fridge. Reheat on the stovetop or in the microwave.

communal casseroles, lasagnas, chilies, stews, and savory pies

nutty portobello chili

 Portobellos, sweet potato, TVP (texturized vegetable protein), cashews, and adzuki beans make a delicious, protein-rich chili. TVP is sold dry; once moistened, it absorbs the flavors around it like a sponge.

SERVES 8

- 3 tablespoons canola oil
- 3 medium onions, chopped
- 2 portobello mushrooms, chopped (stems included)
- 4 garlic cloves, minced
- 2 tablespoons chili powder
- 1 tablespoon ground cumin
- 1 28-ounce can crushed tomatoes, with their juice
- 1 large sweet potato, peeled and cut into ½-inch cubes
- 2 cups TVP (see page 453)

- 4 cups cooked or canned, drained adzuki beans or kidney beans
- 1 teaspoon kosher salt, plus more to taste
- ½ teaspoon freshly ground black pepper, plus more to taste
- 1 green bell pepper, finely chopped
- 1 cup chopped toasted or untoasted cashews (see page 283)
- ½ cup chopped fresh cilantro

  Hot sauce (I like Inner Beauty Hot Sauce)

1 In a large, heavy pot, heat the canola oil over medium heat. Add the onions and sauté, stirring occasionally, until golden brown, 8 to 10 minutes. Add the mushrooms, garlic, chili powder, and cumin and sauté for 2 minutes more.

2 Add the tomatoes, sweet potato, TVP, beans, salt, pepper, and 4 cups water and mix well. Cover, and simmer for 15 minutes, or until the sweet potato is tender.

TVP
versatile could be its middle name

TVP (texturized vegetable protein) is made from soybeans and is usually shaped into flakes. It looks a lot like Grape-Nuts cereal. TVP is as light as confetti, because it's dehydrated. Once it's cooked, it looks deceptively like ground beef, but its flavor and texture are more akin to boiled pasta.

Like pasta, TVP is very versatile. It picks up flavors like a sponge. I use it in soups, chilies, sloppy joes, and veggie burgers. It's inexpensive yet high in protein and potassium and rich in calcium and amino acids.

TVP needs to be reconstituted, usually with 2 parts liquid to 1 part TVP. Look for it in the bulk section of whole food stores.

3 Remove from the heat and stir in the bell pepper, cashews, and cilantro. Add a little hot water if the chili seems too dry. Season with salt and pepper. Serve, passing the hot sauce at the table.

Note
The chili can be made without the cilantro up to 2 days ahead and stored in an airtight container in the fridge. Reheat on the stovetop or in the microwave and stir in the cilantro just before serving.

Variation
Add 1 cup yellow split mung beans (see page 454) in step 2 along with the TVP.

smoky lentil chili

Ⓥ *Here's an easy chili* you can make from a decently stocked pantry (and if you don't have chipotles in your pantry, shame on you!). Skip the fresh cilantro if it means a special trip to the market.

SERVES 6

1 If using fresh corn, cut the kernels off the cobs. Lay one ear flat and make a straight cut down the length of one side. Then rotate the corn a quarter turn and cut down another side. Continue in this manner twice more, until all the kernels have been removed. Repeat with the remaining ear. You should have about 1⅓ cups. Set aside.

2 In a large, heavy pot, heat the olive oil over medium heat. Add the onions and sauté until lightly browned, about 15 minutes. Add the garlic, cumin, and coriander, and sauté for 2 minutes more. Stir in the tomatoes, lentils, chipotles, and 2 cups water and bring to a boil. Reduce the heat to a simmer and cook until the lentils are soft, about 50 minutes. Add more water during the cooking if the mixture gets too dry.

2 ears corn, shucked, or 1⅓ cups frozen (not thawed) corn kernels

2 tablespoons extra-virgin olive oil

2 large onions, finely chopped

4 garlic cloves, minced

2 teaspoons ground cumin

2 teaspoons ground coriander

1 28-ounce can diced or crushed tomatoes, with their juice

2 cups French green lentils (see page 447) or brown lentils

3–5 canned chipotle chiles in adobo, depending on your heat tolerance

½ cup chopped fresh cilantro

1 cup toasted pumpkin seeds (see page 449), coarsely chopped (reserve 1 tablespoon whole seeds for garnish)

Kosher salt and freshly ground black pepper to taste

Sour cream for serving (optional)

3 Add the corn kernels and heat through, about 2 minutes. Stir in the cilantro and chopped pumpkin seeds. Season with salt and pepper. Serve in bowls, topped with sour cream, if desired, and a few whole toasted pumpkin seeds.

Note

The chili can be fully prepared without the cilantro and pumpkin seeds up to 2 days ahead and stored in an airtight container in the fridge. Reheat on the stovetop or in the microwave. Add the cilantro and pumpkin seeds just before serving.

meatless chili is chili too!

Will Rogers once awarded three stars to a chili made from boar testicles. Now I feel right at home using my ingenuity and dissenting from the use of animals in this dish.

Anyone who has even an ounce of creativity should just jump in cold Tofurky. Be conservative with the spicing—chili made from vegetables is more delicate than meat versions, so fewer spices are necessary to achieve great flavor. Now clean out your cast-iron pot and get cookin'!

Rules of the Chili Game

- You must use chiles—whether fresh, dried, or ground—in chili, and their flavor must come through in the finished dish.

- Chili is not soup. The texture should *not* be baby pap. It should take a minimum of three teeth to eat it.

- Be brazen; after all, this is cowboy country food. But be rational as well as bold—stirring in raspberry Jell-O is probably going too far.

- For extra flavor, toast whole spices such as cumin and coriander in a dry skillet until aromatic, then grind them with a spice mill or mortar and pestle. At the very least, cook your spices in the oil before adding the liquid—it helps the spices release their flavors.

- A few recommended chili add-ins: crumbled tempeh browned in oil, chopped green beans, grated chocolate (just a bit added at the end), chopped tomatillos, coffee (the liquid, not the beans), beer, finely chopped cashews, and chopped bell peppers.

couscous stew with tomatoes, olives, and saffron

(V) *The flavors of Persia mingle* in this swift but excellent dish. Make sure you buy Israeli couscous, which has large granules the size of peppercorns and a wonderfully chewy texture. You can find it in whole food stores and Middle Eastern markets. Serve this stew in shallow bowls with warm pita bread to sop up the flavorful broth.

SERVES 4

- 3 tablespoons extra-virgin olive oil
- 1 medium onion, finely chopped
- 2 garlic cloves, chopped
- 1¼ cups uncooked Israeli couscous (see page 447)
- ½ teaspoon ground cumin
- 1 large russet, Yukon Gold, or Yellow Finn potato, peeled and cut into ½-inch cubes
- 12 sun-dried tomatoes (not oil-packed), julienned

- 1 small dried red chile pepper or crushed red pepper flakes to taste
- ½ teaspoon saffron threads
- Kosher salt to taste
- 2 plum tomatoes, cut into ½-inch cubes
- 1 cup frozen, shelled (podless) edamame or peas, thawed
- ¼ cup pitted kalamata olives
- Freshly ground black pepper to taste

1 In a heavy saucepan, heat the olive oil over medium heat. Add the onion and garlic and sauté for 2 minutes. Stir in the couscous, cumin, and 2½ cups water, then add the potato, sun-dried tomatoes, chile or pepper flakes, saffron, and a pinch of salt. Bring to a boil.

2 Reduce the heat to a simmer and cook, stirring occasionally, until the potato and couscous are tender, about 10

If there's lots of food left from your dinner party (and assuming it was good), it's always nice to offer some to your friends when they leave. Guests are usually happy to take it, and who wants to eat the same leftovers day in and out? I'd rather spread the wealth. Save carryout and deli containers for this purpose.

minutes. Add more water during the cooking if the mixture seems too dry. Stir in the tomatoes, edamame or peas, and olives and heat through. Season with salt and pepper. Serve immediately.

Note The stew can be made up to 2 days ahead and stored in an airtight container in the fridge. Reheat on the stove or in the microwave.

Olives

soft polenta with tomato-spinach ragout

In this quick, rustic dish, creamy polenta lies under a rich stew of cherry tomatoes, browned onions, and spinach. A fried egg sautéed in olive oil just before serving and placed on top is a nice addition. If you'd like to try kale or collard greens instead of spinach, use only the leaves, thinly sliced. Serve with a simple green salad dressed with balsamic vinegar and olive oil.

SERVES 4

1½ cups stone-ground cornmeal

1 teaspoon kosher salt, plus more to taste

½ cup freshly grated Parmesan cheese

Freshly ground black pepper to taste

4 tablespoons extra-virgin olive oil

2 medium onions, thinly sliced

1 pint cherry tomatoes

5 garlic cloves, minced

10 ounces fresh spinach, stemmed

1 tablespoon balsamic vinegar

1 In a medium saucepan, combine the cornmeal, 1 teaspoon salt, and 4½ cups water over low heat. Whisk every few minutes for about 25 minutes, or until thickened. Remove from the heat and stir in ¼ cup of the Parmesan and season with salt and pepper.

2 Meanwhile, in a large skillet, heat 2 tablespoons of the olive oil over medium heat. Add the onions and sauté until they are brown around the edges, about 15 minutes. Transfer to a plate.

3 Add the remaining 2 tablespoons olive oil and the cherry tomatoes to the skillet. Sauté for 4 to 5 minutes, then add the garlic and ½ cup water. Cook for 5 to 10 minutes, or until the tomatoes begin to collapse. If they are not collapsing, crush them with a potato masher or pierce them with a fork. Add the spinach and cook, stirring, until it wilts, 1 to 2 minutes. Remove from the

a society of poets

It was a case of poetic inspiration. One day, a friend who teaches poetry at a university in Boston told me that he prays to God before class to help offset the anxiety he feels when lecturing. A few days later when I was attending church, I was entranced by a long poem written and read by our minister.

I decided to bring my professor friend together with the minister to enjoy good food and read poetry. I thought of other people who would love to hear the poems: writers, religious friends, and artists. I took the plunge and asked the minister (whom I barely knew) and the professor to my home for dinner and a reading, and I also invited a cantor who lives down the street from me.

My friends helped themselves to a big buffet dinner, taking seats on the floor, on the sofa, on chairs. As dessert was served, the readings began. I started the set by reading a favorite poem written by my college roommate. The two poets followed, and the cantor and a friend she had brought along sang. The evening finished with everyone joining in the singing. My friends said they felt lucky to have been there. The best parties are born from whims.

heat, add the vinegar, and season with salt and pepper.

4 Spoon the hot polenta onto plates, making a depression in each mound. Spoon the tomato mixture into the depression, then spoon the onions on top. Sprinkle the remaining ¹/₄ cup Parmesan over each dish. Serve immediately.

Note The tomato ragout can be prepared up to 1 day ahead (through step 3) and reheated in a skillet before serving.

communal casseroles, lasagnas, chilies, stews, and savory pies

tofu-shiitake stew

Ⓥ *One day, an article in the* New York Times *about a Korean restaurant that served an intriguing tofu stew caught my eye. The liquid in the stew was soy milk, and the article described it as the sort of stew that should be doctored with lots of fresh and prepared condiments, such as toasted sesame seeds and bean sprouts. The paper provided no recipe, however, so I started to recreate what I had imagined in my kitchen. The first batch went down the drain, but I made some radical changes on the second round, adding dried shiitakes and fresh ginger to the soy milk. Since then I've honed the recipe further.*

In addition to the other condiments, try Lee Kum Kee's Black Bean Garlic Sauce.

SERVES 3 OR 4

½ cup dried shiitake mushrooms

3 cups plain soy milk (*not* sweetened)

3 3-inch-long thin slices fresh ginger

3 garlic cloves, thinly sliced

2 carrots, cut into ¼-inch-thick diagonal slices

1 tablespoon canola oil

10 fresh shiitake mushrooms, stems removed, caps thinly sliced

1 16-ounce carton silken tofu

2 tablespoons soy sauce, plus more to taste

1 tablespoon toasted sesame oil

1 teaspoon Asian chili sauce (see page 443), plus more to taste

2 cups bean sprouts

6 scallions, white and green parts, chopped

¼ cup coarsely chopped fresh cilantro

1 tablespoon toasted sesame seeds (see page 450)

Note This dish can be prepared up to 1 day ahead, through step 5, and stored in an airtight container in the fridge.

1 In a small bowl, combine the dried shiitakes and ³/₄ cup boiling water. Let soak for 20 minutes. Remove the mushrooms, squeezing until the liquid they absorbed falls back into the bowl. Reserve the soaking liquid. Cut off and discard the stems. Thinly slice the caps. Set aside.

2 Meanwhile, in a medium saucepan, bring the soy milk to a simmer over medium heat. Add the ginger, garlic, and carrots and simmer until the carrots are tender, about 15 minutes.

3 In a medium skillet, heat the canola oil over medium heat. Add the fresh shiitakes and sauté until softened, about 5 minutes. Add the fresh shiitakes to the simmering soy milk mixture.

4 Add the dried shiitakes to the simmering soy milk mixture along with the soaking liquid, leaving any sediment behind in the bowl.

5 Using a soupspoon, add the tofu to the liquid in spoonfuls. Bring to a boil, remove from the heat, and stir in the soy sauce, sesame oil, and chili sauce.

6 Ladle the stew into large soup bowls. Top with the bean sprouts, scallions, cilantro, and sesame seeds. Pass more soy sauce and chili sauce at the table.

place-card pitfalls

When a friend of mine had a dinner party recently, she wrote out place cards for the eight or so guests. She put an engaging bachelor between me and another eligible woman, hoping that one of us would hit it off with him. What she didn't anticipate was that *both* of us would hit it off with him. He was amusing and charming, and the three of us talked throughout the dinner. But sometimes when I focused on another conversation, I could overhear the other woman's quips and giggles as the two of them conversed, and I'd have to resist the urge to jump back into their conversation because I didn't want to lose points.

So think before you set out those place cards. For large, fancy parties, they eliminate confusion when guests are trying to find a seat *if* the host has good people sense.

communal casseroles, lasagnas, chilies, stews, and savory pies

burmese squash and tofu stew

V *Perfect for lap-style dining,* this is a casual fall or winter stew that is best eaten with a spoon. It originally featured chicken, and I've revamped it using tofu and yellow split peas. The split peas meld well and add a pleasant nuttiness. You can serve the stew with rice, if you like, but it's quite good without it. If you can't find delicata squash, just use peeled butternut squash.

SERVES 4

1 cup uncooked yellow split peas

1 16-ounce carton firm tofu

Kosher salt to taste

2 tablespoons canola oil

1 large onion, finely chopped

3 garlic cloves, minced

1½ tablespoons peeled and minced fresh ginger

1–3 small, skinny chile peppers, seeded and minced

2 teaspoons ground coriander

1 teaspoon ground cumin

1 delicata squash, unpeeled, cut into 1-inch cubes (about 2½ cups)

1 cup cherry tomatoes, halved

⅓ cup tamarind pulp (see page 452) or 2 tablespoons fresh lime juice (1 juicy lime)

¼ cup minced fresh cilantro or mint, for garnish

1 In a medium saucepan, bring 4 cups water to a boil. Add the split peas and simmer until tender but not mushy, about 35 minutes. Drain well and set aside.

2 Wrap the block of tofu in a clean dishtowel and press it firmly with your hands until you feel the towel become damp. Unwrap the tofu and cut it into ½-inch cubes. Salt the cubes liberally.

tamarind

Inside the pods of the tamarind tree is a delicious, sweet-and-sour pulp. Tamarind adds a tart flavor to many Southeast Asian curries and sauces (as well as Worcestershire sauce). Its sweet tang makes you want to eat tamarind straight from the pod, and in fact many people in the Caribbean, West Africa, and Asia do eat it as a sort of candy. It is vitamin-rich and is reportedly good for the liver and kidney. Tamarind is sold in Asian markets in small, compressed bricks with the seeds still intact. The bricks will keep forever in your pantry. Usually a small portion of the brick is soaked in water, then passed through a sieve to yield the pulp. Leftover tamarind pulp will last in the fridge for at least 3 weeks. Lately, I've heard that people are using a thick, black tamarind concentrate instead of tamarind pulp. No, no, no. Although the concentrate is more convenient, the pulp is where the good flavor is.

3 In a large, well-seasoned skillet (preferably not nonstick), heat the canola oil over medium heat. Add the tofu and onion and cook until the onion is golden brown, 12 to 14 minutes. Use a spatula to lift and turn the tofu and onion once or twice.

Note

The stew can be made up to 2 days ahead and stored in an airtight container in the fridge. Reheat on the stove or in the microwave, adding a bit of water if the stew seems dry. Garnish with the cilantro or mint just before serving.

4 Add the garlic, ginger, chiles, coriander, and cumin to the skillet and sauté for 2 minutes. Stir in the squash, 1 teaspoon salt, and $1^1/_3$ cups water. Cover the pan and cook for 10 minutes, or until the squash is tender. Add the split peas, tomatoes, and tamarind pulp or lime juice and heat through. Season with salt. Transfer the stew to a serving dish and garnish with the cilantro or mint.

communal casseroles, lasagnas, chilies, stews, and savory pies

sweet potato shepherd's pie

This recipe will convince you that you don't need a lamb or cow to produce a memorable shepherd's pie. The sweet potatoes and the nontraditional use of spices in this pie set it apart from all others.

SERVES 4

1 Preheat the oven to 375 degrees. Oil a 9-inch square baking dish.

2 In a small bowl, combine the dried mushrooms and 1 cup boiling water. Let soak for 20 minutes. Remove the mushrooms, squeezing the liquid back into the bowl. Reserve the soaking liquid. Cut off and discard the stems. Chop the caps. Set aside.

3 If using fresh corn, cut the kernels off the cobs. Lay one ear flat and make a straight cut down the length of one side. Then rotate the corn a quarter turn and cut down another side. Continue in this manner twice more, until all the kernels have been removed. Repeat with the remaining ear. You should have about 1^{1}/$_{3}$ cups. Set aside.

4 Bring a large pot of salted water to a boil. Add the sweet potatoes and cook until soft, about 12 minutes. Drain well. Transfer to a large bowl. Add 2 tablespoons of the butter and mash with

8 dried shiitake or porcini mushrooms

2 ears corn, shucked, or 1^{1}/$_{3}$ cups frozen (not thawed) corn kernels

Kosher salt to taste

2 sweet potatoes, peeled and cut into ^{1}/$_{2}$-inch cubes

3 tablespoons butter

^{1}/$_{2}$ cup thinly sliced scallions, white and green parts

Freshly ground black pepper to taste

2 large portobello mushrooms, cut into ^{1}/$_{4}$-inch pieces

1 large onion, chopped

3 garlic cloves, minced

^{1}/$_{2}$ teaspoon ground cardamom

^{1}/$_{4}$ teaspoon freshly ground nutmeg

^{1}/$_{4}$ teaspoon ground cinnamon

1 tablespoon all-purpose flour

^{1}/$_{3}$ cup coarsely chopped toasted walnuts (see page 283; optional)

a potato masher. (It's fine if the mixture is a little lumpy.) Stir in the scallions. Season with salt and pepper. Set aside.

5 In a large skillet, melt the remaining 1 tablespoon butter over medium heat. Add the portobellos and onion and sauté, stirring frequently, for 8 minutes, or until the onion and mushrooms are fully cooked. The mixture will appear to be starving for more butter, but don't worry, just keep stirring. Add the garlic, cardamom, nutmeg, and cinnamon and sauté for 1 minute more. Add the flour, stirring to coat the vegetables. Slowly add the mushroom-soaking liquid, leaving behind any sediment in the bowl, and 1 cup water, stirring constantly. Bring to a simmer and cook, stirring occasionally, until thickened, 2 to 3 minutes. Add the corn kernels and cook for 1 minute more. Remove from the heat. Stir in the dried mushrooms and walnuts, if using. Season with salt and pepper.

6 Transfer the mushroom mixture to the prepared baking dish and spread in an even layer. Top with the sweet potatoes, smoothing the surface with the back of a large spoon. Bake until bubbly and browned on top, about 25 minutes. Serve immediately.

Note The pie can be assembled up to 2 days before baking. Cover with plastic wrap and refrigerate. It will need at least 30 minutes in the oven to become piping hot.

to toast nuts

Preheat the oven to 350 degrees. Spread the nuts on a rimmed baking sheet and toast, stirring occasionally, until golden brown. Be sure not to burn them.

Almonds: Toast whole almonds for 10 minutes, slivered or sliced almonds for 5 minutes.

Cashews: Toast for 5 minutes.

Hazelnuts: Toast for 10 to 12 minutes, or until golden on the inside (bite into one to see). To skin, pour the nuts onto a kitchen towel while they are still hot and form a sack, then rub to remove most of the skins.

Pecans: Toast for 5 minutes.

Pine nuts: Toast for 3 minutes.

Walnuts: Toast for 5 minutes.

communal casseroles, lasagnas, chilies, stews, and savory pies

israeli couscous casserole

My friend Patti coined the term "cannonball couscous" to describe the large granules of Israeli couscous. Don't confuse them with the tiny grains of the more common couscous. These granules are the size of peppercorns and grow larger once they're cooked. I prefer their texture, and it's worth your while to seek them out. Look for them in whole food stores or Middle Eastern markets. Serve this casserole in shallow bowls with crusty bread.

SERVES 4 TO 6

1 In a large saucepan, heat the olive oil over medium heat. Add the couscous, fennel, garlic, and fennel seeds and sauté for 2 minutes, stirring to coat everything with the oil. Add the kale, vegetable broth, and 1 cup boiling water. Cook, stirring frequently, until the couscous is al dente, about 12 minutes. Remove from the heat.

2 Add the feta, tomatoes, and balsamic vinegar and stir until the feta is melted and the tomatoes are heated through. Season with salt and pepper. Serve hot.

- 2 tablespoons extra-virgin olive oil
- 1 cup uncooked Israeli couscous (see page 447)
- 1 fennel bulb, cored and thinly sliced (about 2 cups)
- 6 garlic cloves, minced
- 1 teaspoon fennel seeds
- 3 cups julienned kale leaves
- 2 cups vegetable broth, heated
- 6 ounces creamy French goat's milk feta cheese
- 1 11-ounce can diced tomatoes, drained
- 1 teaspoon balsamic vinegar

  Kosher salt and freshly ground black pepper to taste

Note
The casserole can be made up to 2 days ahead. Transfer to an 8-cup casserole dish, cover, and refrigerate. Reheat in the oven or microwave.

chapter 8

Intimate Gatherings and Celebrations

rebel with a cause

You don't have to grin and bear holidays you loathe. Here are five alternatives:

Super Bowl Sunday: Instead of watching men run into each other and create piles of flesh, have a Southeast Asian dinner party or, better yet, order Asian take-out. If that doesn't suit you, Super Bowl Sunday is a good opportunity for a night out at a restaurant that's normally too packed to get reservations. This day is also a good time for a tea party for football widows (of either gender!).

Thanksgiving: If you dread being with your extended family but like the idea of giving thanks for our bounty, do as a friend of mine in Boston does: hold a "preferred" Thanksgiving. A couple of weeks before the real thing, invite friends over and cook the food that you prefer to eat (see page 311 for vegetarian ideas). Of course you can always do this after Thanksgiving and compare the dramas you endured with your relatives.

The Olympics: Even if you like the sports, who can stand the campy coverage? Instead of grouping around the screen, why not have a nerdy book party? A friend of mine once gave a "favorite book" party. Bring your favorite book (of late or of all time) and have each guest talk about his or her book. At the end of the party, everyone swaps books—or at least knows what book to read next. Table decorations could be ten or twenty of your favorite books standing in a row down your dining room table with bookends.

Kentucky Derby Day: For those who love ruthless competition and betting, Derby Day is a joy. But those who don't care to witness horses being whipped by their riders and sometimes being injured for money and human pleasure need to find other amusement. Why not stage a race of your own? Invite some friends over and organize a piggyback race around the house or the block. There's no better way to crack the ice with someone than to jump on his or her back and yell, "Faster!" You can drink mint juleps and wager as you see fit.

Independence Day: When the best of the country is throwing burgers on the grill, hold a Grilling Without Animals party (see page 131).

spaghetti with green olive pesto

Here's a dish that wins everyone's hearts and stomachs. Use any flavorful green Mediterranean olive (canned olives, by and large, are *not* satisfactory). Instead of the arugula, you could use spinach or watercress. Substituting gnocchi for the spaghetti is also a fine idea. I recommend a light, nonoily salad before or after, such as Jicama-Grape Salad (page 123). Serve with crusty bread. This dish, sans cheese, also makes an excellent cold summer salad. (Use a small pasta shape such as macaroni for the salad version.)

SERVES 6

¼ cup pine nuts

Kosher salt to taste

1 pound dried spaghetti or linguine

1½ cups packed fresh basil leaves

¾ cup pitted Mediterranean green olives, brine reserved

1 cup freshly grated Parmesan cheese

2 garlic cloves

2 tablespoons fresh lemon juice (½ juicy lemon)

⅔ cup extra-virgin olive oil

2½ cups halved cherry tomatoes or 2 tomatoes, cut into ½-inch cubes

1 large bunch arugula, stemmed

Freshly ground black pepper to taste

1 In a small skillet, toast the pine nuts over medium heat, shaking the skillet often, until they are golden brown in spots, about 3 minutes. Transfer to a small bowl and set aside.

2 Bring a large pot of salted water to a boil. Add the spaghetti or linguine and return to a boil, stirring to separate the noodles. Boil for 8 to 10 minutes, or until al dente. Drain, then return the pasta to the pot.

3 Meanwhile, in a food processor, puree the basil, olives, ½ cup of the Parmesan, the garlic, lemon juice, and 2 tablespoons water into a coarse paste.

With the machine running, slowly add the olive oil through the feed tube, and then add 3 tablespoons of the reserved olive brine.

Olives

4 Add the pesto, tomatoes, and arugula to the pot of pasta and mix well to coat everything with the pesto. Season with salt and pepper. Divide among plates, garnishing each serving with some of the toasted pine nuts. Serve, passing the remaining ¹/₂ cup Parmesan at the table.

Menu Suggestion

Cup of Rachel and Felicity's Minestrone (page 96)
Spaghetti with Green Olive Pesto
Cardamom Pound Cake (page 438)
One-Bite-Won't-Suffice Lemon Ice (page 418)

Wine Suggestion

Drink a dry sherry such as amontillado with this meal; it will be perfect. Barbera is another option, or if white wine is preferred, Soave, or a dry Riesling from Germany or New Zealand.

linguine with swiss chard and garlicky bread crumbs

Inspired by one of Michael Romano's pasta dishes from the Union Square Bistro in New York, this dish takes some time (about an hour) to make, but if you like crunchy garlicky bread crumbs with pasta, don't pass it up. Use red Swiss chard if possible, because of its brilliant color.

SERVES 4

1 In a food processor, grind the bread slices into coarse crumbs. In a large skillet, heat 3 tablespoons of the olive oil over medium heat. Add half of the garlic and sauté for 1 minute. Add the bread crumbs and cook, stirring frequently, until the crumbs are brown and crisp. Sprinkle with the balsamic vinegar, stirring constantly. Season with salt and pepper. Transfer to a small bowl and set aside.

2 In the same skillet, heat 2 tablespoons more olive oil over medium heat. Add the chard and sauté until the stems are tender, about 8 minutes. Add the remaining garlic and the red pepper flakes and sauté for 2 minutes more.

3 Meanwhile, bring a large pot of salted water to a boil. Add the linguine

- 4 slices white or whole wheat sandwich bread
- 8 tablespoons extra-virgin olive oil
- 6 garlic cloves, minced
- 1 tablespoon balsamic vinegar

  Kosher salt and freshly ground black pepper to taste

- 1 bunch Swiss chard, leaves thinly sliced, stems finely chopped
- ½ teaspoon crushed red pepper flakes, or more to taste
- 1 pound dried linguine
- 3 tablespoons freshly grated Pecorino Romano cheese
- 1 lemon, cut into 4 wedges

and return to a boil, stirring to separate the noodles. Boil for 8 to 10 minutes, or until al dente. Drain, then return the pasta to the pot. Add the chard mixture, the cheese, and the remaining 3 tablespoons olive oil. Season generously with salt and pepper, and toss well. Top with the bread crumbs and serve with lemon wedges for squeezing.

Note

The bread crumbs can be sautéed and the chard cut up to 1 day ahead and stored separately in airtight containers in the fridge.

Menu Suggestion

Fennel Slaw (page 117)
Linguine with Swiss Chard and Garlicky Bread Crumbs
Blueberry-Peach Cranachan — use strawberries, nectarines or plums instead of blueberries and peaches if desired (page 403)

Wine Suggestion

A Loire red such as Chinon would work well.

how to wash greens

A lot of people wash spinach or Swiss chard by holding it under running water. This is a kitchen "don't!" Greens are tricky, and they'll hold dirt in their crevices unless you drown them in water.

Fill a large bowl with cool (not cold) water; if you're going to cook the greens, you can use warm water. Immerse the greens in the water and swish them around for a few seconds, then let them stand until the dirt settles to the bottom. Lift the greens out of the water and transfer them to a colander (never pour the greens into the colander, which will dump the dirt back onto them). If the greens are very dirty (you can tell by the water), bathe them a second time.

portobello–goat cheese lasagna with flashy green sauce

People always rave about this impressive lasagna. Who wouldn't enjoy putting a fork through layers of mashed potatoes, soft noodles, seared garlicky portobellos, and goat cheese? The brilliant green basil-scallion sauce makes it sophisticated enough for a fancy meal. If you want to go a notch or two higher, use shiitake, oyster, or chanterelle mushrooms instead of—or combined with—the portobellos. Set aside an hour and a half for the first time you make this lasagna.

SERVES 8 TO 10

2½ pounds red or Yukon Gold potatoes, quartered

Kosher salt to taste

6 ounces fresh, creamy goat cheese

2 tablespoons butter

¾ cup milk

Freshly ground black pepper to taste

3 tablespoons plus ½ cup extra-virgin olive oil

1½ pounds portobello mushrooms, caps and top half of stems chopped

4 garlic cloves, minced

½ ounce dried porcini mushrooms or 1 ounce dried shiitake mushrooms, minced while still dry

¾ cup Marsala or Madeira

1 cup red lentils (see page 450)

1 cup sour cream

½ cup freshly grated Parmesan cheese

1 cup packed fresh basil leaves, 4 leaves reserved for garnish

6 scallions, white and green parts, chopped

2 tablespoons fresh lemon juice (½ juicy lemon)

1 pound fresh egg-roll wrappers, or 1 pound lasagna noodles, cooked

1 In a large saucepan, combine the potatoes with cold salted water to cover. Bring to a boil and boil until fork-tender, about 15 minutes. Drain and return the potatoes to the dried pan. Mash with a fork or potato masher, and stir in half of the goat cheese, the butter, and the milk. Season liberally with salt and pepper. Set aside.

2 In a large skillet, heat 3 tablespoons of the olive oil over medium heat. Add the portobellos and sauté until they soften and begin to brown, about 5 minutes. Stir in three quarters of the garlic and sauté for 1 minute more. Stir in the dried mushrooms and the Marsala or Madeira. Season with salt and pepper. Remove from the heat and set aside.

3 In a small saucepan, bring 2 cups water to a boil. Add the lentils and cook until tender, about 5 minutes. Set aside.

4 Meanwhile, in a small bowl, combine the sour cream, the remaining goat cheese, and $1/4$ cup of the Parmesan. Set aside.

5 In a blender or food processor, combine the basil, scallions, and remaining garlic. With the machine running, slowly add the remaining $1/2$ cup olive oil through the feed tube. Add the lemon juice and 2 tablespoons water. Season liberally with salt and pepper. Set aside.

6 Preheat the oven to 375 degrees. Lightly oil a 13-x-9-inch baking pan.

7 Line the bottom of the prepared pan with a single layer of the egg-roll wrappers or noodles, cutting some with scissors if necessary to make a uniform layer. Use a slotted spoon to scatter the mushroom mixture evenly over the pasta, leaving the juices behind. Add another layer of egg-roll wrappers or noodles, and top with the mashed potatoes. Add another layer of egg-roll wrappers or noodles, and top with the sour cream mixture, then the lentils. Add a final layer of egg-roll wrappers or noodles.

8 Cover the pan with foil and bake until heated through, about 45 minutes.

9 Sprinkle the remaining ¼ cup Parmesan over the lasagna and cut it into 8 to 10 squares. Put a large spoonful of the basil-scallion sauce on each plate and place the lasagna on one side of it. Serve immediately.

Note The lasagna can be assembled and the sauce made up to 1 day ahead, covered with foil, and refrigerated separately. Bring the sauce to room temperature while you bake the lasagna. The chilled lasagna will need at least 50 minutes in the oven to become piping hot.

Menu Suggestion

Roasted Pear, Blue Cheese, and Bibb Salad with Cranberry Vinaigrette (page 126) and broken **Pita Chips** (page 43)
Portobello–Goat Cheese Lasagna with Flashy Green Sauce
Hazelnut-Pear Torte (page 440) with vanilla ice cream, or **Pavlova** (page 416)

Wine Suggestion

Mushrooms, lentils, and goat cheese add up to an earthy-tasting dish. Famously earthy red Burgundy is the obvious choice. If you're willing to part with at least $25 — cheap by Burgundy standards — you could hardly do better than a Santenay, named after the wine's village of origin. Less complex but still food-friendly, so-called generic Burgundies can be had for around $15. These wines may be identified on the label as Bourgogne Rouge or Pinot Noir, the grape from which red Burgundy is made.

do you really need to buy parmigiano-reggiano for grating?

Matt Rubiner, owner of the Richmond Store in western Massachusetts, has strong opinions on Parmesan. He says Parmigiano-Reggiano is absolutely worth its price tag: "There is a reliable consistency in Reggiano, because the regulations are strictly controlled. It's made from raw milk, and only a specific region's milk is used. It's sweet and nutty, not too salty, and has lots of complexity." But I find that I just don't want to spend that much when the cheese is used in recipes where its flavor isn't in the forefront. For this, Matt recommends either Parmesan grana, an Italian cheese that's less expensive and a good alternative to Reggiano, or Wisconsin Asiago, a hard grating cheese that's reasonably priced and packs a good punch.

With its sharp flavor, aged goat cheese is not a substitute for Parmesan, but it's one of Matt's favorite grating cheeses.

Avoid

Pecorino Romano: This pungent cheese is too salty to substitute for Parmesan. It is normally used in dishes that can stand up to its sharp flavor.

Argentinean Regginito: Don't be taken in by its cheaper price. Its consistency is not reliable, and the flavor is not terribly complex.

goat cheese flan with arugula salad

This simple first course or light meal makes any occasion special. The recipe came from a friend who got it at the Slow Food Festival 2000 in Turin, Italy. I replaced the original Parmigiano with a local goat cheese—a rather drastic move, but one that worked. If you have any fresh herbs on hand, such as thyme, chives, or marjoram, chop a small handful and add to the food processor. If you're making a meal of this flan, serve with fresh bread.

SERVES 6

flan

- 12 ounces fresh goat cheese
- 1½ cups half-and-half
- ½ cup heavy cream
- 3 large eggs
- 1 teaspoon truffle oil (see page 453; optional)
- Kosher salt and freshly ground black pepper to taste

arugula salad

- 1 bunch arugula
- 1 red onion, thinly sliced
- 2 tablespoons extra-virgin olive oil
- 1 tablespoon balsamic vinegar
- Kosher salt and freshly ground black pepper to taste

1 **To make the flan:** Preheat the oven to 350 degrees. Butter a 9-inch square baking dish or six 1-cup ramekins.

2 In a food processor, puree the goat cheese. With the machine running, slowly add the half-and-half and cream through the feed tube and process until smooth. Add the eggs and process until smooth. Add the truffle oil, if using. Season with salt and pepper. Ladle into the prepared baking dish or ramekins.

3 Place the baking dish or ramekins in a roasting pan and place in the oven. Slowly pour hot water into the roasting pan until it reaches three quarters of the way up the baking dish or ramekins. Bake until a knife inserted in the center of the flan comes out clean, about 45 minutes for the baking pan and 30 minutes for the ramekins. Let cool for 10 minutes before serving.

4 **Meanwhile, to make the salad:** In a large bowl, combine the arugula with the onion, olive oil, and vinegar. Season with salt and pepper. Cover and refrigerate until serving time.

5 Distribute the salad among six plates. Run a paring knife around the edges of the baking dish or ramekins. Cut squares of flan from the baking dish or invert the ramekins onto a plate. Use a spatula to transfer the flan onto the arugula salad. There may be some liquid left in the bottom of the baking pan; just leave it behind. Serve immediately.

Note

The flan can be baked up to 2 hours ahead and kept in a warm (220-degree) oven.

Menu Suggestion

Carrot, Rosemary, and Ginger Minestrone (page 98)
Goat Cheese Flan with Arugula Salad
Hearty French or Italian bread
Lavender Ice (page 420)

Wine Suggestion

Try a dark rosé from Spain or the Rhône with this light yet rich flan.

porcini risotto pudding with truffle oil

This pudding is convenient because it can be made ahead and reheated in the oven. Serve it with crusty bread and a salad of mixed greens tossed with a perky dressing such as Classic Lemon Dressing (page 154) or Cranberry Vinaigrette (page 126).

SERVES 4

1 In a small bowl, combine the porcini and 1 cup boiling water. Let soak for 30 minutes. Remove the porcini, squeezing them so the liquid they absorbed falls back into the bowl. Reserve the soaking liquid. Set aside.

2 Preheat the oven to 350 degrees. Butter a 1½- or 2-quart baking dish.

3 In a large skillet, heat 2 tablespoons of the olive oil over medium heat. Add the scallions and carrots and sauté until softened, 6 to 7 minutes. Add the rice and sauté for 1 minute, stirring to coat with the oil. Reduce the heat to low and add the reserved porcini liquid to the skillet, leaving any sediment behind in the bowl. Add the wine and enough broth to cover the rice. Cover and simmer, adding more

1 ounce dried porcini mushrooms

4 tablespoons extra-virgin olive oil

1 bunch scallions, white and green parts, chopped

2 carrots, peeled and finely chopped

1 cup raw Arborio rice

¾ cup dry white wine

About 2¼ cups vegetable broth

8 ounces fresh cremini or white mushrooms, sliced

½ cup chopped fresh flat-leaf parsley

3 garlic cloves, minced

Kosher salt and freshly ground black pepper to taste

½ cup half-and-half or light cream

1 cup freshly grated Parmesan cheese

1 tablespoon truffle oil (see page 453)

broth every 5 minutes and stirring occasionally, until the rice is tender but still firm, about 30 minutes. Remove from the heat and let cool slightly.

4 Meanwhile, in a medium skillet, heat the remaining 2 tablespoons olive oil over medium heat. Add the fresh mushrooms and the porcini and sauté until the fresh mushrooms are cooked through, about 10 minutes. Stir in the parsley and garlic and sauté for 5 minutes more. Season with salt and pepper.

5 Stir the half-and-half or light cream into the risotto, and mix well. Transfer the risotto to the prepared baking dish and spread the mushroom mixture on top. Sprinkle the Parmesan over the mushrooms. Bake until the top is brown, about 25 minutes. Let cool for 5 minutes before drizzling with the truffle oil and serving.

Note

The pudding can be assembled up to 2 days ahead, covered, and stored in the fridge. Uncover and bake for about 35 minutes. Drizzle with the truffle oil just before serving.

Menu Suggestion

Asparagus Slaw (page 116) or **Bibb lettuce salad with cooked French lentils and a simple vinaigrette**
Porcini Risotto Pudding with Truffle Oil
Espresso Granita with Whipped Cream (page 419)

Wine Suggestion

Drink a simple Bourgogne (an inexpensive red burgundy) or a similar white Burgundy; or a dry sparkling wine.

truffle oil

Truffle oil is one of the sublime pleasures of life. Once you've tasted it on a hot, cheesy potato casserole or on buttered pasta, you'll never forget its flavor.

However, not all truffle oil is created equal. Some have only a trace of ethereal truffle flavor. My favorite brands include Urbani Gocce di Tartufa, Condimento di Tartufo, Truffoil (L'Aquila Importers, London), and Boscovivo (in larger print: Condimento aromatizzato al Tartufo Bianco).

If you buy yourself a bottle of truffle oil, get to know its versatility (see the suggestions below). Even if you use it often, a little goes a long way, so it's best to start with a small bottle. Store truffle oil in the fridge. I've had truffle oil lose all its flavor because I stored it in my pantry during the summer (at which point it tastes like plain olive oil). Because truffle oil is made with olive oil, it will solidify in the fridge. Just pull it out 15 to 20 minutes before using, and it will melt enough to extract the necessary drops. Truffle oil's subtle flavor disappears when cooked, so it is always added to foods just before serving. The following dishes will welcome a drizzle of truffle oil:

- **Grilled cheese sandwich** (I recommend Italian fontina on peasant bread, using either butter or olive oil in the skillet, perhaps with sliced tomato or sautéed mushrooms.) Drizzle the oil onto the cheese as you're making the sandwich.

- **Mesclun salad** (Combine enough mesclun for two with 2 teaspoons red wine vinegar and 1 to 2 teaspoons truffle oil and toss—this also makes an exquisite topping for a pizza with Italian fontina.)

- **Goat Cheese and Roasted Garlic Fondue** (page 72)

- **Shiitakes Stuffed with Goat Cheese, Cranberries, and Pecans** (drizzle on the oil just before serving; page 48)

- **Baked Onion Cheese Soup** (page 106)

- **Escalivada** (page 346)

- Red Cabbage Risotto (page 318)
- Israeli Couscous Casserole (page 284)
- Soft Polenta with Tomato-Spinach Ragout (page 276)
- Mac'n'Cheese (page 256)
- Linguine with Swiss Chard and Garlicky Bread Crumbs (page 290)
- Shiitake Risotto with Edamame (page 320)
- Portobello–Goat Cheese Lasagna with Flashy Green Sauce (page 292)
- Root Stew with Millet Cakes (drizzle it into the stew; page 308)

intimate gatherings and celebrations

crispy rice cakes on spinach with viet red pepper sauce

V *These rice cakes have a lovely crunch* and soft middle, and the red bell pepper–lime sauce plays off it winsomely. (The sauce is also terrific with spring rolls.) The spinach is cleaned well and cooked with its pinkish roots intact. You can find bunches of spinach with the roots in well-stocked supermarkets and whole food stores.

SERVES 6

cakes

- 1¼ cups raw Japanese short-grain rice (see page 447)
- ½ cup minus 1 tablespoon dried, unsweetened coconut
- ½ teaspoon kosher salt
- 3 scallions, white and green parts, finely chopped
- ¼ cup chopped fresh cilantro leaves and stems
- 2 tablespoons canola oil

sauce

- 2 red bell peppers, chopped
- 2 garlic cloves
- ¼ cup chopped fresh cilantro leaves and stems or mint leaves
- 1 tablespoon sugar
- ¼ cup fresh lime juice (2 juicy limes)
- ½ teaspoon kosher salt or 1 tablespoon Asian fish sauce (see page 444)
- 1 teaspoon Asian chili sauce (see page 443), or more to taste
- 2 pounds fresh spinach, washed well, stems and roots left on

  Kosher salt and freshly ground black pepper to taste
- 2 tablespoons dried, unsweetened coconut for garnish

Note The rice cakes can be formed and the sauce made up to 1 day ahead and stored separately in airtight containers in the fridge. The cakes can be fried up to 3 hours ahead and reheated on a baking sheet in a 300-degree oven for 10 to 15 minutes. The spinach is best cooked just before serving.

entertaining for a veggie planet

302

1 **To make the cakes:** In a medium saucepan, bring 2^1/$_2$ cups water to a boil over medium-high heat. Add the rice, coconut, and salt and mix well. Return to a boil, cover, and reduce the heat to a simmer. Simmer gently for 15 minutes, or until the water is absorbed. Remove from the heat and let stand, covered, for 5 minutes. Transfer the rice mixture to a shallow bowl and refrigerate for at least 1 hour. Add the scallions and cilantro and mix well. Form the cooled rice into 6 cakes at least 1 inch thick. Set aside.

2 **Meanwhile, to make the sauce:** In a food processor, puree the bell peppers and garlic until smooth. Add the cilantro or mint, sugar, lime juice, salt or fish sauce, and chili sauce and process until smooth.

3 In a large pot, combine ^{1}/$_2$ cup water and the spinach. Season with salt and pepper. Cook the spinach until just wilted, about 3 minutes. Drain the water from the pot and keep the spinach warm.

4 **To pan-fry the cakes:** In a large, heavy skillet, heat the canola oil over medium-high heat. Add the rice cakes, working in batches if necessary to avoid crowding the skillet, and fry until golden brown and crispy on the bottoms, 6 to 8 minutes. Turn and brown the other sides, 6 to 8 minutes more.

5 Divide the sauce among 6 plates. Place a mound of spinach on the sauce and top with a rice cake. Sprinkle with the dried coconut and serve immediately.

Menu Suggestion

The Prettiest Little Salad Around (page 125)
Crispy Rice Cakes on Spinach with Viet Red Pepper Sauce
Mexican Flan (page 406) or **Blueberry-Peach Cranachan** (page 403)

Wine Suggestion

With flavors that mirror those of the main dish, zesty, lime- and herb-tinged New Zealand Sauvignon Blanc has the right stuff to pair with this meal.

intimate gatherings and celebrations

black rice cakes with tofu and mussamun curry

(V) *Dinner guests love the glamour* of this black rice cake sitting in a bright yellow sauce. The list of spices in this recipe makes it look far more complicated than it really is. The sauce can be served with a variety of dishes, such as fresh Asian rice or wheat noodles or pan-fried tempeh, or used as a dipping sauce with Potato Dosa (page 356) or Roti Jala (page 358).

Use only the stems and roots of the cilantro in this curry and a few of the leaves for the garnish. Since you'll have lots of leftover cilantro leaves, some of my favorite recipes using cilantro are Fresh Cilantro Chutney (page 344), Chinese Noodles in Spicy Lemongrass Sauce with Peanuts (page 246), and Hip Dip (page 36). Cilantro leaves can be stored in a damp kitchen towel in the fridge for up to a week.

One more note: Don't use "forbidden black rice," which is jet black and sold in whole food stores. Its low gluten content will make it impossible to form the rice into cakes.

> *Note*
> The rice cakes can be formed up to 2 days ahead and stored in an airtight container in the fridge. The cakes can be fried up to 3 hours ahead and reheated on a baking sheet in a 300-degree oven for 10 to 15 minutes. The curry can be made, without the cilantro, up to 2 days ahead. Add the cilantro just before serving.

SERVES 4

cakes

½ cup raw jasmine rice

½ cup raw black rice (see page 444)

¼ cup dried, unsweetened coconut

1 teaspoon kosher salt

2 tablespoons canola oil

curry

1 16-ounce carton firm tofu

2 large lemongrass stalks

2 tablespoons canola oil

1 small onion, chopped

4 large garlic cloves, minced

1 tablespoon peeled and minced
   fresh ginger

3 fresh small, skinny green or red chile
   peppers, finely chopped

2 tablespoons ground coriander

2 teaspoons fennel seeds

1 teaspoon turmeric

Pinch of ground cloves

1 13.5-ounce can unsweetened
   coconut milk (see page 446)

6 ounces green beans, trimmed

1 cup cherry tomatoes

⅔ cup finely chopped fresh cilantro,
   roots and stems included, plus
   1 tablespoon leaves for garnish

½ lime, quartered, for garnish

1 **To make the cakes:** In a medium saucepan, bring 1³/₄ cups water to a boil over medium-high heat. Add the jasmine rice, black rice, coconut, and salt and mix well. Return to a boil, cover, and reduce the heat to a simmer. Simmer gently for 15 minutes, or until the water is absorbed. Remove from the heat and let stand, covered, for 5 minutes. Transfer the rice mixture to a shallow bowl and refrigerate for at least 1 hour. Form the cooled rice into four cakes about 1 inch thick. Set aside.

2 **To make the curry:** Wrap the block of tofu in a clean dishtowel and press it firmly with your hands until you feel the towel become damp. Unwrap the tofu and cut it into ½-inch cubes. Set aside.

3 Cut off the bulbous bottom third of the lemongrass stalks (reserve the rest of the stalks for another use). Remove and discard the tough outer leaves. With a large, sharp chef's knife or a plastic vegetable slicer, cut the lemongrass bottoms into thin slices, then mince them. Set aside.

4 In a large skillet, heat the canola oil over medium heat. Add the onion and sauté, stirring occasionally, until soft, about 7 minutes. Add the garlic and the ginger and sauté for 2 minutes more. Add the lemongrass, chiles, coriander, fennel seeds, turmeric, and cloves and sauté for 30 seconds. Stir in the coconut milk and ¹/₂ cup water and simmer for 5 minutes.

5 Add the tofu, green beans, and tomatoes to the skillet, cover, and simmer gently until the green beans lose their raw texture, about 10 minutes. Remove from the heat and stir in the chopped cilantro. Cover and keep warm.

6 **To pan-fry the cakes:** In a large, heavy skillet over medium-high heat, heat the canola oil. Add the rice cakes, working in batches if necessary to avoid crowding the skillet, and fry until golden brown and crispy on the bottoms, 6 to 8 minutes. Turn and brown the other sides, 6 to 8 minutes more.

7 To serve, ladle the curry into four shallow bowls, top each with a rice cake, and garnish the rice cakes with the cilantro leaves and lime wedges.

Menu Suggestion

Chard and Eggplant Salad with Miso-Sesame Vinaigrette (page 134)
Black Rice Cakes with Tofu and Mussamun Curry
Banana–Brown Sugar Spring Rolls (page 423)

Wine Suggestion

Alsatian Pinot Gris, sometimes called Tokay Pinot Gris, sings with this curry. Less aromatic than a Gewürztraminer, it is similarly spicy and full-bodied. A vaguely smoky quality lurks beneath its rich fruit flavor, which can be reminiscent of pears.

offbeat centerpieces

As much as I love fresh flowers, I'm sometimes not up for dropping the cash or going to a flower shop. Here are some of the creative centerpieces I rely on from time to time:

- Once, when there was snow on the ground, I made an eighteen-inch snowman and put him on a platter in the center of the table. By the end of the night, his edges had softened and he had become even more elegant, suggestive of a Henry Moore sculpture.

- I collected a dozen or so large, unusually round, pastel-colored rocks one day on the beach. When they aren't piled on my coffee table, they sit on my dinner table, where their beauty and simplicity make an unobstructive centerpiece.

- I have amassed a collection of animals that I often bring to the table. Sometimes I use a few, sometimes the whole lot. I have a wooden frog, a plastic howling coyote, a stone gargoyle, a rubber monkey, and a large moose. I line them down the center of the table, positioning them so they seem to interact with each other. By the end of the night, you feel as though you have a whole slew of new friends, albeit mute ones.

- Take some frames and find photos of those who will be joining you. Make the framed photos your centerpiece.

- A friend of mine once wound a garden hose around flowerpots and sprinklers, which she placed on the table to give it a spring feel.

intimate gatherings and celebrations

root stew with millet cakes

Created by Jean-Georges Vongerichten, these elegant and indulgent millet cakes are a culinary stroke of genius. They need only a simple stew to make them a special-occasion dish. You can add or substitute other vegetables, such as shiitake mushrooms, tiny potatoes, or winter squash, or top the stew with a garnish of a few garlicky seared oyster or chanterelle mushrooms. Served with a good red wine, it's a guaranteed crowd-pleaser. You can find millet, a humble but hearty grain, in whole food stores.

SERVES 4

stew

2 tablespoons extra-virgin olive oil

2 large onions, diced

3 garlic cloves, minced

1 cup dry red wine

1 pound kale, stemmed and chopped

1 turnip (about 1 pound), peeled and cut into 1/2-inch cubes

2 parsnips or carrots, peeled and cut into 1/2-inch rounds

1/2 ounce dried porcini mushrooms, chopped

2 cups vegetable broth or water

1 tablespoon sherry vinegar

2 teaspoons cornstarch

Kosher salt and freshly ground black pepper to taste

millet cakes

1 1/2 cups raw millet

Kosher salt to taste

4 tablespoons (1/2 stick) butter, melted

3 large eggs plus 1 large egg yolk

1/3 cup milk

2 teaspoons chopped fresh rosemary or sage

1 cup freshly grated Parmesan cheese

Freshly ground black pepper to taste

1 tablespoon extra-virgin olive oil

1 **To make the stew:** In a large pot, heat the olive oil over medium heat. Add the onions and sauté until translucent, 7 to 9 minutes. Add the garlic and sauté for 2 minutes more, then stir in the wine and 1 cup water. Add the kale, turnip, parsnips or carrots, porcini, and vegetable broth or water. Partially cover and simmer until the porcini and vegetables are tender, about 20 minutes.

2 In a small bowl, dissolve the cornstarch in 1 tablespoon cold water. Stir into the stew. Simmer, stirring occasionally, until slightly thickened, about 1 minute. Add the vinegar and season liberally with salt and pepper.

3 **Meanwhile, to make the millet cakes:** Preheat the oven to 350 degrees. In a medium saucepan, combine the millet, a pinch of salt, and 3 cups water and bring to a boil over medium heat. Cover, reduce the heat to a simmer, and cook for 20 minutes. Remove from the heat and let stand, covered, for 10 minutes, or until the liquid is absorbed. Stir in the butter, then add the eggs and egg yolk, one at a time, mixing well after each addition. Add the milk, rosemary or sage, and 3/4 cup of the Parmesan and season with salt and pepper.

Note

The stew and millet batter can be made up to 1 day ahead and stored separately in airtight containers in the fridge. The cooked millet cakes can be kept warm for up to 2 hours on a baking sheet in a 220-degree oven.

4 Heat a large, heavy skillet over high heat. When the skillet is hot, add the olive oil and heat until it is very hot. Spoon the millet batter into the skillet, in batches if necessary, forming four 5-inch cakes. Fry until the edges become firm and bubbles appear in the middles, about 3 minutes. Turn and fry the cakes on the other sides for 2 to 3 minutes, or until they are lightly browned. Transfer the cakes to a baking sheet as they are done. When all the cakes have been browned, place them in the oven for about 10 minutes to add more crunch. Ladle the stew into four shallow bowls and arrange a millet cake, cut in half, on top of each serving. Top with the remaining 4 tablespoons Parmesan and serve.

intimate gatherings and celebrations

Watercress, Cabbage, and Tomato Slaw with Ginger Dressing (page 124)
Root Stew with Millet Cakes
Lemon Square Cake (page 432) with whipped cream

Menu Suggestion

Wine Suggestion

Nearly any flavorful, dry red would complement this stew, but an inexpensive Portuguese selection—look to the Dão and Barraida regions—befits the rustic simplicity of the dish. French country wines (look for "Vin de Pays" on the label) have similar humble origins and a reputation for high quality at a low price. In this instance, cook with the same wine you're drinking.

i have a dream . . .

I harbor a dream that I will move our family's very traditional Connecticut Thanksgiving to Boston, where my entire family (which now numbers twelve) will dine in my cozy apartment. I'll invite six or seven of my friends who are in need of a home to celebrate the day. I'll decorate my table *Wild Kingdom*–style, with my full collection of plastic and wooden animals roaming down the middle of the table, interspersed with three or four glowing candles. I'll have a chair set out next to mine for Henry, my cat (who has been excluded from the Thanksgiving table all his life). The tablecloth will be a mélange of batiks that I bought in Malaysia a few years ago. Music by local musicians will be playing on the CD player.

But the food is really where I'll stir things up. I'll serve a series of the most inventive and scrumptious vegetarian dishes, using local and unusual produce. Everyone at the table will enter a state of bliss, their personalities exuding only love and warmth. Not even my father will notice that meat has been omitted (of course his mashed potatoes will be served, although perhaps I'll throw in some caramelized garlic). In the end, everyone will part with tears and hugs, begging me to do the same next year.

vegetarian strategies for turkey day

For most vegetarians, lentil loaf with gravy or Tofurky won't do the trick on Thanksgiving. Many nonvegetarian homes serve such good side dishes that the turkey fades into the background, so an inspired vegetarian Thanksgiving is well within reach. I think the very notion of trying to find a "main course" for Thanksgiving is dull. Take advantage of local produce, as our country's forefathers (the Pilgrims) did so many years ago. Blue hubbard squash, dumpling squash, turban squash, carrots, cranberries, chestnuts, walnuts, apples, pumpkins, Brussels sprouts, turnips, leeks, shallots, and potatoes are some of the earthly delights you can find at this time of year, depending on where you live. I like to make a meal of a buffet of side dishes, including pilafs and other entrée-like dishes. Here are some suggestions, some of them recipes in this book, others basic ideas that can be easily executed with a small amount of cooking knowledge. Have fun, eat what you like, and don't overwhelm yourself with too much cooking.

Star Anise Pecans (page 9)
Sweet Potato Soup with Chipotle and Sage (page 109)
Rutabaga and apple puree
Maple-glazed acorn squash
Wild rice pilaf
Chestnut and fried sage stuffing
Creamed white beans with onions
Mashed potatoes
Kasha-Crunch Burgers (page 172) or Hazelnut-Mushroom Burgers (page 170)—try these burgers as a turkey substitute and make some gravy with veggie mushroom stock from a box
Wild Rice Curry in Sugar Pumpkins (page 326)
Root Stew with Millet Cakes (page 308)

Spaghetti Squash Wedges with Roasted Vegetable–Feta Stuffing (page 330)
Figgy Walnut Bread (page 382)
Rosemary Roasted Winter Vegetables (page 328)—be creative, use any local winter squash
Savory Hubbard Squash Pudding (page 332)
Cranberry Vinaigrette (page 126)
Cranberry Chutney—use the Peach Chutney recipe on page 343, substituting 5 cups cranberries for the fruit, adding an additional 1/2 cup sugar with the berries
Curried Jack-o'-Lantern (page 212)
Hazelnut-Pear Torte (page 440)

intimate gatherings and celebrations

butternut risotto cakes with portobellos and stilton butter

Serve these hot, crisp, cheesy cakes on a watercress salad dressed with Not-Too-Sweet Caramelized Balsamic Dressing (page 156) or Cranberry Vinaigrette (page 126) or just extra-virgin olive oil and a touch of balsamic vinegar. If you don't have Arborio rice on hand, sushi rice will work fine.

SERVES 6

stilton butter

2 ounces Stilton cheese, crumbled

3 tablespoons unsalted butter, cut into pieces

risotto cakes

3 tablespoons pine nuts

6 tablespoons extra-virgin olive oil

2 portobello mushrooms, caps and upper halves of stems diced

8 garlic cloves, minced

Pinch of freshly ground nutmeg

1 medium onion, finely chopped

$1\frac{1}{2}$ cups raw Arborio rice

$\frac{3}{4}$ cup dry white wine

5 cups vegetable broth or water, heated

$\frac{1}{2}$ small butternut squash, peeled and cut into $\frac{1}{4}$-inch cubes (about 3 cups)

1 tablespoon chopped fresh thyme

$\frac{2}{3}$ cup freshly grated Parmesan cheese

Kosher salt and freshly ground black pepper to taste

All-purpose flour for dredging

Note The risotto and Stilton butter can be made up to 2 days ahead and stored separately in the fridge. In fact, the risotto will be much easier to handle when it's well chilled.

1 **To make the butter:** In a food processor, combine the Stilton and butter and process until well blended. Transfer the Stilton butter to a sheet of plastic wrap and roll it up into a tight, smooth cylinder about 2 inches in diameter. Refrigerate for at least 1 hour.

2 **To make the risotto cakes:** In a small skillet, toast the pine nuts over medium heat, shaking the skillet often, until they're golden brown in spots, about 3 minutes. Transfer to a bowl and set aside.

3 In a large, heavy saucepan, heat 2 tablespoons of the olive oil over medium heat. Add the portobellos and sauté until they are cooked through. Add half of the garlic and sauté for 1 minute more, then stir in the nutmeg. Transfer the mushroom mixture to a bowl and return the pan to the heat. Heat 2 more tablespoons olive oil. Add the onion and sauté for 3 minutes. Add the rice and the remaining garlic, stirring to coat with the oil, and cook for 2 minutes more.

4 Reduce the heat to medium and stir in the wine. Cook until most of the liquid is absorbed, stirring occasionally. Add $1/2$ cup broth or water and simmer, stirring occasionally, until the liquid is absorbed. Continue adding the liquid in this fashion, $1/2$ cup at a time. When half of the liquid has been added, stir in the squash and thyme. Continue to cook, adding the liquid, until the squash is cooked through and the rice is tender but slightly chewy, about 8 minutes more.

5 Fold in the mushrooms, Parmesan, and pine nuts. Season liberally with salt and pepper. Transfer the risotto to a shallow bowl and refrigerate for at least 1 hour. Form the cooled risotto into twelve 3-inch patties, pressing gently so they hold together.

6 **To pan-fry the cakes:** In a large, heavy skillet, heat the remaining 2 tablespoons oil over medium-high heat. Dredge the patties lightly in flour and add to the skillet, working in batches if necessary to avoid crowding the skillet, and fry until golden brown and crispy on the bottoms, 6 to 8 minutes. Turn and brown the other sides, 6 to 8 minutes more.

intimate gatherings and celebrations

7 Place two risotto cakes on each of six plates and sprinkle them lightly with salt. Top each cake with a thin slice of the Stilton butter and serve immediately.

Menu Suggestion

Arugula with orange or clementine segments, shaved red onion, and a drizzle of Creamy Tofu-Lime Dressing (page 159)

Butternut Risotto Cakes with Portobellos and Stilton Butter

Macadamia–Tropical Fruit Salad with Ice Cream (page 412)

Wine Suggestion

Two strong-tasting cheeses point in the direction of an assertive wine. The Aussies call it Shiraz and we call it Syrah, but either way this ripe, smooth-textured red wine with hints of black pepper is a felicitous match with these risotto cakes.

how to throw people out of the kitchen

During a dinner party, you're scrambling to get everything together in the kitchen when a friend strolls in and asks, "Hey, how's your new job going?" Meanwhile, you can't find the wine opener, the entrée is burning, and your garbage disposal is jammed. The best way to deal with talkative guests is to put them to work. Once some of the pressure is off, you might feel like being nice or they may see how stressed out you are and back off. But sometimes you just need to be alone. You might say, "Good question. Let me get back to you on that a bit later—right now I'm experiencing some technical difficulties." I have one brave friend who uses just three words to fend off kitchen loiterers: "Shoo! Shoo! Shoo!" It all depends on your style and on how well you know the person who innocently interrogates.

thanksgiving

My family's Thanksgiving in Connecticut is about as staid as it gets. We have the same menu year after year because if we change it in any way, my father protests. One year I decided to improve things by making creamed onions from scratch, instead of using the frozen kind. As we all dug in, my father scooped up an onion with his fork and then clutched his throat with both hands and coughed up the onion. He tugged on my shirtsleeve and said with a sniffle, "Would you mind warming up some of those nice frozen onions for your poor father?"

My father has made the same mashed potatoes for over twenty-five years, and they're usually the best part of the meal. He wallows in his glory, making an annual speech just after the family blessing: "As hard as it is to believe, I have outdone myself yet *again.* This year's mashed potatoes are absolutely the cream of the crop—ambrosia! Even Paul Bocuse couldn't make potatoes like these."

When I was about seventeen, I interrupted him and announced to our large group, "Just so you know, my sisters and I did all the hard work. *We* bought the potatoes, *we* peeled them, and *we* boiled them. All he did was stroll in at the last minute and whip in a little milk and butter, with an electric mixer no less!"

My father was not in the least bit fazed. "This is how all great chefs must operate," he said.

Next Thanksgiving, things will be exactly the same. If we're lucky.

persian rice with pita crust

This pilaf is adapted from a recipe in *Madhur Jaffrey's World Vegetarian*. The buttery, saffron-infused pita works as a dome and makes the rice and pistachio pilaf all the better.

SERVES 4

3/4 cup raw basmati rice

Kosher salt to taste

1 new potato, peeled and cut into 1/2-inch dice

2 plum tomatoes, coarsely chopped

1/3 cup dried currants or raisins

2 big pinches of saffron threads

Freshly ground black pepper to taste

3 tablespoons unsalted butter

1/4 cup whole shelled pistachio nuts

1 medium pita bread, split into 2 disks

1/2 lime, cut into 4 wedges

1 In a small bowl, soak the rice in cool water for 5 minutes. Drain the rice, then soak for 5 minutes more; drain again. In a medium saucepan, bring 1 3/4 cups salted water to a boil. Add the rice, potato, tomatoes, currants or raisins, and saffron. Cover, reduce the heat to its lowest setting, and simmer for 10 minutes. Remove from the heat and let stand, covered, for 10 minutes. Season with salt and pepper. Set aside.

2 In a medium, nonstick skillet, melt the butter over low heat. Add the pistachios and sauté until crisp, about 2 minutes. (You'll need to taste one to know when they're ready.) Using a slotted spoon, transfer the nuts to the rice.

3 Place one pita disk cut side down in the same skillet, reserving the remaining pita disk for another use. Spoon the pilaf over the pita. (It's OK if the pita doesn't reach the sides of the skillet and the pilaf spills over the edges.) Drizzle 2 tablespoons water over the rice. Cover the skillet tightly with foil and then the lid. Cook for 5 minutes.

4 Remove the cover and foil and place a serving plate on top of the skillet. Invert the skillet and the rice "cake" onto the plate. Let stand for 10 minutes before cutting into wedges with a sharp knife, cutting through the pita crust as you serve. Serve each piece with a lime wedge for squeezing.

Menu Suggestion

Mixed green salad with Tahini-Lemon Dressing (page 157) or **Ana's Yellow Tomato Gazpacho** (page 95)
Persian Rice with Pita Crust
Melon Sago (page 410) or **Hilde's Berry Pudding** (page 409)

Wine Suggestion

With flavors that mirror those of the main dish, New Zealand Sauvignon Blanc is a good match for this meal.

red cabbage risotto

Rice and cabbage have an affinity for each other, making each taste better when they're together. This risotto is a pretty red color from the cabbage, and the caraway, the green apple, and a touch of cider vinegar give it a delicate Alsatian accent. It's a surprisingly pleasing dish, even for people who normally eschew cabbage.

SERVES 4

3 tablespoons unsalted butter

1 medium onion, chopped

6 garlic cloves, minced

4 cups thinly sliced red cabbage

1 teaspoon caraway seeds or anise seeds

1 cup raw Arborio rice

1 cup dry white wine

1 tart green apple, peeled and cut into $1/4$-inch cubes

$1/4$ cup dried currants (optional)

1 tablespoon cider vinegar

Kosher salt and freshly ground black pepper to taste

3 ounces feta cheese, crumbled

2 scallions, white and green parts, chopped

1 In a small saucepan, bring 4 cups water to a simmer over medium heat and keep it hot. In a large saucepan, melt 2 tablespoons of the butter over medium heat. Add the onion and sauté, stirring occasionally, for 5 minutes. Add the garlic and sauté for 2 minutes more, or until the onion is soft. Reduce the heat to low and stir in the cabbage and caraway or anise seeds. Cook, stirring often, until the cabbage is very soft, about 15 minutes.

2 Add the rice, stirring to coat with the butter, then add the wine and stir constantly until it is completely absorbed. Add $1/2$ cup of the simmering water and the apple, and cook, stirring frequently, until the water is absorbed. Add the currants, if using, and $1/2$ cup of the simmering water and stir constantly until the liquid is completely absorbed. Add the remaining water, $^1/_2$ cup at a time, stirring constantly until each addition is absorbed, until the rice is tender but still slightly chewy, 18 to 20 minutes total. Stir in the vinegar and the remaining 1 tablespoon butter and season with salt and pepper. Divide the risotto among four shallow bowls and garnish each with the feta and scallions.

Note The risotto can be prepared through step 1 up to 2 days ahead and stored in an airtight container in the fridge. Put the risotto in a large saucepan and continue as directed.

Menu Suggestion **Mesclun and watercress salad drizzled with Not-Too-Sweet Caramelized Balsamic Dressing** (page 156), topped with halved cherry tomatoes and edamame
Red Cabbage Risotto (serve with crusty bread and extra-virgin olive oil)
Chocolate Buttermilk Cake with Chocolate Sour Cream Frosting (page 426) and whipped cream

Wine Suggestion There's hardly any food that doesn't taste wonderful with an apple-scented German Riesling, but this dish is an especially suitable match. Lighter, less sweet (and typically less expensive) Rieslings carry the Kabinett designation; these are fine to serve with the risotto and, if slightly dry, can be added to the risotto as well.

shiitake risotto with edamame

 Whether you're snowed in on a cold winter day or just don't feel like heading to the store, this unusual pantry risotto is the perfect stay-at-home meal. Lauren, my part-time assistant, created this innovative recipe. The risotto has a cheeselike intensity, though it contains no cheese. Chilled, it makes fabulous risotto cakes.

SERVES 4

1½ cups dried shiitake mushrooms

1 tablespoon red or brown miso (see page 448; optional)

2 tablespoons extra-virgin olive oil

2 garlic cloves, minced

1½ cups raw Arborio rice

2 teaspoons dried tarragon

2 teaspoons kosher salt

½ teaspoon freshly ground black pepper

¾ cup frozen, shelled (podless) edamame (see page 446)

2 teaspoons Champagne vinegar or cider vinegar

1 In a large bowl, combine the shiitakes and 6 cups boiling water. Let soak for 10 minutes. Drain the shiitakes in a colander set over a medium saucepan to reserve the liquid. Place the saucepan over low heat, whisk in the miso, if using, and bring to a simmer. Remove and discard the mushroom stems. Thinly slice the caps and set aside.

2 In a large saucepan, heat the olive oil over medium heat. Add the garlic and sauté for 30 seconds. Add the rice, tarragon, salt, and pepper and sauté for 2 minutes, stirring to coat the rice with the oil.

3 Add ½ cup of the shiitake liquid and the sliced shiitakes to the pan. Cook, stirring frequently, until the liquid is absorbed. Add the remaining

Edamame

shiitake liquid, $^1/_2$ cup at a time, stirring constantly until each addition is absorbed; when there are just 1$^1/2$ cups left, add the edamame. Cook until the rice is tender but still slightly chewy, 18 to 20 minutes total. Stir in the vinegar and serve immediately.

4 **To make risotto cakes:** Follow the method outlined in the Butternut Risotto Cakes with Portobellos and Stilton Butter (page 312) in steps 5 and 6.

Note

The risotto can be prepared up to the point of adding the edamame up to 2 days ahead and stored in an airtight container in the fridge. Reheat the risotto in a large saucepan, adding the edamame and the remaining reheated mushroom liquid, $^1/2$ cup at a time, stirring constantly until the risotto is done. Add the vinegar just before serving.

Menu Suggestion

Fennel Slaw (page 117)
Shiitake Risotto with Edamame
Killer Chocolate Chip Cookies (page 399)

Wine Suggestion

The tastes and textures in this dish cry out for a creamy Meursault, but that's a white Burgundy, and it comes with a hefty price tag. If you're not up to spending at least $35, another Chardonnay-based wine could also do the trick. Oregon Chardonnay can be positively Burgundian in character, and Washington State produces some lovely wines made from this grape. Steer clear of overly oaked California versions—these are poor partners for most foods. Red wine lovers could opt for a simple, fruity Italian wine, such as Dolcetto or Barbera.

smoky corn risotto

 Sweet potato, chipotle chiles, sun-dried tomatoes, and fresh corn strut their stuff in this fiery risotto. When corn is in season, you must try it.

SERVES 4 TO 6

1 Cut the corn kernels off the cobs: Lay one ear flat and make a straight cut down the length of one side. Then rotate the corn a quarter turn and cut down the other side. Continue in this manner twice more, until all the kernels have been removed. You should have about 2 cups. Set aside. If you're using frozen corn, place the kernels in a sieve and run under warm water until thawed.

2 In a small saucepan bring the broth plus ½ cup water to a simmer and keep it hot.

3 In a large saucepan, heat the olive oil over medium heat. Add the sweet potato and onion and sauté, stirring occasionally, until the onion is soft, about 7 minutes. Add the rice, garlic, and salt and sauté for 1 minute, stirring to coat the rice with the oil.

4 Stir in the sherry, chipotles, and oregano and simmer for 30 seconds.

3 ears corn, shucked, or 2 cups frozen (not thawed) corn kernels

4 cups vegetable broth

2 tablespoons extra-virgin olive oil

1 small sweet potato, peeled and diced

1 medium red onion, chopped, 2 tablespoons reserved for garnish

1½ cups raw Arborio rice

3 garlic cloves, minced

1 teaspoon kosher salt, plus more to taste

½ cup dry sherry

2–3 canned chipotle chiles in adobo, seeded if possible, minced

1 tablespoon chopped fresh oregano or 1 teaspoon dried

10 sun-dried tomatoes, drained if oil-packed, thinly sliced

Freshly ground black pepper to taste

Add ½ cup of the broth to the rice mixture and simmer, stirring frequently, until the liquid is absorbed. Add the remaining broth, ½ cup at a time, stirring constantly until each addition is absorbed; when there is just 1 cup left, add the corn and sun-dried tomatoes.

Cook until the rice is tender but still slightly chewy, 18 to 20 minutes total, adding some additional hot water if the rice absorbs all the broth. Season with salt and pepper. Serve immediately, sprinkled with the reserved chopped onion.

Note

The recipe can be prepared through step 4, leaving out at least 1 cup of the broth, up to 2 days ahead and stored in an airtight container in the fridge. Reheat in a large saucepan, adding the remaining reheated broth and stirring constantly until the risotto is done. Add the reserved chopped onion just before serving.

Menu Suggestion

Sliced fresh tomato salad with Mint Vinaigrette (page 155)
Smoky Corn Risotto
Cardamom Pound Cake (page 438)

Wine Suggestion

Pinotage, the red grape of South Africa, makes complex wines with an alluring smoky quality to match this unusual risotto.

fried capers—the sophisticated garnish

Fried capers are crunchy and delicate. They add spunk when sprinkled over pasta, risotto, egg dishes, and salads. They can be made hours ahead and kept at room temperature. Dry 2 to 4 tablespoons capers on paper towels. In a medium saucepan, heat 1 cup canola oil over medium-high heat. Place the capers in a small strainer and dunk the strainer into the hot oil for about 15 seconds, or until the capers blossom. Drain on paper towels.

intimate gatherings and celebrations

bumper crop risotto
with herb butter

This risotto is a celebration of the late-summer harvest. Left-over herb butter can be frozen and used to season noodles, vegetables, or rice. Refrigerate the corn the minute you get it home; unlike tomatoes (which are best kept at room temperature), corn should be chilled to preserve its flavor.

SERVES 4

1 In a small bowl, combine the butter and 1/4 cup of the herbs, mixing and mashing until well blended. Use a rubber spatula to transfer the butter to a sheet of plastic wrap and roll it into a tight cylinder about 2 inches wide. Refrigerate for at least 1 hour, or until ready to serve.

2 Cut the corn kernels off the cob: Lay one ear flat and make a straight cut down the length of one side. Then rotate the corn a quarter turn and cut down another side. Continue in this manner twice more, until all the kernels have been removed. You should have about 2 cups. Set aside.

3 In a small saucepan, bring the broth plus 1/2 cup water to a simmer and keep it hot.

4 tablespoons (1/2 stick) unsalted butter, softened

1/2 cup chopped mixed fresh herbs (basil, dill, chervil, thyme, and/or cilantro)

3 ears corn, shucked

4 1/2 cups vegetable broth

1 tablespoon extra-virgin olive oil

1/2 onion, chopped

1 1/2 cups raw Arborio rice (or sushi rice)

1/2 teaspoon kosher salt, plus more to taste

1/2 cup dry white wine

1 small zucchini, cut into 1/2-inch cubes

1 1/2 cups finely chopped tomatoes

1/2 cup freshly grated Parmesan cheese

Freshly ground black pepper to taste

4 In a large saucepan, heat the olive oil over medium heat. Add the onion and sauté, stirring occasionally, until softened, about 7 minutes. Add the rice and salt and sauté for 1 minute, stirring to coat the rice with the oil.

5 Add the wine and simmer, stirring frequently, until it is absorbed. Add $1/2$ cup of the broth and the zucchini and corn and simmer, stirring frequently, until the broth is absorbed. Add the remaining broth, $1/2$ cup at a time, stirring constantly until each addition is absorbed, until the rice is tender but still slightly chewy, 18 to 20 minutes total. Remove from the heat.

6 Add the tomatoes, Parmesan, and the remaining $1/4$ cup herbs and stir until well incorporated. Season with salt and pepper. To serve, divide the risotto among four shallow bowls, and top each serving with a slice of the herb butter.

Menu Suggestion

Summer salad—find a young tender lettuce, such as any variety of butterhead or mâche. Add tomatoes of all colors, cucumbers, and/or blanched green beans. Make a simple vinaigrette of 1 minced shallot, juice of $1/2$ lemon, and $1/3$ cup extra-virgin olive oil.

Bumper Crop Risotto with Herb Butter
Michel Richard's Fruit "Salad" with
Melted Ice Cream (page 414)

Wine Suggestion

An Italian-style main dish with fresh, subtle flavors calls for a similar wine. Uncork a Pinot Grigio, Gavi, or Vernaccia di San Gimignano from Italy.

Note

The herb butter can be made up to 2 weeks ahead, wrapped in a double layer of plastic wrap, and frozen. The risotto is best made only a few hours ahead, leaving out the last cup of broth, although you can add the tomatoes and herbs. Store the risotto in an airtight container in the fridge for up to 6 hours. Reheat in a large saucepan, adding the remaining reheated 1 cup broth. When the rice is al dente, add the cheese.

wild rice curry in sugar pumpkins

 This dish is chock-a-block full of goodies: dried apricots, pecans, yellow split peas, wild rice, and tempeh, all nestled in roasted sugar pumpkin halves. It's a festive Thanksgiving entrée.

SERVES 4

3 tablespoons extra-virgin olive oil

1 large onion, finely chopped

4 garlic cloves, minced

1 tablespoon curry powder

1/2 teaspoon freshly ground nutmeg

1 cup raw wild rice

1 cup raw yellow split peas

1/2 cup dried apricots, quartered

1 teaspoon kosher salt, plus more
   to taste

2 sugar pumpkins (about 4 pounds each)

4 ounces tempeh, cut into 1/4-inch
   cubes

2 tablespoons peeled and minced fresh
   ginger

Freshly ground black pepper to taste

1/2 cup chopped fresh cilantro leaves
   and stems, reserving 4 nice leaves
   for garnish

1/3 cup chopped toasted pecans
   (see page 283)

1 In a large, heavy pot, heat 1 tablespoon of the olive oil over medium heat. Add the onion and sauté until soft, about 7 minutes. Add half of the garlic, the curry powder, and nutmeg and sauté for 1 minute. Add the wild rice, split peas, apricots, salt, and 5 cups water and bring to a boil. Cover, reduce the heat to a simmer, and cook for 40 minutes, or until the wild rice is tender but al dente.

2 Preheat the oven to 375 degrees. Oil a rimmed baking sheet. Cut about 1/2 inch off each end of both pumpkins so the halves will sit flat without wobbling. With a large, sharp chef's knife, halve each pumpkin crosswise. With a spoon, remove the strings and seeds. Place the halves cut side down on the prepared baking sheet and bake until the flesh is soft, about 1 hour.

3 In a large skillet, heat the remaining 2 tablespoons olive oil over medium heat. Add the tempeh and sauté for 5 minutes. Add the ginger and the remaining garlic and season with salt and pepper. Sauté for 3 minutes more, stirring frequently. Add the tempeh mixture to the wild rice mixture, along with the chopped cilantro and half of the pecans. Set aside and keep warm.

4 To serve, arrange a pumpkin half, hollowed side up, on each of four plates. Reheat the pilaf, if necessary, and divide it among the pumpkin cavities. Sprinkle with the remaining pecans, garnish with the cilantro leaves, and serve.

Menu Suggestion

Sweet Heat Cucumber Salad (page 122)
Wild Rice Curry in Sugar Pumpkins
Peach Upside-Down Cake (page 434)

Wine Suggestion

A California Pinot Noir will tend to be lusher and sweeter than red Burgundy, its French counterpart, but it retains the smoky, earthy flavors characteristic of the Pinot Noir grape. That makes it perfect for drinking with this robust curry, which combines earthy and sweet flavors.

Note

The pilaf can be made up to 24 hours ahead and stored in an airtight container in the fridge. Reheat on the stove over low heat, adding 1/2 cup water. Taste for seasoning. The pumpkins can be cut, wrapped, and chilled for up to 2 days, and baked up to 3 hours in advance. Keep warm in a 250-degree oven until ready to serve.

rosemary roasted winter vegetables

(V) *One day I was running late,* and I had no menu planned for a small dinner party at my private chef job. On the way to Bread & Circus, a glittering supermarket, I tried to come up with a menu—to no avail. I arrived at the market and desperately grabbed a recipe card for roasted vegetables. The resulting dish was so good that I've used variations on it dozens of times since then and gotten raves each time. I've even taught it to the customers and staff at that very supermarket. Of course, I humbly don't take credit for the recipe, my ego firmly in check. Feel free to substitute potatoes, carrots, Jerusalem artichokes, or any winter vegetable for one or more of the choices here.

I have one spunky friend who likes to add halved cherry tomatoes to the mix as well. Serve this dish with brown rice or a simple salad if you'd like to use it for a casual meal.

SERVES 6 TO 8

1 small butternut squash, peeled and cut into 1/4-inch-thick slices

1 small rutabaga, peeled and cut into 1/4-inch-thick slices

1 large red onion, sliced into rings

2 parsnips, peeled and cut into 1/4-inch-thick rounds

6–8 garlic cloves, minced

3 tablespoons finely chopped fresh rosemary

2 teaspoons kosher salt

Freshly ground black pepper to taste

1/3 cup extra-virgin olive oil

Preheat the oven to 375 degrees. In a large casserole dish, combine all the ingredients and mix well with your hands. Roast for 30 minutes. Stir the vegetables to redistribute the seasonings, and bake until everything is tender, about 20 minutes more. Serve.

Note

This dish can be fully assembled but not baked up to 2 days ahead of time and stored, tightly covered, in the fridge. Toss the mixture well before baking and allow a little extra time, since it will be very cold.

Menu Suggestion

Serve the roasted vegetables on a buffet table with two or more of the following:

Double recipe of Brown Basmati or Long-Grain Brown Rice (page 200) or **Short-Grain Brown Rice** (page 201)

French Lentil Salad with Dried Currants and Walnuts (page 150)

Asparagus Slaw—made with green beans if asparagus isn't available (page 116)

Crusty rye bread from a bakery or market—served warm with butter or olive oil

Vegan Chocolate Cake (page 429)

Wine Suggestion

A light- to medium-bodied rustic red would suit the palate and psyche: Bourgueil from the Loire, a Portuguese red, or perhaps a Marsannay (red Burgundy).

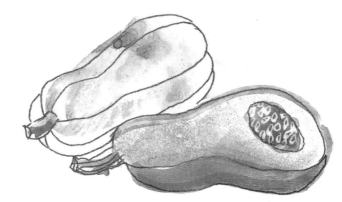

spaghetti squash wedges with roasted vegetable–feta stuffing

This dish belongs in one of the sleek gourmet food cases at Manhattan's Dean & Deluca. Each thick, U-shaped wedge of spaghetti squash is served with its colorful filling intact. This recipe was created by my friend Lauren, and it's as tasty as it looks.

SERVES 4

1 Preheat the oven to 400 degrees. Oil a baking sheet. Halve the spaghetti squash lengthwise. Drizzle 1 tablespoon of the olive oil on the cut sides of the squash and season with salt and pepper. Place the squash halves cut side down on the prepared baking sheet and bake for 45 minutes. Test for doneness by turning the squash over and pulling a bit of the flesh from the cavity; it should be stringy and tender. If the flesh doesn't loosen easily, bake for 10 to 15 minutes more.

2 Meanwhile, place the eggplants and red peppers on gas burners over medium-low heat (1 vegetable per burner). (If you don't own a gas stove, you can halve the eggplant lengthwise, place the eggplant halves and whole bell peppers in a roasting pan and roast

- 1 3-pound spaghetti squash
- 2 tablespoons extra-virgin olive oil
  Kosher salt and freshly ground black pepper to taste
- 2 Asian eggplants (see page 443) or 2 small Italian eggplants
- 2 red bell peppers, roasted
- 2 slices white or whole wheat sandwich bread, cut into ½-inch cubes
- 1 small red onion, thinly sliced
- ½ cup black oil-cured olives, coarsely chopped
- ½ cup feta cheese (my favorite is French goat's milk feta)
- 2 tablespoons chopped fresh basil, plus 8 leaves for garnish
- 2 tablespoons chopped fresh dill
- 2 garlic cloves, minced

in a preheated 425-degree oven, turning occasionally, until the skins are blistered, about 25 minutes.) Use tongs to turn the vegetables every few minutes until they're blackened all over and quite soft. Transfer the vegetables to a cutting board to cool.

3 Remove and discard the charred skins from the eggplants, then coarsely chop the flesh and transfer it to a large bowl. Remove and discard the skins, stems, and seeds from the bell peppers and cut the flesh into 3-inch lengths. Add the peppers to the bowl with the eggplant. Add the bread cubes, onion, olives, feta, chopped basil, dill, garlic, and the remaining 1 tablespoon olive oil and mix well. Season with salt and pepper.

4 When the squash is done, remove the baking sheet from the oven and carefully turn the squash halves cut side up. Stuff the eggplant mixture into each half. Bake for 15 minutes, or until the stuffing is heated through. With a large chef's knife, slice each squash half into 4 wedges. Garnish each wedge with a basil leaf, tucking the stem into one side, and serve 2 slices to each person.

Menu Suggestion

Acorn Squash, Spinach, and Roasted Garlic Soup (page 111)
Spaghetti Squash Wedges with Roasted Vegetable–Feta Stuffing
A salad of shredded napa and red cabbage with **Mint Vinaigrette** (page 155) or a simple **Boston lettuce salad with Classic Lemon Dressing** (page 154) and **roasted beets**
Almond Butter Cake (page 430) with vanilla ice cream

Wine Suggestion

A light, simple red wine, such as Italian Barbera or French Beaujolais, is a good complement to this dish, which is neither heavy nor overly rich.

Note

The squash can be roasted and stuffed up to 1 day ahead, covered with plastic wrap and stored in the fridge. Roast the chilled stuffed squash for 30 minutes.

intimate gatherings and celebrations

savory hubbard squash pudding

Served with a salad, this pudding makes a terrific special-occasion lunch. It's similar to quiche but much easier. A whole hubbard squash is not cheap, even in New England. The bumpy, blue-gray giants often weigh more than 10 pounds and cost more per pound than butternut or acorn squash. You'll get more than rich, nutty flavor for the price — the intriguing monster squash makes a striking "sculpture" in your home for a week or so before you cut it.

SERVES 8

1 3-pound hubbard squash

béchamel

4 tablespoons (½ stick) butter

3 garlic cloves, minced

5 tablespoons all-purpose flour

2¼ cups milk, heated

5 large eggs

1 teaspoon ground star anise, ground cloves, or five-spice powder (see page 446)

Kosher salt and freshly ground black pepper to taste

1 Preheat the oven to 375 degrees. Oil a rimmed baking sheet and butter a 2-quart casserole dish.

2 Cut the squash into large pieces and remove and discard the seeds and strings. Place the pieces on the prepared baking sheet and roast until the squash is tender, about 45 minutes. Set aside to cool.

3 **To make the béchamel:** In a medium, heavy saucepan, melt the butter over medium heat. Add the garlic and sauté for 2 minutes; do not let the garlic brown. Add the flour and cook, stirring constantly, for 2 minutes more. Slowly whisk in the milk, whisking constantly until the mixture comes to a boil. Cook, whisking constantly, until it thickens, about 2 minutes. Remove from the heat and let cool briefly.

4 When the squash is cool enough to handle, scoop the flesh from the skin into a food processor. Add the béchamel and process until smooth. With the machine running, add the eggs through the feed tube, one at a time, stopping once to scrape down the sides of the bowl. Add the star anise, cloves, or five-spice powder and season liberally with salt and pepper.

5 Pour the squash mixture into the prepared casserole dish and bake until it is set and golden brown, about 40 minutes. Serve immediately, cut into squares or wedges.

Note The squash can be roasted and scooped out of its skin up to 2 days ahead and stored in an airtight container in the fridge. The béchamel can also be made up to 2 days ahead and stored in an airtight container in the fridge. One to 2 hours before serving, bring the béchamel to room temperature and add the eggs as directed.

Menu Suggestion **Sweet Heat Cucumber Salad** (page 122) or **Grilled Vegetable Salad with Tarragon-Sherry Vinaigrette** (page 132, but I would roast the veggies instead of grilling them if it's cold out)
Crusty bread and cold unsalted butter
Savory Hubbard Squash Pudding
Macadamia–Tropical Fruit Salad with Ice Cream (page 412) and/or **Killer Chocolate Chip Cookies** (page 399)

Wine Suggestion An Italian Barbera or a French Beaujolais would jibe with this simple pudding.

a miraculously cheap wedding for fifty in ten easy steps

When I was a child, I thought all weddings were the same: a bride, a groom, a church, and then lots of dancing. Now that I've grown up, it's rare when I see a wedding that plays out my preconceptions. Most couples find a way to authentically express themselves, which is what makes a wedding worthwhile.

A caterer multiplies your food cost by about six, and who really remembers the food anyway? (When you do, it's usually because the caterers did a lousy job.) I knew one bride who cooked her own wedding dinner with the help of her friends. This kind of wedding is about as casual as you can get, but you'll save big bucks, which you can use for future vacations, weekly massages, or a hot tub. Here's how. Total prep time, including shopping: about eight hours.

1. Find a friend (perhaps your mate) who's willing to help for a couple of days or evenings. Remind the helper that he or she will be able to boast about the effort throughout the reception.

2. Hire someone to heat the food during the reception and replenish the food trays. This is essential. (You'll need three large trays.)

3. Have another good friend, relative, or neighbor make a large crudité basket or fruit salad.

4. Arrange with an ice cream store to make a cake for fifty people. Make sure it will fit in your freezer! If you're having the wedding at a site with no freezer, order a cake for fifty from a bakery. Tiers are not needed — tiers mean money.

5. Clean out the fridge.

6. Shopping: wake up early two days before the wedding and go shopping with your helper. Besides paper plates, glasses, and napkins, you'll need:

- 8 pints fresh strawberries
- 4 pounds semisweet chocolate
- ½ pint heavy cream
- 1 large wheel Brie (2 kilos) or 2 smaller wheels
- 5 or 6 packages Pillsbury croissant dough
- 1 jar red currant jelly
- 2 bags shelled pecans
- A few boxes of crackers
- Beverages—wine, beer, soda, etc.
- In warmer weather, make a large batch of Potato Salad Niçoise (page 144; multiply the quantities in the recipe by 5). For a winter wedding, make a huge batch of Butternut Squash–Lentil Chili (page 268) and, in any season, buy lots of hearty rolls or French bread.
- 2 or 3 bouquets of flowers

7. Cooking and other prep: cut the Brie in half like an English muffin. Spread on currant jelly then sprinkle with chopped pecans. Top with the second half of the cheese. Wrap the Brie (although not the wooden base) in croissant dough, place on a baking sheet, and bake at 400 degrees until the dough has browned. (The Brie can be prepared and stored unbaked in the fridge for up to 1 day.)

8. Wash the strawberries and let them dry. Melt the chocolate and cream in a double boiler. Oil a baking sheet. Dip the strawberries in the melted chocolate and let harden on the baking sheet (in the fridge, if necessary), then transfer the strawberries to an airtight container in layers, with parchment paper in between.

9. Make the Niçoise salad or chili up to 1 day ahead, cover it with plastic wrap, and store in the fridge.

10. When arranging the food on the trays, clip the flowers from their stems and use them as garnishes.

Toast one another and have a great time!

coconut rice cakes with cathi's thai carrot-chile sauce

V *The sauce comes from my friend* and vegetarian chef Cathi DiCocco. Use as many jalapeños as you can handle; it's supposed to be spicy, and the rice cakes will temper the heat. You can make this dish more substantial if you serve the cakes on a bed of watercress lightly dressed with balsamic vinegar and a touch of canola oil.

SERVES 6 TO 8

cakes

1 13.5-ounce can unsweetened coconut milk (see page 446)

1 teaspoon kosher salt

1¼ cups raw sushi rice (see page 452)

½ cup chopped scallions, white and green parts

¼ cup chopped cilantro leaves and stems

2 tablespoons canola oil

sauce

1 tablespoon canola oil

1 medium onion, chopped

1–3 jalapeño peppers, seeded and minced

1 tablespoon peeled and minced fresh ginger

2 garlic cloves, minced

2 large carrots, peeled and coarsely chopped

2 tablespoons chopped fresh cilantro, plus 6–8 sprigs for garnish

2–3 teaspoons Asian chili sauce (see page 443)

Kosher salt to taste

1 **To make the cakes:** In a medium saucepan, bring the coconut milk, 1 cup water and the salt just to a boil. Add the rice. Return to a boil, cover, and reduce the heat to its lowest setting. Simmer gently for 25 minutes, or until all the liquid is absorbed. Add the scallions and cilantro and mix well. Transfer the rice mixture to a shallow bowl and refrigerate for at least 1 hour. Form the cooled rice into 6 to 8 cakes about 1 inch thick. Set aside.

2 **Meanwhile, to make the sauce:** In a large, heavy pot, heat the canola oil over medium heat. Add the onion and sauté, stirring occasionally, until light golden, about 10 minutes. Add the jalapeños, ginger, and garlic and sauté for 2 minutes more, stirring frequently.

3 Add the carrots and 1 cup water to the pot. Cover and simmer, until the carrots are very tender, about 10 minutes. With a ladle, transfer half of the sauce to a food processor and process with the chopped cilantro until it is smooth. Transfer the pureed sauce to a clean large saucepan and repeat with the remaining carrot mixture. Stir in the chili sauce and season with salt.

4 **To pan-fry the cakes:** In a large, heavy skillet, heat the canola oil over medium-high heat. Add the rice cakes, working in batches if necessary to avoid crowding the skillet, and fry until golden brown and crispy on the bottoms, 6 to 8 minutes. Turn and brown the other sides, 6 to 8 minutes more.

Note
The sauce can be made up to 2 days ahead and stored in an airtight container in the fridge. Reheat on the stove or in the microwave. The cooked rice mixture can be stored in an airtight container in the fridge for up to 2 days. Form the cakes and bring to room temperature if possible before frying. The cakes can be fried up to 30 minutes ahead and kept warm on a baking sheet in a 220-degree oven.

intimate gatherings and celebrations

5 Ladle the sauce onto 6 to 8 plates and top with the rice cakes. Garnish with 1 cilantro sprig on each rice cake and serve immediately.

Menu Suggestion

Mango Slaw (page 120)
Coconut Rice Cakes with Cathi's Thai Carrot-Chile Sauce
Key Lime Pie with Oreo Crust (page 439)

Wine Suggestion

Beer's ability to refresh the palate while dampening the heat of chile peppers makes it the beverage of choice with spicy foods. A crisp sparkling wine is just as good, though, and unlike beer, it immediately signals that the meal and the occasion are special. Both sparkling Vouvray and Champagne designated "extra dry" are good matches with these rice cakes. (Strangely, "extra dry" is the term for a sweet-tasting Champagne—an appropriate choice here because the dish has some sweet accents.) Expect to spend $30 or more for a bottle of French Champagne. Vouvray is a less expensive cousin, but sparkling versions can be hard to find.

chapter 9

'Companyments

if you can't stand the heat,
you're not invited!

Do you sometimes want the world to know that your favorite hot sauce is in fact better than all the others? Do you have more than three varieties of hot sauce in your fridge? If the answers are yes, then it's time to have a hot sauce party.

Invite anyone who shares your evolved palate (the timid-tongued can stay home). Cook three or four dishes that take well to hot sauce. My favorites include Crispy Quesadilla Triangles (page 68), plain deviled eggs, Black Bean Soup in a Hurry (page 103), Lo-Stress Onion Rings (page 195), tostones (fried and smashed plantains), and steamed fresh corn kernels. Serve a cold, hearty microbrewed beer.

If you don't own a good selection of hot sauces, purchase them. Many gourmet shops sell a decent assortment, but for the most varied selection, I suggest a mail-order company called Mo Hotta Mo Betta. These folks are serious chiliheads. Their selection is wide, and many of the sauce labels amuse as much as they singe, such as the one called Smack My Ass & Call Me Sally. My favorite hot sauces? Melinda's XXX and Inner Beauty Hot Sauce, both habanero-based.

chipotle ketchup

(V) *One day soon, we'll be able to buy* chipotle-flavored ketchup and you won't have any work to do at all. Until then, make it yourself. Serve with the Portobello "Burgers" with Chipotle Ketchup (page 174) or with the Kasha-Crunch Burgers (page 172). It's also great with French fries and roasted potatoes.

MAKES ABOUT 1 CUP

2 chipotle chiles in adobo, or more to taste, or 2 dried chipotle chiles

1 cup store-bought ketchup

1 If using dried chipotles, in a small bowl combine them with boiling water to cover. Let soak for 20 minutes, then drain.

2 In a food processor, combine the ketchup and chipotles and puree until smooth. Cover and refrigerate until serving time.

Note The ketchup will keep in an airtight container in the fridge for up to 6 months (when it develops white spots, that's your cue to unload it).

chipotles

raisin ketchup

 This ketchup exists to make veggie burgers—even the super-market variety—taste better. It's also good with home fries, Steak Fries (page 196), and Lo-Stress Onion Rings (page 195).

MAKES 2 CUPS

1 In a large skillet, heat the canola oil over medium heat. Add the onions and sauté, stirring occasionally, until translucent, 7 to 9 minutes. Add the peach or apple, raisins, brown sugar, allspice, Worcestershire sauce, white vinegar, balsamic vinegar, and ¼ cup water. Cook until the peach or apple has softened, about 8 minutes more.

2 Transfer to a food processor and process until fairly smooth. Let cool, uncovered. Season with salt and pepper. Cover and refrigerate until serving time.

2 tablespoons canola oil

2 large onions, chopped

1 ripe but firm peach or apple, unpeeled, pitted or cored, and chopped

1 cup raisins

⅓ cup light or dark brown sugar

1 teaspoon ground allspice

3 tablespoons vegetarian Worcester-shire sauce or Worcestershire sauce

2 tablespoons white vinegar

2 teaspoons balsamic vinegar

Kosher salt and freshly ground black pepper to taste

Note The ketchup will keep in an airtight container in the fridge for up to 8 weeks.

peach chutney

 Chutney is a form of first aid, adding sweet-tart notes to breads, curries, veggie burgers, and more. This speedy chutney goes particularly well with Cashew Korma (page 206). Use when fresh— and preferably local—peaches are available. You can blanch the peaches to remove their skins, but I prefer to leave them on.

MAKES 2 CUPS

- 1 tablespoon canola oil
- 1 large onion (red is nice for color), finely chopped
- 5 ripe or nearly ripe peaches, pitted and finely chopped
- ½ teaspoon crushed red pepper flakes
- 1 tablespoon cider vinegar
- ¼ cup water

  Kosher salt and freshly ground black pepper to taste

In a medium skillet over medium heat, heat the canola oil. Add the onion and sauté until softened, stirring occasionally, about 7 minutes. Add the remaining ingredients, reduce the heat to a simmer, and cook for 10 minutes, or until the chutney has thickened. Let cool, uncovered. Taste and correct the seasoning, adding more salt and pepper if needed. Cover and refrigerate until serving time.

Note
The chutney will keep in an airtight container in the fridge for up to 2 weeks.

fresh cilantro chutney

This raitalike accompaniment has the bright flavors of cilantro, ginger, cumin, and chiles tempered with plain yogurt. I adapted it from a recipe in Yamuna Devi's *Lord Krishna's Cuisine: The Art of Indian Vegetarian Cooking.* Spoon over Potato Dosa (page 356) —the ultimate landing pad for this chutney. It also makes a fabulous sauce for pita sandwiches, veggie burgers (pages 170–174), and curries.

MAKES ABOUT 1 CUP

In a food processor, process the cilantro, coconut, chiles, sesame seeds, and ginger and process until finely chopped. Add the yogurt, cumin, and salt, and process until smooth. Cover and refrigerate until serving time.

Note

The chutney will keep in an airtight container in the fridge for up to 5 days.

1 cup chopped fresh cilantro leaves and stems

¼ cup dried, unsweetened coconut (see page 446)

3 small, skinny chile peppers

3 tablespoons toasted sesame seeds (see page 450)

2 tablespoons peeled and minced fresh ginger

¼ cup plain yogurt

1 teaspoon ground cumin

1 teaspoon kosher salt

romesco sauce

(V) *Silky, sweet, and smoky,* romesco sauce from the Catalan region of Spain is one of my all-time favorites. My version has evolved over time, each time getting a little closer to bliss. This versatile sauce is particularly good with roasted new potatoes or French fries. A spoonful is nice on an omelet, and you can spread it on pizza instead of tomato sauce. For an appetizer, serve it on grilled bread.

MAKES 1 1/2 CUPS

1 dried ancho chile (see page 443)

1/4 cup toasted almonds (see page 283)

1/2 jalapeño pepper, seeded

3 garlic cloves

1 roasted red bell pepper (see page 23)

1 slice whole wheat bread

1 tablespoon red wine vinegar

1/4 cup extra-virgin olive oil

Kosher salt and freshly ground black pepper to taste

A few slivered almonds for garnish

1 In a small bowl, combine the ancho and boiling water to cover generously. Let soak for 30 minutes, turning the ancho occasionally so it softens all over. Drain.

2 In a food processor, puree the toasted almonds, jalapeño, and garlic until smooth. Add the roasted red pepper, bread, ancho, vinegar, and 1/4 cup cool water. With the machine running, slowly add the olive oil through the feed tube and process until the sauce becomes thickened and opaque. Season with salt and pepper.

3 Cover and refrigerate for a few hours to allow the flavors to blend. Let stand at room temperature for 30 minutes before you serve it. Garnish with the slivered almonds before serving.

Note: The sauce can be made up to 3 days ahead and stored in an airtight container in the fridge.

escalivada (smoky eggplant-pepper puree)

Ⓥ *This versatile Spanish vegetable compote* is one of the best I've ever had. You can find smoked paprika in gourmet food stores— it's worth a special trip. The inspiration for this dish came from Ruth Ann Adams, a talented chef who serves it on a good-quality sandwich roll with basil leaves and buffalo mozzarella at the Casablanca restaurant in Cambridge, Massachusetts. Sneak the escalivada into pita bread with some arugula, or just spoon it onto peasant bread. To serve as an appetizer on toast slices or focaccia, increase the vinegar to 3 tablespoons.

MAKES 2½ CUPS

1 small eggplant, cut diagonally into ¼-inch-thick ovals

8 tablespoons extra-virgin olive oil

Kosher salt and freshly ground black pepper to taste

6 garlic cloves, thinly sliced

1 teaspoon smoked paprika

1 roasted red bell pepper (see page 23), cut into ¼-inch-wide strips

¼ cup thinly sliced fresh basil leaves

1 teaspoon ground coriander

1 teaspoon ground cumin

1 tablespoon sherry vinegar or Champagne vinegar

1 Preheat the oven to 400 degrees. In a large bowl, toss the eggplant with 3 tablespoons of the olive oil. Season with salt and pepper. Spread the eggplant in a single layer on a rimmed baking sheet. Bake for about 20 minutes, or until the eggplant starts to turn golden and is soft on the inside. Let cool on the baking sheet. Transfer to a clean large bowl.

2 In a small saucepan, combine the remaining 5 tablespoons olive oil and the garlic over medium heat and cook until the garlic is bubbling, then re-

move from the heat. Add the paprika, stirring until it dissolves. Pour the olive oil mixture over the eggplant. Add the roasted red pepper, basil, coriander, cumin, and vinegar and mix well to combine. Serve at room temperature.

Note

The escalivada can be prepared up to 48 hours ahead and stored in an airtight container in the fridge. Let stand at room temperature for an hour or so before serving.

smoked paprika

Smoked paprika is one of those aromatics, like coffee or cardamom, that just intoxicates me. Sold in gourmet shops, it's becoming the darling of restaurant chefs. It can be used at home to enliven dozens of dishes. Toast it first if you have the time, then add to dishes toward the end of cooking. Toast the paprika in a small, dry skillet over low heat, shaking the skillet, for 2 to 3 minutes, or until it begins to smoke a bit. Taste the paprika, toasting it to your palate's liking. Smoked paprika is available in gourmet stores and from spice companies. Some recipes that would benefit from a teaspoon or so of smoked paprika include:

Black Bean Soup in a Hurry (page 103)
Rachel and Felicity's Minestrone (page 96)
Veggie Sloppy Joes (page 168)
Romesco Sauce (page 345)
Mac'n'Cheese (page 256)
Muhammara (page 26)

caramelized garlic sambal

(V) *In Malaysia almost every meal* consists of rice and a fish or meat dish, and it is sambal that marries the two. Sambals are chili sauces, either raw or cooked, that often contain dried shrimp and vegetables. Street vendors make sambals to serve with the foods they sell, and most families make their own as well. This recipe was given to me by Teh Peng, an excellent chef I once worked with, who got it from his mother. What makes it supreme is that the garlic and shallots are caramelized, imparting a rich, sweet flavor. Serve with veggie burgers (pages 170–174), jasmine rice and Tempeh Rendang (page 232), Curried Jack-o'-Lantern (page 212), Coconut Rice Cakes with Cathi's Thai Carrot-Chile Sauce (page 336), or just the rice alone.

MAKES 1 1/2 CUPS

- 20 2-inch-long dried Mexican red chiles
- 1/2 cup garlic cloves
- 1/2 cup coarsely chopped shallots
- 1/2 cup canola oil
- 3 tablespoons sugar
- 1/2 teaspoon kosher salt
- 1 tablespoon fresh lime juice (1/2 juicy lime)
- Vegetarian stir-fry sauce (see page 453) or Asian fish sauce (see page 444) to taste

1 Crack the dried chiles open and discard the seeds. In a medium bowl, combine the chile pods, garlic, shallots, and 2 cups hot water. Let soak for 30 minutes.

2 Transfer the chiles, garlic, and shallots to a blender or food processor with about 1/2 cup of the soaking liquid. Puree until smooth, then add the rest of the soaking liquid and blend again.

3 In a large skillet, heat the canola oil over medium heat. Add the chile puree, sugar, and salt and cook, stirring occasionally, until the sauce turns dark brown, about 20 minutes. Add the lime juice and stir-fry sauce or fish sauce. Cover and refrigerate until serving time.

I had a dinner party in my driveway, because I couldn't fit everyone in my apartment.

—Roz Cummins

Note The sambal will keep in an airtight container in the fridge for up to 2 weeks.

Garlic

all-purpose peanut sauce

 This is the perfect all-purpose peanut sauce, and it's especially good over Pan-Fried Tofu (page 217) or tempeh and vegetables over rice. Add 1 teaspoon ground star anise for a pleasant licorice accent. (Star anise is often used in Indonesia, the motherland of peanut sauce.) Use tamarind instead of the lime juice if you're feeling rambunctious. Follow the directions on page 452, using $^1/_3$ cup of the strained pulp instead of the lime juice.

MAKES 1$^2/_3$ CUPS

Place the peanut butter in a microwave-safe bowl and microwave for 1 minute or heat in a small saucepan over low heat until it is very soft. In a medium bowl, combine the peanut butter with the remaining ingredients and mix well with a whisk. Serve at room temperature.

$^1/_2$ cup smooth or crunchy peanut butter

3 tablespoons chopped fresh cilantro roots and stems (optional)

2 tablespoons peeled and minced fresh ginger

2 garlic cloves, minced

1 cup unsweetened coconut milk (see page 446)

2 tablespoons fresh lime juice (1 juicy lime)

2 teaspoons Asian chili sauce (see page 443)

   Soy sauce or Asian fish sauce (see page 444) to taste

Note
The sauce will keep in an airtight container in the fridge for up to 2 weeks. Let it stand at room temperature for an hour or so before serving, or warm slightly in the microwave.

peanut dressing

(V) *Try this perky and scrumptious dressing* with cold Chinese noodles (see page 245) or soba noodles or with crunchy greens such as chopped romaine or napa cabbage with grated carrots and apples. It's a perfect dipping sauce for crudités or Pan-Fried Tofu (page 217). Add 2 tablespoons sesame seeds if you want some crunch.

MAKES 2 CUPS

In a food processor, combine all the ingredients except the canola oil and process until completely smooth. With the machine running, slowly add the canola oil through the feed tube and process until the mixture reaches a smooth, thick, saucelike consistency. Serve at room temperature.

- 1/3 cup smooth or crunchy peanut butter
- 3 rounded tablespoons peeled and coarsely chopped fresh ginger
- 1 tablespoon sugar
- 2 garlic cloves
- 1 teaspoon Dijon mustard
- 1/2 cup rice vinegar
- 1 1/2 tablespoons toasted sesame oil
- 1 tablespoon soy sauce
- 2 teaspoons Asian chili sauce (see page 443; optional)
- 1 cup canola oil

Note

The dressing will keep in an airtight container in the fridge for up to 2 weeks. Let stand at room temperature for an hour or so before serving, or warm slightly in the microwave.

pretty pickled red onions

 Sneak these onions into sandwiches, quesadillas, and burritos. They're also delicious strewn on veggie burgers (pages 170–174), pizzas, or almost anything.

MAKES 1 1/2 CUPS

1 large red onion, thinly sliced

1 tablespoon sugar

1/2 cup red wine vinegar

In a small saucepan, combine the onion, sugar, and vinegar over medium-high heat. Bring to a boil, cover, and remove from the heat. Let stand for 15 minutes. Transfer the onions and their liquid to a glass jar or bowl, cover, and refrigerate.

Note

The onions will keep for up to 3 weeks in the fridge.

roasted garlic

(V) *Add roasted garlic to mashed potatoes,* pasta dishes, soups, pizzas, and gravies. There are many ways to roast it, but I find that this method is the most efficient. Store the garlic in the oil in the fridge and use whenever opportunity calls. The oil can be used to sauté vegetables or as a base for tomato sauces and soups. Roasted garlic puree makes a great spread for crusty bread.

MAKES ABOUT ½ CUP

3 **very fresh heads of garlic (make sure they are not soft or sprouted), cloves separated**

About 1 cup olive or canola oil

1 Preheat the oven to 375 degrees. Lightly smash each garlic clove with the side of a chef's knife to release the clove from the skin. Place the peeled cloves in a small casserole dish, then cover the cloves completely with canola or olive oil. Roast for about 40 minutes, or until the cloves are just slightly browned on the edges. Let cool.

Note
The oil and the puree will keep in an airtight container in the fridge for at least 1 month.

2 To make roasted garlic puree, in a food processor, puree the garlic cloves and a few spoonfuls of the oil.

caramelized onions

 Nothing beats these sweet onions hot on a pizza or cold as an onion chutney. They also nestle nicely in wraps, burritos, and veggie burgers (pages 170–174).

MAKES 2 CUPS

¼ cup canola oil

4 large Spanish onions, thinly sliced

2 tablespoons balsamic vinegar

Kosher salt and freshly ground black pepper to taste

In a large heavy pot or skillet, heat the canola oil over medium heat. Add the onions and cook, stirring every 5 minutes (but no more, since stirring will hinder caramelization), for 30 minutes, or until the onions turn a medium brown color. Add the vinegar and season with salt and pepper. Cook for 1 to 2 minutes more.

Note The caramelized onions will keep in an airtight container in the fridge for up to 1 week.

roti (flatbread)

(V) *Roti is a great bread for beginner bakers,* since it's difficult to botch. This one resembles thick pita bread and makes any curry, such as Saag Paneer (page 226), Sweet Potato Badi (page 210), or Curried Cauliflower with Tomatoes and Tofu (page 224), special. Roti, when served alongside soup, makes any occasion splendid.

MAKES 8

1 cup whole wheat flour

1 cup all-purpose flour

1½ teaspoons baking powder

½ teaspoon kosher salt

2 garlic cloves, minced

2 tablespoons canola oil, or more as needed

1 In a large bowl, stir together the flours, baking powder, and salt. Add the garlic and 1¼ cups water, blending to form a soft dough. Knead for 3 to 4 minutes, or until smooth. Cover the bowl with plastic wrap and let stand for 30 minutes.

2 Divide the dough into 8 balls. On a floured surface, roll out each ball as thinly as possible to form eight 6-inch circles.

3 In a medium skillet, heat the canola oil over medium-high heat. Fry the roti, one at a time, until bubbles form on its surface, about 2 minutes. Flip and cook until browned on the second side. Drain on paper towels. Serve warm.

Note The dough can be prepared up to 2 days ahead and stored in plastic wrap in the fridge. Cooked roti can be held on a baking sheet, covered with foil, in a 200-degree oven for up to 30 minutes.

potato dosai (indian pancakes)

These dosai are very different from and far more delicious than the kind one eats in Southern Indian restaurants. Dipped in a bit of Fresh Cilantro Chutney (page 344), they are one of the best treats on the planet. They're as easy to prepare as mashed potatoes. Making them ahead works in your favor, since they get crispier if left in a warm oven for an hour or so. Serve alongside any Indian curry or make a tasty hors d'oeuvre by cutting them into wedges and topping them with chutney.

Don't use rice flour from a whole food store because it is processed differently. The rice flour you want is labeled "glutinous" or "non-glutinous" (both are acceptable here) and should be purchased at an Asian market (see page 444).

MAKES 10

2 small red potatoes (about 2/3 pound total), unpeeled, halved

Kosher salt

1 1/4 cups Asian rice flour (see above)

1/2 cup plain yogurt (nonfat is fine)

1/2 cup chopped cilantro stems and leaves (and roots, if available)

1–2 small, skinny chile peppers, seeded and minced

1 garlic clove, minced

2 tablespoons canola oil, or more if needed

1 In a medium saucepan, combine the potatoes with cold salted water to cover. Bring to a boil and cook until fork-tender, about 15 minutes. Drain in a colander, rinse lightly, and peel off the skins. Transfer the potatoes to a large bowl and mash well with a fork or potato masher. Let cool for 10 minutes.

2 Stir the rice flour into the potatoes, then add the yogurt, cilantro, chiles, garlic, and 1 teaspoon salt. Gradually add about 1 cup water, mixing and mashing until the mixture is the consistency of pancake batter.

3 In a medium, nonstick skillet, heat the oil over medium-high heat. Pour a ladleful of the batter into the skillet and spread it quickly to form a thin cake. Cook until the bottom of the dosa is dark brown around the edges, about 5 minutes. Use a spatula to carefully flip the dosa and cook until the other side is golden, 2 to 3 minutes more. Repeat with the remaining batter, adding more oil as needed (I like to get two skillets going at once, so I'm not making them all day). Serve warm.

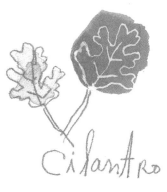

Cilantro

Note

The batter can be made up to 24 hours ahead and stored in an airtight container in the fridge. Cooked dosa will keep, arranged slightly overlapping on baking sheets, for up to 1 hour in a 250-degree oven.

roti jala (malaysian crepes)

Malaysians use these crepes instead of forks to scoop up curries and rice. Serve them instead of rice with Tempeh Rendang (page 232) or with Black Rice Cakes with Tofu and Mussamun Curry (page 304).

MAKES 12

1¼ cups all-purpose flour

1 teaspoon curry powder

Pinch of kosher salt

½ cup unsweetened coconut milk (see page 446)

1 large egg

1 tablespoon canola oil

1 In a large bowl, combine the flour, curry powder, and salt. In a small bowl, whisk together the coconut milk, egg, and 1¼ cups water. Pour the liquid into the flour mixture and whisk to form a smooth batter.

2 In a medium skillet, heat the canola oil over medium-high heat. Pour small ladlefuls of the batter into the skillet to form crepes about 5 inches across, cooking in batches. When bubbles appear around the edges and the roti are golden brown on the bottom, flip them over and fry for 30 seconds more. Transfer to a serving platter and serve immediately.

Note

The roti jala pancakes can be held on a baking sheet, covered with foil, in a 200-degree oven for 1 hour.

chapter 10

Memorable Mornings

Brunch Anyone?

A spot of tea

OJ

seven reasons to have
people over for brunch

1. **Dinner parties require more work than brunch does.** When preparing for a dinner party, you often end up making one or two hors d'oeuvres, a main dish, a salad, and a dessert. Brunch can be much simpler (read: less work).

2. **It's nice for a change.** Few people have brunches, and so it stands out, which automatically makes it more intriguing and fun.

3. **Everyone's expectations are lower early in the day.** People are used to cereal or dried-out store-bought muffins. Your friends will be delighted to eat some homemade food.

4. **It's less expensive.** Brunch means little or no alcohol, which is often the biggest party expense. And brunch food is not as fancy and pricey as dinner-party food.

5. **If you enjoy baking, brunch is the meal for you.** I jump out of bed when I have baking to do, and everyone loves baked goods hot from the oven. Biscuits, scones, coffeecake, muffins, breads, and cookies are only the tip of the iceberg. Churn out a couple of goodies, and your friends will love you more than ever.

6. **Brunch is relatively short.** Once they've eaten, people are generally eager to resume their day. Guests can arrive at noon, then leave around 2:30 or 3:00. When you have people over for dinner, they often drink more, eat more, and linger longer.

7. **Sunday brunch is convenient for both the party-giver and the partygoer.** As the host, you have all of Saturday to prepare. You can relax on Saturday night or go out. Sunday is also a good day because people usually want Saturdays for them-

selves, to accomplish household chores or just to relax from the week. Finally, Sunday brunch leaves you and your guests with Sunday evening free to do your own things.

The food possibilities for brunch are vast enough to fill another book, but I'll pare it down to my three favorite kinds of brunch.

The Omelet Brunch

In this day and age, a good omelet is hard to come by. That's why serving omelets can make a brunch memorable, but you must be enterprising, since they need to be made *during* the party. Because of this, omelet brunches work best for groups of no more than six. See page 362 for details.

The Pancake Brunch

Perennially fun and highly popular, pancakes are easy and delicious, especially when they're made from scratch. Like omelets, pancakes must be made to order, so this brunch works best for small groups. See page 364 for details.

The Baked French Toast Brunch

Baked French toast is the easiest brunch dish of all. You can have eight, twelve, or even twenty friends over, since getting the food ready all at once just means pulling a casserole dish or two out of the oven. See page 365 for details.

the omelet brunch (so simple yet so good)

Omelets are underappreciated in this country, probably because most Americans don't know how to make a proper one. Even in restaurants, omelets are often puffy, brown, dry, and insipid. Interest in omelets also waned because of the egg's cholesterol count. But kinder words are now being spoken of eggs, and it's high time we all learned how to make an omelet.

A good omelet requires nothing more than a well-seasoned skillet and the recipe on page 366. The basic ingredients are eggs, butter, salt, and pepper. Achieving a soft, silky texture hinges on the execution, which takes about three tries to master with the right skillet and a little concentration. This method is almost exactly the same as the one Julia Child put forth forty years ago—a classic method that has probably existed since the omelet's birth in sixteenth-century France. Practice helps, so try making an omelet for yourself for breakfast, lunch, or dinner. Just remember—the worst thing you can do to an omelet is overcook it: this destroys the delicate texture.

Whatever you do, don't aim to serve all your omelets at the same time. The older omelets will cool down too quickly, and keeping them warm will dry them out. It's best to have just three or four guests and to have them eat the omelets as they are made. Serving more than six people is too tiring. It's a good idea to have other food on the table, such as biscuits, fruit, and coffee, so guests will have something to munch on until their omelets arrive.

I make two fillings for a party of four. I usually choose one that includes tomatoes, since eggs and tomatoes have an affinity for each other. Here are some of my favorites:

- Ripe tomatoes with fresh mozzarella and fresh basil

- Asparagus with fresh mozzarella (include a fresh herb, such as dill, basil, or parsley, if you like)

- Creamed spinach and shiitakes (use Creamed Spinach and Shiitakes on Toast—without the toast—on page 194 as the filling)

- Sautéed Swiss chard or spinach and French goat's milk feta

- Porcini mushrooms—rehydrate them according to the directions on page 449, then drain and mince. Add to the egg mixture. When you are ready to fill the omelet, use fresh goat cheese, grated Gruyère, or (for the indulgent) St. André triple-crème cheese.

- Poor man's omelet (a favorite of mine). Pan-fry cubes of French bread in a generous amount of olive oil and pour the eggs over the bread. This alone makes a good folded omelet, but it's also nice served flat, topped with pitted black olives, roasted red bell pepper strips (see page 23), and grated Parmesan.

With the omelets, serve good bread—one with a crust to it, either a slightly sour rustic loaf or a classic French baguette. You can serve it with butter, if desired, but it's mainly there to soak up the juices of the omelet. (Although it may not make Emily Post happy, I like to load my bread with pieces of omelet and eat it like an open-faced sandwich.) The poor man's omelet doesn't need bread on the side, although it won't hurt either.

Another complement for an omelet is Lightlife's Fakin' Bacon. Made from tempeh, it's tasty and satisfying and can be prepared ahead and kept warm in the oven. I also like to serve a seasonal fruit salad. In the winter, try grapes, grapefruit, and kiwis with a teaspoon of sugar. In spring, try blood oranges, toasted walnuts, and bananas. In summer, use peaches, apricots, or mangoes with blueberries. In the fall, use pears, dates, and raspberries. Just chill the fruit salad up to 24 hours ahead. Or serve a simple green salad —nothing fancier than red leaf lettuce with kalamata olives and tomatoes. If you want to go all out, buy biscotti for dessert.

Once you have mastered omelets, you'll see their versatility and practicality. Whether you're serving breakfast, lunch, or dinner, omelets are a great way to use up odds and ends in your fridge, and you can have a marvelous time mixing and matching. When you feel like eating something special but don't want any fuss, omelets are a great option.

the pancake brunch

Everyone loves pancakes. When I was a bed-and-breakfast chef in Cambridge, Massachusetts, the owners required that I make pancakes every other day. The way to serve pancakes at their best is to present them the minute they depart from the stove. I warm the plates in the oven to ensure that the pancakes stay hot. You can drop one pancake onto each person's plate so that everyone can eat close to the same time. It's a good idea to limit the number of guests to no more than six. To placate the people who haven't received pancakes yet, you can place fruit cups on the table as well as coffee and juice.

Offer options such as bananas or blueberries.

Good pancakes don't need much—fresh butter and real maple syrup are about it. Just make sure the butter is soft and the maple syrup is at room temperature by the time the pancakes are ready. Cold maple syrup on hot pancakes is equivalent to a glass of cold water down your back! Fresh fruit —either a fruit salad or just cut melon or berries—will round out the meal. Another option is to mix plain yogurt with jam or brown sugar to use as a topping for the fruit or a low-fat alternative to maple syrup and butter. Either of these can be prepared and chilled up to 24 hours before serving. Another good side dish is Fakin' Bacon by Lightlife.

Homemade orange juice never fails to impress, but it's a lot of work. Just brew good coffee and serve OJ that's not from concentrate. Your friends are lucky that you're making pancakes for them, after all.

the baked french toast brunch

Here's the perfect solution for larger brunches, when you don't want to be bothered by any cooking during the gathering. Baked French toast is easy, and it can be prepared the day before (except for the baking, which takes effort by the oven, not you). I made many versions at my bed-and-breakfast post in Cambridge, Massachusetts. My favorite is Almond Baked French Toast (page 368). If you want to make a more straightforward baked French toast, leave out the sliced almonds.

Do-Ahead Details

You can prepare the egg mixture and slice the bread 1 or 2 days before the brunch. Store the bread in a plastic bag with a few holes poked in it so it will start to get stale. The French toast can be fully assembled the morning of the party and baked for 1 hour before serving.

You can serve baked French toast with:

- Good, fresh butter and real maple syrup
- Fruit salad. Any combination of seasonal fruits is nice. Limit the salad to three fruits so it's not too busy. Add a little lemon juice and a spoonful of sugar, and chill for up to 24 hours before serving.
- Beverages. Orange juice (homemade if you can spare the time!), coffee, tea, or chai.

French toast

one fine omelet

Omelets are fast, and once you learn the simple technique, you can impress your friends to no end. A 2- or 3-egg omelet takes, on average, about 30 seconds, so serving a number of people in quick succession is feasible. (A 4-, 5-, or 6-egg omelet is much trickier to maneuver.)

A well-seasoned skillet, whether nonstick, stainless steel, treated aluminum, or plain or enameled iron, is essential. Some people, like my mother, swear by the classic French omelet pans that are not washed but just wiped with kosher salt and oil after using.

Filling the omelet with cheese, herbs, or vegetables of some sort is a good idea but not necessary.

SERVES 1

2 or 3 eggs, preferably free-range

Big pinch of kosher salt

Big pinch of freshly ground black pepper

1 tablespoon butter

Optional filling, such as herbs, grated cheese, or vegetables (if the vegetables are cooked, warm them)

1 In a medium bowl, beat the eggs, salt, and pepper with a fork until blended; do not overmix.

2 Melt the butter in a 7- to 8-inch pan over very high heat. Tilt the pan so the butter covers the base and sides of the pan. When the foam has subsided and the butter is at the point of coloring, pour in the eggs.

3 Stir the eggs for a few seconds with a wooden spoon, then tilt the pan

Granola Garnish

• • makes 2 cups

Here's a great way to transform granola from the usual humdrum breakfast into something special. The following mixture is also wonderful in pancakes or on top of muffin and cake batter.

In a food processor, process 1 cup frozen cranberries, $2/3$ cup whole almonds, $1/2$ cup Sucanat or sugar, and $1/2$ teaspoon ground cardamom until the nuts and cranberries are chopped fairly fine. Put 3 to 4 spoonfuls on top of some good granola. Add soy milk or regular milk and enjoy.

NOTE: The cranberry mixture will keep, stored in a zip bag, up to 6 months in the freezer.

so the eggs run around the entire base of the pan and onto the sides. Let the eggs set for about 5 seconds and then remove the pan immediately from the heat; the omelet should not be browned.

4 For the filling, if using, place no more than 3 tablespoons filling on the omelet. Using a plastic spatula and tilting one side of the pan toward a plate, fold the omelet so that it rolls onto the plate. Serve immediately.

almond baked french toast

This baked French toast resembles a bread pudding, except the bread is not cubed but left in slices. If you want to serve it without the almonds, it will still be quite good. You'll find that part of each slice of the bread rises above the custard and then becomes rather crisp. The crusty bread makes a good contrast for the soft custard. Steer clear of mediocre supermarket bread. Buy a boule if you can, which is a round, white, French bread. Whole-grain bread is too strongly flavored for this dish. If you use a baguette, you will need 12 slices instead of 6. Serve with real maple syrup.

SERVES 8

5 tablespoons ($^1/_2$ stick plus 1 tablespoon) butter, softened

6 1-inch-thick slices good-quality bread, preferably white and from a round loaf

5 cups milk

1 cup sugar

10 large eggs

$^1/_2$ cup heavy cream

1 teaspoon vanilla extract

Pinch of freshly ground nutmeg

1 cup sliced almonds

1 Preheat the oven to 350 degrees. Butter a 13-x-9-inch baking dish with about $^1/_2$ tablespoon of the butter. Butter one side of each slice of bread with the remaining butter. Place the slices in the baking dish buttered side up, overlapping them slightly.

2 In a large saucepan, heat the milk and sugar over medium-high heat, stirring frequently. Meanwhile, in a medium bowl, beat the eggs with a whisk. Just before the milk mixture boils, slowly whisk it into the egg mixture with the cream. Pour the custard into the saucepan, then strain the custard through a fine sieve back into the bowl. Add the vanilla and nutmeg.

altoids and other party favors

Party favors are always fun on special occasions. My friend Marla invited her girl-friends up to her ski house and gave them dog or cat flannel pajamas, according to which animal they had at home. An industrious and creative friend, Amy, threw a sur-prise fortieth-birthday party for her husband, Wayne. Amy had T-shirts printed with a photo of a buff seventeen-year-old Wayne sunbathing. Her party favors included a tin of Altoid mints. On each tin, neatly glued to the inside cover, was a photocopied pic-ture of Wayne at a particular stage in his life. Mine now sits on my coffee table, an amusing memento of the party.

3 Pour the custard over the bread in the baking dish and let it soak, mov-ing the slices of bread so that at least 1 inch of each slice clears the surface. Bake for 45 minutes. Remove from the oven and scatter the almonds over the top. Bake for 10 minutes more, or until a knife inserted into the center comes out clean. Let cool for 10 minutes before serving. Cut the French toast into 8 pieces and serve.

Note The custard can be prepared (step 2) up to 1 day in advance. Store the custard in an airtight container in the fridge. The unbuttered bread slices can be stored in a sealed bag that has been punctured with a Phillips head screwdriver multiple times to allow the air in.

french toast stuffed with apples and walnuts

This festive and scrumptious French toast is so filling that you'll need only one slice per person. For a zippier filling, substitute chopped frozen cranberries for the currants or raisins. Once it's ready, make sure everyone is sitting down so they can eat the French toast while it's hot. If you'd like to make this for eight people, double the recipe and cook it in two large skillets. Before serving, drizzle a bit of real maple syrup or sift some confectioners' sugar over each slice.

SERVES 4

1 In a food processor, combine the cream cheese, sugar, and cinnamon and pulse a few times to blend. Set aside.

2 In a medium skillet, melt 1 tablespoon of the butter over medium heat. Add the apples and sauté until they soften, about 5 minutes. Add the currants or raisins and Cognac or orange juice and cook until the liquid evaporates, about 3 minutes. Add the walnuts.

3 With a serrated knife, make a pocket two thirds of the way into one bread slice, as wide as possible without

- 3 ounces cream cheese
- 2 tablespoons sugar
- 2 pinches of ground cinnamon
- 2 tablespoons unsalted butter
- 3 apples, preferably Granny Smith, peeled, cored, and finely chopped
- 2 tablespoons dried currants or raisins
- 2 tablespoons Cognac or orange juice
- 1/4 cup chopped toasted walnuts (see page 283)
- 4 2-inch-thick slices soft white bread
- 1 large egg
- 1/3 cup milk

cutting through the sides. With a butter knife, spread one quarter of the cream cheese mixture on the insides of the bread, and spoon in one quarter of the apple mixture. Repeat with the bread, cream cheese mixture, and apple mixture.

4 In a large, nonstick skillet or griddle melt the remaining 1 tablespoon butter over medium-low heat. In a wide, shallow bowl, whisk together the egg and milk. Dip 1 stuffed bread slice into the egg mixture, turn and dip the other side, and place it in the skillet. Continue with the remaining slices and pan-fry until browned on the bottoms, about 5 minutes. Use a spatula to flip the bread and pan-fry until the other sides are brown, 3 to 5 minutes more. Serve immediately.

come and get it *now!*

When I have people over, I tend to get panicky when I put the food on the table and call out, "Come and get it!" and no one stirs. Worse, I've seen people get to the table only to stand in front of their chairs and wait for everyone else to sit. Then you have three or four people standing, vying for the "most considerate guest" award. All I'm thinking is that the food is getting colder by the second.

So I developed a better strategy: I ask a "can-do" friend to round up the group while I'm still in the kitchen so that everyone is seated by the time the food is brought to the table. But I have a chef friend who takes a more direct approach. When she sees that people aren't moving, she clears her throat and announces, "It insults the cook if you let her food get cold. Everyone, please move to the table."

overnight cornmeal-crusted french toast

You need to start this French toast the night before, which is nice because it means less work in the morning. It's a perfect breakfast dish during the busy holiday season. Slather with butter and drizzle with warm maple syrup before serving.

SERVES 4

1½ cups milk

2 large eggs

Pinch of freshly grated nutmeg and/or ground cinnamon

Pinch of salt

8 1-inch-thick diagonal slices French bread, each about 5 inches long

⅓ cup cornmeal

3 tablespoons unsalted butter

1 In a large, shallow bowl, beat together the milk and eggs. Add the nutmeg and/or cinnamon and salt and mix well. Add the bread slices to the milk mixture, turning to coat. Cover with plastic wrap and refrigerate overnight.

2 At serving time, spread the cornmeal on a plate. In a large, nonstick skillet or griddle, melt 1½ tablespoons of the butter over medium-low heat. (Use two skillets with all the butter if you want to make all the French toast at once.) Lift the bread slices out of the milk mixture, squeezing gently to remove some of the liquid. Dredge the bread in the cornmeal and pan-fry in batches until golden brown on the bottoms, about 5 minutes. Don't rush the French toast; cook it slowly so that the batter that has seeped into the bread has a chance to cook. Turn the slices over and pan-fry until the other side is brown, about 4 to 5 minutes. Repeat, using the remaining bread slices and butter. Serve immediately.

Note
This recipe is designed to save you time in the morning, since the bread and batter are prepared the night before.

healthy but luscious pancakes

I tried a recipe in Gourmet magazine for cornmeal-yogurt pancakes and found them very nice. But I tinkered with the recipe, cutting down on the butter to make them lighter and adding wheat germ to up the fiber. Serve with maple syrup.

MAKES 12 PANCAKES, SERVES 4

1 cup all-purpose flour

1/2 cup cornmeal

1/2 cup toasted wheat germ or bran

3 tablespoons sugar or Sucanat (see page 451)

2 teaspoons baking powder

1 teaspoon baking soda

1/2 teaspoon salt

3 tablespoons unsalted butter, chilled

3/4 cup plain yogurt mixed with 1/4 cup water

1 large egg, lightly beaten

2 tablespoons unsalted butter or canola oil, or more as needed

1 In a food processor, pulse the dry ingredients to combine. Add the chilled butter and pulse until the mixture forms coarse crumbs. Transfer to a medium bowl and make a well in the center; add the yogurt mixture and egg. Whisk to blend the wet ingredients, gradually incorporating the flour mixture just until blended. (One secret to tender pancakes is to never overstir the batter at any point; this makes them tough.)

2 Heat a large skillet or griddle over medium heat. Add the butter or oil, and when it is hot, ladle the batter into the pan to form 5-inch cakes, working in batches if necessary to avoid crowding the pan. Pan-fry until the pancakes are golden brown on the bottom and large bubbles appear on the top, about 3 minutes. Turn the pancakes and brown the other sides, 2 minutes more. Serve immediately.

Note

The pancake batter can be made up to 24 hours ahead and stored in an airtight container in the fridge.

testy cat muffins (banana– chocolate chip, carrot, or fig muffins)

Not so long ago, I ran an informal business called Testy Cat Bakery in honor of Henry, my skittish and food-obsessed cat. For many months, I sold these muffins to a progressive community store near my home. They can be made with 1½ cups Sucanat and no other sweetener if desired.

MAKES 8 JUMBO OR 12 STANDARD MUFFINS

master recipe

- ¾ cup buttermilk
- ¾ cup canola oil
- 3 large eggs
- ¾ cup packed dark brown sugar
- ¾ cup sugar or Sucanat (see page 451)
- 1 cup plus 2 tablespoons whole wheat flour
- ¾ cup plus 2 tablespoons all-purpose flour
- ⅓ cup toasted bran-flake cereal or unprocessed bran
- 2 tablespoons wheat germ (optional)
- 1½ teaspoons baking soda
- 1½ teaspoons baking powder
- ½ teaspoon salt

for banana–chocolate chip

- ⅔ cup walnut pieces (optional)
- 2 ripe bananas, mashed
- ½ cup chocolate chips
- ¼ cup raisins
- ½ teaspoon ground cardamom
- ½ teaspoon ground cinnamon

for carrot

- 1 cup walnut pieces
- 2 large carrots, grated
- ¼ cup raisins
- 1 teaspoon ground cinnamon
- ¼ teaspoon allspice

1 Preheat the oven to 350 degrees. Lightly oil 8 jumbo or 12 standard muffin cups. Spread the walnuts, if using, in a single layer on a rimmed baking sheet and toast for 5 minutes, or until golden brown. Set aside to cool.

2 In a large bowl, combine the buttermilk, oil, eggs, brown sugar, and sugar or Sucanat and mix well. Set aside.

3 In a medium bowl, combine the whole wheat and all-purpose flours, bran, wheat germ (if using), baking soda, baking powder, and salt and mix well.

4 Fold the flour mixture into the buttermilk mixture and blend well, but gently. Add the additional ingredients for the type of muffin you're making (including the soaking liquid, if using figs), and stir only until incorporated. Don't overmix.

5 Divide the batter among the prepared muffin cups and bake until a knife inserted in the center of a muffin comes out clean, about 35 to 40 minutes for jumbo muffins and 30 minutes for standard muffins.

for fig

2/3 cup walnut pieces

1 cup dried mission figs, soaked in boiling water for 30 minutes, drained (reserve 1/4 cup soaking liquid), and quartered

1 small apple, unpeeled, cored, and chopped

2 tablespoons poppy seeds

1 1/2 teaspoons ground ginger

1/2 teaspoon ground cinnamon

1/4 teaspoon ground allspice

6 Cool in the pan for 10 minutes, then run a knife around the edges to loosen the muffins from their cups. Serve.

Note The muffins can be wrapped in plastic wrap and frozen for up to 2 months.

vegan banana-walnut muffins

Ⓥ *I used to bake a vegan butternut squash bread,* but one day I decided to use ripe bananas instead of the squash. Eureka! What a brilliant loaf of bread. I turned the banana bread into muffins without changing a thing. (If you'd like to make banana bread, bake the batter in a loaf pan in a preheated 375-degree oven for 45 to 50 minutes, or until a knife inserted in the center of the bread comes out clean.) Serve plain or with butter or jam.

MAKES 8 JUMBO OR 12 STANDARD MUFFINS

4 ripe bananas

1 cup plain or vanilla soy milk

½ cup plus 2 tablespoons canola oil

2 cups all-purpose flour

1 cup Sucanat (see page 451) or brown sugar

1½ teaspoons baking powder

½ teaspoon baking soda

1½ teaspoons freshly ground nutmeg

½ teaspoon salt

2 cups chopped walnuts

1 Preheat the oven to 350 degrees. Lightly oil 8 jumbo or 12 standard muffin cups.

2 In a large bowl, mash the bananas with a fork or potato masher. Stir in the soy milk and canola oil.

3 In a medium bowl, combine the flour, Sucanat or brown sugar, baking powder, baking soda, nutmeg, and salt and mix well. Add in 3 batches to the banana mixture, stirring only until incorporated, and adding the walnuts with the last batch.

4 Divide the batter among the prepared muffin cups and bake until a knife inserted in the center of one of the muffins comes out clean, about 30 minutes for jumbo muffins and about 20 minutes for standard muffins.

5 Cool in the pan for 10 minutes, then run a knife around the edges to loosen the muffins from their cups. Serve.

Note The muffins will keep for 2 days if they are wrapped in plastic wrap. A better solution is to prepare the batter up to 24 hours ahead and store in an airtight container in the fridge.

Bananas

tofu corn muffins

 Tofu helps produce moist, fluffy muffins that are good with soup or chili. They also make good use of leftover tofu.

MAKES 6 JUMBO OR 10 STANDARD MUFFINS

- 1 cup cornmeal
- 3/4 cup all-purpose flour
- 2 teaspoons baking powder
- 2 teaspoons minced fresh or dried rosemary
- 1 teaspoon salt
- Half a 16-ounce carton firm tofu, drained
- 5 1/2 tablespoons canola oil
- 1 tablespoon sugar or maple syrup

1 Preheat the oven to 350 degrees. Lightly oil 6 jumbo or 10 standard muffin cups.

2 In a large bowl, combine the cornmeal, flour, baking powder, rosemary, and salt and mix well.

3 In a medium bowl, squeeze the tofu through your hands until it has the consistency of scrambled eggs. Stir in the canola oil, 1 cup water, and the sugar or maple syrup. Add to the cornmeal mixture and stir just until moistened.

4 Divide the batter among the prepared muffin cups and bake until a knife inserted in the center of one of the muffins comes out clean, about 30 to 40 minutes for jumbo muffins and about 25 to 30 minutes for standard muffins.

5 Cool in the pan for 10 minutes, then run a knife around the edges to loosen the muffins from their cups. Serve.

Note The batter can be made up to 1 day ahead (through step 3) and stored in an airtight container in the fridge.

blueberry-cardamom coffeecake

One slice of this breakfast cake will restore your faith in the world—or at least in coffeecake. Instead of blueberries, try this cake with fresh pitted cherries or raspberries.

SERVES 10 TO 12

1 Preheat the oven to 350 degrees. Butter and flour a 13-x-9-inch baking pan.

2 In a large bowl, cream the butter and sugar with an electric mixer until fluffy. Add the eggs, one at a time, and beat until incorporated.

3 In a medium bowl, combine the flour, baking powder, baking soda, cardamom, and salt and mix well. In a second medium bowl, toss the blueberries with 1/2 cup of the flour mixture. Add the remaining flour mixture to the butter mixture in three batches, alternating with the sour cream. Fold in the blueberries. Spread the batter in the pan.

4 In a small bowl, combine the sugar, pecans or walnuts, and nutmeg and mix well. Scatter the topping over the batter. Bake until a knife inserted in the center of the cake comes out clean, 35 to 40 minutes. Serve warm.

12 tablespoons (1½ sticks) unsalted butter, softened

1 cup sugar

2 large eggs

2 cups all-purpose flour

1 teaspoon baking powder

1 teaspoon baking soda

1 teaspoon ground cardamom

1 teaspoon salt

1½ cups blueberries (if frozen, do not thaw)

1 cup sour cream

topping

3/4 cup light or dark brown sugar

1/2 cup chopped pecans or walnuts

1 teaspoon freshly ground nutmeg

Note The batter can be made up to 1 day ahead and stored in an airtight container in the fridge. The topping can also be prepared up to 1 day ahead and stored in a zip bag at room temperature.

world's best vegan coffeecake

 If you're a vegan, make haste and bake this cake! Studded with bits of cranberries and almonds, it's tender, moist, and excellent. The poppy-seed streusel adds crunch and character. If you like, substitute whole wheat flour for half of the all-purpose flour. You can also use chopped fresh strawberries instead of cranberries. If you serve it for dessert, call it the World's Best Vegan Streusel Cake.

SERVES 10

cake

- 1 **cup almonds**
- 2 **cups frozen cranberries (*not* thawed)**
- 2 **cups all-purpose flour**
- 1 **cup sugar or Sucanat (see page 451)**
- 2 **teaspoons ground cinnamon or 1 rounded teaspoon ground cardamom**
- 2 **teaspoons baking powder**
- ½ **teaspoon salt**
- 1 **cup plain or vanilla soy milk**
- ½ **cup canola oil**

streusel

- ⅓ **cup almonds**
- 4 **tablespoons (½ stick) soy margarine, cut into 6 pieces**
- ⅓ **cup sugar or Sucanat**
- ¼ **cup all-purpose flour**
- 2 **tablespoons poppy seeds**

1 Preheat the oven to 350 degrees. Grease a 2-quart tube or Bundt pan.

2 **To make the cake:** In a food processor, finely pulverize the almonds. Add the frozen cranberries and process until they are coarsely chopped. Transfer to a large bowl and add the flour, sugar or Sucanat, cinnamon or cardamom, baking powder, and salt and mix well. Make a well in the center. Add the soy milk and canola oil and stir until the mixture comes together. Transfer the batter to the prepared pan.

3 **To make the streusel:** In a food processor, coarsely pulverize the almonds. Add the margarine, sugar or Sucanat, flour, and poppy seeds and process until the mixture resembles wet sand. Sprinkle the streusel evenly over the batter. Bake for 50 to 55 minutes, or until a knife inserted in the center of the cake comes out clean. Let cool for at least 15 minutes before cutting and serving.

Note

This coffeecake can be baked 1 day ahead, wrapped in plastic wrap, and stored in the fridge. It can be reheated in a 250-degree oven for about 20 minutes. The baked cake can be frozen for up to 3 months. Double-wrap it in plastic wrap, then wrap once in foil. Let the cake come to room temperature before reheating in the oven.

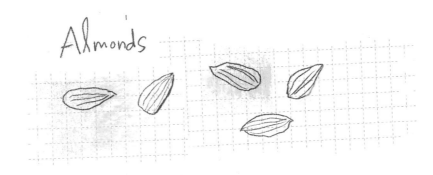

Almonds

figgy walnut bread

(V) *Here's one of my all-time favorite* quick breads. It's dairy-free and loaded with good-for-you ingredients, yet through the magic of applesauce, bananas, and canola oil, it's rich and moist. The figs are left whole, which makes for handsome slices. Flaxseed can be found in whole food stores in the bulk section.

MAKES 2 LOAVES

2 cups walnuts

2¼ cups dried Calimyrna figs

2½ cups plus 2 tablespoons whole wheat flour

2 tablespoons ground flaxseed (see page 447; optional)

1½ teaspoons ground cardamom

1½ teaspoons baking soda

½ teaspoon salt

1 overripe banana, mashed (optional)

1 cup plus 2 tablespoons applesauce

2 small unpeeled Granny Smith apples, grated

1 cup plus 2 tablespoons packed dark brown sugar

¾ cup canola oil

½ cup poppy seeds

1 Preheat the oven to 350 degrees. Spread the walnuts in a single layer on a rimmed baking sheet and toast for 5 minutes, or until golden brown. Set aside to cool. Increase the oven temperature to 375 degrees. Oil two 9-x-5-inch loaf pans.

2 In a medium bowl, combine the figs and boiling water to cover. Let soak for 15 minutes. Drain well. Set aside.

3 In a second medium bowl, combine the flour, flaxseed (if using), cardamom, baking soda, and salt.

4 In a large bowl, blend the banana (if using) and applesauce with a fork. Add the figs, apples, and brown sugar and mix well. Gradually whisk in the canola oil and 6 tablespoons water until well blended. Add the dry ingredients, folding until they are completely incorporated, then add the walnuts and poppy seeds. Divide the batter between the prepared pans.

Note

The bread will keep, wrapped in plastic wrap, for 3 to 4 days. Or double-wrap it and freeze for up to 3 months.

5 Bake for about 1 hour, or until a knife inserted in the center of a loaf comes out clean. Cool in the pans on a cooling rack for 30 minutes, then invert the loaves onto the rack and cool completely.

Figs

whole wheat communion bread

(V) *St. John's is a unique Episcopal church* in Jamaica Plain, Massachusetts. For Communion, the priest offers homemade wheat bread instead of those cardboard-like wafers that adhere to the roof of your mouth. I asked for the recipe and began making the bread at home. It owes its moist texture and flavor to a large dose of molasses or honey. I recommend it for the Emmons Egg Salad Sandwich (page 190). Unbleached bread flour is available in bulk at whole food stores.

MAKES THREE 9-INCH ROUND LOAVES

6 tablespoons molasses or honey

4½ teaspoons (2 packets) active dry yeast

3 tablespoons canola oil

1 teaspoon salt

1 cup rolled oats

2¾ cups whole wheat flour

2½ cups unbleached white bread flour, plus more if needed

1 In a large, warmed bowl (use the bowl of a stand mixer if you own one), combine 2¼ cups very warm water and a drop of the molasses or honey. Sprinkle the yeast over the water and wait for it to foam slightly, about 5 minutes. Stir in the remaining molasses or honey, canola oil, and salt until well combined. Add the oats and gradually add the flour, using a spoon or the dough hook of an electric mixer until the dough comes together. If you're kneading by hand, transfer the dough onto a floured work surface and knead for 5 to 7 minutes, adding more flour if the dough still seems very sticky, until it springs back when pressed with a finger. If using a mixer, knead the dough on low speed with the dough hook for 5 minutes, or until smooth and elastic.

2 Transfer the dough to a large, oiled bowl. Cover with plastic wrap and a dishtowel, and let rise in a warm place until doubled in bulk, about 1 hour. Oil a baking sheet. Divide the dough into 3 pieces and roll each piece into a ball. Arrange the balls on the prepared baking sheet, cover with plastic wrap and a dishtowel, and let rise again for 30 minutes.

Note

The bread can be baked, double-wrapped in plastic wrap, and frozen for up to 2 months.

3 Preheat the oven to 350 degrees. Use a razor blade or very sharp knife to slash a cross on the top of each loaf. Bake until the loaves sound hollow when tapped on the bottom, 30 to 40 minutes. Cool to room temperature on cooling racks. Wrap well with plastic wrap.

pipérade

I first tasted pipérade in Paris. It was a revelation to me that this simple, slow-cooked tomato and bell pepper dish from the Basque area of France could be so good. It is common to serve pipérade with an egg or two baked on top. You may feel that you could cut down on the olive oil a bit, but in fact it gives the dish its needed richness. Encourage your guests to sop up the extra sauce with crusty bread.

SERVES 4

4 tablespoons extra-virgin olive oil

1 large onion, sliced

2 red, orange, or yellow bell peppers, cut into strips

2 green bell peppers, cut into strips

4 plum tomatoes, chopped (about 2 cups)

4 garlic cloves, minced

Kosher salt and freshly ground black pepper to taste

8 large eggs

8 large fresh basil leaves, thinly sliced for garnish (optional)

1 Preheat the oven to 400 degrees. Lightly oil four 2-cup ramekins or one large, shallow casserole dish.

2 In a large skillet, heat 2 tablespoons of the olive oil over medium heat. Add the onion and bell peppers and sauté, stirring occasionally, until the onion is soft, about 7 minutes. Reduce the heat to low, add the tomatoes and garlic, and cook, stirring occasionally, until the bell peppers are very soft, about 25 minutes more. Season with salt and pepper.

3 Divide the bell pepper mixture among the prepared ramekins or spread evenly in the casserole dish. Carefully break 2 eggs into each ramekin, without breaking the yolks. For the casserole dish, make 8 evenly spaced indentations in the bell pepper mixture with a spoon and break an egg into each one.

4 Bake the pipérade until the eggs are as set as you'd like. (Touch one gently with your finger to check its firmness.) Drizzle with the remaining 2 tablespoons olive oil and scatter the basil, if using, on top of the eggs. Serve hot.

Note

The bell pepper mixture can be sautéed up to 1 day ahead and stored in an airtight container in the fridge. Let stand at room temperature for 30 minutes before adding the eggs and baking as directed.

Variation

To serve as an hors d'oeuvre:

Bake the pipérade in the casserole dish just until heated through, omitting the eggs. Serve with sliced bread or croutons. Serves 6 to 8.

tomato-tarragon quiche

This quiche is rich and creamy, yet it's lighter than most. Silken tofu replaces the usual cream. The sesame seed crust is made partly with canola oil, and its crunch complements the soft tarragon-infused custard. It has no cheese, and you'll see that it doesn't need it.

SERVES 6

crust

- 1 cup all-purpose flour
- 3/4 cup whole wheat flour
- 1/4 cup toasted sesame seeds (see page 450)
- 1 teaspoon kosher salt
- 4 tablespoons (1/2 stick) butter or margarine, chilled, cut into pieces
- 5 tablespoons canola oil

filling

- 1 garlic clove
- 1 tablespoon fresh tarragon leaves
- 1 16-ounce carton silken tofu
- 1/2 cup sour cream
- 2 large eggs
- 1 tablespoon extra-virgin olive oil
- 1/2 teaspoon kosher salt
- Freshly ground black pepper to taste
- 2 medium tomatoes, seeded, coarsely chopped, drained in a sieve

1 **To make the crust:** In a food processor, combine the all-purpose and whole wheat flours, sesame seeds, and salt and pulse a few times to blend. Add the butter or margarine and pulse until it is cut to the size of peas. Add the canola oil, 1 tablespoon at a time, pulsing between spoonfuls. Add about 1/4 cup cold water, 1 tablespoon at a time, pulsing between tablespoons to add just enough so the dough comes together.

2 Transfer the dough to a sheet of plastic wrap and gather it gently into a disk. Wrap it tightly and chill until cold and somewhat firm, about 30 minutes.

3 Preheat the oven to 375 degrees. On a floured surface, roll out the dough to form an 11-inch circle and transfer to a 9-inch pie pan, fitting it gently into the bottom. Prick the crust all over with a fork and refrigerate for 15 minutes. Line the crust with foil, fill it with pie weights (or dried beans or raw rice), and bake until the crust looks dry when the foil is lifted, about 10 minutes. Reduce the heat to 350 degrees.

4 **Meanwhile, to make the filling:** In a food processor, combine the garlic and tarragon and process until finely chopped. Add the tofu, sour cream, eggs, olive oil, salt, and pepper and process until smooth. Transfer to a bowl and fold in the drained tomatoes.

5 Pour the filling into the crust, smoothing the top. Bake until the quiche is just set, about 15 minutes. Let cool for 10 minutes before serving.

Note The crust and filling (without the tomatoes) can be made up to 1 day ahead and stored separately, well wrapped with plastic wrap, in the fridge. Stir the tomatoes into the filling and assemble the quiche just before baking. Bake an extra 5 minutes if the filling is cold. The baked quiche will hold for 30 minutes in a 200-degree oven, and leftovers are fine reheated.

throwing yourself a birthday party

Throwing yourself a birthday party may have once been considered taboo, but these days it's the thing to do, especially if you're single.

To welcome the end of my third decade, I invited my twelve closest friends to celebrate on a cold, snowy day in February. I pondered many dreamy cake combinations for weeks, then finally chose a fudge cake with a coconut buttercream. I baked the cake in a large bowl so that when iced and coated with coconut, it looked like a giant mound of snow. I also held a scavenger hunt. The hunt was memorable, mainly because my friends were allowed only one question if they got perplexed. About twenty seconds after the hunt started, I had nine or so of my friends queued up waiting impatiently to ask me a question. My clues were so cryptic that only I could crack their meanings, and a couple of times even I had no idea what I had meant! It was great fun, and everyone finally found their destination (once I upped the quota of questions), where a gift of chocolates and a gag gift from a joke shop awaited them.

Other throw-yourself-a-party ideas:

- One friend had a sweet-sixteen party, *doubled*. (She was turning thirty-two.)

- Another friend who will be turning forty plans to invite an artist friend to show her work on the walls. She feels that this will deflect the attention onto the drawings and her artist friend, giving everyone a topic for conversation.

- A friend of a friend threw a party for her "lost year." She had always maintained that her misspent teens owed her at least one additional year, so when she turned thirty, she held her "Lost Year" party and turned back the clock. All of her friends were there to make it legit.

chapter 11

Sweet Eats (and Drinks)

surprise!

Some years I walk into my apartment on my birthday wondering if (and wishing that) people will pop out from behind the furniture. If you're thinking about surprising someone, consider these ideas:

Try kidnapping the person. Very early on one Saturday, my good friend Jean and I grabbed our friend Marty by surprise, blindfolded her, jammed a cheap, imitation seventeenth-century farmer's hat on her head, then dragged her to my car. When she asked where we were going, we gave her misleading clues while we drove to Plimoth Plantation, a well-known living history museum near Boston. Once there, we took off Marty's blindfold and spent a few hours cavorting with professional actors and actresses in the seventeenth century. We had a good time testing their knowledge of colonial life with questions like, "How do you prepare squirrel?"

Then we blindfolded Marty again and drove her to Newport, Rhode Island, where she had just spent the summer developing a crush on a local schoolteacher. We had arranged for him to meet us at a bar. After a few drinks, some good food, and plenty of quality flirting, we escorted Marty back home.

Another equally successful surprise party was the one I threw for my cat, Henry, on his tenth birthday, along with two (human) friends who find his "entitled" manner as adorable as I do. We all yelled, "Surprise!" and threw green beans, his favorite snack, into the air. He scurried past us and dove for cover under the bed, where he stayed for the entire party. Nevertheless, *we* had fun eating butternut squash with roasted garlic over penne, one of Henry's favorite dinners. We even sang "Happy Birthday."

Surprise Party Guidelines

Be considerate. If you aren't sure how the person will react, rather than springing it on him or her, probe the surprisee months earlier. ("I'm thinking of throwing my friend Judy a surprise party. What do you think about surprise parties?")

Be original. Give the surprise party at an unexpected place or time, i.e., the bedroom of the surprisee, a bowling alley, a beach or skating pond, a favorite restaurant, or on a Saturday morning for a pancake breakfast. Some friends had a small gift-giving party for my dad on the ninth hole while the four of them were golfing.

Create some structure. Plan an activity so that the surprisee doesn't feel responsible for the entire flow and mood of the party. Some ideas: open presents, organize a game of charades (you can limit the subjects to any event, movie, song, or book that relates to the birthday boy or girl), or have a make-your-own sundae or pizza activity.

one big, bad hot chocolate

Warning: this cocoa is so rich that it's more of a dessert than a beverage! When you drink it, your senses are engulfed in the flavors of the chocolate. I offer it either in lieu of dessert or with biscotti for dipping. Amanda Hesser of the *New York Times* asked John Scharffenberger, the manufacturer of fine baking chocolate, "What is the best way to enjoy the flavor of dark chocolate?" Scharffenberger replied, "Hot cocoa—*real* hot cocoa."

SERVES 4

½ cup heavy cream

4 tablespoons plus 1 teaspoon Scharffen Berger or other good-quality cocoa powder

4 tablespoons plus 1 teaspoon sugar

2½ ounces bittersweet chocolate (70%–75% chocolate liquor), finely chopped

Pinch of salt

5 cups whole milk

1 In a medium bowl, whip the cream with 1 teaspoon of the cocoa and 1 teaspoon of the sugar; beat until stiff peaks form. Set aside.

2 In a medium saucepan, combine all but 2 tablespoons of the chocolate, the remaining 4 tablespoons cocoa and 4 tablespoons sugar, salt, and milk over medium heat and whisk gently. When the chocolate melts and the cocoa dissolves, increase the heat to medium-high and whisk vigorously to form froth on the surface. When the mixture bubbles around the edges and seems ready to boil, remove from the heat. Don't let it boil.

3 Divide the cocoa among four cups and spoon a dollop of the whipped cream on top of each cup. Sprinkle with the remaining 2 tablespoons chopped chocolate and serve.

tealess chai

Chai in the afternoon or after dinner really hits the spot. It's easy to make for friends: just heat milk or soy milk in a saucepan to a near boil and add the syrup to taste. I don't think this flavorful chai syrup needs a tea boost at all, but if you like, add a bag or two of either green or black tea to the milk. You can find dried licorice root in the herb/spice section of whole food stores.

SERVES 4; MAKES 2½ CUPS CHAI SYRUP (ENOUGH FOR 20 DRINKS)

- 12 whole star anise pods (see page 451)
- 1⅓ cups sugar or honey
- ¼ cup chopped unpeeled fresh ginger
- 1 tablespoon cardamom pods (see page 445), coarsely ground with a spice mill or mortar and pestle
- 1 teaspoon whole cloves
- Fresh or dried orange rind (optional)
- Up to 2 tablespoons dried licorice root (optional)
- 4 cups milk or soy milk, heated to steaming

1 In a medium saucepan, combine all the ingredients with 4 cups water over medium heat. Bring to a boil, then reduce the heat to a simmer and cook for 1 hour.

2 Strain the liquid through a sieve into a large bowl. Let cool completely. Transfer to an airtight container and refrigerate.

3 To serve four, mix ½ cup chai syrup with 4 cups steaming hot milk.

Note The syrup will keep indefinitely in an airtight container in the fridge.

maple-peanut popcorn balls

These are fun to make, especially for a birthday party. You can even buy pink-hued plastic wrap, wrap them up, and give them out as party favors. I use grade B syrup so that the maple flavor comes through loud and clear. With grade A, the kind that is most common, the popcorn balls will still be quite tasty. You can also substitute pecans for the peanuts.

MAKES 6

- 2 tablespoons canola oil
- ½ cup popcorn kernels
- ¾ cup grade B maple syrup
- 2 tablespoons melted unsalted butter
- ¼ cup sugar
- ¾ cup unsalted roasted peanuts (see page 449)
- ½ teaspoon salt

1 In a large, heavy saucepan, heat the oil over medium-high heat. Add the popcorn kernels. Cover the pan and shake it lightly as the kernels pop. When the popping sound slows markedly, remove the pan from the heat. Transfer the popcorn to a large bowl and set aside.

2 Set a small bowl of cold water next to the stove. In a small, nonreactive saucepan, combine the maple syrup, butter, and sugar over high heat. Bring to a boil, stirring constantly until the sugar dissolves. Reduce the heat to medium and boil without stirring for about 3 minutes, or until it reaches the soft ball stage and is about the color of an old penny. (To see if it's ready, remove from the heat and quickly spoon a bit of the caramel into the bowl of cold water. Collect the blob of caramel with your fingers; it should form a soft ball. If it's too soft, cook the caramel for 1 minute more and then test again.)

3 As soon as the caramel is ready, quickly pour it over the popcorn, swirling the caramel to distribute it evenly. Be careful not to burn yourself on the hot caramel. Add the peanuts and salt and mix quickly with a long wooden spoon.

4 When the mixture is cool enough to handle, form it into 3-inch balls. You'll probably need to wash your hands every other ball to keep the mixture from sticking. Serve.

Note
The popcorn balls will keep in an airtight container at room temperature for 2 weeks.

crunchy peanut butter balls

This is a perfect birthday party (or afterschool) activity for kids who are hungry and in need of being occupied but not heavily supervised—the recipe is that easy. These crunchy balls are dense and nutritious and will stave off hunger until the next meal arrives. They also make tasty snacks for hiking, since they travel well. Don't use natural peanut butter that has a layer of oil on top—any ordinary supermarket brand will work.

MAKES 25

2 cups smooth or crunchy peanut butter

1/2 cup honey

4 cups dry milk flakes

1/2 cup carob chips (optional)

1/2 cup dried, unsweetened coconut (see page 446; optional)

1 In a large bowl, stir together the peanut butter and honey with a strong spoon until well mixed. Add 2 cups of the dry milk and mix well; this will take a few minutes if the peanut butter is stiff. Stir in the carob chips and/or coconut, if using.

2 Place the remaining 2 cups dry milk in a wide, shallow bowl. Coat your hands with some of the dry milk and roll the peanut butter mixture into balls the size of walnut shells. Dredge the balls in the dry milk before serving.

Note The peanut butter balls will keep in an airtight container in the fridge, in a single layer or with plastic wrap between the layers, for up to 2 months.

killer chocolate chip cookies

I've adapted this recipe from one in *Jim Fobel's Old-Fashioned Baking Book*. I increased the butter and sugar, which produces a richer, more delicate cookie. The baking times given are a little short; slightly underbaking the cookies gives them an irresistible crispy-chewy texture.

MAKES 18

1 Preheat the oven to 350 degrees. Spread the nuts in a single layer on a rimmed baking sheet and toast for 5 minutes, or until golden brown. Set aside.

2 In a large bowl, beat the butter with an electric mixer until creamy, about 1 minute. Gradually add the brown sugar and sugar, beating well until the mixture is very light in texture. Add the vanilla and salt, and then the egg, beating just to incorporate. With a rubber spatula, fold in the flour, baking soda, chocolate chips, and nuts.

3 Spoon rounded tablespoons of dough 2 1/2 inches apart onto ungreased baking sheets. Bake for 6 to 8 minutes, or until the cookies are just a tiny bit golden around the edges but are still white in the centers. Let cool for 5 minutes on the baking sheets before serving.

1 cup chopped walnuts or pecans

9 tablespoons (1 stick plus 1 table-spoon) unsalted butter, softened

1/2 cup packed light brown sugar

1/2 cup sugar

1 1/2 teaspoons vanilla extract

1/2 teaspoon salt

1 large egg

1 cup plus 2 tablespoons all-purpose flour

1/2 teaspoon baking soda

8 ounces semisweet chocolate chips

Note

The cookies can be baked up to 1 week ahead and stored in an airtight container. The dough can be made and frozen in an airtight container (or formed into a log shape and wrapped in plastic wrap, and then sliced for baking) for up to 2 months. Bring to room temperature or thaw overnight in the fridge before baking.

sweet eats (and drinks)

stowe brownies

Years ago, I was asked to develop a intensely rich brownie for an opening café. After dozens of failed attempts, I took a break and headed up to Stowe, Vermont, for a weekend at my friend Marla's. One night I made brownies and went freeform, following no exact formula. Well, I should take breaks in Stowe more often. This was just the brownie I wanted—rich and slightly gooey with a crisp, tender exterior. Luckily, I had measured the ingredients so I was able to recreate it. I always eat these with ice cream.

MAKES 12

- 1½ cups chopped walnuts
- 8 tablespoons (1 stick) unsalted butter
- 8 ounces semisweet or bittersweet chocolate
- 1 cup sugar
- 2 large eggs
- 2 tablespoon Kahlúa or 1 teaspoon vanilla extract plus 1 tablespoon water
- 6 tablespoons all-purpose flour

1 Preheat the oven to 350 degrees. Butter a 9-inch square baking pan. Spread the walnuts in a single layer on a rimmed baking sheet and toast for 5 minutes, or until golden brown. Set aside. Increase the oven temperature to 375 degrees.

2 In a small saucepan, melt the butter and chocolate over low heat, stirring occasionally. (Or microwave in a bowl on high for 1 minute, then stir, allowing the heat of the melted butter to melt the chocolate; microwave again if necessary.)

3 In a large bowl, beat the sugar and eggs with an electric mixer on high speed until light yellow, about 3 minutes. Add the chocolate mixture and Kahlúa or vanilla mixture, then the flour and walnuts, stirring only to combine. Pour into the prepared pan.

4 Bake until the top is glossy and cracked and a toothpick inserted in the center comes out with gooey crumbs, about 25 minutes. You can serve them immediately, but they will cut more easily after they have cooled for at least 20 minutes.

Note

The brownies can be baked up to 2 days ahead, cooled completely, wrapped in plastic wrap, and stored in the fridge. They can also be double-wrapped and frozen for up to 2 months.

Bittersweet Chocolate

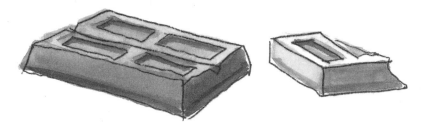

hermit bars

Chewy and mildly spicy, yummy hermit bars make excellent picnic fare or a great afternoon pick-me-up with a cup of spice tea.

MAKES 24

1 Preheat the oven to 350 degrees. Oil a 12-x-16-inch rimmed baking sheet and set aside. Spread the walnuts in a single layer on an ungreased baking sheet and toast for 5 minutes, or until golden brown. Set aside.

2 In a large bowl, beat the brown sugar or Sucanat and butter with an electric mixer until creamy and smooth. Add the molasses and eggs and beat on low speed until the mixture is thick and light, 1 to 2 minutes. Stir in the sour cream.

3 In a medium bowl, combine the flour, poppy seeds, cinnamon or star anise, baking soda, and salt. With a spoon, stir the dry ingredients into the butter mixture in two batches. Stir in the walnuts, figs, and raisins.

4 Spread the mixture evenly onto the prepared baking sheet. Bake until a knife inserted in the center comes out clean, 25 to 30 minutes. Let cool for 10

1 cup chopped walnuts

2 cups brown sugar or Sucanat (see page 451)

1 cup (2 sticks) unsalted butter

½ cup molasses

2 large eggs

¾ cup sour cream

2¼ cups all-purpose flour

2 tablespoons poppy seeds

1½ teaspoons ground cinnamon or ground star anise (see page 451)

1½ teaspoons baking soda

½ teaspoon salt

1 cup dried figs, quartered

1 cup raisins

Note The bars will keep in an airtight container at room temperature for at least 2 weeks.

minutes, then cut into 24 bars. With a spatula, transfer the bars to a plate to cool completely before serving.

blueberry-peach cranachan

I first tasted cranachan, a Scottish pudding made of whipped cream, toasted oats, raspberries, Drambuie, and sugar, at my upstairs neighbor's apartment. My neighbor got the recipe from Sheila Lukins's *All Around the World Cookbook.* In my version, I use pecans, blueberries, peaches, dates, and granola instead of the oats. It's one of my favorite desserts, and it's so darn easy. In the winter, you can use chopped bananas and pears instead of blueberries and peaches.

SERVES 6

1 cup granola

2/3 cup chopped pecans

   Pinch of salt

3 tablespoons melted unsalted butter

2 cups heavy cream

1/2 cup sugar

2 tablespoons dark rum or Drambuie

3 peaches, unpeeled, pitted, and chopped

2 heaping cups blueberries

1 cup pitted, chopped dates (preferably Medjool)

1 Preheat the oven to 350 degrees. Spread the granola, pecans, and salt in a single layer on a rimmed baking sheet. Drizzle the melted butter over the mixture. Bake until the pecans are toasted and fragrant, 8 to 10 minutes. Let cool to room temperature.

2 In a medium bowl, whip the cream to soft peaks. With a rubber spatula, gradually fold in the sugar. Fold in the rum or Drambuie, then the peaches, blueberries, and dates. Fold in the cooled nut mixture and refrigerate for at least 1 hour before serving. Serve in small bowls or parfait cups.

Note The cranachan can be prepared up to 1 day ahead and stored in an airtight container in the fridge.

bionic chocolate pudding

One fan says this tastes like topflight chocolate ice cream. Check out the variations—they're worth making. Serve the pudding in espresso cups or small goblets. It definitely needs the whipped cream to cut the intensity.

SERVES 8

$2/3$ cup plus 1 tablespoon sugar

$1/4$ cup good-quality cocoa powder, preferably Dutch-processed

3 tablespoons cornstarch

3 cups whole milk

4 ounces good-quality bittersweet chocolate, chopped

2–3 tablespoons Grand Marnier or 1 tablespoon vanilla extract

$2/3$ cup heavy cream

1 In a medium bowl, sift or stir together the $2/3$ cup sugar, cocoa powder, and cornstarch. Whisk in $1/2$ cup of the milk until smooth. Set aside.

2 In a large, heavy saucepan, bring the remaining $2^1/2$ cups milk to a strong simmer over medium-high heat. Pour about 1 cup of the hot milk into the cocoa mixture, whisking constantly, and then pour this mixture back into the pan of hot milk. Whisk constantly over medium-high heat until the mixture comes to a boil. Boil gently for 5 minutes, whisking vigorously, then reduce the heat to low. Continue cooking and whisking until the pudding thickens to the texture of cold yogurt. Remove from the heat.

3 Add the chocolate and Grand Marnier or vanilla, stirring until the chocolate is melted and incorporated. Pour the pudding into a shallow bowl

and cool, uncovered, in the refrigerator for at least 2 hours.

4 In a medium bowl, whip the cream with the remaining tablespoon sugar until soft peaks form.

5 To serve, spoon the pudding neatly into 8 small cups and top each with a dollop of whipped cream.

> I have learned the joy of being organized for a party, especially if it's a real party and not just an informal dinner with friends. I love to set the table. I always do that first thing in the morning. It gives me a great deal of pleasure to spend time with fabrics and dishes and flowers.
>
> —**Deborah Madison, author of *Vegetarian Cooking for Everyone***

Variations

Vegan Chocolate Pudding: Substitute soy milk (vanilla is best) for the milk and omit the whipped cream.

Banana Chocolate Pudding: Puree 2 ripe (but not black) bananas in a food processor and add along with the chocolate in step 3.

Cinnamon Chocolate Pudding: Make the pudding with vanilla, not Grand Marnier. Whisk 1 teaspoon ground cinnamon into the milk before it simmers in step 2.

Chocolate Cream Pie: Divide the warm pudding between two 8-inch store-bought graham cracker crusts and chill for several hours until set. Top with whipped cream and chocolate curls, if desired.

Note

The pudding can be made up to 2 days ahead and stored in an airtight container in the fridge. The cream should be whipped the same day it's served.

mexican flan

Flan never did much for me —until I tried this recipe. It was inspired by a recipe in Molly O'Neill's *New York Cookbook*. The milk is reduced through simmering to half its original quantity for an unusually rich, creamy flan. It's as scrumptious as crème brûlée but not as sinful. A garnish of sliced strawberries would be festive.

SERVES 6

6 cups whole milk

8 cardamom pods (see page 445)

1 teaspoon vanilla extract

3/4 cup plus 6 tablespoons sugar

3 large eggs

4 large egg yolks

Pinch of salt

1 Preheat the oven to 325 degrees. In a large, heavy saucepan, bring the milk and cardamom pods to a boil. Reduce the heat to medium-low and simmer until the milk is reduced to 3 cups, about 40 minutes. Remove from the heat and stir in the vanilla.

2 Meanwhile, in a small, nonreactive saucepan, combine 3/4 cup of the sugar and 1/4 cup water over high heat. Bring to a boil, stirring constantly. Reduce the heat to medium and boil without stirring for about 10 minutes, or until it turns golden amber. Remove from the heat and carefully pour the hot caramel into a 1 1/2-quart baking dish, tilting to coat the bottom. (Work fast, or the caramel will harden before it covers the dish.) Place the caramel-lined baking dish inside a large roasting pan. Set aside.

3 In a large bowl, combine the remaining 6 tablespoons sugar, the eggs, egg yolks, and salt, whisking until well blended. Strain the hot milk mixture through a sieve into a clean large bowl, then gradually pour the hot milk over the egg mixture, whisking constantly.

4 Pour the egg mixture into the caramel-lined baking dish. Cover the dish loosely with foil, and place the nested pans in the center of the oven. Slowly pour hot water into the roasting pan until it reaches halfway up the baking dish. Bake until the flan is set but still slightly wobbly, about 1 hour.

5 Remove the flan from the water bath, leaving the water bath in the oven to cool. Let the flan cool to room temperature, then refrigerate it, uncovered, for at least 4 hours before serving. To serve, run a knife around the edge of the baking dish to loosen the flan and invert it onto a rimmed serving platter.

Note

The flan can be baked up to 2 days ahead and stored in its baking dish, covered with plastic wrap, in the fridge. Bring to room temperature to unmold, and then chill for up to 2 hours before serving.

crunchy almond rice pudding

One of my favorite desserts, this pudding is wonderful hot-weather food. If you want to get fancy, add melon, nectarine, or peach cubes to the pudding. Also, try using pistachios or cashews instead of the almonds. You can make the pudding with vanilla soy milk instead of milk and cream; it will be lighter but still good. Either way, this pudding needs about 1 1/2 hours to cook and another 2 1/2 hours to cool and chill.

SERVES 4 TO 6

- 1/2 cup chopped almonds
- 4 cups whole or low-fat milk
- 1/2 cup heavy cream
- 1/2 cup raw jasmine rice
- 1/2 cup sugar
- 8 cardamom pods (see page 445)
- Large pinch of salt

1 In a small skillet over medium heat, toast the almonds until they start to color and become fragrant, about 3 minutes. Let cool to room temperature, then grind in a blender or food processor. Don't overprocess, or the almonds will become pasty.

2 In a medium heavy saucepan, combine 3 1/2 cups of the milk, the cream, ground almonds, rice, sugar, cardamom pods, and salt over medium heat. Bring to a simmer, reduce the heat to low, and cover the pan. Cook for 1 1/2 hours, stirring occasionally, until the rice is very soft and the pudding is creamy. Remove from the heat and stir in the remaining 1/2 cup milk. Spoon out the cardamom pods. Transfer to an airtight plastic container and let cool, uncovered, to room temperature. Cover and refrigerate until cold, about 2 hours.

Note The pudding must be made at least 4 hours and up to 24 hours before serving.

hilde's berry pudding

My aunt Hilde, who grew up in Austria, is an enterprising woman, but her refreshing fruit pudding is surprisingly simple. In winter, you can make it with frozen berries; in the summer, use fresh berries. Make sure you start the dessert 3 to 4 hours before serving, since it takes time to chill and set. This pudding is best eaten with vanilla or cherry ice cream or One-Bite-Won't-Suffice Lemon Ice (page 418).

SERVES 6

1 In a medium saucepan, combine the berries, sugar, and ¹/₂ cup water over medium heat. Bring to a simmer, stirring until the sugar dissolves. Simmer for 5 minutes.

2 Meanwhile, in a small bowl, combine the cornstarch or arrowroot with ¹/₄ cup cold water and mix until smooth. Add to the berry mixture and cook, stirring constantly, until thickened and bubbly, about 4 minutes. Remove from the heat and stir in the lemon juice. Transfer to a shallow serving dish and refrigerate until cold. Serve with ice cream.

- **6** cups fresh or frozen berries (one kind or a mixture: blueberries, strawberries, raspberries, or pitted cherries)
- **³/₄** cup sugar
- **3½** tablespoons cornstarch or arrowroot
- **3** tablespoons fresh lemon juice (about 1 juicy lemon)
- **1** pint superpremium cherry or vanilla ice cream

Note The pudding must be made at least 3 to 4 hours and up to 48 hours ahead. Store in an airtight container in the fridge. Leftover pudding will keep for up to a week in the fridge.

melon sago (tapioca)

Pureed ripe melon and coconut milk form the base of this dreamy pudding, with the tapioca contributing subtle but necessary texture. Sago means "tapioca" in Malay, and I first tried this pudding upon my return from Malaysia, having become smitten with many Malaysian desserts. When shopping for a melon, look for one with a soft, fragrant stem end.

SERVES 6

3/4 cup small pearl tapioca

1/2 very ripe cantaloupe or honeydew melon, peeled, seeded, and cut into 1/4-inch cubes

1 cup unsweetened coconut milk (see page 446)

1 cup plus 2 tablespoons sugar

Juice of 1 lime or lemon

Mint leaves for garnish (optional)

1 In a large bowl, soak the tapioca in 2 cups cool water for 15 minutes. Drain through a fine-meshed sieve.

2 Meanwhile, in a blender or food processor, puree half of the melon cubes and transfer to a large bowl, along with the remaining melon cubes and the coconut milk.

3 In a medium saucepan, bring 3 cups water to a boil. Add the tapioca and cook until there is only a faint white dot left in the center of each tapioca pearl, about 5 minutes. (To check, taste one of the pearls; it should be soft, not crunchy.) Remove from the heat and add the sugar, stirring until the sugar dissolves.

4 Add the tapioca mixture to the melon mixture and stir well. Taste the pudding and add enough lime or lemon juice to balance the flavors. Pour into a serving bowl or six individual cups and chill until the sago is cold, about 2 hours. The consistency should be like that of fruited yogurt. Garnish with the mint leaves, if desired, before serving.

Note The sago must be made at least 2 hours ahead so that it chills properly. It's best served within 24 hours, but the leftovers will keep for 3 more days stored in an airtight container in the fridge.

if you hate parties

My good friend Jon detests parties and avoids both going to them and hosting them. But when he bought a home with an expansive living room that had a window running the length of the room overlooking some pine trees, I saw the need for a party. "It'll be fabulous, Jon. I'll make the food." His response: "But what if no one shows?"

A few weeks later, Jon attended a benefit that was auctioning folk singers for an evening of home entertainment. When two musicians were still not taken, Jon, who is as passionate about folk singers as he is about avoiding parties, bought both on the spot. With the entertainment secure, he was suddenly undaunted by the prospect of a celebration. As the date approached, his excitement grew, and he invited people whenever he could. I asked him how many he expected, and he said, "Gee, I don't know. Somewhere between fifty and two hundred. Could you pick up some ice?"

As I drove toward his house, I was amazed to find his street lined with cars. My next thought was that I wasn't sure if he could handle such a crowd. But as I entered the party, it was clear that Jon was doing just fine. He had invited people of all ages and from all walks of life, and everyone was talking and mingling. I helped him make ice creams using fresh mint and lemongrass from his garden. As people listened to the musicians, we passed it out in plastic bowls to the swaying guests' delight.

Three Morals to the Story

1. Parties that aren't meticulously planned can be the best kind.

2. If you're a reluctant party-giver, build the party around something you love.

3. If you're serving only one kind of food, make it homemade ice cream.

sweet eats (and drinks)

macadamia–tropical fruit salad with ice cream

I've found that even those who don't like dried coconut enjoy this dessert. Feel free to use whatever fruits you like. Alternatives include: kiwis, strawberries, raspberries, bananas, and sliced, canned litchis. If you have fresh mint on hand, add ½ cup coarsely chopped mint leaves to the salad.

SERVES 6 TO 8

1 Preheat the oven to 350 degrees. Spread the nuts in a single layer on a rimmed baking sheet and toast for 5 minutes, or until golden brown. Set aside.

2 Cut all the fruit into ½-inch cubes. To dice the mango, see page 120.

3 In a large bowl, combine the fruit, lime juice, nuts, coconut, and sugar together and toss well. Serve immediately, topped with the vanilla ice cream.

1 cup coarsely chopped macadamia nuts, or more to taste

1 ripe papaya or ½ small cantaloupe, peeled and seeded

1 ripe but firm mango, peeled

1 pineapple, peeled and cored, or additional mango or cantaloupe, or oranges, pears, or strawberries

1 Fuji or Gala apple or Asian pear, cored

Juice of 1 lime

1 cup toasted dried, unsweetened coconut (see page 446)

3–4 tablespoons sugar

1–2 pints vanilla ice cream

Note
The fruit can be cut up and tossed with the lime juice up to 4 hours ahead and stored, covered, in the refrigerator. Add the nuts, coconut, and sugar just before serving.

molly's successful birthday party

When my friend's daughter Molly turned twelve, she wanted a party that was different and very much her own. With the help of her mom and me, she pulled it off with flying colors. First Molly and six of her girlfriends went to see a play at the local theater. Then Molly's mom brought them back to her house for a sleepover. It was now 10:00 p.m., ordinarily bedtime, but instead the girls went into the kitchen to build their own pizzas. I supplied partially baked doughs and the sauce. For toppings, there was grated "yellow" and "white" cheese and roasted veggies. Later the girls built their own sundaes, including World's Best Peanut Butter–Hot Fudge Sauce (page 421), various ice creams, Stowe Brownies (page 400), and some store-bought toppings. The kids then painted one another's faces with the leftover hot fudge. Hopefully they washed their faces before hitting the sack.

michel richard's fruit "salad" with melted ice cream

Reading the New York Times, I was intrigued that the French chef Michel Richard, when at home, often takes good vanilla ice cream and runs it through a food processor instead of making crème anglaise. What a fabulous idea. Here I have adapted one of his recipes.

SERVES 4

3 tablespoons unsalted butter

¼ cup sugar

4 cups fresh rhubarb, cut into ½-inch pieces, or 3 cups fresh cranberries

1 ripe cantaloupe, peeled, seeded, and cut into bite-size pieces

12 fresh basil or mint leaves, plus more for garnish

1 pint Häagen-Dazs or other superpremium vanilla ice cream, softened slightly

1 In a large skillet, melt the butter and sugar over medium heat, stirring until the sugar dissolves. Add the rhubarb or cranberries and cook for 30 seconds. Reduce the heat to a simmer, cover, and cook until the rhubarb or cranberries are softened but not mushy, 2 to 3 minutes more. Remove from the heat, add the melon, and set aside.

2 In a blender or food processor, chop the basil or mint. Add the ice cream and puree until the mixture is smooth. Transfer to an airtight container and refrigerate for up to 3 hours before serving.

3 To serve, divide the warmed fruit mixture equally among four small bowls, and top each with a spoonful of the ice cream mixture. Serve immediately, garnished with a single perfect basil or mint leaf.

Note The rhubarb compote can be prepared up to 24 hours ahead. Cool, cover tightly, and refrigerate. Reheat the compote in a saucepan just before serving.

Bananas in Rum-Raisin Caramel with Ice Cream

• • serves 4

Sometimes the simplest desserts are the best.

    8   tablespoons (1 stick) unsalted butter
    1   cup packed light or dark brown sugar
    ½   cup raisins
    ½   cup dark rum
    4   bananas, peeled and halved lengthwise
    4   scoops vanilla ice cream

1 In a wide saucepan over medium heat, combine the butter, brown sugar, raisins, and rum. Bring to a boil, stirring occasionally. Reduce the heat to a simmer and cook for 10 minutes.

2 Add the bananas and cook for 5 minutes more. Scoop the ice cream onto small plates and top with the bananas, distributing the rum-raisin caramel evenly among the servings.

NOTE: The rum-raisin caramel can be prepared up to 3 hours ahead (through step 1) and left at room temperature before reheating and adding the bananas.

pavlova

In this dessert, a white meringue the size of a throw pillow holds a beautiful array of chopped fruit, and atop this rests a large cloud of whipped cream. If you're near an Eastern European market, pick up some orange flower water; it adds an intriguing flavor. Pavlova is an Australian dessert, inspired by the Russian ballerina Anna Pavlova.

SERVES 10

1 **To make the meringue:** Preheat the oven to 300 degrees. Line a baking sheet with parchment or foil, and trace a 10-inch-wide circle on it. (If using parchment, flip it over.) In a large bowl, beat the egg whites and salt with an electric mixer on low speed until frothy. Increase the speed to medium-high and beat until stiff peaks form, 2 to 3 minutes. Gradually add the sugar and increase the speed to high. Beat until stiff, glossy peaks form, 3 to 5 minutes more. Sprinkle the cornstarch, vinegar, and vanilla or orange flower water over the egg whites and gently fold in.

2 Using a large spoon and a spatula (or a pastry bag), fill in the traced circle on the baking sheet with the meringue, smoothing the top and building up the sides so that they are about 1 inch higher than the base. Place in the

meringue

4 large egg whites, at room temperature

Pinch of salt

1 cup plus 2 tablespoons sugar

2 teaspoons cornstarch

1 teaspoon white vinegar

1/2 teaspoon vanilla extract or 2 tablespoons orange flower water (see page 449)

2 cups heavy cream

2 tablespoons Grand Marnier or triple sec

1/2 teaspoon orange oil or 1 teaspoon grated fresh orange rind

8 cups fresh fruit: any combination of sliced bananas and kiwis, strawberries, blueberries, and raspberries

The whipped cream and fruit can be prepared and stored separately in the fridge up to 4 hours ahead. The baked, undecorated meringue can be stored at room temperature (unless the weather is very humid) for up to 2 days, wrapped in plastic wrap. The pavlova must be assembled at the last minute.

center of the oven and bake for 1 hour, then turn off the oven, leaving the meringue inside the oven to dry for about 4 hours.

3 When the meringue is completely cool, remove it from the oven. Carefully remove the paper or foil and transfer the meringue disk to a serving plate.

4 In a large bowl, whip the cream with the Grand Marnier or triple sec and orange oil or rind until soft peaks form. Pile it on top of the meringue. Arrange the fruit on the cream. Serve immediately, cut into wedges.

BluebeRRies

one-bite-won't-suffice lemon ice

(V) *My mom would make this ice* for dinner parties. For some reason, this was the only time she made it, perhaps because the lemon squeezing took some time. My sisters and I just loved it, and we would sneak tiny spoonfuls of it on the day of the party. Now that I have my own kitchen, I can eat all the lemon ice I want and not get into trouble.

A fun way to serve lemon ice is in hollowed-out lemon halves (level the bottom of each half with a paring knife). You can fill them ahead of time and keep them in the freezer.

SERVES 6

3 juicy lemons

1 cup plus 2 tablespoons sugar

Fresh mint leaves for garnish (optional)

1 Grate the rind from 1 1/2 lemons. Juice all the lemons, straining out any seeds.

2 In a medium, heavy saucepan, combine the lemon rind, sugar, and 2 cups plus 2 tablespoons water over medium heat, stirring until the sugar dissolves. When the mixture comes to a boil, remove from the heat and let stand for 20 minutes.

Note The ice will keep in an airtight container in the freezer for up to 2 weeks, but is best eaten within the first 4 or 5 days.

3 Stir the lemon juice into the sugar mixture. Transfer to a 9-inch square baking pan and freeze for 1 hour. Take the pan out of the freezer and rake the ice with a fork. Return the pan to the freezer for 1 hour, then rake again. When the ice is thoroughly frozen, store it in an airtight container in the freezer. Serve in small cups or bowls, garnished with mint leaves, if desired.

espresso granita with whipped cream

This granita is unusual, elegant, and effortless. Serve it as the finale to a warm-weather meal. One note of caution: this dessert is only as good as the espresso you buy. I always buy eight shots of high-quality decaf espresso; I don't use my own espresso maker since its espresso pales in comparison to the high-pressure commercial version. Perhaps you are like me and will bargain with your neighborhood espresso shop since you are buying so many shots. I get eight shots for the price of six.

SERVES 6

3/4 cup sugar

1 cup brewed espresso (about 8 shots; decaf or regular)

1 cup heavy cream, whipped to soft peaks

1 In a medium heavy saucepan, bring the sugar and 2 cups water to a boil over medium heat, stirring. Remove from the heat and stir in the espresso.

2 Transfer to a 9-inch square baking pan and freeze for 1 hour. Take the pan out of the freezer and rake the ice with a fork. Return the pan to the freezer for 1 hour, then rake again. When the ice is thoroughly frozen, store it in an airtight container in the freezer. Serve in small cups or bowls with the whipped cream.

Note

The ice will keep in an airtight container in the freezer for up to 2 weeks but is best eaten within the first 4 or 5 days.

sweet eats (and drinks)

419

lavender ice

(V) *A neighbor has a huge lavender bush,* and I often pluck myself a sprig from its backside just to smell as I take a walk. One day I was inspired to cook with it and took more than one sprig — then went home and made this ice. Serve it with cookies or biscotti.

SERVES 6

1 cup sugar

¼ cup fresh lavender flowers still on the stems, plus a few sprigs for garnish

Juice of ½ lemon

1 In a medium, heavy saucepan, combine the sugar and 2½ cups water over medium heat, stirring until the sugar dissolves. When the mixture comes to a boil, remove from the heat, stir in the lavender flowers, and let stand for 20 minutes, covered.

2 Stir the lemon juice into the lavender mixture, then strain through a fine sieve into a 9-inch square baking pan and freeze for 1 hour. Take the pan out of the freezer and rake the ice with a fork. Return the pan to the freezer for 1 hour, then rake again. When the ice is thoroughly frozen, store it in an airtight container in the freezer. Serve in small cups or bowls.

Note The ice will keep in an airtight container in the freezer for up to 2 weeks but is best eaten within the first 4 or 5 days.

world's best peanut butter– hot fudge sauce

How do I know that this is the "World's Best"? I tested the sauce on a panel of half a dozen twelve-year-old girls, and they unanimously decided that it was.

MAKES 1 1/2 CUPS; SERVES 6

In a heavy saucepan, heat the cream and butter over medium heat. When the mixture simmers, add the sugar and brown sugar, stirring until they are dissolved. Reduce the heat to low and add the cocoa powder, peanut butter, and salt. Whisk until smooth. Remove from the heat. Serve immediately or keep warm.

1/2 cup heavy cream

3 tablespoons unsalted butter, cut into small pieces

1/3 cup sugar

1/3 cup firmly packed dark brown sugar

1/2 cup sifted good-quality cocoa powder

1/4 cup smooth peanut butter

Pinch of salt

Note

The sauce can be made up to 3 weeks ahead and stored in an airtight container in the fridge. Reheat in the microwave or in a heavy saucepan over low heat, adding water if it's too thick.

"seizing" hot fudge sauce

This hot fudge sauce seizes and hardens over ice cream. It doesn't become an intractable chocolate rock but turns a bit gooey, with some fudgy Tootsie-Roll-like nugget action. Once refrigerated and boiled again, it gets even harder when spooned over the ice cream.

MAKES 1 1/2 CUPS; SERVES 8

In a medium, heavy saucepan, bring the sugar, corn syrup, cream and 2 tablespoons water to a boil, whisking occasionally. Boil for 2 minutes, then reduce the heat to low and add the chocolate. Whisk until the chocolate is melted. Return to a boil, whisking constantly, and boil for at least 30 seconds. Remove from the heat and add the espresso, liqueur, or vanilla and salt. Serve immediately or keep warm.

2/3 cup sugar

1/2 cup light corn syrup

1/4 cup heavy cream

6 ounces unsweetened good-quality chocolate, coarsely chopped

2 tablespoons brewed or instant espresso, Grand Marnier, or triple sec, or 1 tablespoon vanilla extract

Pinch of salt

Note

The sauce can be made up to 2 weeks ahead and stored in an airtight container in the fridge. Leftovers, if there are any, will last, in the fridge, for up to 2 weeks.

banana–brown sugar spring rolls

If you need a dessert that's a cinch to prepare but will really wow your friends, make these spring rolls. Lumpia spring roll wrappers are made from wheat flour and can be found in the frozen section of many Asian markets. If you want to get really fancy, drizzle each plate with melted chocolate or chocolate sauce.

SERVES 4

4 bananas

8 spring roll wrappers (also called lumpia wrappers; see page 448)

8 tablespoons dark brown sugar

2 tablespoons butter

1 pint ginger or maple walnut ice cream

1 Cut the bananas in half lengthwise. On a clean work surface, lay down 1 spring roll wrapper, with a corner facing you. Place a banana half in the middle of the wrapper, and top it with 1 tablespoon brown sugar. Then, starting at the bottom corner, roll up the spring roll, folding the left and right points inward over the filling, and rolling up to enclose the filling tightly. Repeat with the remaining spring rolls.

2 Just before serving, in a large skillet over medium heat, melt 1 tablespoon of the butter. Add 4 of the spring rolls and pan-fry until golden brown on the bottoms, about 2 minutes, then turn and pan-fry the other side. Transfer the spring rolls to a plate and repeat with the remaining 1 tablespoon butter and 4 spring rolls. Serve 2 spring rolls per person, and scoop some ice cream onto each plate.

Note The spring rolls can be made up to 1 day ahead and stored on a plate covered with plastic wrap in the fridge.

nutella fondue

Nutella is a silky, smooth chocolate-hazelnut spread from Italy made with lots of sugar. I like to serve this fondue after a cheese fondue dinner, making the evening a world-class dipping event. Welsh Rabbit (page 69) and Goat Cheese and Roasted Garlic Fondue (page 72) are two of my favorite cheese fondues. I like to assemble my friends around my coffee table, everyone sitting cozily on the rug with lights on low and candles burning nearby to set a European chalet mood. Sometimes I use a Sterno setup, but if it's just three or four of us, I use a heavy casserole dish that I've warmed on the stove (with the fondue in it) and set on a trivet. You'll find Nutella next to the peanut butter in well-stocked supermarkets and Italian grocery stores.

SERVES 4

1 In a fondue pot or small, heavy saucepan, bring the cream to a boil over medium heat. Reduce the heat to low and add the Nutella in three or four additions, whisking until smooth. Remove from the heat.

²/₃ **cup heavy cream**

¹/₂ **cup Nutella**

2 **tablespoons Frangelico (hazelnut liqueur)**

¹/₂ **cup very finely chopped toasted hazelnuts or almonds (see page 283)**

1 **quart cherries or strawberries and 4-5 cups of cubed French bread and/or pound cake, cut into small cubes**

Note
The fondue can be prepared through step 1 up to 3 days ahead and stored in an airtight container in the fridge. Just before serving, reheat the mixture over low heat, and continue with step 2.

unplain jane and her cakewalk

Years ago, my friend Jane Gillooly needed to raise money fast. She and eight other artists had been thrown out of their Boston studio space due to a large commercial takeover. They had found a massive raw space, and they needed to build a darkroom, printmaking studio, and living space if they were to continue pursuing their art. Jane decided to host a cakewalk like the ones she remembered from her elementary school years. They work like this: while music plays, children walk on numbers inside a circle painted on the floor. When the music stops, they all scramble for the number nearest them. A number is then randomly drawn from a basket, and whoever is standing on the winning number gets to choose one of the cakes baked by the members of the PTA.

Jane took the basic idea and elevated it a few notches. Instead of playing records, she asked some musician friends to play live in the large studio space. In place of the more subdued painted circle of her youth, she painted a large area with numbers, and in atomic lettering she painted the phrase "Every good boy deserves fudge." Then she and her friends handed out fliers to everyone they knew. Her good friends made the cakes, which ranged from conventional to bizarre. (One was covered with Barbie doll heads.)

But the one that "took the cake" was Jane's. The recipe was from her grandmother —a chocolate sheet cake in which the ingredients are mixed right in the cake pan. Suspended above the cake from the ceiling was a sparkly red high-heeled shoe dripping with marshmallow fluff. The fluff hypnotically oozed out of the shoe and down to the cake, where it became the frosting. The cakewalk drew more than four hundred people, and Jane and a friend of hers acted as the emcees. Her only regret is that she charged a measly two-dollar admission.

2 Stir in the Frangelico and hazelnuts or almonds. If you're not using a fondue pot, transfer the mixture to a clay pot or heavy bowl that will retain the heat. (You can warm the bowl in the oven first, if you like.) Set the bowl on a large, heatproof platter and arrange the fruit, bread, and/or cake around the bowl, with forks for dipping.

sweet eats (and drinks)

chocolate buttermilk cake with chocolate sour cream frosting

This cake is a no-fail, impress-everyone kind of dessert. The recipe comes from my dear friend Deirdre. You can serve it with whipped cream and your choice of berries instead of the frosting, if you like.

SERVES 10

1 In a small bowl, melt the chocolate in the microwave on 50-percent power for 1 minute; stir and repeat if necessary. Or melt it in a small saucepan over very low heat, stirring constantly. Set aside to cool.

2 Preheat the oven to 325 degrees. Butter and flour a 9- or 10-inch cake pan or an 8-cup Bundt pan. In a large bowl, sift together the flour, cocoa powder, baking soda, and salt. Set aside.

3 In a large bowl, cream the butter and sugar with an electric mixer on medium speed until it is light in color. Add the eggs, one at a time, mixing well after each addition. Add the vanilla. Reduce the mixer speed to low and pour in the melted chocolate, scraping the sides and bottom of the bowl with a

4 ounces unsweetened chocolate, coarsely chopped

1½ cups all-purpose flour

¼ cup good-quality cocoa powder

2 teaspoons baking soda

Pinch of salt

8 tablespoons (1 stick) unsalted butter, softened

2 cups sugar

2 large eggs

2 teaspoons vanilla extract

2 cups buttermilk

Chocolate Sour Cream Frosting (page 428)

rubber spatula. Mix in the dry ingredients in 3 additions, alternating with 2 additions of buttermilk.

4 Pour the batter into the prepared pan, filling it two thirds full. Bake in the center of the oven until a knife inserted in the center of the cake comes out clean, 40 to 50 minutes. Let cool in the pan for 20 minutes, then loosen the sides of the cake with a knife and invert onto a serving plate.

5 When the cake is completely cool, frost it with the Chocolate Sour Cream Frosting.

Note The baked, cooled, unfrosted cake can be double-wrapped in plastic wrap and frozen for up to 2 months. Thaw at room temperature before frosting and serving.

chocolate Cake

chocolate sour cream frosting

Use this frosting at room temperature; don't even try to whip it while it's cold! I've adapted it from *Jim Fobel's Old-Fashioned Baking Book*.

MAKES 1½ CUPS, ENOUGH TO FROST 1 CAKE

6 ounces bittersweet chocolate, coarsely chopped

8 tablespoons (1 stick) unsalted butter, softened

1 tablespoon brandy or 2 teaspoons vanilla extract

¾ cup sifted confectioners' sugar

About ⅓ cup sour cream

1 In a small bowl, melt the chocolate in the microwave on 50-percent power for 1 minute; stir and repeat if necessary. Or melt it in a small saucepan over very low heat, stirring constantly. Set aside to cool.

2 In a large bowl, beat the butter with an electric mixer on medium speed until fluffy, about 1 minute. Add the brandy or vanilla, then gradually blend in the sugar, beating well. Add the cooled chocolate, and when it is incorporated, add enough sour cream to give the frosting a good spreading consistency.

Note The frosting will keep for up to 4 days stored in an airtight container in the fridge. Bring to room temperature for at least 1 hour before whipping again with a mixer to soften.

vegan chocolate cake

Ⓥ *Here is a vegan chocolate cake* that beats all others I've tried. It was inspired by a recipe in *Saveur* magazine.

SERVES 8

3 ounces unsweetened chocolate, coarsely chopped

1 cup dark brown sugar

2 cups all-purpose flour

1/3 cup good-quality cocoa powder, preferably Dutch-processed

1 teaspoon baking soda

2/3 cup canola oil

1 cup vanilla or plain soy milk

2 teaspoons vanilla extract

1 medium zucchini, grated (2 cups packed)

1½ cups chopped toasted walnuts (see page 283; optional)

Confectioners' sugar

1 In a small bowl, melt the chocolate in the microwave on 50-percent power for 1 minute; stir and repeat if necessary. Or melt it in a small saucepan over very low heat, stirring constantly. Set aside to cool.

2 Preheat the oven to 350 degrees. Butter and flour a 9- or 10-inch cake pan or an 8-cup Bundt pan. In a large bowl, combine the dry ingredients and mix well. Add the melted chocolate and the oil and mix until well blended. Whisk in the soy milk and vanilla until smooth. Fold in the zucchini and nuts, if using.

3 Pour the batter into the pan, smoothing the top. Bake until a knife inserted in the center comes out clean, 35 to 45 minutes. Cool for 10 minutes in the pan, then invert onto a rack.

4 When the cake is completely cool, pour some confectioners' sugar into a small sieve and sift it over the top before serving.

Note The cake can be stored in the fridge, covered with plastic wrap, for up to 3 days. Bring to room temperature before eating (and add the confectioners' sugar just before serving). It can be frozen, double-wrapped in plastic wrap, for up to 2 months.

almond butter cake

This cake was inspired by both my love for almond biscotti and an almond cake recipe by Flo Braker. It's only biscotti-like at the bottom; toward the top the texture is soft, reminiscent of the filling in a good almond croissant. Serve with coffee in the afternoon or as a dessert with a dollop of whipped cream on each slice.

SERVES 8

1½ cups almonds

2 cups light brown sugar

16 tablespoons (2 sticks) unsalted butter, softened

5 large eggs

½ teaspoon almond extract

1 cup all-purpose flour

1 teaspoon baking powder

¼ teaspoon salt

Confectioners' sugar

1 Preheat the oven to 350 degrees. Grease a 9-inch cake pan. Spread the almonds in a single layer on a rimmed baking sheet and toast for 10 minutes, or until golden brown. In a food processor, process the almonds until they are finely ground.

2 In a large bowl, beat the brown sugar and butter with an electric mixer until fluffy, about 2 minutes. Add the eggs, one at a time, beating well after each addition. Add the ground almonds and the almond extract, then fold in the flour, baking powder, and salt and mix well.

3 Pour the batter into the prepared pan and bake until the cake is golden brown and a knife inserted into the center comes out clean, 40 to 45 minutes. Let the cake cool in the pan for 10 minutes, then invert onto a cooling rack and let cool completely. Pour some confectioners' sugar into a small sieve and sift it over the top of the cake. Cut into wedges and serve.

Note

The cake is best made 1 day ahead and stored in the fridge wrapped with plastic wrap. It will keep for up to 1 week. It can also be frozen, double-wrapped in plastic wrap, for up to 3 months.

going with the flow

Cheryl Schaeffer is a computer geek and a good friend. One summer day, she set out to bake a cake (from a box) for another friend's birthday. After she put the rectangular cake in the oven, things went downhill, so to speak. She peeked at the cake and saw that the batter had shifted to the same troubling decline of her warped kitchen floor. Then a light bulb went on: "Aha! I'll make a shoreline cake!" When Cheryl was done, there was no question that the cake was one of a kind.

You'll need:

- Blue frosting for the sea section
- White frosting for a whitecap effect and the sandy area
- Turbinado sugar to sprinkle on the sandy area
- Small triangular pieces of chocolate for shark fins
- Fruit roll-ups cut into small rectangles for beach towels (cut fringes with scissors)
- Tiny crumpled pieces of paper for trash
- Anything else that strikes you as fitting (matchbox dune buggies are good, as are small plastic animals, small dolls, etc.)

For those without the built-in advantage of a warped floor, place a baking sheet under the cake pan. Wedge an ovenproof gadget, such as a metal vegetable peeler or butter knife, under one side of the cake pan and bake as directed.

lemon square cake

When I was growing up, I had a good friend named Heidi Craig. Her mother made delectable, crumbly, gooey lemon squares that dissolved in your mouth. Recently, I have converted them into a cake that can be eaten on a plate with a fork as a dinner-party dessert. It's lemony on top and somewhere between pie crust and cake on the bottom. I consider it one of my great baking successes. Whipped cream is the appropriate garnish if you're having a dinner party. Toss a few raspberries on top for glamour, if you like.

MAKES ONE 9-INCH CAKE, SERVING 8

crust

- 1 cup all-purpose flour
- ½ cup sugar
- ½ teaspoon salt
- 8 tablespoons (1 stick) unsalted butter, chilled, cut into 8 pieces
- 1 large egg, beaten
- 1 teaspoon vanilla extract

custard

- 3 large eggs
- 1 cup plus 2 tablespoons sugar
- Grated rind of 2 lemons
- ½ cup fresh lemon juice (about 2 juicy lemons)
- 2½ tablespoons all-purpose flour
- 1 teaspoon baking powder
- Pinch of salt

1 Preheat the oven to 350 degrees. Butter a 9-inch springform pan or an 8-inch square baking pan.

2 **To make the crust:** In a food processor, combine the flour, sugar, and salt.

Add the butter and pulse until the mixture is crumbly, about 10 seconds. Add the egg, vanilla, and 2 teaspoons water and pulse just until the dough comes together.

maple whipped cream

One step above homemade whipped cream is maple whipped cream. I use a grade B maple syrup so I can taste the maple clearly. I fold it in after the cream is stiffly whipped—2 to 3 tablespoons seem to do the trick, but let your own palate guide you. Serve with cobblers, upside-down cakes, tarts, and tortes. I particularly like it with Almond Butter Cake (page 430).

3 Transfer the dough to the prepared pan, pressing down lightly to make an even layer. Bake for 15 minutes, or until the crust begins to brown around the edges. Transfer the pan to a cooling rack. Leave the oven on.

4 **Meanwhile, to make the custard:** In a large bowl, combine the eggs and sugar and beat with an electric mixer until the mixture is very pale, about 5 minutes. Add the lemon rind and juice, and when it is incorporated, sift the flour, baking powder, and salt over the egg mixture and fold them in.

5 Pour the custard over the crust. Bake until the custard is golden brown and a knife inserted in the center comes out clean, 25 to 30 minutes. Transfer the pan to a cooling rack and let cool completely.

6 For the springform pan, unmold the cake and cut it into wedges. For the square baking pan, cut into wedges in the pan before serving.

Note The cake can be prepared up to 4 days ahead. Try making it at least 1 day ahead, since it's even better on the second day. Let cool, cover with plastic wrap, and refrigerate overnight. Bring to room temperature at least 30 minutes before serving.

peach upside-down cake

This handsome cake is a delight with a little ice cream or whipped cream. The recipe is adapted from a restaurant called Good in Manhattan.

SERVES 6

topping

- 8 tablespoons (1 stick) unsalted butter
- ½ cup plus 3 tablespoons packed light brown sugar
- 4 peaches, halved, pitted, and each cut into 6 wedges

cake

- 1 cup plus 1 tablespoon all-purpose flour
- ¼ cup cornmeal
- 1 teaspoon baking powder
- ½ teaspoon salt

- 8 tablespoons (1 stick) unsalted butter, softened
- 1 cup packed light brown sugar
- ½ cup sugar
- 3 large eggs
- ⅓ cup sour cream (low-fat is fine)
- 1 teaspoon vanilla extract
- ⅔ cup heavy cream, whipped to soft peaks with 1 tablespoon amaretto (optional)
- ¼ cup toasted sliced or blanched almonds (see page 283; optional)

1 Preheat the oven to 350 degrees. Lightly butter a 9-inch cake pan and line it with parchment or waxed paper.

2 **To make the topping:** In a small saucepan, melt the butter with the brown sugar, stirring until smooth. Pour into the prepared cake pan and let cool slightly. Arrange the peach wedges over the butter mixture. Set aside.

3 **To make the cake:** In a medium bowl, sift together the flour, cornmeal, baking powder, and salt. Set aside.

4 In a large bowl, beat the butter with an electric mixer until light, about 3 minutes. Add the brown sugar and sugar and beat until light and fluffy, about 5 minutes. Add the eggs, one at a time, beating well after each addition.

Beat in the sour cream and vanilla. On low speed, add the flour mixture to the batter in 3 additions, scraping down the sides of the bowl. Don't overmix.

5 Pour the batter over the peaches in the cake pan. Bake until the top of the cake is golden brown and a knife inserted in the center comes out clean, 50 to 60 minutes. Cool for 5 minutes, then invert onto a serving platter. Serve plain or garnish each slice with a spoonful of amaretto-flavored whipped cream sprinkled with a few almonds.

Peach

Note The cake can be baked up to 1 day ahead. Store the cooled, unmolded cake, covered with plastic wrap, in the fridge. Bring to room temperature about 1 hour before serving. The whipped cream can be made up to 5 hours ahead, covered, and chilled.

u-choose ice cream cake

Children love making and eating this cake. So does my mom, who's seventy years old. You get to choose which flavor(s) of ice cream to buy as well as what kinds of cookies or cake to use. It's a practical and yummy way to use or extend the life of any kind of leftover cake, because it gets frozen with the ice cream. I like a creamy ice cream for this, but not a superpremium one such as Ben & Jerry's, which is just too rich for this purpose.

SERVES 8 TO 10

"Seizing" Hot Fudge Sauce
(page 422)

1/2 gallon (2 quarts) ice cream, any
flavor, softened

filling options

Four 2-inch-thick slices leftover
cake, cut into 1/2-inch-thick fingers

15 small cookies (Oreos, Girl Scout
Thin Mints, graham crackers,
vanilla wafers, etc.), coarsely
ground in a food processor

1/4 cup toasted sweetened coconut
(optional)

1/4 cup toasted walnuts, unsalted
peanuts, or almonds (see pages
283 and 449; optional)

2 Heath bars, broken into small
pieces

1 Wrap the outside of a 9-inch springform pan (preferably nonstick) with foil. If the fudge sauce is hot, transfer 3/4 cup of it to a small bowl to cool.

2 Spread half of the ice cream in an even layer in the springform pan. Distribute any or all of the filling options over the top, and drizzle with the 3/4 cup cooled hot fudge. Freeze for 5 minutes to allow the fudge to set. Spoon the remaining ice cream over the filling, smoothing the layer carefully to keep the filling in the center.

3 Cover the pan with foil and freeze until firm, about 4 hours. To serve, reheat the remaining 3/4 cup fudge sauce over low heat. Remove all the foil from the pan and wrap a hot, wet dishtowel around the sides. Run a wet knife around the inside of the pan to loosen the cake if necessary, and release the pan sides. Smooth the sides of the cake with a wet knife, if desired, drizzle with the hot fudge sauce, and serve immediately.

Note

The cake must be prepared at least 4 hours before serving so it will have time to freeze. It can be prepared up to 5 days in advance. Leftovers will last for weeks.

cardamom pound cake

My idea of heaven would be to sleep in a bed where the pillow and mattress are stuffed with ground cardamom. This cake is good plain or served with whipped cream or ice cream. If you have lots left over, freeze it for the U-Choose Ice Cream Cake (page 436).

MAKES 2 LOAVES, SERVES 16

- 2½ cups all-purpose flour
- 1 tablespoon ground cardamom
- ½ teaspoon baking powder
- ½ teaspoon salt
- 1½ cups (2½ sticks) unsalted butter, softened
- 1⅓ cups sugar
- 5 large eggs
- ½ cup sour cream
- 2 tablespoons Grand Marnier or triple sec, or 1 tablespoon vanilla extract

1 Preheat the oven to 325 degrees. Lightly butter and flour two 8-x-4-inch loaf pans. In a medium bowl, stir together the flour, cardamom, baking powder, and salt. Set aside.

2 In a large bowl, cream the butter with an electric mixer until very light and fluffy, about 5 minutes. Gradually add the sugar, beating until incorporated. Add the eggs, one at a time, beating well after each addition. Add the sour cream and the Grand Marnier, triple sec, or vanilla and mix well. Gradually fold the dry ingredients into the butter mixture until blended.

3 Divide the batter between the prepared pans. Bake until a knife inserted in the center of a loaf comes out clean, about 55 minutes. Don't overbake. Let cool in the pans for 10 minutes, then invert the loaves onto a cooling rack and cool completely before serving.

Note The cake can be baked up to 3 days ahead, wrapped in plastic wrap, and stored in the fridge. Let the cake come to room temperature before serving, although I also like it cold. It can be frozen, double-wrapped in plastic wrap, for up to 2 months.

key lime pie with oreo crust

Why aren't all Key lime pies made with Oreo crusts? This dessert is an old standby that never fails to please, and it requires barely any effort at all.

SERVES 8

- 3 cups slightly broken Oreo cookies (less than a 1-pound bag)
- 2 tablespoons unsalted butter, softened
- 1¼ cups sweetened condensed milk
- ¾ cup fresh lime juice (from 6–7 juicy Key limes)
- 1 cup heavy cream, whipped to soft peaks

1 In a food processor, pulverize the Oreos and butter until they form a fine, crumbly paste. Press the mixture into the bottom and sides of a 9-inch pie pan.

2 In a large bowl, whisk together the condensed milk and lime juice until well blended. Gently fold in the whipped cream. Pour the mixture into the crust. Refrigerate for at least 2 hours before serving.

Note
Refrigerate the pie uncovered for at least 2 hours, then cover it loosely with plastic wrap and return it to the refrigerator for up to 2 days before serving.

hazelnut-pear torte

This dessert is an entertainer's dream: not only is it speedy and delicious, it's also visually impressive. Feel free to use toasted almonds (see page 283; skin on is fine) instead of the hazelnuts, if you like. Serve the torte warm, with superpremium vanilla ice cream.

SERVES 8

1 1/3 cups hazelnuts

1/2 cup plus 6 tablespoons (1 3/4 sticks) unsalted butter, softened

1 cup plus 4 tablespoons sugar

2 large eggs, at room temperature

2 tablespoons Frangelico or Cognac

1/2 teaspoon almond extract

1/2 cup plus 2 tablespoons all-purpose flour

3 Bosc pears, peeled (they need not be soft)

1 Preheat the oven to 350 degrees. Butter a 9-inch springform pan (a 9-inch cake pan will do in a pinch). Spread the hazelnuts in a single layer on a rimmed baking sheet and toast for 10 to 12 minutes, or until golden in the center (you'll need to cut into one to see). While the nuts are still hot, pour them onto a clean dishtowel, form a sack, then rub the nuts in the towel to remove the skins. Don't worry about removing every last bit of skin. Open the towel and transfer the hazelnuts to a small bowl with your hands, leaving the paperlike skins behind.

2 In a large bowl, cream the butter and 1 cup plus 3 tablespoons of the sugar with an electric mixer until light. Add the eggs, one at a time, mixing well after each addition. Add the Frangelico or Cognac and almond extract. Using a rubber spatula, fold in the hazelnuts and flour.

Note

The torte can be baked up to 1 day before serving, wrapped in plastic wrap, and refrigerated. Reheat in a 300-degree oven for 20 minutes, and cut the torte in the pan.

coffee *after* dessert?

Coffee's bitterness and robust flavor can easily drown out dessert. Only chocolate desserts can withstand the force of a cup of coffee alongside. This is why Europeans drink coffee *after* dessert, not with it.

I always serve decaf (and I use a French press), since many people are kept awake by the real thing. It's vital that you purchase the highest-quality decaf possible. Mediocre decaf doesn't taste good, but high-quality decaf tastes every bit as good as high-quality regular coffee.

If you are having a nonchocolate dessert and want to sip something with it, try a demitasse of sweetened Moroccan mint tea, Tealess Chai (page 395), sweetened ginger tea, Wu Wei tea (available at tea shops), or Celestial Seasonings' Cinnamon Apple Spice tea.

3 Spoon the batter into the prepared pan and smooth the surface. Cut each pear in half lengthwise and neatly scoop out the seeds with a spoon or melon baller. Slice each half crosswise into thin half-moons, and arrange, overlapping slightly, in concentric circles on top of the batter. Sprinkle the torte evenly with the remaining 1 tablespoon sugar.

4 Place the pan on a baking sheet and bake the torte until a knife inserted in the center comes out clean, 55 to 60 minutes. Let the cake cool for 10 minutes, then remove from the pan and serve.

sweet eats (and drinks)

simplify your dessert course with wine

I love the notion of a dessert that consists only of something sweet to nibble on and a fine dessert wine. A chilled half-bottle (375 ml) of sweet wine will serve at least four people. It can be the entire dessert course. If you'd like to serve coffee or tea, you can do so after the wine course.

If you want to serve a dessert with your sweet wine, remember that the wine should be sweeter than the dessert. You can place bowls of nuts, such as walnuts, pecans, and hazelnuts, on the table for your guests to shell. Dried fruits, such as dates, figs, and apricots, also work well with most dessert wines. When you have time to bake, dishes with the flavors of honey, berries, apricots, peaches, nectarines, and some tropical fruits are good matches for sweet, full-bodied dessert wines. Or, you can serve some simple biscotti.

Most dessert wines are white; the finest and most expensive are the Sauternes and Barsacs from France, the Hungarian Tokajis, and the German Beerenausleses and Trockenbeerenausleses (TBAs). You can find an affordable French Muscat wine, such as Muscat de Beaumes de Venise, in most good wine shops. Late-harvest wines, especially Rieslings, vary in price and are made in many areas of the world, including Australia, Austria, California, and South Africa. Lately, there have also been some good American late-harvest wines from the Niagara areas of Canada and upstate New York's Finger Lakes, as well as from Canada's western regions.

If you're serving a chocolate dessert, it's best to search out a red dessert wine. Port and many of the red dessert wines are fortified; they have a higher alcohol content and can taste sweeter than late-harvest wines. Some of the most available reds are the classic French Banyuls (fortified) or Andrew Quady's Elysium, a black Muscat wine from California that goes well with chocolate and fruit desserts. You may also be able to find a variety of California late-harvest Zinfandels. Many people like port with chocolate, including ruby, tawny and LBV (Late Bottled Vintage), or Vintage Character Ports. These wines can be quite sweet, and they are best paired with cocoa or dark chocolate flavors and nuts.

a friendly guide to unfamiliar ingredients

I recommend two excellent books on exotic ingredients:

- *Asian Ingredients* by Bruce Cost (Quill, 2000)
- *The Asian Grocery Store Demystified* by Linda Bladholm (Renaissance Books, 1999)

Adzuki beans (also called red beans): Small, burgundy-colored Asian beans. Traditionally used in Japanese and Chinese desserts and drinks, they are also attractive in salads. I do not soak adzuki beans, which cook in about 45 minutes.

Ancho chiles: Dried, dark brownish red poblano chile peppers, about 4 inches long and 1 to 2 inches wide. The heat of anchos is not intense, but if multiple chiles are used, the heat can build. Anchos are used in many Mexican sauces and soups. They need to be softened before using. Either soak them in hot water for 30 minutes or hold them with a fork or tongs over a flame until they become crisp but not blackened. Ancho chiles can be found in well-stocked supermarkets, Latin supermarkets, and whole food stores. As a last resort, you can substitute 2 teaspoons chili powder per ancho chile.

Asafetida powder: A gum resin derived from the milky juice of a huge fennel-like plant. It has a marked fruity/garlicky smell and is used often in Indian cooking. It is sold in small plastic jars in Indian markets. A minced garlic clove and a chopped celery stalk make an adequate substitute.

Asian chili sauce: A spicy, thick hot sauce made from red chiles and vinegar. My favorite brand has a rooster on the container and is made by Huy Fong Foods (I prefer the one in a plastic jar with chile seeds visible). It can be found in Asian markets as well as many supermarkets. Stored in the fridge, it'll keep for at least a year.

Asian eggplants (also called Chinese eggplants): Slender, 8-inch-long, magenta eggplants that hold their shape when cooked. Their major advantage is that they are not as bitter as large eggplants because they contain no seeds. They can be found in Asian markets as well as some whole food stores. Large eggplants that are heavy for their size with taut skins can be substituted, since today's strains are less bitter than in the past.

Asian fish sauce: A sauce usually made of an extract of fermented anchovies. Fish sauce is used like soy sauce throughout most of Southeast Asia. The best fish sauce comes in glass bottles. It's available in Asian markets as well as most supermarkets and whole food stores. Although it is not vegetarian, there really is no substitute, but in some dishes I replace it with salt or Lee Kum Kee's Vegetarian Stir-Fry Sauce. Fish sauce keeps indefinitely at room temperature. For more on fish sauce, see page 219.

Asian pears: Resemble large, golden apples with tiny flecks of brown. Asian pears are mild, watery, and crunchy. They can be found in gourmet shops, Asian markets, and whole food stores. If you can't get one, I recommend a juicy apple, such as Fuji.

Asian rice flour: Flour made from ground rice. It's whiter and more refined than the rice flour sold in whole food stores. It comes in two forms: nonglutinous (from long-grain rice), which is used to make rice noodles, and glutinous (from short-grain sticky rice), which is used for dumplings and pastries. Asian rice flour is available in Asian markets. Stored in an airtight container, it will keep for 6 months.

Barley miso: See Miso.

Basil, Thai: See Thai basil.

Basmati rice (brown): Basmati rice with the bran covering intact. It should be soaked or rinsed before cooking and takes about 20 minutes longer than white basmati to cook.

Basmati rice (white): A slender rice originally grown in India. It swells to three times in length when cooked (in about 20 minutes), although the thickness of the grain remains unchanged. Its fragrance, especially when cooking, is sweet and pleasant. Soak or rinse basmati rice before cooking so it doesn't clump.

Black beans, Chinese fermented: See Chinese fermented black beans.

Black rice (also called purple rice): A sticky rice from Thailand with a black-brown coating that turns an intense purple when cooked. Black rice is mainly used for desserts. When making savory rice cakes, I like to mix it half and half with sushi rice to mellow its slightly bitter flavor. Black rice can be found in Asian markets in 1- to 5-pound bags. Don't buy black rice that is jet black with no white specks, called "forbidden rice," which is found in whole food stores; it's not glutinous and will not form cakes.

Black sesame seeds: Like regular sesame seeds, but black in color. Black sesame seeds are striking in slaws and salads. Toasting them is essential, since otherwise they have very little flavor. Black sesame seeds are available in plastic bags in Asian markets.

To toast: Preheat the oven to 350 degrees. Spread the seeds in a single layer on a rimmed baking sheet and toast for 10 to 15 minutes, stirring occasionally, until one of the seeds has a marked sesame flavor when you taste it.

Black vinegar: A flavored Chinese vinegar made from glutinous rice. Complex, smoky, and sweet like balsamic vinegar, it's excellent with stir-fried eggplant or bok choy and in dipping sauces with soy sauce and sesame oil. I recommend only Chinkiang brand—all other brands are medicinal in flavor. You can find it in Asian markets.

Brown miso: See Miso.

Cardamom pods: An aromatic spice. Cardamom is used in curries, pilafs, pastries, and lassis. Before using, place the pods on a flat surface and give them a light thwack with a heavy saucepan so they crack open slightly to release their flavor. Remember to remove the pods from the dish before serving. They are sold in Indian markets, gourmet stores, and whole food stores.

Cellophane noodles (also called bean thread noodles or vermicelli): Vermicelli-width noodles made from mung beans. They become translucent when cooked and are a bit chewier than rice noodles. Soak them in hot water for 15 minutes before adding them to soups or stir-fries. They are sold in Asian markets, whole food stores, and larger supermarkets.

Chickpea flour (also called besan): A dense and nutty-tasting flour used in Indian cooking, it is used in pakoras and other treats. It is sold in paper bags in Indian markets and whole food stores. Store chickpea flour in the fridge, in its bag or an airtight container, for up to a year.

Chinese fermented black beans: Pungent beans that are partially decomposed, then dried. Use them in small amounts to flavor Chinese dishes. They are often very salty: do not rinse them, just salt your dish less. They are available in jars in Asian markets. They keep indefinitely in the fridge.

Chinese rice noodles: See Rice noodles, fresh.

Chinese wheat noodles (also called mein): Fresh noodles that come in varying widths. These noodles cook in 3 to 4 minutes. They are available in 1-pound bags in Asian markets and many supermarkets and are a bargain, costing half the price of fresh Italian pasta. I usually keep a few bags in my freezer and thaw a bag an hour or two before cooking. For more on Chinese wheat noodles, see page 245.

Chipotle chiles: Smoked jalapeños available dried or canned in a spicy, brick-red adobo sauce. I prefer the flavor of dried chipotles, but canned ones are more convenient. Dried chipotles must be soaked in boiling water for 30 minutes. One canned chipotle is equal to 1 seeded dried chipotle. Chipotles are sold in well-stocked supermarkets, Latin markets, and whole food stores.

Chipotle chile sauce: A smoky hot sauce. It's found in large supermarkets and gourmet shops. I like Mo Hotta Mo Betta's Chipotle Adobo Hot Sauce or Frontera's Chipotle Hot Sauce (see page 70).

Coconut, dried, unsweetened (also called

desiccated coconut): Do not confuse it with the dried, *sweetened* coconut used in baking. It looks like artificial snow and can be found in Asian and Indian markets (in bags) and whole food stores (often in the bulk section).

To toast, spread coconut on a rimmed baking sheet and bake in a 350-degree oven, stirring occasionally, for 5 to 8 minutes.

Coconut milk, unsweetened: A liquid processed from grated coconut, essential in many Southeast Asian curries and soups. Check the label to be sure you aren't buying sweetened coconut cream —a common error. Good coconut milk has a thick, creamy layer over a clear, watery liquid. Asian markets usually carry many brands in cans. My favorites are Chao Koh and Mae Ploy. Store opened cans in the fridge for up to 4 days.

Couscous: See Israeli couscous.

Curry leaves: A Southeast Asian plant not related to curry powder that smells like curry but tastes of citrus and musk. Crush curry leaves in your hand to release their essence before you add them to stews or soups. They are sold fresh in plastic bags in the refrigerator or produce section of Indian markets. There is no substitute.

Curry paste: See Madras-style curry paste; Red curry paste.

Edamame: Young, blanched soybeans. Although they are commonly eaten in their pods as a snack, you want to buy the *podless* edamame for cooking, since the pod is inedible. They are found in bags in the frozen section of large supermarkets, whole food stores, and Asian markets. For more on edamame, see page 37.

Eggplants: See Asian eggplants.

Feta cheese: A firm cheese that is often fairly salty, made from cow's milk (the most common), sheep's milk, or goat's milk. My favorite is sheep's milk feta from France, which is creamier than most. French goat's milk feta has a pleasant tang. Both types can be found in cheese shops, whole food stores, some Middle Eastern markets, and supermarkets.

Fish sauce: See Asian fish sauce.

Five-spice powder: A mix of star anise, cinnamon, cloves, fennel, and Sichuan peppercorns, used in savory dishes. It's found in Asian markets, whole food stores, and gourmet shops.

Flaxseed: Small, shiny brown (or yellow) seeds about the size of sesame seeds. Flaxseeds are high in alpha-linolenic acid, an omega-3 fatty acid that offers health and heart benefits. Add them to breads, cereals, and the like. Ground flaxseeds provide more nutritional benefits than whole. Grind them in a food processor or coffee grinder. They can be found in whole food stores and many supermarkets. Store unground flaxseeds in an airtight container in the fridge for up to 6 months.

French green lentils (also called lentilles du Puy): Dark green lentils that are thicker and smaller than the more common brown lentils. They don't get as mushy as brown lentils, and their color is appealing. They take only about 25 minutes to cook. They are found in whole food stores, gourmet markets, and some Middle Eastern markets.

Fresh rice noodles: See Rice noodles, fresh.

Galangal: A pale yellow rhizome with dark concentric circles in the same family as ginger, which it resembles. It tastes peppery and almost medicinal and is used in curry pastes, soups, and Southeast Asian cooking. It can be found in Asian markets. It should be peeled, then finely chopped. You can substitute ginger.

Garam masala: A blend of ground, dry-roasted spices, including star anise, cloves, cinnamon, and coriander. See page 209 for a homemade version. Garam masala is found in Indian markets, whole food stores, and well-stocked supermarkets.

Green lentils: See French green lentils.

Hatcho miso: See Miso.

Israeli couscous: A grainlike pasta made from semolina. Larger than ordinary couscous, the uncooked grains of Israeli couscous are about the size of peppercorns. It cooks in about 10 minutes in boiling water (no soaking necessary). Israeli couscous can be found in whole food stores and gourmet stores. In a pinch, you can substitute barley, although barley takes about 45 minutes to cook.

Japanese short-grain rice: See Sushi rice.

Jasmine rice: A popular aromatic rice from Thailand. Traditionally, no salt is added during cooking, but I salt mine.

Kaffir lime leaves: Leaves from a wild lime tree, similar in size to bay leaves, that smell like a cross between an intense lemon and a lime. They are excellent in soups, sauces, and curry pastes. Like bay leaves, they are usually added to a simmering liquid and should be removed before serving. They can be found frozen in Asian markets or sometimes fresh in the produce section. There is no real substitute for these perfumed leaves, although grated lime rind will do in a pinch. Substitute 1 teaspoon lime rind for every 6 leaves.

Lemongrass: Long stalks that impart a heady, sweet lemon scent to dishes, with none of the acidity of citrus. Don't buy the dried version, which tastes like sawdust. Fresh lemongrass is found in the produce section of Asian markets, well-stocked supermarkets, and whole food stores.

Lentils: See French green lentils; Red lentils.

Lumpia spring roll wrappers: Spongelike wheat wrappers for pan-fried or deep-fried spring rolls. They're tender and flaky when cooked. Remove them from the freezer 2 hours before using. No moistening is needed—they seal naturally. They are available in the frozen section in Asian markets.

Madras-style curry paste: The most common Indian yellow curry in paste form. It's more convenient than Madras curry powder because it can be added directly to dips, cold sauces, or soups, without any cooking. I think it's tastier too. Sold in glass jars, it's available in well-stocked supermarkets and many Asian and Indian markets. I buy the D & D brand.

a friendly guide to unfamiliar ingredients

Miso: A Japanese soybean paste originally produced as a food preservative but now used as a seasoning. Miso is made by fermenting soybeans with salt and a grain, usually rice or barley, with the help of a mold. All misos will last for at least 1 year in an airtight container in the refrigerator. The type of grain used determines miso's color, aroma, and flavor. The lighter the color of the paste, the blander the flavor.

Barley miso (also called mugi miso): Brownish gray in color. Use it in dressings, soups, and sauces.

Brown miso (also called genmai miso): Made from brown rice and soybeans with a medium-strong taste. It's great for soups and salad dressings.

Hatcho miso: A dark-colored miso made only from soybeans. It's aged for at least 9 months. Used only in soups.

Red miso (also called aka miso): Made from barley or rice and soybeans. It has an intense, salty flavor, and it is commonly used in Japanese soups.

White miso (also called shiro miso): Made from rice and soybeans. It's used mainly in salad dressings and soups.

Mung beans: See Yellow split mung beans.

Mu-shu pancakes: Soft wheat-flour wrappers. They're traditionally used for Chinese dishes. I use them for Malaysian spring rolls instead of popiah skins. Let them thaw for at least 1 hour before using. They're found in the frozen section of Asian markets and whole food stores.

New Mexican chile, dried: Originally from Mexico, this dark red chile is popular because its heat does not overwhelm. Often sold in large bags, bundles, or wreaths, these chiles are 3 to 8 inches long and about 1 inch wide and are cultivated not only in New Mexico but in California, Texas, and Arizona. They are perfect for stews, sauces, soups, and many vegetable dishes. They can be found in Asian markets, South and Central American markets, whole food stores, and some gourmet stores. Store at room temperature.

Orange flower water: A flavoring made from orange blossoms distilled in water. Used often in Middle Eastern cooking, it can be added to lemonade, meringues, puddings, and whipped cream. Sold in small bottles in gourmet shops, Armenian markets, and some Middle Eastern markets.

Peanuts, unsalted raw: Much fresher and better-tasting than store-bought roasted peanuts. Buy them in Asian markets and whole food stores.

To roast: Preheat the oven to 350 degrees. Spread the peanuts in a single layer on a rimmed baking sheet and roast for 12 to 15 minutes, stirring occasionally, until golden brown. Store roasted peanuts in a zip bag in the freezer; they'll stay fresh there for at least 5 months.

Pickled sliced ginger (also called *gari*): A condiment served with sushi. It's found in the refrigerated section and/or jars among the condiments in Asian markets, whole food stores, and well-stocked supermarkets. It keeps indefinitely in the fridge.

Pomegranate molasses: A slightly sweet and very sour syrup made from sour pomegranates. It adds a great tang to dressings, sauces, and desserts. It's found in Armenian markets, Middle Eastern markets, Indian markets and, increasingly, in gourmet shops. I prefer the Cortas brand. It will keep indefinitely at room temperature.

Popiah skins: Very thin, crepelike spring roll wrappers made from wheat flour. They are used for *popiah,* the classic unfried spring roll of Malaysia. They are difficult to find, but look for them in Asian markets. I use mu-shu pancakes instead.

Porcini mushrooms, dried: Richly flavored mushrooms, worth their high price. They add a delightful flavor to soups, stews, risottos, and more. They should be rehydrated in a hot liquid, such as water or brandy, for at least 20 minutes. The soaking liquid can be used as well. They're found in specialty food stores and larger supermarkets. They will last for at least a year in an airtight container.

Pumpkin seeds: The seeds of pumpkins, with the white hulls removed. Buy them at whole food stores and many Latin markets. They are best when toasted.

To toast: Preheat the oven to 350 degrees. Spread the seeds on a rimmed baking sheet and toast for 10 to 15 minutes, stirring occasionally, or until they taste toasted and are lightly browned.

Red curry paste: A Thai seasoning made from red chiles, lemongrass, garlic, galangal, and sometimes shrimp. It's sold in small cans and plastic jars in Asian markets and some supermarkets.

Red lentils: Actually orange, despite their name. These small lentils cook in about 5 minutes, although in some traditional *dal* ("cooked lentil" in Hindi) recipes, they are cooked for up to 30 minutes. You can get them in Indian markets and whole food stores.

Red miso: See Miso.

Rice noodles, fresh (also called *chow fun* or *sha he fen* or *gueyteow*): Wide Asian noodles made from rice flour, they unfold to a 12-inch square sheet. They are best used the same day they are purchased. They can be refrigerated for up to 5 days, but they will stiffen. If that happens, cook them in boiling water until they soften, about 3 minutes. Then you can pan-fry them. They are sold in plastic bags in well-stocked Asian markets, usually *not* in the refrigerated section and often near the produce. For more on fresh rice noodles, see page 243.

Rice vinegar: A mild vinegar made from fermented rice. It can be used interchangeably with brown rice vinegar, which is somewhat blander. Rice vinegar can be found in most supermarkets and Asian markets; brown rice vinegar can be found in whole food stores.

Rose water: A flavoring extracted from rose oil. It's used in baking and in salads in India and the Eastern Mediterranean. A little goes a long way. It's found in Middle Eastern and Asian markets and some whole food stores and supermarkets.

Saffron: The stigmas of a crocus, gathered by hand, which are prized for their

a friendly guide to unfamiliar ingredients

unusual, delicate flavor. Make sure to buy the threads, not ground saffron. It's expensive, but you need only a small amount for each dish. It's available in gourmet shops and most supermarkets.

Seitan: Wheat dough from which the starch has been washed away, leaving only the gluten, which is then boiled. Seitan is probably a vegetarian's best substitute for meat. I prefer "chicken-style" seitan, which has been marinated in a garlicky brine. Buy it in whole food stores and some large supermarkets in the refrigerated section, usually near the tofu. For more on seitan, see page 189.

Sesame seeds: One of the oldest edible seeds. They should be stored in the freezer, since they'll go rancid at room temperature. They're found in supermarkets, Asian markets, and whole food stores.

To toast: Preheat the oven to 350 degrees. Spread the seeds in a single layer on a rimmed baking sheet and toast for about 5 minutes, stirring occasionally, until they have a nice sesame flavor and are golden brown.

Sesame tahini: A paste made of sesame seeds. It's found in Middle Eastern markets and whole food stores and adds flavor and richness to salad dressings, dips, and sauces, including baba gannouj and hummus. Store opened cans and jars in the fridge.

Shiitake mushrooms, dried (also called black mushrooms): Flavorful dried mushrooms used in Asian cuisine. They must be soaked in hot water for 30 minutes before using. It's best to store the bag in the freezer, since freezing will kill any tiny moths that hatch from larvae that may be lurking in the bag. They're sold in Asian markets, whole food stores, and well-stocked supermarkets in bags that frequently bear no English words. You can recognize them by their gray-brown caps and beige stems.

Sichuan peppercorns: Rust-colored berries that are very fragrant, almost perfumed. They work best mixed with other spices, and they're great in pickling brines. They can be found in Asian markets.

Soba noodles: Japanese noodles made with buckwheat flour. Silky and a bit nutty, they're perfect for soups or stir-fries. The highest-quality soba, called *nihachi,* have two parts wheat flour to eight parts buckwheat flour. Although soba noodles can be found fresh in Japan, they are sold mostly dried in this country. Found in Asian markets, whole food stores, and well-stocked supermarkets.

Spring roll wrappers (also called lumpia wrappers): Spongelike wheat wrappers that are used for pan-fried spring rolls, both sweet and savory. These wrappers yield a tender yet crispy roll. I like the large 8-inch square wrappers. I recommend the Wei-Chuan and Spring Home brands. They are found in the frozen food section of Asian markets.

Star anise: The licorice-flavored head of Chinese magnolia trees, resembling inch-wide, mahogany-colored stars. They can be ground or left whole for sauces or soups and then removed. You can find it in Asian markets and whole food stores.

Sucanat: A registered trademark that stands for SUgar CAne NATural. Its flavor is similar to brown sugar, with a slightly stronger molasses flavor. It's made from freshly cut, nutrient-rich sugar cane. The juice is pressed from the cane, then concentrated into a thick, rich syrup that retains nutritious mineral salts, vitamins, and trace elements. The syrup is dehydrated without being refined and with no chemicals added, then milled into a powder. You can substitute it for sugar in almost any recipe in this book, except desserts that are delicate in texture or light in color. Look for it in whole food stores and well-stocked supermarkets.

Sushi rice (also called Japanese short-grain): A white rice with short, almost round grains that become sticky when cooked. Popular in Korean and Japanese cuisine, it is often mixed with sugar and rice vinegar and used in sushi. Look for the Kokuho Rose brand from California, Japanese Nishimoto, or Hikari Imperial Quality. It is available in Asian markets, whole food stores, and well-stocked supermarkets.

Sweet potato noodles (also called yam noodles or *tangmyon*): Brownish gray noodles made from a mixture of sweet potato and mung bean starch. They become translucent when cooked, and like cellophane noodles, which can be substituted, they readily absorb other flavors. They're great for soups, stir-fries, stews and cold salads. Check the ingredients to see if sweet potatoes or yams are present, since the English name of the noodles often is not given on the package. You can find them in Asian markets.

Tahini: See Sesame tahini.

Tamarind: The pod of the tamarind tree. It imparts a sweet-and-sour flavor to Indian, Malaysian Senegalese, Vietnamese, and Thai cuisine. Buy the kind that has been pressed into small bricks and wrapped in plastic, with the seeds still intact. Don't buy the more convenient tamarind concentrate sold in jars, because the flavor pales in comparison with the seeded bricks. Tamarind can be found in Asian markets and some Hispanic markets. In a pinch, you can substitute $1/4$ cup fresh lime juice and 1 teaspoon sugar for $2/3$ cup tamarind pulp. For more on tamarind, see page 281.

To extract the pulp from a brick: cut off a 2-inch-square piece of tamarind. In a small bowl, cover the tamarind with $3/4$ cup boiling water. Let stand for 15 minutes, then use your fingers to loosen the tamarind from the seeds. Strain through a sieve, discarding the seeds and any fibrous pulp. The remaining tamarind pulp should be the consistency of thick gravy. You should have about $2/3$ cup. It will keep in an airtight container in the fridge for at least 2 weeks.

Tempeh: A dense cake made from fermented cooked soybeans. (The process is similar to the one used to make blue cheese, but a mushroom-based culture is used to promote the fermentation.) Tempeh is best pan-fried until golden brown.

a friendly guide to unfamiliar ingredients

Its strong flavor needs an intense sauce to match, such as peanut sauce. It's found in most supermarkets, whole food stores, and some Asian markets. For more on tempeh, see page 231.

Thai basil: Darker green in color than ordinary basil, often with purple buds. It's much stronger than other basils, with a pronounced anise flavor. Thai basil is excellent in Asian soups and salads and good in Mediterranean dishes. Look for it in the produce section of Asian markets. Any other form of basil can be substituted for it, although it won't have the same punch.

Thai chiles (also called bird chiles): Skinny, 1-inch-long red or green chiles. Far spicer than jalapeños, they pack a quick sting, leaving in their wake a particularly fresh and clean chile flavor. Buy them in Asian markets and many large supermarkets. Freeze them in zip bags, double-bagging them to guard against freezer burn. They will keep for up to 4 months. Thawing is not necessary, since you can cut through the chile even when it's frozen.

Tofu: Made from pressed soy milk, tofu comes in several forms, all of which are available in supermarkets and whole food stores, from soft to extra-firm. Firm and extra-firm tofu holds its shape in stir-fries and soups. This is the tofu I use most often. Silken tofu is a pillowy version that's nice in soups and stews. Tofu should be stored in the fridge covered with water for up to 4 days; change the water daily. For more on tofu, see page 217.

Truffle oil: Olive oil infused with black or white truffles. Imported from Italy, it can transform a mundane dish into a sublime one. I prefer the oil made from the more pungent white truffle. See page 300 for specific brands, since the quality varies widely. It's found in specialty food stores and gourmet shops. Store in a cool, dry place with the cap tightly sealed. It will last for 6 to 8 months.

TVP (texturized vegetable protein): A dehydrated food made from soybeans. It looks a lot like Grape-Nuts, but it is much lighter. Once cooked in liquid, it resembles ground beef. Use TVP in sloppy joes and chilies. Buy it in whole food stores in the bulk section. For more on TVP, see page 271.

Udon noodles: Japanese noodles made of wheat flour and water. They are used mainly in soups and stews. They're found in Asian markets, whole food stores, and well-stocked supermarkets.

Vegetarian oyster sauce: Made from sugar, salt, yeast, caramel color, and a variety of starches, this Chinese sauce is remarkably tasty, almost preferable to real Chinese oyster sauce. It works well in fried rice or Asian noodle dishes and Asian-inspired soups. Look for the Amoy brand. It can be found in Asian markets. Store in the fridge once opened.

Vegetarian stir-fry sauce: Similar to oyster sauce in flavor, but less sweet. It gets its intensity from mushrooms. I prefer the Lee Kum Kee brand. It makes a passable vegetarian substitute for fish sauce. It's available in Asian markets and many whole food stores.

entertaining for a veggie planet

Wasabi powder: A green powder made from the root of an Asian plant. It's most often used to make the pungent paste that adds kick to sushi. It's found in small tins in Asian markets, many whole food stores, and larger supermarkets.

Yellow split mung beans: A bit crunchy with a nutty flavor. I particularly like them in Asian slaws. They should be boiled for about 10 minutes, or until al dente. You will find them in bags near the other beans in Asian markets.

Yellow split peas: Similar in appearance to green split peas, but yellow. I find their flavor and texture preferable to that of green split peas. Buy them in whole food stores, Indian markets, and many supermarkets in the Spanish section.

index